INVOKING THE INVISIBLE HAND

RHETORIC AND PUBLIC AFFAIRS SERIES

INVOKING THE INVISIBLE HAND

SOCIAL SECURITY AND
THE PRIVATIZATION DEBATES

Robert Asen

Michigan State University Press • *East Lansing*

 Michigan State University Press
East Lansing, Michigan 48823-5245

Printed and bound in the United States of America.

18 17 16 15 14 13 12 11 10 09   1 2 3 4 5 6 7 8 9 10

LIBRARY OF CONGRESS CATALOGING-IN-PUBLICATION DATA
Asen, Robert, 1968–
Invoking the invisible hand : social security and the privatization debates / Robert Asen.
p. cm.—(Rhetoric and public affairs series)
Includes bibliographical references and index.
ISBN 978-0-87013-843-0 (cloth : alk. paper) 1. Social security—Government policy—United States. 2. Privatization—United States. 3. Social security individual investment accounts—United States. I. Title.
HD7125.A775 2009
368.4'300973—dc22
2008029583

Cover and book design by Sharp Designs, Inc., Lansing, Michigan

g **green** Michigan State University Press is a member of the Green Press Initiative
press and is committed to developing and encouraging ecologically responsible
INITIATIVE publishing practices. For more information about the Green Press Initiative and the use of recycled paper in book publishing, please visit *www.greenpressinitiative.org*.

Visit Michigan State University Press on the World Wide Web at *www.msupress.msu.edu*

To Simone
May your future be secure

Contents

Acknowledgments

Among its many benefits, Social Security affirms the importance of community in our everyday lives. Benefiting from the support and wisdom of many friends and colleagues, I experienced a powerful enactment of community as I wrote this book.

John Murphy, Mike Hogan, Daniel Béland, and Danielle Devereaux-Weber provided extensive feedback on the entire manuscript. Their insights led me to reconsider my approach to the Social Security debates in important ways, and this book has improved significantly as a result. Marty Medhurst enthusiastically supported this book through the initial drafting and revision processes. On this project and others, Marty has offered excellent editorial direction that trenchantly discerns the key issues at stake in my writing and lucidly articulates revisions for realizing its potential.

Jean Goodwin, Jim Jasinski, Jim Aune, Tom Goodnight, Steve Browne, Rosa Eberly, Cara Finnegan, Lisa Foster, Vanessa Beasley, Barb Biesecker, Charles Pfeifer, Rasha Diab, Pam Conners, Jeff Drury, Kathryn Palmer, Ryan Solomon and others have discussed with me aspects of this manuscript during its development. Their feedback helped me clarify ideas and themes as well as refine aspects of my analysis. In this way, too, I have benefited from the advice of innumerable others—people who, in conversations at coffee shops and conventions, have affirmed the importance of this project and shared their perspectives on Social Security.

I have been especially fortunate to receive the support and good counsel of many wonderful colleagues, past and present, including Rob Howard, Sue Zaeske, Steve Lucas, Erik Doxtader, Chris Garlough, and Mike Xenos. Together, we have built an outstanding intellectual community in Madison that has inspired me and greatly improved my scholarship. My colleagues have offered encouragement and feedback on the overall structure and specific content of this book. They have sustained a collaborative environment of inquiry and achievement.

Every academic needs a posse, and mine consists of Dan Brouwer, Chuck Morris, and Alex Hivoltze-Jimenez. These good friends have generously provided advice, support, and fun, which should never be neglected over the course of an extensive writing project. Alex passed away as this book went to press. He was a dear soul who departed this earth too soon, but Alex survives in the memories of the many people touched by his generous spirit.

The Market Reaches for Social Security

Every individual necessarily labours to render the annual revenue of the society as great as he can. He generally, indeed, neither intends to promote the public interest, nor knows how much he is promoting it. By preferring the support of domestic to that of foreign industry, he intends only his own security; and by directing that industry in such a manner as its produce may be of the greatest value, he intends only his own gain, and he is in this, as in many other cases, led by an invisible hand to promote an end which was no part of his intention. Nor is it always the worse for the society that it was no part of it. By pursuing his own interest he frequently promotes that of the society more effectually than when he really intends to promote it.[1]

In this famous passage from *The Wealth of Nations*, Adam Smith employs a powerfully evocative metaphor that bursts through his prose to escape the confines of political economy and obtain the status of a common sense. Resonating across national contexts and historical eras,

1

the metaphor of the "invisible hand" has spoken to many people as an intuitive description of how the world works and an unparalleled prescription for ethical individual action. The invisible hand artfully captures the spirit of a market ethics by insisting that in working for oneself, an individual works for the good of others. The invisible hand connects individuals to society by coordinating their activities without their conscious participation. Through their labors, individuals neither intend nor exhibit cognizance of their role in promoting a greater good. Individuals desire and know only one aim: self-enrichment. Yet the invisible hand enacts a kind of magical transubstantiation, turning self-interest into collective action by leading individuals "to promote an end which was no part of [their] intention." Moreover, the invisible hand achieves societal amelioration more efficaciously than purposefully directed and consciously coordinated activities. Individuals serve society more ably when they leave its betterment to the magic of the invisible hand: "By pursuing his own interest he frequently promotes that of the society more effectually than when he really intends to promote it."

Exemplifying the social power of language, the metaphor of the invisible hand offers a potentially compelling ethical justification of ostensibly self-interested behavior. Individuals act most selflessly when they pursue self-interest, whereas conscious efforts to improve the condition of others actually reveal a kind of selfishness and self-importance. A desire for public acclaim or a misplaced sense of pity drives social reformers—rather than a genuine concern for the well-being of the people they purport to serve. Further, charity seizes individual respect and autonomy. In another famous passage, Smith writes: "It is not from the benevolence of the butcher, the brewer, or the baker, that we expect our dinner, but from their regard to their own interest. We address ourselves, not to their humanity but to their self-love, and never talk to them of our own necessities but of their advantages. Nobody but a beggar chuses to depend chiefly upon the benevolence of his fellow-citizens."[2] In adopting the status of a beggar, an individual relinquishes agency as a market actor, an essential activity that makes us human. Moreover, this move breaks the ethical contract that ensures everyone's well-being, since markets can only advance a greater good when individuals abide by market norms.

Common sense can fail us, however, and individuals and nations often have experienced the market not as a benevolent actor but as a producer of misery and strife. In the United States in the 1930s, as the nation suffered through a severe and seemingly endless economic depression, policymakers and citizens alike questioned their faith in the market as an ameliorative, self-regulating realm. In his 1935 State of the Union address, President Franklin Delano Roosevelt challenged the very basis of a market ethics—individual gain did not redound to a greater good. FDR asserted that citizens understood "that Americans must forswear that conception of the acquisition of wealth which, through excessive profits, creates undue private power over private affairs and, to our misfortune, over public affairs as well."³ Instead of solitary advantages, citizens sought mutual benefits. Moreover, citizens demanded purposeful government action to alleviate people's suffering. Sustained advocacy and economic depression spurred intense legislative activity, resulting in one of the most important pieces of legislation in U.S. history: the 1935 Social Security Act. This landmark Act included a little known and modestly supported provision for a contributory pension system. Over time, Old-Age Insurance, as this provision was originally titled, would grow in size, scope, and popularity such that insurance-based retirement benefits—Social Security—would come to stand for the Act itself.

As Social Security has matured, political winds have shifted. In the final third of the twentieth century, some policymakers and citizens shifted their judgments of governments and markets. Carrying the banner of privatization, advocates have championed the market as a solution to pressing social problems and, more fundamentally, as a model of human relationships. Advocates have called for privatization of various public services ranging from municipal trash collection to federal environmental protection.⁴ Proponents of privatization have discerned in the market a powerful set of incentives and rewards promising to reduce the costs and increase the returns on ostensibly public goods and services. Despite its popularity, Social Security has not escaped this call to comport with market norms. To the contrary, as policymakers increasingly have scrutinized the program's finances from the 1970s onward, just as the larger movement toward privatization has taken shape, advocates increasingly have argued that Social Security's supposed bulwark against economic insecurity—its social-insurance basis—constituted the source of its woes. Advocates of privatization have called for a fundamental restructuring of Social Security from an insurance-based to an investment-based retirement system.

This campaign for privatization has faced multiple obstacles, since markets and social policies typically operate in accordance with different norms and practices that do not submit to easy reconciliation.

Whereas market actors aim for profits, social policies may undertake the nonprofitable aims of prevention, redress, or protection. As the invisible hand demonstrates, markets situate human agency in individual terms, while social policies often promote coordinated or collective agency among members of a polity. Market actors employ criteria of costs and benefits to evaluate opportunities and endeavors, whereas social policy invokes criteria of justice and fairness. While the market promotes a culture of competition, social policy fosters an environment of cooperation. Given these differences, calls to privatize Social Security raise questions regarding how policymakers and other debate participants have attempted to reconcile potentially competing aims. How has privatization emerged historically? How have debate participants reinterpreted Social Security through a market lens? How have debate participants articulated collective commitments and citizens' obligations to each other?

Of course, actual policies are never as clear-cut as analytic frameworks, and Social Security has pursued both individual and collective goals since its inception. From the very beginning, policymakers have pursued contributory and noncontributory aims. Contributory aims highlight the dedicated financing of Social Security, whereby workers and employers contribute to retirement pensions through payroll-tax deductions. Policymakers and others have invoked this financing structure to represent Social Security as a rights-based program through which retirees receive benefits in proportion to their contributions plus interest. In this way, they have positively distinguished Social Security from other social policies that, in Adam Smith's terms, position recipients as dependent beggars. Noncontributory aims focus on the adequacy of retirement benefits. Invoking values of justice and fairness, policymakers and others have insisted that Social Security pay retirees sufficient benefits, which historically have exceeded workers' payroll-tax contributions, in order to insure a decent and respectable retirement. In this way, policymakers have been concerned with retirees' material and psychological well-being; both have been deemed necessary to avoid the stigma of the beggar.

This book examines debates over Social Security from 1995 to 2005, a period of intensive advocacy and deliberation about the future of the program, culminating in President Bush's widely publicized barnstorming tour for private accounts in 2005. Although the privatization debates did not produce specific legislation, the debates destabilized insurance as the founding principle of Social Security. In this way and others, the privatization debates will inform any future change to Social Security, thereby influencing the lives of the millions of Americans who receive benefits through the program. Further, the debates reveal important qualities about the world in which we live. Although advocates of privatization did not succeed in restructuring Social Security according to the principle of investment, the duration, expansiveness, and visibility of their campaign evidence the power of market-based appeals in contemporary political discourse. If supporters of a program as popular as Social Security have to battle mightily to resist privatization, then what hope may supporters hold for creating new government programs that pursue nonmarket aims like justice and fairness? How Americans answer this question will say a great deal about how they imagine their nation. If markets reign triumphant, will an investment nation continue to fulfill the hopes and dreams of Americans who see their country as a place to live a better life—not just in terms of wealth, but also vibrant democratic practices?

As these stakes suggest, debates over Social Security do not represent technical debates best left to the "experts." While Social Security raises important technical issues, such as estimates of the long-term solvency of the trust fund, policymakers and citizens too often have treated the topic as a specialized inquiry. However, in a healthy democracy, experts ought to take their charge from citizens, not the other way around. As noted champion of democracy John Dewey has written, "Expertness is not shown in framing and executing policies, but in discovering and making known the facts upon which the former depend."[5] At a basic, unavoidable level, the key questions confronting Social Security concern the values that citizens want to affirm in their public policies. Neither actuarial tables nor market forecasts will answer these questions for citizens. Rather, answers must emerge through an honest and vigorous debate among diverse groups of Americans. To understand how we got here and where we need to go, we must direct our attention to rhetoric—not as a distraction from or supplement to public policy, but as constitutive of policy itself.

Rhetoric, Public Policy, and Materiality

During the heat of the 2004 presidential campaign, in an unsettling essay in the *New York Times Magazine*, journalist Ron Suskind revealed a central tenet of the Bush administration's thinking about the nature of public policy. Suskind recalled a conversation with an unnamed senior presidential advisor who rebuked him for living in a "reality-based community," which, ironically, ignored how the "world really works." The aide asserted unapologetically that "we're an empire now, and when we act, we create our own reality. And while you're studying that reality—judiciously, as you will—we'll act again, creating other realities."[6] This statement, a crude expression of the belief that "might makes right," created a stir among the administration's opponents. *New York Times* columnist Bob Herbert responded indignantly that while "we may think there are real-world consequences to the policies of the president, real pain and real grief for real people," the White House regarded such thinking as "passé."[7] In the virtual world, left-leaning bloggers adopted the phrase as an affirmative self-description, with some bloggers appending the statement "a proud member of the reality-based community" to their mastheads. By reversing the administration's disdain for reality, these responses rightly rebuked the president for dismissing evidence and ignoring the views of others in formulating public policy. However, reality does not speak for itself, nor does it orient action transparently and objectively. Embracing reality as an ethical guide enacts a rhetoric, even though journalists, bloggers, and others typically treat reality and rhetoric as opposites. To the extent to which we oppose these two forces, retreating into the realm of a supposedly secure reality against the distortions of "rhetoric," we misunderstand the constitution and conduct of public policy.

Policymakers and media commentators are not alone in their efforts to free reality from rhetoric, for scholars of public policy also have insisted on separating or, more precisely, placing the two in battle as "rhetoric" versus "reality." In an article comparing the "rhetoric and reality of work-based welfare reform," Maria Cancian identifies and tests three propositions guiding pro-work rhetoric in the policy debates: "Work is the norm, work is good for families, and work leads to self-sufficiency." For each proposition, Cancian considers the evidence gathered by scholars and government agencies, finding in each case that reality chastens an incautious rhetoric. Against the rhetorical assertion that "work is the norm," for instance, she counters that "the reality, however, is that most women with children, poor and not poor, do not work even 30 hours a week year-round."[8] On this point and others, Cancian engages in an important process of testing claims by considering supporting and contrary evidence, but her investigation does not appeal to a "reality" divorced from "rhetoric." As the rhetorically trained readers of this book know well, the injunction to test claims and evaluate evidence forms an important part of the foundation of rhetorical scholarship and pedagogy. Indeed, rhetorical practices of inquiry and deliberation enable this very process.

If rhetoric and reality do not exist independently of each other, then we need to consider the role of rhetoric in public policy. In the following chapters, I approach public policy as a mediation of rhetorical and material forces.[9] In terms of materiality, public policies provide money, goods, and services to target populations to achieve particular outcomes, such as offering retirement incomes and disability benefits to millions of American workers and their families. A Social Security check engenders a qualitative improvement in the lives of its recipients, enabling elderly couples to pay utility bills and purchase groceries while offering younger recipients the chance to pursue long-term goals like obtaining a college education in the event of the tragic death or disability of a working parent. Without Social Security, people would suffer. A rhetorical analysis of public policy must appreciate this basic point, even as it must not reduce public policy to its material components, nor establish a material "reality" as the arbiter of public policy.

Since material outcomes require human participation, rhetoric plays an equally important role in public policy through the ineluctable operation of meaning. At a fundamental level, policies create, sustain, negotiate, and redefine the meanings of the very money, goods, and services provided. Consider the phrase "providing retirement benefits," which might appear at first glance as a rudimentary description of the non-rhetorical nature of Social Security. However, this phrase already implicates rhetoric, for it presumes a shared understanding of each of its three terms, which participants in the privatization debates have vigorously contested. In these debates, "provision" has meant a federally administered pension system as well as a system of private accounts, "retirement" has meant both a carefree and a worrisome period of life, and "benefits" have assumed a wide variety of shapes and forms. These differences illustrate Frank Fischer's claim that policies entail "struggle over ideas and their meanings."[10] In this sense, a benefits check is never simply a benefits check. Offering the material advantages of the amount promised to its bearer, a check circulates in a system of meaning that invokes particular institutions (e.g., banks) as well as the meanings that we ascribe to the beneficiaries, their money, and other members of society.

Implicated in struggles over meaning, policies express a nation's values, principles and priorities, hopes and ideals, and beliefs about citizens' responsibilities and obligations to each other. As I argue in this book, advocates of privatization affirmed values of ownership, choice, control, and individualism, while supporters of the existing Social Security system upheld values of community, security, wide-ranging protection, and poverty alleviation. Further, as rhetorical artifacts, policies do not seek out existing and objectively apparent populations for receipt of benefits. Instead, policy debates enact powerful processes of representation, casting retirees, for example, as frugal grandparents enjoying fulfillment in retirement, or as "greedy geezers" pursuing conspicuous consumption over the long-term well-being of their children and grandchildren. Whether positively or negatively, policies may force these identities on individuals, or individuals may actively adopt these identities. Reiterating the mediating character of public policy, representations constituted in policy debates may expand or restrict individuals' opportunities for agency in their everyday lives by conferring different levels of status on recipients, such as contrasting images of Social Security and welfare recipients.

As my reference to agency suggests, policies often enact and enforce symbolic hierarchies that unite and divide people, and synthesize and oppose values. In these ways, policies can bring people together, creating a target population that overcomes individual differences, and policies can pull people apart, constituting some individuals and groups as "other" and inferior to conventional practices and beliefs. In this respect, Social Security has participated in a prominent symbolic hierarchy that has shaped the landscape of American social policy, namely, insurance versus assistance.[11] As the dominant partner in this hierarchy, Social Security has obtained an honorific position in national politics as much for what it does not promote as for what it does. From the beginning, supporters of Social Security championed its insurance basis as promoting independence, while chastising assistance for perpetuating dependence. Insurance benefits represented a return on workers' contributions, and retirees claimed benefits as a right. Paling in comparison, assistance supposedly transferred money from workers to idlers, casting recipients as shameful beggars. To sustain this hierarchy, supporters of insurance have advanced arguments opposing work and nonwork, and independence and dependence. However, we can imagine an alternative discourse that supports insurance-based retirement benefits not by demonizing assistance, but by celebrating the contributions (paid and unpaid) that seniors make to their communities.

As policies mediate rhetorical and material elements, the process of *policymaking* foregrounds the role of rhetoric as a constitutive force. Congressional hearings, floor debates, presidential speeches, media campaigns—these all represent irreducibly rhetorical acts. Policymaking occurs as debate participants attempt to persuade others to support particular programs and outcomes. Like ongoing policies themselves, policymaking ineluctably involves meaning and engages symbol systems. Policymaking also mediates the material, often in the form of institutional power, officially sanctioned authority and privilege, and money. However, policies and policymaking differ in their explicit use and mode of rhetoric. In terms of mode, I distinguish policymaking from policies as a difference between *making* meaning (policymaking) and *maintaining and enforcing* meaning (policies). Of course, practice complicates my analytic distinction, as administrators and field agencies, for instance, can make their own meaning by following the letter of a law while undermining its spirit. Welfare policy betrays a sad history of administrators turning away legally eligible applicants for assistance. The so-called "welfare crisis" of the 1960s arose as a consequence of poor people successfully claiming their legal entitlements. On this score, James Patterson reports that whereas only 33 percent of eligible families in the early 1960s participated in the Aid to Families with Dependent Children program, by 1971 over 90 percent of families participated.[12] As this statistic illustrates, varying levels of maintenance and enforcement can expand, restrict, and shift policy meanings.

Policymaking nevertheless represents atypical moments in the "lives" of policies where meaning-making appears as the central task occupying participants. Over its seventy-plus year history, Social Security has only periodically undergone explicit legislative revision, with important amendments and changes occurring in 1939, 1950, 1972, and 1983. In these moments—and, as advocates of privatization hope, in the contemporary period—questions of aims and methods become primary concerns. Participants in policy debates ask, "What do we want to do?" and "How do we want to do it?" Policymaking thus constitutes paramount rhetorical moments in the lives of policies. However, since no policy arises ex nihilo, policymaking does not inaugurate unprecedented meanings as much as it intervenes in an ongoing symbolic field. Negative attitudes toward assistance already circulated publicly in the 1930s, when supporters of insurance invoked this distinction to champion their preferred vision of retirement pensions. In a similar spirit, contemporary advocates of privatization draw on public hostility toward government in their case for individual investment accounts. In these ways, policymaking provides participants with opportunities to constellate meaning, creating and re-creating multiple associations and dissociations, in making policy. Drawing on different constellations, debate participants may articulate social problems requiring a government response, imagine target populations, evaluate histories, and envision futures for public policies.

My conception of policy debate challenges theories of deliberative democracy that regard institutional forums as restricted problem-solving arenas. Notably, in his discourse theory of democracy, Jürgen Habermas distinguishes legislative bodies as "contexts of justification" from public spheres as "contexts of discovery." In the former, Habermas asserts, participants focus on the "cooperative solution of practical questions, including the negotiation of fair compromises." Deliberation in legislatures "consists less in discovering and identifying problems than in dealing with them; it has less to do with becoming sensitive to new ways of looking at problems than with justifying the selection of a problem and the choice among competing proposals for solving it."[13] This formulation presumes a one-way flow of information from public spheres, which conduct the preliminary investigation of problems, to legislatures, thereby discounting the meaning-making capacities of the latter. Neither problems nor solutions circulate plainly in the public sphere, waiting for policymakers to notice them. Sometimes, with great courage and hard work, citizens may convince policymakers to address their needs and interests, as civil rights activists urged politicians to enact legislation in the 1960s. At other times, policymakers may impose a problem and its solution on their constituents. On this score, citizens had not been clamoring for investment accounts prior to the start of the privatization debates in the mid-1990s. Rather, ideologically driven politicians and their allies, especially conservative think tanks, created a sense of crisis about the future finances of Social Security and presented investment as the answer. Their efforts received a significant boost when a Social Security Advisory Council addressed the issue in the mid-1990s, but this too represented an institutional site of discourse. Had policymakers uniformly reassured citizens that Social Security would meet its obligations well into the future, the debates effectively would have ended.

My association of rhetoric and public policy may generate concerns for some readers, and I want to assure my readers that a rhetorical approach to public policy does not grant debate participants license to say whatever they please. I shall develop a normative critique in the conclusion, but for now I shall stress the importance of critically evaluating policy debates. In dismissing reality, the unnamed Bush aide excused the administration's repeated misrepresentations of events in Iraq and its unremitting intimidation of opponents of the war. With respect to "workfare," work may raise an individual's self-esteem and contribute positively to society, but, as Cancian suggests, work also happens in contexts—valued and undervalued, with and without institutional supports, and paid and unpaid. Different types of work may produce fulfillment and alienation, while prompting celebration and denigration. However, in distinction from Cancian, we may appreciate how rhetoric shapes our understanding of work, even as we object to the reductive and duplicitous character of many calls for "workfare."

The Rise of Market Talk

As an intervention into ongoing symbolic fields, policymaking connects debates and contexts—economic, political, cultural, and discursive. I discuss these various contexts in the following chapters, but one contextual theme ties together the various episodes of the privatization debates: the rise of "market talk." Contemporary advocates have rediscovered their love for the market as an ameliorative set of practices, norms, and institutions. Writing in the 1990s, Robert Kuttner observed that the United States had once again fallen into "one of its cyclical romances" with a utopian view of the market.[14] Forgetting past infidelity, media commentators and policymakers especially embraced markets as essential elements of human liberty, efficacious forces for financial gain, and superior governing structures.

Recognizing the rise of market talk enables us to appreciate the constitutive power of *discourse* as a social force. While participants in policy debates craft rhetorical appeals to advance their case, rhetoric sometimes obtains a force of its own that exceeds the transitory participation of specific people. In this way, I invoke "discourse" to refer to bodies of rhetoric that serve as publicly articulated ways of collectively understanding and evaluating our world that propagate and enforce social norms with material consequences. Discourses speak publicly in a variety of forums, including official pronouncements in state-sponsored reports, technical expositions in quarterly journals, and informal expressions in popular culture. Discourses promote collective understanding by offering explanations for societal events and developments. For example, when a company explains that market forces compelled its movement of manufacturing facilities from the United States to a developing nation, market talk facilitates our understanding of this decision. Discourses foster collective evaluation by providing criteria for judging institutions and practices. We can see this characteristic in evidence when advocates call on the "discipline of the market" to improve the performance of public schools. By enabling understanding and evaluation, discourses propagate and enforce social norms. Market talk privileges norms of self-enrichment over potentially competing norms of justice in prescribing the rights and obligations of citizenship. In these ways, discourses produce material consequences. One example concerns the prevalence of Americans without health insurance, because many policymakers have discounted a universal plan as contrary to market principles.

As a discourse, market talk does not depend on some previously agreed-upon definition of a societal phenomenon. Rather, market talk derives part of its power from its capacity to define such phenomena. Along these lines, economist Eckehard Rosenbaum explains that "defining a market is essentially a *normative* enterprise that has to be judged by its usefulness for the chosen purpose rather than its truth or falsity." Rosenbaum favors the purpose of distinction, namely, distinguishing markets from other forms of human interaction and exchange. However, his reference to a normative enterprise intimates a more fundamental purpose for defining a market: constituting the phenomena specified in the definition. Addressing this purpose, rhetorical theorist Edward Schiappa notes that "definitions represent claims about how certain portions of the world are." Successfully redefining a term "changes not only recognizable patterns of linguistic behavior but also our understanding of the world and the attitudes and behaviors we adopt toward various parts of that world."[15] If we regard markets as ameliorative social forces rather than uncertain and potentially harmful realms (as many policymakers in the 1930s believed), then we are more likely to place our retirement savings under the market's discipline.

Market talk functions variously in debates over public policy, which importantly includes framing policy debates. Market talk shapes the societal problems identified by citizens and policymakers as requiring policy solutions. Judgments that subsequent generations of workers would receive lower rates of return on their payroll-tax contributions than previous generations partially motivated proposals for private accounts in Social Security. In this case, market talk highlighted lowered rates of return as a problem requiring a solution. Framing also proceeds by creating a wider context for considering policy proposals. For debates over Social Security, this wider context included shifts in private pensions from defined-benefit to defined-contribution arrangements. In this context, private accounts comported with a larger shift in financing people's retirements. Further, drawing on market talk's capacity to discern relevant histories for policy debates, advocates of private accounts pointed to a declining worker-to-retiree ratio from the 1930s onward as a reason for switching from an insurance model.

Market talk also functions to circulate models—both descriptive and prescriptive—for public policies and institutions. The circulation of descriptive models recalls the explanatory power of a discourse: market talk takes complex and varied human and social relationships and makes them comprehensible. In the process, market talk distinguishes the inessential from the essential, ornamentation from structure. For example, in asserting that self-interest primarily motivates humans, market talk simplifies potentially complicated questions about why people behave as they do. Prescriptively, models circulate exemplars, standards for imitation. Market talk seeks to reform nonmarket institutions (e.g., schools) in the image of the market. This impulse constitutes a process of homogenization, an effort to make commensurate seemingly incommensurable realms of public life. Rather than accepting that matters of basic justice and economic gain may invoke different evaluative criteria and, when in conflict, present difficult policy decisions, market talk asserts that policymakers can decide all matters according to a single measure. In this way, market talk prescribes solutions to pressing social problems: make the "problem" comport with the model of the market.

Market talk serves as a mode of reasoning for participants in policy debates by providing substantive content as well as strategies of inference that enable participants to develop arguments. The content of market talk includes values like efficiency and slogans that encapsulate shared ways of thinking, such as the promises by software firms to develop applications that function "at the speed of business," which reinforces notions of business as highly performing. Market talk also provides premises for arguments (e.g., markets waste less money than governments) and stories of success and failure, such as the stories of entrepreneurs who risk personal financial ruin to develop a needed product or service. The strategies of inference offered by market talk enable debate participants to interpret and weigh evidence. For instance, advocates of private accounts regarded lowered rates of return as evidence of the limits of an insurance-based approach, rather than a consequence of the maturation of Social Security, which collected fewer taxes from retirees during its first few decades of operation. Strategies of inference also offer debate participants methods for analyzing problems and moving from premises to conclusions, such as the prominence in many policy domains of cost-benefit analysis as a method for reaching decisions.[16]

In terms of its discursive style, market talk exhibits a realist pose that also serves idealist ends. Market talk perpetuates a distinction between nature and artifice, and places itself in line with the former. Market talk purports to reveal the true nature of things, whereas other discourses belie particular ideologies in addressing public issues, thereby imposing constraints on humans and their environment. Refusing to heed social convention, market talk dispenses with pretense. Rhetorical theorist James Aune explains that "realism is the default rhetoric for defenders of the free market." Market talk treats language as a veil over nature. Investigators may discover truth by progressively uncovering symbolic elements until one locates an essence. Aune writes that "the realist economic style works by radically separating power and textuality, constructing the political realm as a state of nature, and by depicting its opponents as prisoners of verbal illusions."[17] Nonmarket approaches remained constrained by language, mistaking artifice for nature. Market talk circulates the ostensibly objective voice of the economist at a societal level. Portraying the economist's authorial pose, Deirdre McCloskey explains that "it is not I the scientist who makes these assertions but reality itself."[18] In this way, market talk seeks to deny its own status as a discourse.

Still, for market talk, the real is the ideal insofar as discerning the true nature of things enables individuals to realize their full potential. The idealist qualities of market talk appear in frequent associations of democratic practices with the practices of the market itself. Thomas Frank notes that in the view of market advocates in the 1990s, "the market was *more* democratic than any of the formal institutions of democracy. . . . The market was infinitely diverse, permitting without prejudice the articulation of any and all tastes and preferences." And the market would protect its democratic character unfailingly: "It had no place for snobs, for hierarchies, for elitism, for pretense, and it would fight these things by its very nature." Rather than betraying utopian thinking, these claims represented an embrace of an essential quality. Markets thus constituted an inherently ethically superior realm of society because they enabled more authentic expressions of human activity. Frank observes that advocates embedded markets in human nature: "Markets are where we are most fully human; markets are where we show that we have a soul. To protest *against* markets is to surrender one's very personhood."[19] Markets act compassionately, but without compulsion and constraint.

As real and ideal, market talk presents itself as the culmination of a progressive history of human development. This quality of market talk appears as both triumphant and inevitable. In terms of the former, markets have triumphed over competing modes of organizing economic and political affairs. Communication theorist George Cheney explains that this perspective situates markets at "the end of history," espousing "the post–Cold War position that the market has triumphed over socialist and communist economies. With this position, capitalism is usually equated with democracy, such that mentioning one neatly accounts for the other."[20] As this association suggests, the triumph of markets represents the victory of democracy over nondemocratic alternatives. Whereas this victory highlights human agency, as millions of market actors have worked individually to defeat collective foes, inevitability situates history as an agent. From this perspective, individuals may have hastened the worldwide arrival of markets, but this development would have occurred eventually as part of an evolutionary process. The inevitable quality of market talk appears frequently in policy debates over global economic development, as indicated in the distinction between "developing" and "developed" nations. In these terms, developed nations possess mature market economies and compliant governing institutions, while developing nations occupy a point on an evolutionary path toward a full-fledged market economy. Officials from organizations such as the World Bank push these nations to relinquish nonmarket practices and commitments.

The Rhetorical Life of a Public Policy

Policies do not attend youth soccer games or read Harry Potter books, but they do lead lives. Policymakers create policies, and subsequent policymakers adopt or disown existing policies. In this process, some policies grow strong and self-assured, receiving praise from policymakers and citizens alike, while other policies scrape out a meager existence, suffering the scorn of the populace. Any policy that lives long enough will confront varied challenges and opportunities, which force a policy to find its way in a society different from its birth. Some policies may maintain their values and principles during changing times, whereas others will adapt to their environments, abiding by new principles and pursuing alternative goals. The following chapters focus on a specific period in the seventy-plus year life of Social Security, when policymakers and others scrutinized the program's founding principle.

I first consider Social Security's founding, since debates in 1935 raised important tensions that continue to inform policymaking for Social Security. The New Dealers struggled to balance contributory and noncontributory aims for Social Security. On the one hand, they sought to distinguish Old-Age Insurance from assistance by emphasizing its contributory character. On the other hand, they sought to affirm values of justice, fairness, and decency, which exceeded a strict contributory logic. A second tension arose between the universal aspirations of Social Security, as a right earned through a contribution, and its particular application, which excluded a majority of black workers. I refer to these tensions as sites of policy polysemy because the disjunctures they produce have created spaces for subsequent advocates to imagine Social Security in contrary ways.

My analysis of the privatization debates begins in the second chapter as I examine the fundamental conflict in the debates between the long-standing principle of insurance and the privatizing principle of investment. I explicate how both principles function metaphorically, inviting debate participants and observers to regard Social Security through a distinctive value framework. I have indicated the values associated with each principle, but insurance and investment also enabled corollary metaphorical clusters in the debates. For instance, the association of insurance and community enabled supporters of the existing program to invoke repeated "family" metaphors to defend the existing structure of Social Security, while advocates of investment reversed this metaphor to charge the insurance-based system with a dereliction of parental responsibility.

In addition to guiding principles, policymaking connects policies to target populations, demonstrating rhetoric's power of representation. As I explain in chapter 3, representation implicates debate participants in ethical and aesthetic choices regarding Social Security beneficiaries. Ethical choices arise because representation grants social status rather than involving participants in a neutral, transparent process. Artistic choices may hide the constructed character of representation, as eloquent images "effortlessly" report on populations. Representations during the privatization debates highlighted age: many participants perceived young people, baby boomers, and seniors as having different—and potentially conflicting—interests. Some advocates linked privatization with equal opportunity, imagining an investment nation that would overcome differences of class, race, and gender.

In the 1990s, advocates pointed to soaring stock markets as proof of the superiority of investment. However, as the new millennium began, stock markets crashed, fueled by the bursting of the dot-com bubble. Moreover, high-profile cases of scandal shook public faith in the integrity of corporate America. Although these events suggested caution, advocates continued to insist on the need for an immediate change to Social Security. In chapter 4, I amplify how debate participants engaged the rhetorical notion of *kairos*, which refers to discourse "at the right time in the right measure."[21] Debate participants negotiated time as a contextual factor, and they invoked time as a rhetorical appeal. Advocates sought to maintain a sense of urgency for investment by historicizing market declines and isolating scandals. Advocates also foregrounded what they regarded as the system's imminent insolvency.

In 2004, President Bush won his reelection campaign, while Republicans increased their majorities in the House and Senate. In this context, in the days after the election, Bush identified Social Security as a top priority for his second term. That winter, he launched a barnstorming tour for private accounts. My analysis in chapter 5 examines how Bush and other debate participants shifted their rhetoric from the comparatively esoteric realms of hearing rooms to the public sphere. Interest groups on both sides of the issue developed extensive media campaigns, utilizing fear and humor appeals to accentuate or downplay "crises." For politicians accustomed to having their way, the egalitarian self-understanding of the public sphere created the problem of appearing to facilitate unrestricted debate while sustaining one's privilege. Bush drew on his image as a regular, likeable guy to speak plainly to Americans on their own terms.

The privatization debates offer many important lessons for Social Security, as well as policy debates more generally. Since "reality" does not serve as a transparent and interest-free guide, I sketch a framework for ethical policy debate in the conclusion. Ethical debate obligates participants to speak honestly, contextualize their claims, exhibit openness to contrary evidence, appeal to audiences' better selves, and engage each other vigorously. Judged in this light, the privatization debates provided ample evidence of failure amid the occasional instance of inspiring deliberation. Redressing this situation requires a reversal of the trajectory of market talk. Social Security serves this end as a powerful model of democracy in action that provides people with the symbolic and material resources for engaged citizenship.

1

Policy Polysemy and the 1935 Social Security Debates

A mericans know Social Security. They likely know it better than any other public policy. Whereas many policies appear distant from Americans' everyday lives, seemingly addressed only to Washington insiders, Social Security touches ordinary citizens directly. For millions of Americans, Social Security has provided irreplaceable benefits to compensate for income lost through the tragic injury or death of a breadwinner. For millions more, Social Security has provided steady retirement benefits for oneself, a parent, or a grandparent, affirming, in the process, the honorific status of senior citizen. And virtually all Americans have experienced the rite of passage enacted by obtaining a Social Security card—the nearly universal entry credential into the world of work. Once working, Americans receive a regular (and sometimes irritating) reminder of Social Security in the form of a dedicated payroll-tax deduction.

Yet familiarity with Social Security has not produced a universal understanding or judgment of the program. Americans disagree about what Social Security does, and they judge its successes and failures differently. Some Americans recognize the intergenerational financing of Social

Security, whereby workers pay taxes to sustain the benefits of current retirees, while other Americans construe Social Security as a system of individual retirement accounts. This latter interpretation does not represent a
simple case of misunderstanding, since the Social Security Administration
encourages this very understanding by sending out periodic statements
to Americans explaining the status of their retirement contributions.
Americans also express varying degrees of confidence in Social Security's
future. Some indicate complete confidence that they will receive benefits
in retirement, whereas others—especially younger workers—doubt that
Social Security will survive into their golden years. Although these interpretations differ, they share a common history and origin—the growth
of Social Security in the United States and, importantly, the founding
debates over the 1935 Social Security Act. Policymakers in the 1930s did
not speak with one voice on Old-Age Insurance (OAI), what we today
call Social Security, even when they supported it. Disagreements over
the purposes and populations for the program produced tensions in its
legitimating discourses, which have enabled different prescriptions for the
proper conduct of, and a propitious future for, Social Security.

I call this range of interpretations and meanings "policy polysemy."
Policy polysemy indicates that debate participants may understand the
objects of their deliberation differently, sometimes holding in view different objects under the same subject heading. These differences do not
merely signal support or opposition to a policy, what Celeste Condit right-
fully characterizes as "polyvalence,"[1] but differences in kind. However,
my reference to polysemy itself invokes a polysemous term. In an engaging essay, Leah Ceccarelli explains that rhetorical scholars have employed
the term "polysemy" variously to refer to multiple meanings created by
rhetors, audiences, and critics.[2] Rhetor-induced polysemy refers to strategic ambiguity introduced by the creator of a text to negotiate potentially
competing situational demands, such as multiple audiences with opposing interests. Audience-induced polysemy indicates a "resistive reading"
that understands a text differently from the dominant message intended
by its creator. Critic-induced polysemy alludes to the intellectual dexterity
of the analyst, who discerns multiple meanings in a text to appreciate
more fully its rhetorical dynamics.

Policy polysemy crosses these categories, raising questions of author-
ship and temporality differently than single, discrete texts. In comparison to a single speech, for example, a policy debate involves not a single

public author, but hundreds, if not thousands. This complicates a clear-cut identification of polysemy as strategic ambiguity or resistive reading, for both senses presume a readily identifiable author and audience. And yet, we cannot simply turn to the critic, because policy polysemy does not fit easily with Ceccarelli's characterization of critically induced polysemy as "not mak[ing] a claim about how audiences 'actually' read a text, but instead, offers a new expanded way that audiences *should* read a text."[3] To be sure, this chapter engages the 1935 debates to gain a fuller understanding of their tensions, but policy debates resist appreciative criticism as much as they enable it through their multiple authors and audiences. Like the stubborn cats frustrating the hypothetical shepherd, the participants and audiences of policy debates do not relinquish their independence graciously in constituting a larger textual entity. The critical work of analyzing policy debates focuses on discovering *how* participants and audiences understand a policy, as well as arguing that a critic's readers *should* understand the debates in a particular way.

In terms of temporality, policy debates represent an ongoing engagement of text and context. Debate participants disagreed over the purposes and populations for OAI in 1935, and subsequent participants have interpreted and reinterpreted the meanings of the founding debates ever since. Both advocates of investment and supporters of insurance have asserted that their preferred purposes comport with the guiding spirit of Social Security. In this way, rhetor, audience, text, and context operate in cross-historical perspective. Compare the development of debates over Social Security to Ceccarelli's illustrations of resistive readings and strategic ambiguity. For resistive readings, she cites Southern newspaper interpretations of President Lincoln's Second Inaugural Address. For strategic ambiguity, she references, among other examples, Henry Grady's 1886 speech "The New South." In both cases, the elements of the rhetorical situations constellated at a particular historical moment. In contrast, Social Security constitutes a "living" text with over seventy years of experience. Whether we consider the founding debates, the privatization debates, or their interaction, we cannot avoid the observation that policy debates—unlike a single rhetorical act—unfold over time. Moreover, subsequent debate participants cannot avoid the influence of past debates in shaping their perspectives.

My purpose in this chapter is to investigate tensions in the 1935 debates that help explain how Social Security—as insurance or investment, sturdy or shaky, a just retirement or government theft—has come to mean different things to different people. The founding debates stand as a symbolic resource for participants in the privatization debates, who implicitly and explicitly have revisited earlier themes. My analysis focuses on two key issues: eligibility, the basis on which retirees would receive benefits; and coverage, the classes of workers who would be able to participate in the program. Supporters of OAI framed eligibility in terms of a contributory right: payments made during one's working years would entitle one to receive benefits during retirement. However, in making their case for the program, supporters departed from the strict logic of a contributory right. They held that OAI should represent values of fairness, decency, and social justice, which could not be met through attention to contributions alone. These noncontributory values also threatened to confuse the clear distinction that supporters wished to uphold between insurance and assistance. With respect to coverage, Social Security's designers appreciated the universality of old age, and they understood that insurance programs operated best with a diverse coverage pool. However, the designers quickly ceded to the politics of the Congress in agreeing to exclude particular classes of workers. Although debate participants recognized the clear racial implications of these exclusions, most participants avoided explicit references to race, utilizing instead the language of administration to neutralize this potentially volatile question. Before addressing these two issues, I discuss the context of the 1935 debates. In the penultimate section of this chapter, I discuss the growth of OAI in the decades after 1935 from a little-known contributory pension system to the embodiment of Social Security itself.

From Industrial Pensions to Social Security

Before Social Security, as the nation began its second century, Americans lived uneven lives in retirement—if they retired at all. The same inequities that characterized Americans' working years shaped their retirement possibilities. Owning property sometimes provided white men with security, but most Americans had to rely on the kindness— or, at least, the absence of outright cruelty—of others. Women, blacks, and immigrants often experienced their advanced years as anything but golden.[4] The world of work transformed dramatically during this period, as industrialization produced rapid change in the United States toward the end of the nineteenth century. Between 1880 and 1890, the number of people employed in manufacturing increased by 67 percent.[5] With the rise of manufacturing came a shift in the locus of economic decision making and control; corporations superseded much of the decision-making authority of local merchants.[6] Even as these economic transformations arose, old age remained the same for most Americans. Estimates from the early twentieth century indicate that roughly half of the elderly lived comfortably. Another 15 percent of elderly men and women lived on a budget that provided for their basic subsistence. The remaining 35 percent of the elderly lived in near-subsistence or impoverished conditions.[7] As these figures suggest, the experience of old age in industrial America varied for different people and groups.

Motivated mainly by self-interest, employers started offering company pensions in the late-nineteenth and early-twentieth centuries.[8] Fearful of labor-union organizing and uncertain about the implications of mass production, employers wished to establish more stable and predictable relationships with their employees. In a 1932 study of industrial pensions in the United States, Murray Latimer, who would later serve as one of the main designers of the Old-Age Insurance provision of the Social Security Act, reported that employers increasingly turned to pensions after 1910. Of the 397 pensions in operation in 1929, 211 were established between 1911 and 1920, and 126 were established between 1921 and 1929. Existing pensions were heavily concentrated in the railroad, utility, and metal industries. For instance, 82 percent of railroad employees and 90 percent of telephone and telegraph employees worked for companies offering pension plans.[9] However, the percentages for workers in general contrasted sharply with these figures. At no point before the 1940s did even one-tenth of the entire civilian work force receive pension coverage.[10] Moreover, concerns about employer manipulation and control persisted. Abraham Epstein, a noted social-insurance and pension expert, wrote in 1933 that "practically all plans include in their rules a number of conditions which materially limit the chance of the average employee to qualify. In some cases the rules also make it possible to use the pension system to enforce plant discipline."[11]

One significant public alternative to industrial pensions existed in the late nineteenth century and early twentieth century: Civil War pensions. Begun as a relatively modest system of benefits for Union veterans disabled in the Civil War, this system eventually developed, in the words of Theda Skocpol, into a "kind of precocious social security system for those U.S. citizens of a certain generation and region who were deemed morally worthy of enjoying generous and honorable public aid." In this way, the percentage of veterans enrolled as pensioners grew from just 5 percent in 1870 to over 93 percent in 1915.[12] However, as Civil War pensions continued into the Progressive Era, social reformers raised questions about patronage, fraud, and waste. In 1913, Isaac Rubinow, a social-insurance analyst, called for an honest assessment of veterans' pensions. He asserted as a matter of "common knowledge" that "pensions are obtained upon fraudulent representation of past services, forged records, fictitious marriage certificates, etc." The problems of the federal pension system led Rubinow to conclude that "the most singular feature of the American pension system is that it primarily redounds to the advantage of a class least in need of old-age pensions."[13] Partially in response to the perceived corruption and excesses of Civil War pensions, states did not adopt similar measures for citizens.

More basic objections blocked the adoption of state pensions, however. In 1910, for example, the Massachusetts Commission on Old Age Pensions issued a report denouncing old-age pensions. The commission concluded that "the adoption of any scheme of non-contributory pensions in Massachusetts, or any other American state, seems inadvisable and impracticable."[14] Pensions threatened family integrity, since intergenerational bonds depended on children supporting their aged parents. Pensions also threatened self-reliance, potentially expanding the class of dependents to previously independent segments of society. The commission also questioned the constitutionality of pensions. Instead, the commission proposed measures to reaffirm thrift, including compulsory education in the public schools. The commission adamantly rejected appeals to citizenship, regarding as "distinctly un-American" the doctrine that "a citizen may claim a pension from the state as a right."[15] After 1920, attitudes toward pensions shifted, as the elderly emerged as a key issue in politics and new leadership arose in the social-insurance movement.[16] More ominously, the Great Depression worsened the conditions of the elderly and revealed the limits of private voluntary efforts to provide security in old age.

Producing massive disruptions to economic and social life, the Great Depression forced collective rethinking in public attitudes regarding the proper role of the federal government in bolstering the economy and fostering social well-being. Statistics tell part of the story. Between 1929 and 1933, the gross national product fell by one-half, and business investment sank to one-eighth of its previous value. During the same period, official unemployment climbed from 3.2 to 24.9 percent. In some places, unemployment reached truly catastrophic levels. Fifty percent of the workers in Cleveland were unemployed, and 80 percent of workers in Toledo, Ohio, could not find work.[17] In the South, many sharecroppers and tenant families—already living in ramshackle houses without electricity, plumbing, or running water—received no income for years.[18] For many observers, the Great Depression portended a bleak national future. Historian David Kennedy writes of a spreading feeling that "the nation had turned a historic corner, to find itself facing an endless future of pervasive, structural unemployment."[19] Rather than producing widespread unrest, misery reduced many Americans to passive, stoic acceptance.

Within this context, observers reported on the desperate situation of the elderly. Abraham Epstein wrote of "the tragedy that is old age."[20] He held that specialization in modern industry practically eliminated the need for the skill and experience of the older worker. He noted that "it is now an established fact that modern American industry does not want men and women past middle age."[21] Employers frequently limited their hiring searches to people under forty-five years of age. Older workers suffered from a 50 percent higher unemployment rate than workers under sixty-five years of age. Moreover, periods of unemployment lasted longer—in some cases twice as long—for older workers than for younger workers. The Depression only worsened the situation for older workers, leaving Epstein to conclude that the chances of an older worker finding employment had "almost completely vanished." The pervasiveness of old-age unemployment and dependency compelled a reassessment of the supposed causes of economic distress. Epstein urged his readers to abandon explanations that placed fault with individuals. The elderly suffered despite their best efforts. Poverty in old age constituted a national problem: "The nature and extent of old age dependency in the United States clearly indicate that it is not due to individual maladjustment but rather to social and economic forces altogether beyond the control of the individual."[22] Nor could charities respond adequately. Between 1929 and 1932, one-third of the nation's private agencies disappeared for lack of funds.[23] In 1932, community chests raised more money than ever before, but they still could not meet existing needs.[24] A private, local response seemed impossible.

Under these conditions, social movements clamored for political change. Historians have written about the widespread social influence of figures like Louisiana senator Huey Long and the Detroit radio priest Father Charles Coughlin,[25] but members of Congress considering OAI devoted most of their attention to a movement led by California physician Francis Townsend.[26] Edwin Witte, who served as executive director of the Committee on Economic Security, recalled that Townsend's congressional testimony created unusual excitement. Witte recounted that "his appearances before the two congressional committees were widely advertised in advance, attracted the largest audiences of the entire hearings, and received front-page publicity in nearly all daily newspapers."[27] The movement started modestly in September 1933 when Dr. Townsend sent a letter to his local newspaper in Long Beach, California, proposing a monthly pension of $200 for people over age sixty who agreed to withdraw from the work force. He would require recipients to spend their entire pension check every month, which, in turn, would revive the economy. Townsend planned to pay for the pensions with a 2 percent national tax. Support for the proposal grew quickly. Townsend Clubs formed throughout the country to advance the plan. In 1934, Townsend incorporated his movement, and he launched a national newsletter in 1935 called the *Townsend National Weekly*. As congressional committees considered the Social Security Act, Townsend attracted millions of members to his clubs, and many millions more signed petitions calling on Congress to adopt old-age pensions. Townsendites flooded members of Congress with letters urging adoption of the doctor's proposal.

Although he appreciated the influence of social movements, FDR championed his own plan for economic security. In a June 8, 1934, message to Congress, President Roosevelt announced that "next winter we may well undertake the great task of furthering the security of the citizen and his family through social insurance."[28] On June 29, Roosevelt issued Executive Order no. 6757 establishing a Committee on Economic Security (CES), an Advisory Council on Economic Security, and a Technical Board on Economic Security. Secretary of Labor Frances Perkins chaired the CES, acting as its driving force. In her biography of FDR, Perkins recounted his reaction when she suggested that the attorney general serve as chair. Roosevelt retorted: "No, no. You care about this thing. You believe in it. Therefore I know you will put your back to it more than anyone else, and you will drive it through. You will see that something comes out, and we must not delay."[29] Perkins shared the president's enthusiasm for social insurance. Other members of the committee, Harry Hopkins especially, pressed for combining relief and social-insurance payments. Hopkins believed that people should receive relief as a matter of right. Perkins and FDR believed that a combined approach would effectively turn social insurance into a "dole." The report of the CES strongly advocated differentiation. Comparing assistance and insurance for the elderly, the CES report judged that "contributory annuities are unquestionably preferable to noncontributory pensions. They come to the workers as a right, whereas the noncontributory pensions must be conditioned upon a 'means' test."[30]

While the Advisory Council on Economic Security primarily represented different interests and bolstered political support for the president's agenda, the Technical Board on Economic Security and its subcommittees handled the task of designing and drafting the components of the Social Security Act. Although they recognized the need to provide assistance to the elderly, the three subcommittee members drafting the old-age provisions of the Act—pension experts Murray Latimer, J. Douglas Brown, and Barbara Armstrong—saw in social insurance an exciting policy future. They argued that OAI would lower costs and encourage thrift. The subcommittee explained that "since insurance benefits would be received as a matter of right, based on contributions related to wages, workers would be encouraged to maintain the best possible record of employment and wages in order to earn the right to a high rate of benefits. Savings or other assets would in no way reduce the amount of benefits received but would provide a means of augmenting income in the later years of life."[31] Led by its chair, Armstrong, the subcommittee pressed for a national approach to guarantee a uniform system of benefits while preventing destructive interstate competition.

The Social Security Act appeared as part of what some historians have referred to as the "Second New Deal." In 1933, facing the immediate problem of economic misery, the new administration worked with Congress to enact a flurry of legislation aimed at recovery. By 1935, as work remained elusive and families still suffered, the administration increasingly considered reform efforts geared toward shaping the nation's future. In this spirit, OAI promised no immediate relief to families—it would not even begin to distribute benefits until 1942—but OAI did promise a reconstructed experience of retirement. Further, the Second New Deal exhibited a change in methods, moving away from the national economic-planning approach of 1933 toward an ameliorative relationship with a decentered market economy. As Arthur Schlesinger Jr. has prominently explained, "the First New Deal characteristically told business what it must do. The Second New Deal characteristically told business what it must *not* do."[32] In this spirit, OAI sought to establish the limits of just economic activity by enabling a secure retirement that accounted for individual work histories.

Yet neither the First nor the Second New Deal escaped judicial scrutiny and, in the case of the former, Supreme Court rejections. On May 27, 1935, "Black Monday," as policymakers considered the Social Security Act, the Supreme Court handed down three unanimous decisions that infuriated and embarrassed FDR. Most prominently, in *Schechter Poultry Corporation v. United States*, the Court declared the National Industrial Recovery Act unconstitutional. In a meeting with reporters four days after the decision, FDR famously fumed: "We have been relegated to the horse-and-buggy definition of interstate commerce."[33] Concern over future Supreme Court decisions extended to CES staff. Thomas Eliot—a young lawyer who served as counsel to the CES and an associate solicitor in the Department of Labor—recalled that he "could not honestly assure the committee that a national plan for old age insurance would be upheld by the Supreme Court." He wondered if the Court would "say that a law levying a payroll tax and spending the proceeds in paying old age benefits was really nothing else but a federal insurance scheme to provide annuities to the elderly, and that the Constitution gave Congress no authority to go into the insurance business."[34] Yet CES staff felt that they had no choice: the limits of state plans committed the CES to recommending a national plan.

On January 17, 1935, President Roosevelt, calling for prompt action, sent a message to Congress announcing the Social Security legislation. In January and February, the Ways and Means and Finance committees held hearings. Committee chairs Rep. Robert "Farmer Bob" Doughton and Sen. Byron "Pat" Harrison—both Southern conservatives—pledged to work with the administration to report a bill. Yet their congressional colleagues displayed greater enthusiasm for Old-Age Assistance (OAA). For members of Congress, assistance fit the situation faced by their elderly constituents in 1935. Assistance promised help right away, and its benefits appeared more generous than the amounts contemplated for Old-Age Insurance. Indeed, in the years after the enactment of the Social Security Act, assistance benefits to individuals exceeded insurance benefits. For these reasons, OAA provided a more appealing response to the proposals of Long and Townsend than social insurance.

Representatives of business derided OAI as an unwarranted intrusion into employer-employee relations. Companies with existing pension plans sought exemptions from OAI. If exemptions had been granted, Social Security would be a very different program—and likely a considerably less consequential program—than it is today.[35] The status of business exemptions rested on the fate of a provision known as the Clark Amendment. The product of an intensive lobbying campaign, the amendment was introduced by Finance Committee member Sen. Bennett Clark, a conservative Democrat from Missouri. The amendment alarmed the Roosevelt administration, which pressed the House to exclude any such amendment from its bill. The ensuing conference committee struggled over the amendment. Thomas Eliot recalled that "it even seemed possible that the whole bill would go down the drain, owning to the inability of conferees to agree on whether to include the Clark Amendment."[36] Eventually, conferees reached a compromise by establishing a special committee to revisit the amendment the following year. By the time the committee met, business opposition to OAI had waned. Employers discovered that federal OAI actually bolstered private pensions by allowing employers to reward higher-income workers with supplemental benefits at a comparatively low cost.[37]

Congressional opposition to OAI appeared most explicitly in the minority report of the House Ways and Means Committee. Signed by all seven Republican members of the committee, the report singled out OAI as the objectionable title of the Social Security bill. The minority members of the committee approved of the assistance provisions of the bill, including aid to states for public health, maternal and child welfare, care of dependent children, and, importantly, noncontributory old-age pensions. They also indicated cautious support for the principle of unemployment insurance. However, when they came to contributory old-age pensions, the Republican members of the committee categorically rejected the idea. They questioned the constitutionality of the provision, holding that the "Federal Government has no power to impose this system upon private industry."[38] The minority members asserted further that OAI would offer no relief from present economic conditions, and it could even retard economic recovery. The signees maintained that OAI would "impose a crushing burden upon industry and upon labor."[39] The administrative apparatus required by such a system would result in the establishment of an unwieldy bureaucracy that would compete unfairly with private businesses and destroy private retirement systems. Nevertheless, all but one minority committee member, in addition to overwhelming majorities of Republicans and Democrats, voted for the Social Security Act on the House and Senate floors.

On August 14, 1935, President Franklin Roosevelt signed the Social Security Act into law. Old-Age Insurance appeared as the second title of the Social Security Act, after Old-Age Assistance.[40] Its funding provisions appeared in Title VIII. The legislation stipulated that the levying of payroll taxes would begin on January 1, 1937, and the distribution of benefits would commence on January 1, 1942. The legislation established a reserve account, prescribing that reserve funds could be invested only in interest-bearing obligations of the United States, or in obligations guaranteed in principal and interest by the United States. The Act specified a 3 percent return for reserve-fund investments. Taxes and benefits covered the first $3,000 of annual income. The legislation excluded certain categories of employees, including federal, state, and local government employees; employees of nonprofit organizations; and, importantly, agricultural, domestic, and casual laborers.

Security in a New Era

President Roosevelt's June 8, 1934, message to Congress previewed many of the important themes that characterized congressional consideration of the Social Security Act. Roosevelt explained that the nation faced a changed and challenging social environment, which Congress had to address in any effort to spur economic recovery. Roosevelt's description of this environment evidenced both temporal and spatial features. With respect to the former, the nation needed to strike a balance between historical transformation and timeless values. For Roosevelt, history—or at least American history—did not proceed as a sequence of contiguous yet entirely disparate eras supplanting those that came before. Social change did not sweep away existing practices and values, nor did change render these values and practices obsolete. Policymakers could foster economic recovery by remembering values forgotten in the speed of social change. FDR explained that economic "reconstruction does not require the creation of new and strange values." Rather, reconstruction consisted of "finding the way once more to known, but to some degree forgotten, ideals and values. If the means and details are in some instances new, the objectives are as permanent as human nature." Later in his message, Roosevelt described his plans as a "return to values lost in the course of our economic development and expansion."[41] The temporal balance informing Roosevelt's advocacy appeared in his linkage of newness and permanence. Recovery required return and remembrance.

Spatial features of this altered landscape included Americans' connection to their physical environment, as well as connections among local and national spaces. Unlike their ancestors, modern Americans could not simply find new and better spaces to alleviate suffering. Roosevelt noted that nature's bounty had offered seemingly endless opportunities to previous generations. When their land had worn out, "our ancestors moved on to better land. It was always possible to push back the frontier." Yet the physical environment had changed, and this required a different sense of exploration and ingenuity. For modern Americans, the "frontier has now disappeared. Our task involves the making of a better living out of the lands that we have."[42] Movement entailed reordering existing spaces. This involved a second important spatial feature: a reconfiguration of national and local space. In past eras, local communities provided sufficient resources for citizens' security. Familial and economic arrangements made this possible, and local governments could handle the dislocations that periodically impacted their communities. In contrast, "the complexities of great communities and of organized industry make less real these simple means of security." The economy had become national in scope; networks of interdependence replaced relatively autonomous local economies. This change, in turn, required a changed government response. Roosevelt held that "we are compelled to employ the active interest of the nation as a whole through government in order to encourage a greater security for each individual who composes it."[43] Rather than suggesting a loss of independence, interdependence signaled the changed scale of economic activity and dislocation, and a corresponding change in scale of an appropriate government response.

In this situation, security had become a national objective. For
Roosevelt, security entailed decent homes, productive work, and safeguards against misfortune. Safeguarding the nation against misfortune
meant responding to the hazards and vicissitudes of life. The specter
of unseen harm produced fear and worry in the populace, which only
exacerbated social unrest and economic suffering. An appropriate government response thus fit Roosevelt's assessment of the situation: the
federal government needed to act to provide a counterweight of stability and predictability against seemingly uncontrollable and unforgiving
change. Security lay in a reduction of uncertainty by offering assurance
amid change. Moreover, Roosevelt insisted, the Constitution compelled
the federal government to act. Roosevelt observed that "if, as our Constitution tells us, our Federal Government was established among other
things 'to promote the general welfare,' it is our plain duty to provide
for that security upon which welfare depends."[44] In this way, Roosevelt
articulated an anticipatory retort against those who would subsequently
question the constitutionality of the Social Security Act.

Social insurance stood as the method for obtaining security against
misfortune. Roosevelt informed members of Congress that "next winter
we may well undertake the great task of furthering the security of the
citizen and his family through social insurance."[45] Expressed immediately after Roosevelt's declaration of constitutional sanction for federal
action, this statement linked security and insurance as aim and method.
Security also appeared as the third, progressive step in a program of
economic recovery. FDR developed this theme in his first Fireside Chat
of 1934. Reviewing the accomplishments of the seventy-third Congress,
he told his radio listeners that legislation enacted during the congressional term initially addressed the pressing need of relief. Recovery came
next, which entailed reforming and reconstructing institutions and
practices in various sectors of the economy. Whereas relief and recovery
focused on the present, security looked to the future. Securing a future
meant using "the agencies of government to assist in the establishment
of means to provide sound and adequate protection against the vicissitudes of modern life—in other words, social insurance." Once again,
FDR's discourse evidenced temporal balance: one could not predict the
future, but a measure of confidence could be achieved through proper
government action. Moreover, security in the future entailed remembering the past, reviving "well-known, long-established but to some

degree forgotten ideals and values."[46] Timeless values offered stability in times of change.

Social insurance promised benefits to recipients as a right. For Roosevelt, this was true of security in general. He proclaimed that "these three great objectives—the security of the home, the security of livelihood, and the security of social insurance—are, it seems to me, a minimum of the promise that we can offer to the American people. They constitute a right which belongs to every individual and every family willing to work."[47] In the case of social insurance, a sense of right emerged from its contributory financing structure. Roosevelt insisted that general tax dollars must not finance social insurance. Instead, funds should be generated by dedicated contributions. This would establish social insurance as an independently financed program paid for by the beneficiaries themselves. In his history of the New Deal, Arthur Schlesinger Jr. notes a subsequent response by FDR to concerns about the regressive character of a payroll tax. Roosevelt conceded this point, but he explained that "we put those payroll contributions there so as to give the contributors a legal, moral, and political right to collect their pensions and their unemployment benefits. With those taxes in there, no damn politician can ever scrap my social security program."[48] As the congressional hearings revealed, this right did not free itself from constraint, nor did the program truly finance itself. For Roosevelt, however, insurance stood in stark contrast to relief. Whereas insurance tied benefits to contributions, relief simply dispersed funds. Although relief may have been a necessary first step in a program of economic recovery, it could not serve as the basis of future federal policy. In a speech to the Advisory Council of the CES later in the year, Roosevelt insisted on a clear distinction between insurance and relief. He instructed that "we must not allow this type of insurance to become a dole through the intermingling of insurance and relief. It is not charity. It must be financed by contributions, not taxes."[49] In practice, the financing of OAA and OAI would display strong similarities. In the discourse of FDR and his supporters, the symbolic import of assistance and insurance would be quite different.

In his 1935 State of the Union message, Roosevelt pressed the themes of his Social Security program with greater urgency. He reiterated his firm belief that only social insurance could enable Americans to achieve security, while sharpening his objections to relief. FDR focused on unemployment and his preference for public-works projects over cash and in-kind

benefits, but his critique of relief applied more widely, especially considering the contributory character of OAI versus noncontributory assistance.
Indeed, contemporary conservatives often have cited FDR's 1935 State of
the Union message in support of their attacks on federal social-welfare
policy. Roosevelt characterized relief as a necessary first response to economic pain and suffering, but he warned that long-term reliance on relief
transformed this medicine from remedy to disease. Relief threatened the
body politic with physical and spiritual addiction. History demonstrated
"conclusively that continued dependence upon relief induces a spiritual
and moral disintegration fundamentally destructive to the national fibre.
To dole out relief in this way is to administer a narcotic, a subtle destroyer
of the human spirit."[50] Taken too long, relief acted as a dangerous drug
that warped the body and mind of its user. Like other dangerous drugs
that appear initially to give their users a newfound sense of independence
and vitality, relief ultimately destroyed a person's self-reliance and self-
respect. Insidiously, relief positioned agents of the federal government,
whose duty was to help make Americans secure, as dealers. This could not
stand. Roosevelt announced unequivocally that "the Federal Government
must and shall quit this business of relief."[51] Contrary to contemporary appropriations of Roosevelt's remarks, the president did not believe that the
federal government had no role to play in social-welfare policy. Given the
national scope of the economic problems facing the country, the federal
government had to act. FDR stressed that "the Federal Government is the
only governmental agency with sufficient power and credit to meet this
situation."[52] Opposed to inaction, and convinced that private responses to
social problems would not succeed, FDR favored public employment and
insurance.

On January 17, 1935, President Roosevelt sent a message to Congress announcing his Social Security legislation. Like his advocacy in the
preceding months, the president's initiative sought balance in uncertain
times. Warning against extravagant action, and implicitly rebuking the
proposals of Long and Townsend, Roosevelt described social insurance
as a "sound idea" that would develop into a "sound and workable project." He instructed Congress to follow three principles in passing the
legislation. With respect to those programs that called for federal-state
cooperation, he encouraged deference to state officials in the management of the programs. Second, he envisioned the trust funds of the social-
insurance programs as public and federal accounts. Policymakers should

guarantee their sound management by "retaining federal control over all funds through trustees in the Treasury of the United States." Of most consequence for congressional consideration of OAI, Roosevelt insisted that social insurance adhere to the principle of self-support. He prescribed that "the system adopted, except for the money necessary to initiate it, should be self-sustaining in the sense that funds for the payment of insurance benefits should not come from the proceeds of general taxation."[53] Although advocates of OAI turned to a dedicated payroll tax for funding, some of their aims for the program presented challenges to notions of self-sufficiency.

Financing Rights

Like the president, members of Congress and committee witnesses believed that the nation faced a changing economy. The Great Depression upset an ostensibly natural cycle of recession and recovery. A more ominous trajectory of reduced economic output threatened the nation's well-being. Many members of Congress doubted whether the economy could offer a decent livelihood to all Americans. Older workers especially suffered. Witnesses testified that older workers disproportionately experienced the destabilizing effects of technological change and geographic mobility. Their support networks dissolved as children moved away from parents and local communities succumbed to disruptive social forces. The Depression dissolved whatever savings the elderly had accumulated. Industry had simply abandoned older workers. A zero-sum game characterized the job market. Industry required fewer workers, and employers increasingly chose lower-paid younger workers when making hiring decisions. Testifying before the Ways and Means Committee, Rep. James Mott lamented the problem of permanent unemployment. He explained that "it is no longer necessary for industry to employ more than a portion of our population." In this situation, older workers could not survive. Employers regarded them as obsolete parts: "People over 60 years of age have reached the end of their real economic usefulness in modern industry."[54]

Others saw pensions and insurance as ways to help all workers. Removing older workers from the labor force would open paths to employment and promotion for younger workers, raising overall economic productivity and employee morale. Martin Folsom, a member of the

Advisory Council on Economic Security and an executive at the Eastman Kodak Corporation, expressed precisely this rationale for existing industry plans. With private annuities, "you are able to retire persons after they have outgrown their period of usefulness and replace them by more efficient workers. Therefore in the long run they pay for themselves."[55] OAI accorded older workers a central role in the federal government's response to economic distress. Indeed, invoking the Townsend plan, Murray Latimer saw the purchasing power of old-age annuities as a potentially strong force for economic stimulus. As a long-range objective, he envisioned "a marked rise in the level of the social welfare generally if we made some arrangement whereby there would be continuously a clearance of the aged persons from among those who seek jobs."[56] Reflecting the increasingly interdependent nature of the national economy, social-welfare policies enacted in one area could spur improvements in other areas.

Nor could policymakers ignore the cost of caring for the elderly. As Edwin Witte explained to both the Finance and Ways and Means committees, "whether you enact pension laws or not, that cost is there."[57] And costs would only increase. Several committee witnesses—including Witte, Latimer, Sen. Robert Wagner, Frances Perkins, and Henry Morgenthau Jr.—warned that the percentage of elderly as a proportion of the total population would increase dramatically in the years ahead. Witte, for example, indicated that the proportion of elderly would double in thirty years. Elderly dependency already constituted a national problem that would only worsen without federal action. Increased national costs meant that a cost-effective response required national design and implementation. Observing that "old age is national in nature," Frank Graham, chair of the CES Advisory Council, raised an important actuarial principle. He explained that "the only way you could set up a sound actuarial old-age insurance plan would be on the whole population in the nation and not by geographical patches."[58] Just as the soundness of a private insurance plan increased with the diversity of the population covered, so, too, would a national plan better distribute risk than numerous state plans.

Supporters of OAI asserted that the elderly would receive benefits as a matter of right. Several committee witnesses stated this position unequivocally. Edwin Witte emphasized the contractual character of old-age annuities. Frances Perkins stressed the right to OAI repeatedly in her testimony. She described the administration's goal as establishing a "secure and systematic method of providing for the old-age necessities of persons who are young and of middle age and in the midst of their working years and therefore theoretically able to contribute to the funds which will be used in the future, as a matter of contractual right." Workers' contributions toward OAI would go toward a fund that "will later be used to pay them an insurance benefit which they have as a contractual right when they become 65 years of age."[59] Douglas Brown may have put the matter most directly, holding that the old-age annuity "is contributory and contractual and affords an annuity as a matter of right." Brown pressed for a clear distinction between insurance and assistance, insisting that people earned their insurance benefits, whereas dependents received assistance as largesse. He stated that "it is insurance not relief. . . . The amounts paid to the aged are related to contributions made to the fund, not to need."[60] Brown proposed the distribution of stamp books so that workers could watch their savings accumulate. Pushing for the same distinction, Edwin Witte noted that assistance, which appeared in the form of old-age pensions, addressed the needs of the presently impoverished elderly. He explained that "the old-age pension is a gratuity paid to people that have nothing to live on—that is the essence of it." By contrast, insurance invoked entitlement, alleviating the need for a pension. Witte maintained that "contributory annuities are something that the man with the matching contributions of his employers builds up for himself."[61]

This distinction bore clear value implications. Speaking of OAI as something earned ascribed an honorific status to the program, its benefits, and its beneficiaries. Insurance carried with it the prestige and obligations of a contract. Its parties appeared as autonomous agents, and their claims could not be denied. In a seemingly literal sense, insurance benefits did not constitute "benefits" at all. Annuities represented payment with interest on a worker's own money. And both parties to the contract benefited: the federal government induced elderly workers to withdraw from the labor force, and workers envisioned a more secure retirement. Assistance paled in comparison, constituting, in FDR's terms, a potentially harmful and addictive drug. Relief met an immediate need, but relief threatened its users with long-term injury. Relief sapped the vigor of the body politic. Further, relief represented a one-way flow of resources. The source of funding for assistance ostensibly came from the general tax revenues paid by citizens who received nothing in return. Assistance positioned nonrecipients as independent and beneficiaries as dependent.

Yet the rights status of OAI was not as clear as its supporters suggested. The design of the program raised questions about the nature of the right ascribed to OAI, and whether the program deserved the appellation of right at all. These questions interested Sen. Thomas P. Gore, who remained unconvinced by the administration's assertion of the contributory character of the program. To Gore, the program raised the specter of wealth redistribution, which suggested an attenuated version of Huey Long's proposal. Expressing concerns for the security of private property, Gore wondered: "What guarantee is there? Has the citizen got any constitutional guarantee? Has the citizen got any legal or moral guarantee under this plan that some man might not come into power who would take more than he ought to take from one and give to another?"[62] These questions intimated the particularity of the right to insurance. OAI certainly did not stand as a natural right or a birthright. Neither did it signal a right of citizenship or membership. The program's supporters spoke specifically in terms of a contributory right: a person paid in to obtain a right to benefits. Even this opportunity did not extend to all workers. On its own terms, the discourse of contributory rights ran contrary to other goals and values ascribed to the program.

The logic of a contributory right called for a program that no one seemed prepared to defend. A strict contributory right implied that no retiree would receive benefits exceeding what he or she had paid in, plus interest earned on one's contributions. This meant that a contributory insurance program could not function fully for more than thirty years, when workers just entering the labor force in 1935 would begin to retire. A strict contributory program would also require payroll taxes sufficient for workers to fund their retirement. Lower taxes or less than a full career spent paying premiums would result in small annuities upon retirement. Further, a strict contributory program would create large reserves from workers' contributions, which policymakers would have to protect against political pilfering and invest wisely. Supporters of OAI did not wish to create this sort of program. They believed that the distribution of benefits had to begin soon. They felt that the payroll tax should not exact too heavy a toll on current workers. They insisted that retirees should be paid decent benefits. And they did not want to create a large reserve.

Supporters of OAI acknowledged that retirees would receive more than their contributions. Their defense of this situation relied on appeals that exceeded the bounds of the supposedly value-free contract. Justice and decency called for the payment of sufficient benefits. Douglas Brown explained that his subcommittee recommended paying larger-than-earned annuities because they wished to "obtain the social and economic advantages of contractual annuities as soon as possible in order to secure the 'lift' of self-sufficing and self-respecting old-age."[63] Respect appeared as an important goal for OAI, but this quality did not arise as an intrinsic aspect of the contractual relationship: policymakers explicitly had to cultivate this characteristic. Edwin Witte spoke of the "psychological factor" involved in determining benefit levels. If the federal government provided small annuities to people who paid payroll taxes for only a portion of their working lives, the benefits "will never be satisfactory to them. It will seem to them that they are being cheated."[64] Despite Witte's efforts to distinguish between insurance and assistance, both raised attitudinal and spiritual issues. The president likened relief to a drug, but insurance, if improperly implemented, also caused potential psychological harm. Relief and insurance appeared similar in this respect. Just as too much relief induced physical and spiritual deterioration, too-strict insurance produced the same effects. The word "relief" appeared explicitly in Sen. Robert Wagner's defense of paying larger than earned annuities. Wagner appealed to a sense of fair play for older workers. He held that "fairness would be outraged if we gave relief in form but not in substance to those whose only disqualification is that society has too long neglected them already."[65] Fairness appeared alongside respect as a quality that policymakers explicitly needed to foster.

An additional quality of social justice also held sway. On this point, Frances Perkins explained, assistance and insurance shared the same principle: "the prevention of poverty and need among aged persons." Yet this also required a departure from the logic of a contributory right. Insurance ostensibly dispensed benefits independently of need. Need invoked the very stigma of charity that the supporters of insurance wished to avoid, which added urgency to the "need" to create a program that connoted respect and fairness. The shared goal of preventing poverty also pointed to the need for a valuational difference between assistance and insurance. Under a strict contributory program, the annuities of a poor worker seemed unlikely to offer the prospect of a bountiful retirement. Interest might offer marginal improvement, but low wages meant low contributions, and low contributions meant a comparatively small accumulation of funds over the course of one's working life. Under these circumstances, insurance might do more harm than good by reducing, in the form of payroll taxes, a low-wage worker's already meager income. Once more, insurance threatened to take shape as the harmful drug of relief. A strict contributory right would have enabled a clearer distinction, but it could not meet the goal of social justice. The supporters of insurance did not wish to forsake this goal, nor did they wish to abandon the values they attached to insurance. Respect, fairness, and justice demanded a departure from the logic of a contributory right.

Opponents of OAI argued that the program helped older workers at younger workers' expense. Sen. Daniel Hastings argued that OAI placed the federal government in the position of supporting discriminatory practices. Hastings objected that a younger worker paying into the system more than twice as long as an older worker would receive only 25 percent higher monthly benefits, which amounted to only $10 more per month than the older worker. Hastings suggested that the younger worker might not sit idly by upon learning of this disparate treatment. Raising this scenario with Douglas Brown, he predicted that younger workers might someday press Congress to change the legislation: "The fellow who goes in at 20, with that staring him in the face, may reach the conclusion that that is not fair and he may compel the Congress to change it in some form." Forecasts of potential intergenerational animosity did not sway Brown. He acknowledged a disproportionate return in benefits, but retorted that the younger worker would not experience unfair treatment. Brown appealed to the noncontributory values associated with the program to make his case. He maintained that "we are not giving the young man less but we are giving the older man more. And we are giving him more for a social purpose—that is providing him with a decent income in his old age, despite the fact that the government had provided no facilities for many years for doing so."[66] This exchange evidenced different understandings of fairness. Hastings regarded fairness as adhering to a strict proportionality between one's contributions and one's benefits. Brown (and others) believed that fairness had to account for other values like decency, and he intimated, too, that the older worker effectively had made many unrecorded payments in the years before 1935.

Negotiating contributory and noncontributory values presented policymakers with a crucial choice regarding the financing of OAI. For Frances Perkins, this decision was paramount. She explained to the Senate Finance Committee that "the matter of policy really to be considered is whether or not you want to build up your reserve or whether it is better not to build up your reserve and pay as you go." The CES supported the pay-as-you-go option. To be sure, a large reserve fit with the idea of a contributory right. Building up a large, dedicated reserve could have created a situation where recipients claimed benefits as a return of their money with interest. However, Perkins and others believed that large reserves would create investment problems. They worried, too, that large reserves would encourage future Congresses to raise benefits in a spendthrift manner. Building large reserves would require higher tax rates that might be met with ire by the very workers who stood to benefit from such reserves. Lower tax rates also would enable economic recovery to continue. Policymakers would need to increase taxes eventually, but this could wait. Further, a fully funded system would require most of the current generation of workers to pay twice for insurance: once to fund the annuities of older workers near retirement, and a second time to fund their own future retirements. Still, in Perkins's view, old-age insurance could rely on a reserve of sorts: "The real security back of the system is the security of the government and the large reserve is not needed." [67] Perkins expressed confidence in the creditworthiness of the federal government.

Perkins's view, which also represented the position of the CES, did not prevail. Others objected that a pay-as-you-go system passed on present responsibilities to future generations. The CES acknowledged future funding shortfalls. In its report to the president, the CES noted that low initial tax rates would require OAI to obtain additional sources of revenue in thirty years. It recommended supplementing workers' dedicated contributions with general tax revenues. Although all committee members signed the report, ongoing discussions raised doubts about this arrangement, especially from Treasury Secretary Morgenthau, who threatened to withdraw his support if the CES did not increase the tax rates for the contributory insurance program. FDR, too, objected to the possibility of general-revenue financing. He directed the committee to calculate a revised tax schedule. Morgenthau subsequently presented a proposal to increase the payroll tax to the Ways and Means Committee, which the committee adopted. In his testimony, Morgenthau expressed concern about burdening future generations. He held that a stepped-up tax schedule would "establish this system on such sound foundations that it can be continued indefinitely in the future; and, at the same time, to meet the highly desirable social objective of providing an adequate annuity without a means test to all eligible workers upon retirement."[68] However, as Morgenthau's reference to social objectives intimated, concerns about financing did not compel supporters of OAI to adopt the strict logic of a contributory right. Adequacy remained an objective. Moreover, means tests compromised the honorific status of OAI, which policymakers needed to cultivate explicitly.

Increased payroll tax rates did not satisfy opponents of OAI. They also appealed to social objectives and values. Far from bolstering the case for insurance, a concern with noncontributory criteria revealed the limits of the program. Opponents argued that OAI violated principles of fairness and justice in its treatment of future generations. Noel Sargent of the National Association of Manufacturers asked the Finance Committee: "Have we a moral right to now impose upon the next generation, possibly against what may be its will, the burdens of our generation?" Similarly, Elon Hooker queried: "Our children and grandchildren will have their wars and their depressions to pay for, and if we pass on to them the cost of our war and our depression can anyone, from a reasonable point of view, assume that it is fair on top of that for us to indulge our desire for what we would like to do in welfare work unless we pay for it ourselves?"[69] A departure from the logic of a contributory right circumscribed the autonomy of program participants, and this held both for present generations and future generations. A contributory right implied a contract that all parties entered into willfully, and from which all parties received an equitable benefit. Future generations could not make a decision about public policy in 1935. And yet, opponents maintained, OAI would bind future generations to a contract entered into without their consent.

Supporters of OAI pushed for higher benefits for retirees than a strict contributory approach would have allowed, but they represented themselves as standing firm against social pressures to adopt more generous and fiscally irresponsible measures. The Townsend Plan drew the most criticism by far. Nearly every witness queried on the plan dismissed it as an impossible and propagandistic measure. Witnesses insisted that the nation simply could not afford to give $200 monthly pensions to people over sixty. Merely discussing the plan raised false hopes among the elderly and set back the cause of old-age pensions. More dangerously, the Townsend Plan threatened the insurance by conflating it with relief. Frances Perkins objected that the Townsend Plan "is not insurance. It is a dole." Perkins explained that the plan "is a mere appropriation of a large monthly income without any preliminary contribution."[70] Both the Townsend plan and OAI promised to increase purchasing power among the elderly by placing cash in their hands. If citizens regarded the Townsend plan as insurance, they would reject the contributory basis of OAI as unnecessarily punitive. In this respect, the extravagance of the Townsend Plan aided supporters of OAI. Against this fiscally irresponsible proposal, a contributory insurance program conveyed a cautious and measured approach.

Dr. Francis E. Townsend appeared before the Finance and Ways and Means committees with great fanfare, yet he professed modesty in his testimony, describing himself as "simply a country practitioner of medicine." He deferred specific questions about his plan to associates who accompanied him during his appearances. Townsend spoke with a religious fervor. He predicted that "we are on the verge of something tremendous. Millions of inventions are ready to go the minute the market is assured for the products that those inventions will produce."[71] Surpassing their usefulness in industry, the elderly could serve as agents of amelioration by stimulating consumer demand. Townsend proclaimed that "'plenty' will be the word of the day, and in a time of plenty competition is going to take care of any advanced costs." Businesses would share the windfall: "The augmentation of business, which would accrue from the spending of this money, would probably immediately double the volume of business which we are doing, and it would continue to increase as we continue to increase the list of pensioners."[72] Circulating money held the key to economic prosperity—the faster the circulation, the greater the prosperity. Townsend envisioned only rising prosperity if the Congress simply would allow his plan to do its work. The elderly had already done theirs. The elderly earned a pension because they "have created all the wealth that exists practically in the country today." In this way, Townsend, like others, highlighted the contributions of the elderly. They had paid their premiums by leading the nation to a new age of possibility. Now the nation needed to respond generously. Further, Townsend, like others, promised that the nation would reward itself by rewarding the elderly.

Coverage and Race

The strength of an insurance program arises importantly from its coverage pool. As the number and diversity of enrollees increases, an insurance program is better able to spread risk. And shared risk is the basic principle of insurance. The designers of OAI understood this principle. They also held to a principle of inevitability in designing a program that would cover all workers. As Edwin Witte told the Ways and Means Committee, "everybody grows old; and they all have to make provision for their old age or somebody has to take care of them."[73] Although they did not deny the inevitability of old age, members of Congress and other committee witnesses did not concur with the universal approach of the CES. As I explained above, businesses with existing pension plans unsuccessfully sought exemptions from OAI by lobbying for passage of the Clark Amendment. Various nonprofit groups—including churches, hospitals, and colleges—succeeded in obtaining exemptions from OAI. Nonprofits based their appeals on need. Robert Jolly, president of the American Hospital Association, maintained that "if we should have to pay this tax, that would take just that much money out of our hospitals to take care of the indigent people that come in."[74] Nonprofits called on policymakers to depart from insurance principles in implementing federal old-age pensions. They gave greater weight to principles of charity—the very notion that policymakers wished to avoid.

In a move with clear racial implications, policymakers denied coverage to casual, domestic, and agricultural workers, perpetrating the most significant exclusion in the Social Security Act.[75] However, with only a few exceptions, witnesses did not raise the issue of race explicitly; witnesses purged race under the guise of administrative efficiency. The CES had recommended the inclusion of all workers in its report, but the issue of exclusion arose during Edwin Witte's committee testimony. Rep. Fred Vinson asked Witte if the exclusion of domestics, farm workers, and the casually employed would "tend to better administration and be particularly beneficial in respect of the removal of the nuisance feature if these three groups were excluded." Witte had previously stressed the neediness of these workers, and he had explained that higher assistance costs would cancel out savings in OAI. Still, in responding to Vinson, he accepted the line of administrative efficiency. He explained that "it would certainly be easier of administration initially, there is no question about that. On the other hand, if you wish to solve the problem permanently, you will probably bring them in at some later date. But initially certainly it would be much easier of administration."[76] Witte's reference to solving the problem permanently reflected the administration's desire to minimize and eventually eliminate relief expenditures for the elderly. Yet by denying some workers the opportunity to obtain insurance, he weakened the administration's claims to insurance as a contributory right.

Objections to universal coverage ridiculed the idea as impractical—if not preposterous. On the first day of Finance Committee hearings, Sen. Hastings asked incredulously: "I am correct, am I not, in assuming that every housewife who employs one maid will be required to make a tax return, and every farmer who employs one farm hand will be compelled to make a tax return?" Hastings's question, directed to Sen. Wagner, invoked an image of ill-prepared and overburdened housewives and farmers suddenly confronted with the intrusion of the federal government in their daily lives. Universal coverage would bureaucratize the seemingly innocuous tasks of seeking extra help in the home or extra hands on the farm. Individual housewives and farmers would lose their freedom as federal agents monitored their activities.

Others saw different threats. Like Witte, Henry Morgenthau Jr. appreciated that workers in all sorts of occupations would benefit from OAI. He even expressed a personal wish that policymakers provide coverage for domestics, farm workers, and casual laborers at a future date. However, he believed that beginning with universal coverage threatened social insurance in its entirety. Morgenthau conceded that "we recognize, without question, the need of these classes of workers for the same protection that is offered other employed workers under the bill." He believed that policymakers could meet the needs of these workers in different ways, and a less-than-universal system would balance competing kinds of necessity. Morgenthau asked members of Congress "to consider the question whether it is wise to jeopardize the entire contributory system, as well as, possibly, to impair tax-collecting efforts in other fields, by the inclusion under the system of the necessity for far-flung, minutely detailed, and very expensive enforcement efforts."[77] Morgenthau foresaw financial jeopardy if policymakers installed a universal system. The costs of tax collection would overwhelm the system, and the damage might not be confined to OAI.

A reference to "jeopardy" intimated other kinds of threats—threats suggesting that political fights lay beneath the seemingly sanitary language of administrative efficiency. Appeals to efficiency deflected attention from these threats, but the threats did not disappear. Some established interests resisted OAI and its potential to reconfigure social relations and relieve social inequities. Abraham Epstein broached this topic in his testimony to the Ways and Means Committee. He initially objected to including domestics and farm workers on the grounds of efficiency, maintaining that "you are going to have to spend more money in administering the act than you will ever collect." Epstein urged legislators to begin modestly in constructing social-insurance programs. Overly ambitious plans would set back the progress of social insurance for a generation or more. However, after reiterating the impossibility of collecting from domestics and farmers, Epstein suddenly shifted ground in his objection to universal coverage: "Frankly, I do not want the farmers to come in here and fight us. We will have enough of a fight with the manufacturers' association. Why take on the farmers at the same time?" The real threat to OAI arose from the opposition of powerful interests—not small farmers and housewives—that resisted the "intrusions" portended by the legislation. Epstein believed that the combined opposition of farming and manufacturing interests would defeat the legislation. He pleaded with legislators not to "undertake too much now. Do not let us undertake a fight that will defeat us. Do not try to take a bite that will choke us in trying to swallow it. We just cannot do it."[78]

Only a few witnesses directly discussed the racial implications of less-than-universal coverage. Two of these witnesses were George Haynes and Charles Houston, representing the Federal Council of Churches and the National Association for the Advancement of Colored People, respectively. Haynes and Houston provided some of the most detailed analyses of the legislation of any witnesses to appear before the Finance and Ways and Means committees, save the staffers from the CES. They focused their testimony on the likely consequences of the legislation, and they proposed changes to ensure fair treatment for black and white workers. Both noted the disparate impact on blacks of the exclusions of certain classes of workers. Houston maintained that "from a Negro's point of view it [the legislation] looks like a sieve with the holes just big enough for the majority of Negroes to fall through." He explained that of the 5.5 million black workers in the country, 3.5 million were employed in agricultural and domestic labor. Under the banner of administrative efficiency, policymakers would deny more than three out of every five black workers the opportunity to contribute to security for their old age.[79] The Depression hit black workers harder than white workers, compounding the blatant unfairness of this situation. A greater proportion of black workers had lost their jobs, and those who remained employed struggled in comparatively lower-wage positions. A positive principle also supported greater inclusion, one that challenged the implicit individual orientation of a contributory right. The Great Depression had demonstrated the interconnectedness of workers' fates; suffering in one sector of the economy threatened the economy as a whole. George Haynes insisted that "the welfare of the Negro population is bound up with the welfare of the whole people." Policies that did not "treat Negroes on the same basis as other persons not only does an injustice to them but retards the general welfare."[80] Haynes sought to redeem the promise of an interdependent community implicit in the idea of social insurance.

Haynes also pressed the House and Senate for specific language in the legislation barring discrimination on the basis of race in the administration of services and benefits. He advanced a straightforward argument: in cases where such language existed, one could discern equity in the administration of public policies; in the absence of such language, blatant inequalities persisted. Haynes presented a detailed analysis of existing federal legislation to support this viewpoint. In the 1890 and 1907 amendments to the Morrill Act establishing land-grant colleges, for example, language prescribed the disbursal of funds irrespective of race or color. This resulted in an equitable distribution of funds among white and black land-grant colleges. Yet, the Morrill Act stood as an exception—discrimination represented the rule. The appropriations under the Smith-Hughes Act for vocational education, for example, revealed serious discrepancies in salaries for black and white teachers. White teachers in the South typically received salaries seven times greater than the salaries of their black peers. Past experience led Haynes to the conclusion that "unless this bill requires the distribution of benefits irrespective of race or color there is grave danger that in the regulations covering eligibility and other conditions for receiving benefits unfair practice against Negro aged will arise."[81]

The most important proposal advocated by Haynes and Houston called for the merger of insurance and assistance, which went to the heart of the symbolic structure of the Social Security Act. Defenders of occupational exclusions maintained that the federal government would not abandon elderly domestics, farm workers, and others: they could receive assistance benefits. However, Haynes and Houston understood the import of this differentiation. Policymakers supported OAI through the honorific language of rights, whereas OAA connoted relief—the very practice that FDR and others wished to reduce and eventually cease. Moreover, OAI established a direct relationship between the federal government and eligible workers, whereas OAA set up state governments as "middlemen," raising the specter of capricious local decision making. For these reasons, policymakers could not regard OAI and OAA as fungible, and retirees prohibited from participating in one program could not receive benefits under another program without consequence. Only by merging the two programs could retirees experience similar treatment. As Houston explained: "The old-age annuity is a direct Federal right with the worker receiving his old-age annuity direct from the Federal Social Insurance Board; but the old-age assistance benefits are operative only after the states have acted. Under our proposal we would give the worker a direct Federal right under the old-age-assistance plan."[82] Merging OAI and OAA would frame both insurance and assistance through the discourse of rights.

Merger presented a stronger rights claim than the nondiscriminatory application of OAI. Had domestics, farm workers, and casual laborers been permitted to participate in OAI at the outset, they, too, would have been able to claim a right in retirement. However, this right would have remained a contributory right: the basis of retirees' benefits, in principle, would have been contributions made during their working years. Merger promised to expand the contributory right of insurance to a general right of old age. It has always been the case that retirees' Social Security benefits have exceeded their contributions, but merger would have undone the symbolic distinction between earned and unearned benefits by detaching employment histories from receipt of benefits. Old age as such would have been the basis for benefits: Social Security might have been cast as a right of citizenship and, in this way, as a policy affirmation of social citizenship.[83] Detaching benefits from employment also would have helped overcome some of the consequences of discrimination. Even if all workers could have participated in OAI, differences in benefits would have remained. Haynes observed that "it is commonly accepted knowledge that the wages of Negro workers are frequently lower than those of white workers in the same plant and on the same jobs or occupations."[84] Contributions from wages did not represent the deposit of individual income as a preparation for old age, nor did contributions reflect a percentage of one's earning potential in a pure labor market. Rather, the contributory right to OAI obscured the social dimensions of employment and remuneration. Differences in income evidenced racial discrimination.

For the most part, the testimony of Haynes and Houston elicited no response. Those who did respond demanded direct evidence of racial discrimination and sought to redirect the entire issue of race under the theme of proper administration. During Haynes's testimony to the Ways and Means Committee, Rep. Samuel Hill asked: "Is there any discrimination in this bill against the colored race?" Haynes replied that in past cases where federal legislation included language prohibiting discrimination, officials administered policies fairly. In the absence of such language, one could discern clear inequities based on race. Hill did not follow up, but his question implied dissatisfaction with Haynes's view. Comparisons to past legislation were insufficient, and even improperly provocative, for discerning discrimination in the Social Security Act. Evidence had to come from explicit language authorizing discrimination in the Act itself. Indeed, when confronted with the possibility of discrimination, policymakers adamantly denied any nefarious motives. In his appearance before the Ways and Means Committee, Rep. Howard Smith was asked whether any loophole in the legislation enabled discriminatory practices. Denying any connection between race and eligibility conditions, Smith retorted that "it just so happens that that [Negro] race is in our state very much of the laboring class and farm laboring class." Even sympathetic witnesses sought to minimize the issue of race. Asked by the Finance Committee about the possibility of "so-called 'racial discrimination,'" Abraham Epstein affirmed the fairness of competent administration. He maintained that "the success of a law depends very much more on the proper kind of administration and clear conception in the bill than it does in just putting it on the statute books."[85]

While Epstein and others looked to proper administration as a safeguard against discrimination, talk of administration functioned importantly in the debates themselves. Administrative talk absolved policymakers of responsibility for the consequences that likely would arise from their policy choices. It just so happened, Rep. Smith remarked, that black workers held jobs in excluded occupations in greater proportions than white workers. Administrative talk also obscured the social conditions attending the development of OAI. Debate participants, save Haynes and Houston, simply did not ask questions about the reasons for income disparities across race. Administrative talk also shifted attention away from the symbolic privileging of insurance over assistance. In this context, even though assistance payments exceeded insurance payments in the years after the passage of the Social Security Act, recipients of assistance did not participate in the honorific status and independent (rather than dependent) relationship connoted by insurance. Race thus informed the debates obliquely. Race functioned as an important influence and a potentially powerful issue, but participants purged race and purified the debates through the language of administration.

From a Cruel Hoax to a Household Name

Amendments in 1939, 1950, and 1972 would help OAI grow from a small pension for select workers into a cornerstone of American public policy. But first, OAI needed to survive its initial years after passage. FDR's signing of the Social Security Act did not stop many elderly Americans from demanding generous, universal pensions. The Townsend movement reached a peak of 2.2 million members in 1936, totaling 10 percent of the population aged sixty and over in the United States.[86] In addition, as OAI awaited its 1942 start date, OAA quickly expanded. By the end of 1936, all but four states had established programs for Old-Age Assistance. On the political front, Republican presidential nominee Alf Landon campaigned forcefully against OAI, famously rebuking the program as a "cruel hoax" in a September 1936 speech in Milwaukee.[87] Landon held that OAI made promises that the federal government could not keep. He warned his audience that politicians and bureaucrats could divert money collected through the payroll tax to other operations of government. Only a stack of IOUs would remain. This arrangement amounted to a "cruel hoax. . . . The workers asked for a pension and all they have received is just another tax." By compelling workers to save for their retirement, OAI also treated citizens paternalistically: "It assumes that Americans are irresponsible." Landon suggested that OAA should serve as the foundation of a national pension plan. However, the following months adumbrated a brighter future for OAI: FDR's reelection provided political support for OAI, and an affirmative 1937 Supreme Court decision answered the lingering question of constitutionality.

Turning toward expansion, the 1938 Advisory Council on Social Security—the first of its kind—recommended incorporating more noncontributory components into OAI. Initially, the Advisory Council praised insurance as a secure retirement foundation, for "it is only through the encouragement of individual incentive, through the principle of paying benefits in relation to past wages and employment, that a sound and lasting basis for security can be afforded." However, the Advisory Council called for increasing benefits paid out in the early years of the program to ensure retirees a minimum subsistence. Seeking to enhance "public understanding of the method of contributory social insurance,"[88] the Advisory Council urged policymakers to move up the start date of OAI two years to 1940. Responding to criticisms of the reserve, the Advisory Council encouraged the establishment of a trust fund, but indicated that contributions need not fully fund it. The Advisory Council also proposed benefits for wives, widows, and children, as well as extending coverage to domestics and farm workers.

During hearings over the 1939 Amendments, supporters of OAI urged Congress to bolster social insurance right away. Martin Folsom, treasurer of Eastman Kodak and a member of both advisory councils, put the matter plainly. He explained that OAI benefits, under the current schedule, compared unfavorably to OAA benefits. In some cases, a retired person could receive twice as much through assistance as through insurance. This situation had to be changed: "The contributory system should be strengthened, because we are so convinced that it is a much better plan than either old-age-assistance plan, in the long run, or any of the plans for giving free grants to everyone over 65 on a uniform basis."[89] "Strengthening" referred both to the benefits offered by insurance and to its public image. Treasury Secretary Morgenthau recommended that "the taxes under Title VIII be termed 'contributions' . . . to improve public understanding of the purposes for which the funds are collected."[90]

Policymakers responded favorably to the major recommendations of the Advisory Council, save the extension of coverage to farm workers and domestics. Arguing for adoption, John Davis of the National Negro Congress recounted the desperate situation of many domestics and agricultural workers. He characterized domestics as "the least economically secure occupational group in urban America." Poverty forced some domestics into prostitution to supplement their meager wages. Nor could policymakers view farm life as rosy. Other witnesses stressed the common humanity of all workers. Gerard Swope, president of General Electric, asserted that domestics and farm workers "should be treated as human beings, just as the others are."[91] But committee members stood firm, questioning whether farmers (albeit not farm workers) would want coverage for themselves and their employees, and doubting that farmers could handle the administrative aspects of coverage. Rep. McCormack, for example, expressed the position of his colleagues when he indicated that Congress should wait for farmers to request coverage. He also proposed a public education campaign to increase farmers' understanding of the program.

Although the policy context had changed by 1950, assistance still loomed as a threat to insurance. Old-Age and Survivors Insurance (OASI), as it had been renamed in 1939, no longer named a tiny future program. Policymakers had ten years of experience with OASI, which now distributed benefits to almost 3.5 million people. In its report, the 1948 Advisory Council envisioned OASI as the foundation of Social Security. The Advisory Council anticipated a "time when virtually all persons in the United States will have retirement or survivorship protection under the old-age and survivors' insurance program."[92] In 1948, however, OASI had not yet achieved standing as the primary retirement program in the United States. OAA still paid elderly people higher benefits. Members of Congress and policy administrators and analysts envisioned OASI and OAA locked in a portentous battle for preeminence as the nation's retirement program, with most observers wishing to see OASI emerge victorious.

Several witnesses worried that OAA, in view of its comparatively higher benefits and broader coverage than OASI, threatened the very existence of insurance for the elderly. Martin Folsom—who by 1950 had served on all three advisory councils, the most recent appointment in 1947—urged immediate action. He insisted that "if the insurance system is not strengthened soon, there is a grave risk that the plan will come into disrepute and be abandoned for either the old-age assistance or the free-pension method." A sense of urgency informed the statements of numerous witnesses. Sumner Slichter, an economics professor at Harvard University and associate chair of the 1948 Advisory Council, also called on Congress to act quickly to strengthen OASI. He warned that "if the old-age and survivors plan is not made adequate in the very near future, we are likely to become so dependent upon straight out-and-out relief measures that we shall never build up our insurance."[93] If left to develop according to the trajectory engendered through existing legislation, OASI would not attract enough of the popular support presently enjoyed by assistance programs.

Rights talk surfaced prominently both in support and opposition to OASI. In a revealing exchange, Rep. Walter Lynch and Social Security

Administration commissioner Arthur Altmeyer grappled with the continuing tension over a "right" to Social Security. Noting that persons employed after age sixty-five and earning above a specific amount would forfeit their OASI benefits, Lynch wondered why. If elderly persons obtained a right to benefits on the basis of contributions made during their working years, then why should employment after sixty-five disqualify someone from receiving what he or she had already earned? Altmeyer responded by distinguishing an old-age annuity from a retirement annuity. OASI amounted to a retirement annuity; receipt of benefits required withdrawal from the work force. Lynch refused to concede: "If a person from the age of 18 to 65 years of age contributes to social security, both on his own behalf and through the employer, he has a certain vested right." Altmeyer again insisted on a distinction. OASI offered insurance against wage loss; if a person continued to work after sixty-five, then this person suffered no loss of wages. Lynch retorted: "Do you think the average American workingman knows that he is being insured against a wage loss, or do you believe the average American man feels, when he is contributing to OASI, that he is going to get, as a matter of right, an annuity when he reaches the age of 65 or retires from work?" Altmeyer's response that workers understood the program did not satisfy Lynch. He asserted that "either you are entitled to that [annuity] or you are not, when you pay for it."[94] This exchange revealed the malleability of rights for supporters of OASI. They invoked rights to privilege insurance over assistance, but subordinated rights when pursuing other goals.

In 1950, buoyed by the endorsement of groups like the American Farm Bureau and the American Federation of Labor, policymakers agreed to expand OASI coverage to domestics and farm workers. Labor Secretary Maurice Tobin held that "the expanded industrial economy has contributed to the insecurity of the average home, the average family, that plus the fact of the change in our economy whereby the corner store credits are no longer available to the workers' families and cash must be paid. . . . There is a great fear in the hearts of workers looking forward to a loss of jobs."[95] If uncertainty characterized the lives of industrial workers, then domestic and farm employment only exacerbated this condition. Organized by the Baltimore Urban League and Young Women's Christian Association, a few women testified about their experiences with the low pay, irregular hours, and minimal benefits of domestic labor. In addition to these more immediate concerns, Lucille Lewis explained how the need for assistance denied domestics standing as citizens. Lewis asserted that "it is embarrassing to most people to receive something that they have not had a chance to contribute to; and they also feel that they have lost citizenship."[96] Recalling the critiques of Haynes and Houston, domestics and farm workers understood how the prevalent symbolism of social policy demeaned them.

Policymakers in the late 1960s and early 1970s focused squarely on money. Over the previous two decades, OASI secured its position as the central component of federal retirement policy. Many policymakers believed that the remaining task consisted of compensating retirees for a lag in benefits against inflation, and making sure that future benefits would keep pace with increases in the cost of living. On the first count, policymakers acted decisively in a short time. Congress passed benefit increases of 15 percent in 1969, 10 percent in 1971, and 20 percent in 1972 (with the Amendments). This constituted a benefit increase of 23 percent in real terms—adjusted for inflation—in a period of just three years.[97] Even so, this increase did not represent the upper limit of the debates. Some members of Congress in 1972 advocated for benefit increases as high as 50 percent.[98] Proposals to index benefits to inflation had surfaced in the late 1960s, but indexing did not become law until the 1972 Amendments.

The locus of congressional action shifted in 1972. Previously, the authorizing committees in each chamber—the Ways and Means Committee in the House, and the Finance Committee in the Senate—had prepared Social Security legislation that the larger bodies adopted with little modification. Representatives particularly deferred to Wilbur Mills, chair of the Ways and Means Committee, whom they regarded as both a powerful figure and an unparalleled expert on the intricacies of Social Security policy. Further, the authorizing committees tended to work in a relatively bipartisan manner, reaching agreement on key issues before bringing legislation to the floor of the House and Senate. Deliberation occurred primarily in the committee rooms. In June 1972, Mills and Sen. Frank Church, chair of the Special Committee on Aging, introduced amendments on the floor to increase benefits by 20 percent and to add an automatic cost-of-living adjustment to benefits. They did not attach the amendments to a Social Security bill, but to an otherwise technical bill to raise the federal debt ceiling. Neither Mills nor Church brought these amendments to their respective committees. Nevertheless, the amendments passed the Senate by a vote of 82 to 4, and the House by a vote of

302 to 35. This strong bipartisan support evidenced the obligation that both Democrats and Republicans felt toward recipients of Social Security, as well as the political cachet of the program.

Making a case for their amendments, Church and Mills drew attention to poverty among seniors. Sen. Church observed that one out of four seniors lived in poverty—a rate that was twice as high as the poverty rate for the general population. Under these circumstances, a 20 percent increase in benefits would produce immediate positive effects, lifting 1.4 million seniors out of poverty.[99] Social Security represented a major—and in many cases, the only—source of income for seniors. Rep. Mills stressed to his colleagues that "social security benefits are the major reliance of the great majority of retired workers and the sole reliance for about half of them."[100] Moreover, inflation reduced the value of these benefits, even though Congress had passed regular increases in the past. Senators and representatives agreed that inflation exacted an especially painful toll on seniors, whose fixed incomes did not enable them to adjust to the rising prices of necessary goods and services. A nominal increase in Social Security benefits would not improve the financial situations of seniors, and a sufficient increase without an automatic cost-of-living adjustment would succumb to inflation in only a few years.

Members of Congress characterized Social Security as an earned right, while highlighting the moral worthiness of seniors. Although an earned right intimated distributing benefits without considering deservingness, moral worthiness signaled clear support for seniors as a special group. Some policymakers noted how seniors could unite a diverse and sometimes fractious nation. "Aging is the common denominator of mankind," maintained Sen. Williams. He observed that "whatever our social or economic standing, ethnic background, sex, aptitudes, or beliefs, we share the fact that we all grow older. What we do to aid today's older citizens, we potentially do for each of us." Others stressed the hard work that retirees had performed in their younger years. Sen. Hartke exhorted that "there is no reason why anyone who has worked hard all of his life and contributed to his family, his community, and his country should be forced to live in poverty and despair." Still others extolled the proud heritage that seniors have passed on to successive generations. Sen. McClellan insisted that seniors deserved recognition, for "they have given America its traditional standards, its traditional values, and its traditional precepts." The unqualified deservingness of seniors created a moment of moral choice. The nation could repay its debt to seniors, or it could renounce the ideals that citizens had long espoused. As Sen. Church put the issue to his colleagues: "If this country cannot afford that [increase], it is bankrupt, indeed."[101]

Bankruptcy soon arose as a pressing concern, however. In the first few decades of the program, policymakers could increase benefits and expand coverage while delaying scheduled tax increases, thereby keeping the costs of expansion low. An immature system also kept the numbers of retirees receiving benefits artificially low, which sustained a deceptively high ratio of workers to beneficiaries. In 1945, there were nearly forty-two workers for every eligible retiree. In 1950, this ratio remained high at sixteen workers for every retiree. Not until the mid-1970s did the ratio stabilize at roughly three workers for every retiree, where it remains today.[102] Although Social Security's designers anticipated this trajectory, policymakers ignored it in the interest of expediency. The stabilization of the worker-to-retiree ratio in the mid-1970s thus appeared as a financial shock to the system. Demographics magnified this trend as the end of the baby boom of the 1950s and 1960s portended a gradually aging population.

Larger economic developments also raised doubts about Social Security's financial future. By the mid-1970s, the long, virtually unbroken post–World War II economic boom that had strengthened the U.S. economy came to an end. Between 1948 and 1972, real median family income more than doubled. Increased worker productivity fueled a growing economy, and a growing economy provided greater resources for social programs. After 1972, real median income stalled and then fell. In 1980, the United States suffered the largest single decline in real median family income—5.5 percent—since the government began keeping records of this statistic in 1947.[103] The 1970s also witnessed stagflation: simultaneous inflation and economic stagnation. Stagflation confounded accepted Keynesian approaches to macroeconomic policy. Inflation and unemployment increased in tandem, while wage increases for employed workers could not keep pace with the rising cost of living. In this context, the automatic cost-of-living adjustment adopted by Congress in 1972 greatly—and unintentionally—exacerbated projected deficits and increased benefits promised to workers. Members of Congress did not anticipate these conditions, nor could they wait for the economic woes to subside. The economic downturn of the 1970s had an immediate and long-lasting impact on Social Security.

By the 1980s, a financial crisis loomed. The 1982 trustees' report warned that "without corrective legislation in the very near future, the Old-Age and Survivors Insurance Trust Fund will be unable to make benefits on time beginning no later than July 1983." Social Security had sustained itself over the past few years by drawing down assets of the trust fund, which could not continue. The trustees explained that "the assets of the OASI Trust Fund have been reduced to such a low level that they will not be able to continue making up the difference between outgo and income much longer."[104] The public, too, sensed that times had changed. The news media began reporting stories that expressed Americans' increasing doubts about the future of Social Security. A *Washington Post*–ABC News survey found that 66 percent of respondents under forty-five doubted that Social Security would survive into their retirement. Seventy-four percent of respondents aged eighteen to thirty expressed similar skepticism.[105]

Within this context, President Reagan announced in December 1981 the formation of a National Commission on Social Security Reform. The commission consisted of fifteen members appointed equally by the White House, the Democratic congressional leadership, and the Republican congressional leadership. Known by the name of its chair, Alan Greenspan, the commission issued its report in January 1983. The Greenspan Commission recognized that a "financing problem" existed both in the short-term and long-term for the Social Security trust fund. Unlike the trustees' reports, however, the commission did not address the potential exhaustion of the fund. Further, the commission, objecting to fundamental changes, affirmed the principle of insurance as the basis for Social Security. The commission's first recommendation stated that "the Congress, in its deliberations on financing proposals, should not alter the fundamental structure of the Social Security program or undermine its fundamental principles."[106] On the specific matter of the trust funds, the commission noted the widespread public discussion of investment procedures. It rejected suggestions that the funds had been invested poorly, or the returns spent on other operations of government. The commission retorted that the procedures followed by the trust funds in the past have been "proper and appropriate." Still, the commission appreciated the need to increase public understanding in the operations of the trust funds and, in turn, increase confidence in their integrity. Among the proposals recommended by the Greenspan Commission and adopted by the Congress were the acceleration of scheduled increases in the payroll tax rate and an increase in the retirement age from sixty-five to sixty-seven.[107]

Policy Polysemy and Privatization

In understanding Social Security differently, contemporary Americans stand in good company with the participants in founding debates over the Social Security Act. Developing this theme, I have explicated sites of polysemy in founding discussions of rights and coverage. However, my references to founding debates and contemporary debates may understate the powerful connection between these two periods. Both represent efforts to understand a dynamically unfolding text; both constitute a larger "living" text; and earlier debates create a policy context for subsequent debates. In these ways, policy polysemy exhibits a cross-historical temporality absent from single, synchronic rhetorical texts. G. Thomas Goodnight captures this dynamic in his definition of controversy as "temporally pluralistic, extended argumentative engagements."[108] If we accept the "noncontroversial" claim that Social Security sometimes has generated controversy, then Goodnight's definition illuminates the temporality of policy polysemy. As pluralistic argumentative engagements, controversies may persist for days, months, years, or—as Social Security demonstrates—decades. Participants in the 1990s entered into a debate that had been thriving for over sixty years. Their understanding of Social Security—what the program does, how well it has worked, what it may achieve—has been shaped by previous debates. Contemporary disagreements find support and opposition in the statements of previous participants. The ongoing "text" of the debates has authorized multiple meanings for Social Security.

Although Social Security's founders supported a contributory *insurance* program, their right-based arguments have authorized potentially conflicting future trajectories for Social Security. Designers understood the basis of Social Security as a contributory right—something akin to paying a premium to a private insurer. Contributions bought a right to protection: if disaster, death, or unemployment (i.e., retirement) struck, workers and their dependents would not have to worry about paying rent and buying groceries. The noncontributory values of justice, fairness, and decency bolstered the goals of security and protection, but loosened the moorings of a contributory right to benefits. In the founding period and subsequent expansion, this looser connection aided supporters of insurance, since it permitted supporters to promote the cooperative and interdependent character of insurance while deferring the latent individualism of a contributory right. Yet a loosened connection to contributions also opened supporters up to the charge that they had betrayed the promise of Social Security and misled workers. Advocates of privatization have reasserted the contributory character of Social Security with a vengeance, reinterpreting the contributory right as tantamount to a property right. From this perspective, accounts owners emerge as the property managers of their assets—as opposed to some faceless bureaucrat in Washington who holds no claim on the account.

Founding debates over coverage, too, served as sites of polysemy. A universal program at inception would have situated Social Security as a right of old age or, if supporters followed the lead of Haynes and Houston, a right of citizenship. Moreover, an originally universal program would have established the expectation of uniform treatment of beneficiaries. On matters of basic justice, citizens tend to accept differential treatment reluctantly, preferring instead to operate under the principle of equal treatment under the law. Unwavering commitment to universality would have bolstered insurance, both pragmatically and thematically. Pragmatically, as Social Security's designers knew well, a diverse insurance pool better distributes risk. Thematically, universality underscores values of community and interdependence, which buttress insurance. Instead, in the founding debates themselves, supporters of OAI accepted differential treatment of the nation's retirees. Advocates of privatization thus could implicitly draw on this history in arguing that workers ought to choose the type of plan for their retirement. Like the supporters of insurance who deflected the critiques of Haynes and Houston, advocates of privatization could argue that all workers would plan for their retirement, even if the means differed.

Attention to policy polysemy also encourages us to consider the relative influence and circulation of multiple meanings. As Social Security grew, the principle of insurance managed to negotiate the founding tensions in the debates. Objections to Social Security as a mandatory contributory pension occasionally appeared—for example, in a portion of Milton Friedman's *Capitalism and Freedom*[109]—but these remained at the margins of policy debates. By the mid-1990s, the situation had changed. Insurance no longer reigned supreme as the guiding principle of Social Security. For many policymakers, investment constituted a viable alternative.

2

Competing Metaphors of Insurance and Investment

Privatization promised a policy revolution born in the legitimating discourses of Social Security. In this spirit, advocates of privatization, who made their case through multiple congressional hearings beginning in earnest in the mid-1990s, pressed the logic of the rights claims asserted by the original supporters of Social Security. They, too, saw Social Security benefits as a right secured by a worker's contributions, but advocates rebuked government control of these contributions as usurping the title to an individual's property. Since rights rested properly with their bearers, any break in this connection by another party without the full consent of the rights holder amounted to tyranny. In this respect, insurance improperly converted an individual right into communal property. Only investment fully respected the rights basis of Social Security by ascribing freedom and control to individuals.

Revealing larger stakes in the debates over Social Security, insurance and investment expressed wider values and beliefs about relations between individuals and communities, the proper role of government in society, and the qualities of a good life. And they did so *metaphorically.* To appreciate this point, we can represent the contesting purposes of Social Security in the form of the metaphorical statement "A is B." Defenders of the existing system held that Social Security is an insurance program. Advocates of privatization retorted that Social Security is (or should be) an investment program. Neither of these statements conveys a literal truth. The cumbersome character of supporters' original claim that Social Security offered workers insurance against unemployment in old age revealed their efforts to underwrite an event that did not necessarily function by actuarial principles. Rather than guarding against potential loss, Social Security facilitated the very "loss" (nonwork in old age) it ostensibly sought to prevent. But investment does not provide a better fit for Social Security. The program's near-universal coverage of the workforce, even if reconfigured as a system of individual accounts, militates against the idea that individuals should weigh risk and reward in deciding where to invest their money. Some compelled contributors might have otherwise decided that retirement constitutes a bad investment.

In making these points, I am not insisting on a literal rendering of public policy to determine the true nature of Social Security. Doing so would discount the primary role of rhetoric in policymaking, which some policy analysts seemingly devalue. Reflecting on the uneven economic performance of the 1990s, which overwhelmingly benefited higher earners, Joseph Stiglitz, former chairperson of President Clinton's Council of Economic Advisors, recalls that "we put too much faith in words, in mystical notions of confidence, in the so-called wisdom of financial markets; we paid too little attention to the underlying *real* economics."[1] In an important sense, Stiglitz is right: policymakers *did* pay too much attention to the purpose of investment in the 1990s. However, as I argue in the introduction, an alternative policy does not require a flight from rhetoric toward an underlying reality. To the contrary, we make policy through our rhetoric—in hearing rooms, on op-ed pages, and elsewhere. Nor can we hope for a neutral policy language, since our words express our commitments. In particular, metaphors of insurance and investment enabled policymakers to craft different visions for Social Security. These purposes connected policy to shared values and enabled understanding and evaluation of existing policy.

This chapter considers how debate participants envisioned different retirement programs in the values they associated with insurance and investment. Supporters of privatization believed that a system of individual accounts would lower the risk and increase the return on a worker's payroll contributions. They upheld the values of individualism, wealth creation, ownership, and market superiority. Supporters of social insurance defended the existing structure of Social Security. They rejected the focus on individual rates of return, responding that Social Security provided workers and their families with social benefits that investment did not recognize. Supporters of social insurance upheld the values of community, security, wide-ranging protection, and the alleviation of poverty. Before investigating these associations, I consider the function of metaphors in policy debate and the larger context of the 1990s debates.

Metaphors and Public Policy Debate

Theories of metaphor developed alongside classical theories of rhetoric itself. In the *Poetics*, Aristotle exalts metaphorical dexterity. He holds that "the greatest thing by far is to be a master of metaphor. It is the one thing that cannot be learnt from others; and it is also a sign of genius, since a good metaphor implies an intuitive perception of the similarity in dissimilars." In the *Rhetoric*, Aristotle identifies ordinary language and metaphor as the techniques best suited for prose style.[2] Although Aristotle offers high praise for metaphor, modern and contemporary theorists frequently have charged that he unjustly circumscribes its function and significance. Rejecting his attribution of an innate gift of metaphor, they criticize him for casting metaphor as adornment and for explaining its meaning through a one-way process of substitution. We need not resolve this dispute to see that an expansive understanding of metaphor may illuminate how purposes of insurance and investment functioned in the privatization debates.[3]

Since at least I. A. Richards, theorists have held that metaphor does not serve as a stylistic technique apart from the invention of discourse, but it functions prominently in our understanding of ideas and events. Richards challenged the notion of metaphor as "something special and exceptional in the use of language, a deviation from its normal mode of working, instead of the omnipresent principle of all its free action."[4] In our contemporary intellectual milieu, a view of language as irreducibly metaphoric has obtained the status of common sense. Indeed, this position is infectious. Once we call attention to the role of metaphor in language, we discover its presence everywhere, as in my exposition of the role of metaphor in policy debate. Inquiries into the rhetoric of economics have highlighted the constitutive power of metaphor in interpreting our world. In this way, "constitutive metaphors determine what makes sense and what does not."[5] This applies equally to metaphors in public policy debate. Investment and insurance offer different frames for considering Social Security. They remember particular and distinct pasts and envision alternative futures for the program. These metaphors identify different problems confronting Social Security and propose different solutions.

Enabling understanding, metaphors do not operate in isolation. Metaphors do not function as words that appear simply in sequence with others, the meaning and significance of which disappear as soon as one reads or listens "past" them. Instead, metaphors invoke and inform other ideas, values, and beliefs. This quality of metaphor engenders the organizational structure of my analysis, as I discuss the values debate participants associated with investment and insurance. In a famous essay, rhetorical theorist Kenneth Burke illuminates this quality of metaphor through the notion of perspective: "To consider A from the point of view of B is, of course, to use B as a *perspective* upon A."[6] In a similar vein, George Lakoff and Mark Johnson speak of metaphoric "entailment" to indicate how conceptual metaphors invoke wider systems of belief.[7] In carrying ideas across different realms, metaphors travel with baggage. Investment and insurance invite different standards for judging success in retirement policy. These purposes foreground particular social relations while backgrounding others.

The perspective or entailment carried by metaphor means that metaphors do not function innocently. In framing debates over Social Security, the purposes of investment and insurance make implicit value judgments. They act as alternative ethical frameworks. Ruth Malone illustrates this function in her analysis of the prevalence of market metaphors in debates over contemporary health-care policy. These metaphors cast health care as a product that rational consumers may purchase according to their individual needs and interests. However, while advocates of a market-based approach celebrate individual choice as a virtue, Malone holds that a lack of perspective-taking constitutes the ethical failing of market metaphors: "The market seems to have no concept that corresponds to policy's moral mandate to understand problems from the point of view of the affected other."[8] Still, we should not think that a solution lies in discovering a value-free metaphor: all conceptual metaphors carry entailments. The point is to make "plain" the values we support. This holds for insurance, too, which operates more like a dead metaphor given its longstanding role as the guiding principle of Social Security.

Metaphors make meaning through processes of mediation. Richards famously introduces the elements of metaphor as tenor (the underlying idea) and vehicle (its figuration). Rather than locating stable meaning in either element, Richards explains that "in many of the most important uses of metaphor, the co-presence of vehicle and tenor results in a meaning . . . which is not attainable without their interaction."[9] If metaphor takes the form of a statement "A is B," then meaning arises in the interplay of A and B. In this spirit, Paul Ricoeur locates metaphorical meaning in the spaces in between larger discursive contexts (represented in sentences and statements) and particular deployments (represented in words). Metaphor resides "*between* the sentence and the word, *between* predication and naming."[10] The notion that metaphorical meaning arises fundamentally through mediation is crucial to understanding the purposes that debate participants ascribed to Social Security. Investment does not take a purpose from a properly financial realm and transfer it to the realm of public policy. Rather, advocating investment as the purpose of Social Security imagines a retirement system that exists in neither the private nor the public sector. Investment through Social Security constitutes a purpose particular to Social Security, just as insurance has distinguished Social Security from private workplace pensions. Whether we think of Social Security as investment or insurance, we rethink our understandings of both the purpose and the program.

As a process of mediation, metaphorical meaning refuses to stay in one place. For this reason, metaphors invoke difference in their very expression. Ricoeur explains this invocation as a tension in the copula—the "is"—of metaphor. Insofar as they enable understanding, metaphors imply a referential claim that asserts a literal reading. Social Security *really is* an investment system. Understanding the program through an investment frame invites a corresponding ontological judgment. With respect to economic rhetoric generally, Klamer and Leonard observe that economists often forget the important lesson of Milton Friedman, who held that economists reason "as if." Economists frequently gesture toward the constructed character of their models, but they "think of their work as making true statements about the world."[11] Yet this does not hold, for supply and demand curves do not *really exist*, even as they explain many significant operations of the economy. Ricoeur maintains that we can elucidate the tension informing metaphorical reference by exposing an "is not" implied in the act of metaphorical assertion. We can appreciate the nature of metaphorical truth by including the "critical incision of the (literal) 'is not' within the ontological vehemence of the (metaphorical) 'is.'"[12]

This admittedly abstract discussion of difference in metaphor helps us understand how competing purposes of investment and insurance interacted in the Social Security debates. Because metaphorical meaning invokes difference, no metaphor—no matter how prevalent—can eliminate the possibility that its constituents (in Richard's terms, tenor and vehicle) may be understood in new and/or alternative ways. For advocates of privatization, the social-insurance basis of Social Security meant something very different from what it had meant during the program's expansion in the mid-twentieth century—namely, that insurance meant shameful dependence on government. For many advocates of privatization, when supporters of Social Security articulated the language of insurance, they propagated a scam. Further, difference in metaphorical meaning suggests that metaphors may imply contrasting assertions by invoking other cultural discourses. In this way, Philip Eubanks argues that the statement "Abortion is murder" cannot be heard in American culture without invoking a counterclaim about the rights of women. He asserts that "statements need to be considered with respect to relevant statements already afoot."[13] Insisting that investment is the purpose of Social Security requires breaking with the traditional purpose of insurance. Doing so contrasts the two purposes, either explicitly or implicitly. However, the metaphor of investment cannot erase insurance or force forgetfulness. Reframing the purpose of Social Security enacts a conflict of contrasting metaphors. Before we can investigate these metaphors, we need to consider the larger context of the 1990s debates.

The Ideological, Political, and Economic Contexts of the 1990s Debates

Ideological, political, and economic forces converged in the 1990s to facilitate the emergence of the privatization debates. Conservative think tanks promoted market-based solutions to social problems. The 1994 midterm congressional elections created a political environment favorable to privatization. Advocates of privatization saw in the rise of a "New Economy" confirmation of their belief in the superiority of investment. And the 1994–1996 Advisory Council on Social Security considered various investment ideas. All of this occurred in a highly polarized political environment.

The 1990s witnessed the maturation of a conservative intellectual infrastructure inaugurated two decades earlier by public officials and private executives who believed that conservative policy ideas had been marginalized by the rise of the New Deal. In 1971, two months before President Nixon nominated him to the Supreme Court, Lewis F. Powell Jr. wrote a memorandum for the U.S. Chamber of Commerce titled "Attack of the American Free Enterprise System." In this document, Powell outlined the threats facing capitalism from developments in education, media, and, sadly, business itself. Powell asserted that "few elements of American society today have as little influence in government as the American businessman, the corporation, or even the millions of corporate stockholders."[14] Sounding a similar alarm, William Simon, who served as Treasury secretary in the Nixon and Ford administrations, called for the rise of a "conservative counterintelligentsia" in his 1978 book *A Time for Truth*. These subversive intellectuals would serve "to raise the unnamed issues, to ask the unasked questions, to present the missing contexts, and to place a very different set of values and goals on the public agenda."[15] Although conservatives had to battle liberal ideas directly, Simon, who served as president of the Olin Foundation during this time, understood that the development of a counterintelligentsia would require significant financial backing. Simon asserted that "what this means is nothing less than a massive and unprecedented mobilization of the moral, intellectual and financial resources which reside in those who still have faith in the human individual." He estimated that the money involved likely would reach the "multimillions."[16]

In this milieu, a number of conservative think tanks emerged to become significant players on the national policymaking scene. Some were formed in the 1970s; others had existed before, but constituted a scarcely perceptible presence in the policymaking arena.[17] For instance, the American Enterprise Institute, which was founded in 1943 but operated modestly for most of its history, increased its annual budget from $1 million to $10.4 million, and its staff from 19 to 135 people between

1970 and 1980. During the Carter administration, the American Enterprise Institute became a refuge for Republican officials. With respect to policy analysis, in 1981, the Heritage Foundation presented the Reagan administration with the monumental volume *A Mandate for Leadership*. Over three hundred contributors helped to produce the 1,093-page document, which addressed policy areas in all of the Cabinet departments, several independent regulatory agencies, and other government agencies.[18] Conservative think tanks combined substantial research and writing with marketing savvy. William Baroody Jr., president of the American Enterprise Institute from 1978 to 1986, acknowledged this approach unapologetically: "I make no bones about marketing. . . . We pay as much attention to dissemination of the product as to the content."[19]

With the Heritage Foundation and the libertarian Cato Institute leading the charge, conservative foundations took direct aim at Social Security. In its 1981 book *Agenda for Progress*, the Heritage Foundation dismissed the program as a glorified Ponzi scheme: "With its 'social insurance' rhetoric peeled away, [Social Security] is nothing more than a gigantic, government-operated Ponzi scheme, in which earlier, smaller investors (workers now retired) are paid off with the receipts from later, larger investors (currently active workers)."[20] Like all such schemes, this structure would eventually fail. To make Social Security actuarially sound, policymakers needed to separate the "earned" and "unearned" components of monthly benefits. The Heritage Foundation insisted that earned benefits consisted exclusively of a retiree's contributions plus interest. Heritage held that if policymakers wished to distribute assistance above this level, they should do so through a welfare program targeted to needy seniors.

In 1983, the Cato Institute devoted a special issue of its *Cato Journal* to Social Security. Like analysts at the Heritage Foundation, the contributors to this volume argued that the present system wrongly conflated insurance and welfare functions. Yet Cato went beyond Heritage (at this historical moment) in rejecting the public provision of insurance altogether: any public program of retirement insurance represented an unwarranted intrusion into the marketplace. Peter Ferrara suggested that the proper course of action lay in devolving the functions of Social Security to different institutions, "allowing the welfare function to be performed by a separate program explicitly and carefully designed to help the poor, and allowing the insurance function to be performed by the private sector."[21] Private retirement accounts would provide individuals with higher returns uncorrupted by the distributional impact of welfare. To accomplish this fundamental change, contributors called for a "Leninist strategy" toward Social Security. They instructed advocates to divide Social Security's beneficiaries generationally. Workers nearing retirement needed reassurance that they would receive their full benefits, whereas younger workers needed to understand "just how much of a loss they are taking by participating in the program."[22] Further, advocates needed to build a pro-privatization coalition of banks, insurance companies, and other institutions that would benefit from an IRA-based system. In these ways, conservative think tanks advocated privatization of Social Security throughout the 1980s.

The 1994 congressional elections promised widespread circulation of these policy proposals. Republicans captured majorities in the Senate and—for the first time in forty years—the House of Representatives. News-media accounts of the election and the statements of politicians portended dramatic change. A revolution had occurred. The recently elected members of Congress (in the House, especially) appeared as revolutionaries. In this spirit, the *Wall Street Journal* led: "Just two years after losing the White House, Republicans rose up to stage a political revolution." The *Los Angeles Times* predicted that "the Republicans' triumph will turn Washington upside down, marking the rise of a new kind of ideological politics." *Washington Post* columnist David Broder wondered if "the Republican midterm election victory, as deep as it was wide, could be one of those rare events that reshapes the landscape of American politics."[23] By interpreting the election results as a revolution, commentators and policymakers constructed a political environment ripe for fundamental change. The new majorities in the House and Senate would not simply reform existing policies, but they would evaluate and restructure the basic framework of the government's approach to various policy domains. Nothing was sacred. Legislators would not exempt any policy from this stringent evaluation, regardless of its longstanding and celebrated history. Moreover, the revolution possessed democratic legitimacy, since voters expressed their strong desire for revolution by installing new majorities in Congress.

Sensing their opportunity, political leaders exuded a confident, visionary tone. Presumptive House Speaker Newt Gingrich, widely regarded as the architect of the House victories, promised to adhere to a core set of conservative principles. Characterized by the *Washington Post* as "a new political powerhouse," Gingrich expressed an interest in working with the Clinton administration, but he rejected the idea of compromise. He asserted that "we will cooperate with anyone, and we'll compromise with no one."[24] Compromise would undermine the revolution that Gingrich struggled to accomplish. During the campaign, Gingrich spearheaded efforts to persuade over three hundred candidates to sign a Contract with America. Unveiled in September 1994, the Contract sketched a conservative policy agenda by calling for a balanced-budget amendment to the Constitution, capital-gains and other tax cuts, toughened public-assistance and crime laws, increased defense spending, and congressional term limits. The Contract did not mention Social Security privatization, but it did promise to end a style of governance "that is too big, too intrusive, and too easy with the public's money."[25]

Although only a minority of prospective voters had heard of the document, the Contract still served important functions during and after the campaign. The Contract reflected Republican efforts to inject a national focus into local congressional races and thereby contrast their views with a president unpopular in many regions of the country. *CQ Weekly* observed that "perhaps more than at any time in the past twelve years, this year's House elections are being run as a referendum on the party in control in the White House."[26] Outlining an alternative approach, the Contract enabled Republicans to join together around a common set of themes and policies. Adhering to this agenda, the new House majority demonstrated impressive unity as the 104th Congress began its work. Further, the Contract offered the news media a ready-made frame for interpreting the significance of the election.[27] Republicans had offered a contract accepted by a majority of voters: once voters "signed" this document, Republicans had to fulfill their contractual obligations.

Shifting loci of policymaking promised advocates of privatization a full hearing for their proposals. Although privatization would receive some bipartisan support, new committee chairpersons would enable more hearings on the subject and friendlier witness lists. Further, the more conservative leadership of the 104th Congress likely would turn to likeminded think tanks for analysis and advice. For instance, in a December 1994 article exploring the increased popularity of the Cato Institute among Washington insiders, the *Wall Street Journal* characterized Cato's new headquarters as "one of this city's new power addresses."[28] The notion of shifting power centers went so far as to question the president's relevance to the policymaking process. In an April 1995 press conference, a reporter asked President Clinton if he worried about his voice being heard. Clinton responded: "The Constitution gives me relevance. The power of our ideas gives me relevance. The record we have built up over the last two years and the things we're trying to implement give me relevance."[29] Of course the president remained relevant. The succeeding months proved this basic point when the press and public blamed congressional Republicans for an unpopular shutdown of the federal government over disagreements about the 1995 federal budget.[30] However, as Republicans maintained congressional majorities throughout the 1990s, the links between conservative intellectuals and policymakers remained strong.

Economic events seemingly confirmed revolutionary visions. A new economy ostensibly arose in the 1990s, promising prosperity for everyone. Propelled by powerful innovations in computer technology, the new economy rendered obsolete old ways of doing business and measuring national economic well-being.[31] This new economy stressed knowledge over manual labor, information over physical capital, technology over mass production. Bulky old-economy companies, which built such weighty goods as cars and refrigerators, stressed expansiveness, hierarchy, and order. A new economy rewarded fast and flexible firms whose products and managerial philosophies comported with the weightlessness of the new era. Governments that followed suit would prosper, while others would languish. Importantly, the new economy would replace cycles of boom and bust with steady economic growth. In a 1996 *Business Week* article, Michael Mandel celebrated the strength of the new economy. Observing the incredible rise in the stock market over the past year, Mandel sought to calm potentially anxious readers. He held that "the stock market's rise is an accurate reflection of the growing strength of the New Economy."[32] Globalization and information technology had combined to raise productivity and corporate profits (but not wages), and investors would enjoy the returns. His confidence notwithstanding, Mandel's assessment appeared conservative and cautious when compared to predictions by other market watchers. In their boldly titled book *Dow 36,000*, James Glassman and Kevin Hassett predicted limitless wealth. They insisted that "the stock market is a money machine: Put dollars in at one end, get those dollars back and more at the other end."[33] Glassman and Hassett chided less aggressive analysts, whom they dismissed as holding onto old-economy notions of stock valuation.

More than anything else, the stock market emblematized the cel-
ebratory qualities of the new economy. In the 1990s, the stock market
became the people's market. In the view of its advocates, the stock market constituted a realm where regular people could achieve extreme
financial success. The operations of the popularized stock market bolstered
democracy—better than many putative democratic institutions. Thomas
Frank has referred to this view as "market populism," which holds that "in
addition to being mediums of exchange," markets function as "mediums
of consent."[34] As such, markets express the voice of the people. Markets
enable individuals to assert their interests and indicate policy preferences.
Brokerage advertisements in the 1990s represented the stock market as
a populist vehicle.[35] The Discover company portrayed a series of average Americans—tow-truck drivers, bartenders, grandmothers—who had
struck it rich in the market, much to the surprise of the condescending
representatives of old Wall Street who appeared in the ads. These everyday
millionaires kept their humble ways even as they experienced tremendous
wealth. Online broker E*Trade stressed a direct connection between the
people and the market in its slogan "The power is in your hands." Citing
"democratizations" of technology, finance, and information, commentator
Thomas Friedman predicted that "soon everyone will have a virtual seat
on the New York Stock Exchange."[36] As these examples demonstrate, market populism sought to replace elitist representations of the stock market
with portrayals emphasizing regularity and accessibility.

Many workers had become familiar with investment-based approaches
to retirement as private employers increasingly shifted their plans from
defined-benefit to defined-contribution schemes.[37] Defined-benefit plans
operate like Social Security by providing fixed monthly pensions to retirees. Defined-contribution plans specify employer and employee contributions made during one's working years; a worker's retirement benefits
depend on the returns received on accumulated benefits. Between 1983
and 1998, the number of full-time pensioned employees participating in
defined-benefit plans declined from 87 to 44 percent. During this same
period, the percentage of full-time pensioned employees participating in
defined-contribution plans increased from 40 to 79 percent.[38] This shift
has been motivated importantly by companies' efforts to develop more
fluid corporate structures in the "new economy." They have replaced strict
department boundaries with more flexible product "teams." In this new
structure, employers effectively subcontract the skills of their employees.

Defined-contribution plans, especially 401(k) plans, fit the flexibility and mobility of this new structure. These plans permit portability and enable employers to attach benefits more directly to a worker's performance.

Sometimes grudgingly, policymakers also felt pressure to pursue agendas that facilitated the growth of markets. Campaigning in 1992, Bill Clinton promised to advance programs that improved the situations of workers suffering through recession and global economic changes. However, President Clinton quickly discovered the difficulty of obtaining the necessary funds for this goal in light of congressional interest in reducing the federal deficit. Angered by congressional objections to his first economic stimulus package, Clinton sarcastically complained: "We're Eisenhower Republicans here. . . . We stand for lower deficits and free trade and the bond market. Isn't that great?" At another moment, he thundered: "We're doing everything Wall Street wants! . . . We're losing our soul."[39] Former labor secretary Robert Reich recalled that these discussions were influenced significantly by Federal Reserve Board chairperson Alan Greenspan. Reich bemoaned that "Greenspan haunts every budget meeting, though his name never comes up directly. . . . It is repeatedly said that we must reduce the deficit because Wall Street needs to be reassured, calmed, convinced of our wise intentions." Similarly, Joseph Stiglitz noted that the Council of Economic Advisors closely observed Greenspan. Although he initially expressed some concern about stock prices, Greenspan quickly became a "cheerleader for the market's boom, almost egging it on, as he repeatedly argued that the New Economy was bringing with it a new era of productivity increases."[40] However, new-economy policies geared toward investment bankers on Wall Street did not help ordinary folks on Main Street. Although productivity rose steadily throughout the 1990s, real wages hardly improved—and the gap between the wealthy and everyone else continued to widen.[41]

In addition to these larger political and economic developments, the report of the 1994–1996 Advisory Council on Social Security signaled the possibility of fundamental reform. For the first time since their initiation in 1937, an advisory council recommended that policymakers dedicate a portion of the payroll tax to the creation of individual investment accounts. Reflecting the tensions in debates over Social Security, the Advisory Council did not offer a unanimous recommendation. Instead, the Advisory Council issued three separate recommendations for bolstering the finances of Social Security, each supported by a minority of the board members. One plan, the maintenance of benefits (MB) plan, upheld the principle of social insurance. The MB plan would "maintain the present Social Security benefit and tax structure essentially as is."[42] Supporters of the MB plan called for further study of a plan to invest a portion of the trust fund in the stock market. A second plan, the Individual Accounts (IA) plan, sought to combine aspects of insurance and investment. The IA plan envisioned individual accounts administered by the federal government and converted to an indexed annuity upon a worker's retirement. A minimum guarantee provision would ensure some (albeit not full) payment to a worker's survivors in the case of death. A third plan, the Personal Security Accounts (PSA) plan, foregrounded the principle of investment. The PSA plan sketched a two-tiered system with private accounts to replace the existing Social Security system. The first tier would provide a flat retirement benefit for workers unrelated to income or contributions, while the second tier "would provide fully funded, individually owned, defined-contribution retirement accounts."[43]

Despite the differences in their plans, members of the Advisory Council cast themselves as "breaking new ground" by recommending that policymakers improve "returns" for younger workers. Of course, possible methods for improving "money's worth" for younger workers produced significant disagreement among Advisory Council members. Still, they worried that young workers and future generations would pay considerably more in taxes than they would receive in benefits. Increasing public awareness of this possibility contributed to unprecedented low levels of confidence among younger workers that Social Security would be available for them upon retirement. To bolster the system's financial prospects and regain public confidence, the Advisory Council agreed that Social Security should provide "a reasonable money's worth return on the contributions of younger workers and future generations, while taking account of the redistributive nature of the Social Security system."[44]

The unanimous identification of "money's worth" as a proper objective for Social Security gave momentum to calls for privatization. Supporters of the MB plan accepted money's worth with great hesitation, insisting that this criterion could offer only a partial evaluation of Social Security. Indeed, in their follow-up statement to the main report, supporters of the MB plan held that the comparative aspects of the Advisory Council report placed too great an emphasis on money's worth. Supporters of the MB plan characterized money's worth as "inadequate and indeed misleading when used as the primary basis for comparing these proposals."[45] These objections notwithstanding, the very appearance of money's worth in the Advisory Council report shifted the evaluative criteria for Social Security away from the reigning principles of social insurance that had guided the program in the decades after its passage. Moreover, the strong criticism of money's worth advanced by the supporters of the MB plan appeared as only one of three views on Social Security. In this way, their adherence to social insurance appeared as a minority view, since supporters of the other plans exhibited greater comfort invoking money's worth to compare the proposals.

In a related manner, supporters of all three plans turned to the stock market to increase revenues, whether for the system generally or for individual accounts. Supporters of the MB plan sought a strict delimitation of this aspect of their plan as well—this time to obtain a higher return for the system than could be obtained by investing in government bonds alone. However, once invoked, the stock market could not be easily contained. If the stock market offered the promise of greater returns for the system, then it might also enable greater returns for individual retirees. Both the IA plan and the PSA plan utilized the stock market to benefit individuals, thus blurring any clear line in the report between system-wide and individual investing. Once again, the strong adherence to insurance principles represented in the MB plan appeared as only one of three positions on the relationship between Social Security and the stock market.

Although animated debates had been ongoing, President Clinton drew even greater attention to the issue when he called for a national conversation on Social Security in his 1998 State of the Union address. President Clinton began his 1998 address by praising the improved structure and finances of the federal government. The new economy had produced rapid economic and technological change, and his administration acted affirmatively to create "a new kind of government for the information age." This new approach enabled the seemingly impossible elimination of the federal deficit. President Clinton proudly announced that "tonight I come before you to announce that the federal deficit, once so incomprehensibly large that it had 11 zeros, will be, simply, zero." Soon budget surpluses would create new possibilities for public policy. Clinton identified his primary priority plainly: "Save Social Security first." He insisted that policymakers reserve "every penny of any surplus" until they had fixed the long-term financial problems facing Social Security. However, Clinton did not announce a plan, and he did not spend much time discussing the topic of Social Security. Instead, Clinton called for a national dialogue on Social Security sustained by all Americans before policymakers pursued a specific course of action. He proposed regional discussion forums and promised a White House conference at the end of the year. Clinton urged a "nonpartisan" approach to the issue that included citizens and lawmakers from both major political parties. He hoped that a year-long discussion might provide a "true consensus on how we should proceed."[46]

In his 1999 State of the Union address, Clinton proposed using the budget surplus to restore the long-term solvency of Social Security. Connecting Social Security's troubles to the "aging of America," Clinton did not rebuke the program as improperly designed or inefficiently managed. An aging population presented challenges for all policies, as the elderly population would double over the next three decades and "the baby boom will become a senior boom." Clinton highlighted Social Security's insurance functions by linking its early achievements and the present day. He observed that "when President Roosevelt created Social Security, thousands wrote to thank him for eliminating what one woman called 'the stark terror of penniless, helpless old age.' Even today, without Social Security, half our nation's elderly would be forced into poverty."[47] This statement framed Social Security as an antipoverty program that guaranteed the well-being of seniors. This frame excluded investment as a proper criterion for judging the program's success. Concerns about money's worth did not mandate a fundamental restructuring of Social Security, because money's worth did not capture its central function.

Clinton did not abandon ideas of individual investment, but he kept these separate from Social Security. He affirmed that "we must help all Americans, from their first day on the job, to save, to invest, to create wealth." Identifying this goal, Clinton reframed the problem: larger systems of savings and investment—and not Social Security—had failed to address the needs of millions of workers and their families. To remedy this situation, Clinton proposed the creation of individual savings accounts outside of Social Security. He called for dedicating "11 percent of the surplus to establish universal savings accounts—USA accounts—to give all Americans the means to save."[48] This proposal exemplified what rhetorical critic John Murphy has termed Clinton's "power of metamorphosis."[49] Co-opting his opponents' position, Clinton affirmed the need to create investment opportunities for all Americans. However, this constituted a larger problem distinct from Social Security, which remained fundamentally sound.

Clinton delivered both addresses in a highly polarized political environment manifest in the Republican-initiated impeachment proceedings. In this context, President Clinton sustained the approval of a majority of Americans (as measured by polls) by playing to his strengths as a competent executive.[50] Americans recognized his imperfect character, but they judged his policy competence as more important. Clinton's attention to Social Security presented a significant opportunity to demonstrate his competence. Moreover, Clinton's approach to this issue placed him above the partisan fray. His call for a national dialogue demonstrated a willingness to consider diverse viewpoints. His proposal for USA accounts illustrated his "nonideological" character in employing a range of policy options. Clinton thus occupied a moderate political position vacated by his congressional prosecutors. However, in a polarized climate, the likelihood of bipartisan compromise necessary for fundamentally restructuring Social Security appeared slim. Instead, the political conflicts of the 1990s—from the Contract with America to impeachment—portended contesting metaphors.

The Values of Investment

Privatization respected individual freedom, choice, and control. Privatization enabled workers to pursue their individual desires and plan their lives as they saw fit. In his opening statement to a House Budget Committee hearing, Rep. John Kasich proclaimed that "if we can begin to have a program that develops more savings and more investment, our workers, I believe, will be set free." Privatization promised to restore workers' independence, whereas the present system perpetuated their dependence. Sen. Conrad Burns identified this as a fundamental problem with efforts to bolster the system. Doing so would weaken individual initiative and autonomy. In making this claim, Burns and others rejected the longstanding view that social-insurance programs fostered independence, while public-assistance programs encouraged dependence. Burns worried that bolstering Social Security would lead workers to expect benefits "without any kind of responsibility to themselves, and taking care of themselves for old age, or building estates, that they become more reliant on government."[51]

For Burns, this spelled disaster, portending the very imprisonment that Kasich wished to overcome. He held that "once you become reliant on government, then government sort of infringes on freedoms."[52]

Supporters of privatization maintained that it facilitated wealth creation. In a Finance Committee hearing, Sen. Phil Gramm explained to his colleagues that they faced a choice between "staying in a system based on debt, where we have to raise payroll taxes and cut benefits continuously, or transitioning to a system based on wealth." According to Gramm, the present system spent money, whereas a privatized system could create money. The present system placed the federal government in the difficult position of having to choose among its citizens in deciding whose well-being it wished to promote. On this score, Ways and Means Committee chair Bill Archer asked his colleagues to reflect on whether they were comfortable with this role. He queried: "Is the role of the government simply to redistribute existing wealth or to foster conditions that enable everyone to make more wealth?" For Archer, redistribution represented a policy of pessimism and envy. It treated finances as a zero-sum game whereby wins experienced by one party would be felt as losses by another party. Holding that the present system punished hard work, Archer asked whether policymakers should take "away from those who have, denying the fruits of the labor to those who work harder, or do we create opportunity so others can have more?"[53] Privatization constituted an expression of faith in an ever-expanding economy that would create wealth for all.

Evaluated in terms of wealth creation, the existing Social Security system failed miserably. Supporters of privatization charged that the system produced significantly lower rates of return than could be obtained through stock-market investing. For this reason alone, the existing system needed a fundamental restructuring. Michael Tanner, a policy analyst at the Cato Institute, argued that "even if you could find a way to keep Social Security solvent, that does not solve the other problem with Social Security, and that is that Social Security is increasingly a bad deal for younger workers." This stemmed from "the basic nature of Social Security," which utilized pay-as-you-go financing. Tanner explained that "in a pay-as-you-go system, your Social Security taxes are not saved for you or invested in any way." He and others identified this as a primary reform objective; they contended that Social Security provided younger workers a negative rate of return. Underscoring Social Security's costs for younger workers, Jagadeesh Gokhale, of the Federal Reserve Bank of Cleveland, held that people born after 1945 "pay roughly 5 percent in terms of a lifetime net tax rate by participating in the Old Age and Survivors' Insurance program."[54] Far from creating wealth, Social Security actually cost workers a significant amount of money.

Transitioning to an investment-based system would also cost taxpayers money, but advocates sought to reframe these costs as debts from the present system. Sylvester Schieber explained that the Advisory Council's PSA plan "assumes that the cost of transitioning from the current system to the proposed one would be paid by an explicit tax. We have dubbed this the liberty tax because it would free us over time from the completely unfunded retirement program that we currently have." The liberty tax promised transparency as well as emancipation. Like other advocates of privatization, Schieber held that "the accruing debt [of transferring to a new system] would be simply an explicit recognition of the implicit obligation that already exists in Social Security." Similarly, Carolyn Weaver, a scholar at the American Enterprise Institute and also a member of the 1994–96 Advisory Council, contended that "it is not a new debt, but is simply a new debt that is not currently shown on the federal books."[55] In this way, Schieber and Weaver argued that all future Social Security benefits should count as costs of the present system. By promising benefits to future retirees, supporters of the present system committed financial resources of the federal government. Transitioning to a new system would make these costs explicit, and perhaps prompt society-wide reflection on the distribution of financial resources across generations. Besides, the returns on private accounts would more than reimburse taxpayers for the "costs of liberty."

Advocates of privatization envisioned fantastic potential for wealth creation through investment. Stephen Entin, a resident scholar at the Institute for Research on the Economics of Taxation, promised that "retirees could get three times the benefits for one-third the cost through a real saving program." This meant that private accounts could "double or triple people's retirement income for the last 20 years of their lives." On this basis, Entin and others could not imagine why policymakers would deny retirees such windfalls. Confident that the long bull run in the stock market had not yet reached its peak, supporters of privatization predicted greater and greater highs. Roger Ibbotson, a professor of finance at Yale University, predicted that the Dow Jones Industrial Average would increase from its recently attained level of 10,000 to 100,000 over the next twenty-five years. Responding to a concern about unfounded optimism, he defended this prediction of a ten-fold increase in the value of stocks by explaining that he simply had forecasted the premium that stocks had historically returned in comparison to bonds. Similarly, Ibbotson held that $1 of stock purchased in 1926 would be worth $2,351 today.[56] In the statements of Entin, Ibbotson, and others, the stock market appeared to be an untapped resource. Mining this resource would create riches for Americans, and it would enable policymakers to avoid difficult decisions. In fact, the stock market had been working its magic all along, but previous generations of policymakers lacked the insight or courage to pursue it. Privatization presented an opportunity to cash in on the wealth of the nation.

Perhaps the most suggestive case where a debate participant represented the stock market as an unlimited source of money arose in a discussion of developments abroad. In a 1999 Ways and Means Committee hearing, David Harris, a research associate at Watson Wyatt Worldwide, drew on his past experience as a financial-services regulator in Australia to discuss that country's experience with private accounts. Switching to a system of private accounts required a public education campaign so that workers could understand how their accounts operated and appreciate the value of these accounts. A series of advertisements served these functions in Australia. Harris recounted one advertisement that depicted a "person watering a tree, and the tree is sprouting leaves which are money. And it suggests that if the employee can be encouraged to contribute to the individual accounts, he'll be a lot better off in the future."[57] With private accounts, money really did grow on trees. This image and other accounts, like fantastic forecasts for the stock market, suggested that private accounts would create wealth with minimal attention and skill. An investor only needed to provide a basic source of nourishment—whereas money trees required water, private accounts used money to grow money—and wealth would appear. For their part, policymakers simply had to give individuals this opportunity.

Private accounts would enable Social Security to function as a money tree through the power of compound interest, which advocates of privatization repeatedly invoked during the debates. Pursuing this theme, Brian Keane, representing the advocacy organization Economic Security 2000, remarked that "what we're talking about, though, is actually creating money." Keane regarded as beyond dispute the idea that "if you give a person a chance to save money, and if that is able to grow through compound interest, that person who had no wealth will have wealth." The power of compound interest promised benefits for the Social Security system as well as individuals. Sen. Pete Domenici warned that "if we cannot find a way to empower the Social Security system to be affected by the power of compounding, then it is going to be very difficult to maintain the system into the next century." Domenici remained optimistic for the future of Social Security because "the power of compounding is a fantastic instrument in terms of asset growth."[58] The structure of the present system had imperiled future retirement benefits for some time, but compound interest could recover lost ground. Compound interest could overcome past policy mistakes and provide a bountiful policy future.

Advocates of privatization depicted compound interest as an almost mystical force that individuals could harness if they took the time to understand and appreciate it. Sen. Phil Gramm repeatedly invoked the power of compound interest during committee hearings. Gramm disclosed that "throughout history, only a very small number of people have ever truly understood the power of compound interest. And very few people have ever been able to put it to work for them. They have become very wealthy as a result." Privatization presented an opportunity to share this secret with all Americans. No longer would the power of compound interest be reserved for the privileged few—private accounts would make its power available to all. The magic of compound interest did not require the few to succeed at the expense of the many—it enabled magnanimity. Such was the power of compound interest that it effected a complete reversal of traditional class politics. On this point, Gramm could barely contain his excitement: workers' contributions to their private accounts would be multiplied by "what Einstein called the most powerful force in the universe, which is the power of compound interest, to literally make working people in America wealth owners, to turn Karl Marx on his head by literally having workers own the means of production."[59] In Gramm's view, advocates of privatization constituted the intellectual vanguard; they would use the power of compound interest to smash class barriers and bring about revolution.

In generating wealth, the power of compound interest promised to overcome divisive barriers of income inequality in the United States. Sam Beard, founder of Economy Security 2000, made this case passionately in his testimony before a few congressional committees. Bemoaning the emergence of "two separate societies," Beard insisted that addressing the gap between rich and poor represented a matter of basic economic justice. He exhorted that "we need to address the issue of fairness in terms of asset accumulation and wealth and economic opportunity."[60] Privatization presented a tremendous opportunity for redress. In this spirit, Jack Kemp called for "democratizing the capitalist system." Under present conditions, poor people lacked access to capital. Kemp maintained that "the only thing a poor person has is his or her labor. This idea allows you to convert labor into capital."[61] In this way, policymakers could eliminate income inequality—or at least leftist class distinctions. Supporters of privatization envisioned all Americans as capitalists participating in an economy of increasing wealth.

The values I have identified so far demonstrate how the investment metaphor expressed optimism about the nation's future that implicitly contrasted with a putative pessimism attributed to insurance. Advocates of privatization repeatedly cast their position in terms of growth and expansion: investment would *increase* wealth, create *more* capital, *raise* the returns on Social Security. These claims tap into the notion that the future is always better, which, as Lakoff and Johnson note, resonates powerfully in American culture. Moreover, these claims tie investment to a directional metaphor that associates increases with improvement. As Lakoff and Johnson bluntly write: "Good is up; bad is down."[62] Investment enabled an association of increases in the stock market, which rose steadily during the 1990s, predicted increases in Social Security benefits, and a happy future. Advocates of privatization looked into the future and saw more wealth for everyone. By contrast, insurance implicitly accepted a static view of the economy that denied increases in wealth. In this view, insurance operated with the assumption that policymakers could only redistribute existing wealth. Whereas investment expressed hope, insurance engendered envy. Further, associations of investment and freedom, as Rep. Kasich asserted at the outset of this section, bolstered this sense of optimism. By enabling freedom, investment exhibited faith in an individual's ability to make sound decisions about one's future. Investment affirmed the "can-do spirit" of American culture, while insurance appeared stodgy and restrictive. Doubting people's abilities, insurance sought to impose constraints on individual decision making. A desire to free oneself from constraint appeared in Sylvester Schieber's characterization of the cost of private accounts as a "liberty tax." When compared to investment, insurance pined for the past while casting a suspicious eye on the future.

An insurance-based system clung to the precepts of a lumbering industrial economy, but the rise of an information-based, high-tech economy required more mobile and adaptable public policies that workers could tailor to their specific employment situations. Rep. Newt Gingrich called for a retirement system for the "information age." He complained that "we have a 1935 paper-based, bureaucratic, Social Security information system, which cannot tell you what taxes you paid, cannot tell you what interest you earned, cannot tell you what's in your account, and can't track you as an individual. It is a highly obsolete, precomputer, pre-information age model."[63] Looking confidently to the future, investment promised innovation and individuality. In the industrial era, large-scale enterprises powered the economy, propelling economic growth through the sheer volume of their output. This process treated human and nonhuman resources alike as parts of a giant machine; assembly-line workers performed specifically prescribed tasks to achieve a larger end. Workers' routines taught them to expect uniformity in the workplace and, as an extension, in retirement. But the rules had changed. The new economy demanded flexibility, and new technologies allowed people to work in previously unimaginable ways. Investment affirmed these changes in its core values. Its commitment to individuality synchronized retirement policy with workers' mobile and fluid careers. Its ability to create wealth through the power of compound interest enabled workers to free themselves from binding workplace attachments and pursue opportunities without constraint.

In a surprising turnaround, Sen. Daniel Patrick Moynihan, regarded by many of his colleagues as the Senate's foremost expert on social-welfare policy, embraced new-economy thinking in his eventual advocacy of private accounts.[64] Moynihan characterized private accounts as the next step in the development of retirement policy. He noted that in the course of deliberations over Social Security, "there has emerged a new dimension appropriate to the end of this century—as the basic Social Security annuity was appropriate to the end of the last century when it began in Europe—the personal retirement account." Moynihan praised the private account as "a lifelong savings and investment system which would leave the citizen not simply with a retirement income, but an estate that would quite change the relationships in society which we have come to think of as the hierarchical relations of an industrial society. This is a wholly new idea." Although the new economy required new thinking, private accounts participated in a long tradition of innovative policymaking. Moynihan identified a "grand sequence" in public policy as "society has organized itself in sequence, to deal with the wholly new experience of industrialism and the modern economy." Each successive step in this sequence brought about a cumulative improvement in workers' lives. A history of progress engendered confidence that policymakers could act affirmatively across different historical eras and ideological environments. Moynihan celebrated an "agenda of wealth" as appropriate for the twenty-first century.[65]

Investment also served an immediate instrumental function by promoting ownership for the holders of private accounts. Signaling a property right to one's account, ownership meant that politicians could not control one's retirement benefits. Sen. Judd Gregg stressed that private accounts meant that workers "actually have physical ownership" of their retirement savings, which they could invest as they wished. The possession of a stock certificate conferred an otherwise unattainable right. Only through ownership could workers and retirees act in their own interests and direct others to do so. Michael Tanner maintained that the absence of ownership created uncertainty in the present system. He explained that "because workers have no ownership rights to their pension funds, the government has no fiduciary duty to those workers." Workers had to rely on the goodwill of politicians. So long as members of Congress felt a duty to workers and retirees, they would support Social Security benefits. However, if congressional sentiment shifted, benefits might disappear. In this way, supporters of privatization once again challenged longstanding claims that social insurance bolstered independence. They retorted that insurance, in the form of the present system, left workers and retirees dependent on others. Connecting the values of individualism and ownership, Sen. Robert Kerrey asserted that "the source of real independence that comes in old age comes from ownership of financial assets."[66]

Appealing to individual control and ownership, some supporters of privatization characterized investment rather than insurance as a protection against risk. Individuals could make decisions about their investments, whereas insurance required central decision makers (either politicians or bureaucrats) to determine outcomes for others. Loss of control and lack of ownership meant exposure to risk. Along these lines, Rep.

Jim Kolbe insisted that "the current system provides a mere statutory right to benefits, which Congress can cut at any time in the future. Thus, such security is really illusory." Kolbe and others making this argument held little faith in laws, because laws suggested greater contingency than property. Property could change hands, but only with the full consent and participation of the buyers and sellers. Laws appeared to change in response to arbitrary and unknown elements—political whims, special pleading, influence peddling, etc. Laws, as the products of legislative bodies, also located decision making in groups rather than individuals. Whereas individual owners could determine the fate of their property, no single legislator could determine the fate of a law. Moreover, laws appeared more easily subject to demagoguery and manipulation. An un-scrupulous legislator could persuade a majority to adopt an unwise course of action, or a majority could enforce its views on an unwilling minority. Expressing these concerns, Rep. Jim McCrery asserted that "a law is just a law and any future Congress can change the law with a simple majority vote."[67] For these reasons, these advocates contended, whatever economic risk one might wish to associate with investing, the political risks of the present system loomed larger.

The market constituted a superior realm for secure investment. Ex-pressing the viewpoint of many supporters of privatization, William Beach, of the Heritage Foundation, proclaimed that "there is not a government program on the face of the earth that can't be made more efficient and better for the people that it is supposed to serve." This statement implied that government programs propagate waste and inefficiency (if not out-right fraud and abuse) by their very nature; the same action undertaken by government agencies and the private sector would cost more and de-liver less through the former. In contrast, markets inherently promoted efficiency and innovation. Markets fostered competition, which acted as a testing mechanism for discerning better and worse approaches to public problems. In a competitive environment, decision making rested with in-dividuals, who could choose freely among a range of goods and services. Whereas cronyism in the public sector might support inferior policies, individual choice in the marketplace ensured the utilization of superior ones. Lawrence White, a professor of economics at New York University, testified that private accounts would "bring the creative and competitive forces of the financial services sector into the picture to devise appropriate instruments and educate the program's participants."[68] Politicians could not be trusted, but markets could. A turn to markets necessarily would offer optimal solutions.

Supporters of privatization often anthropomorphized the market. Rather than referring to an abstraction, institution, or set of social arrangements, the market stood as an agent that responded to incentives and disincentives. The market paid attention to public policy, evaluated policy outcomes, and acted accordingly. Alan Greenspan depicted the market as actor in his appearances before congressional committees. According to Greenspan, the market understood that transitioning from a public to a private system would take time and (temporarily) increase costs, but the market appreciated the long-term benefits of such a transition. Greenspan explained to policymakers that "if you have a period of significant surpluses and you temporarily go into deficit . . . the market won't be penalizing you for that." The market could act quickly, but it did not make snap judgments. The market weighed multiple options in determining the best course of action for the short term and the long term. Greenspan held that the market's reaction to any change in Social Security policy depended on "where the markets perceive the longer term is." However, just as the market appreciated that short-term sacrifices could facilitate long-term gains, the market would not be deceived by quick fixes or "surface" reforms. Policymakers had to convince the market that they were committed to an optimal course of action. A positive market response to policy change would only occur if the "market [held] . . . the view that the Congress and the administration are serious about fiscal policy."[69]

Greenspan's personification of the market highlighted several virtues that bolstered its standing as a low-risk investing partner. Because it responded to incentives and disincentives, the market exhibited a consistent, knowable psychology that investors could learn and appeal to when conducting business. In this way, the market maintained a stable, steady demeanor that elicited trust. Whereas governments acted capriciously, the market offered justifications for its decisions. Exhibiting patience and reflection, the market did not "penalize" people for undertaking difficult tasks. However, the market was no fool—it could discern whether politicians proceeded seriously with reforms. Greenspan's stature in Washington positioned him as a close confidant of the market who could speak authoritatively about its character. Although he spoke with special insight, Greenspan did not disclose proprietary information, for the market wished to advertise its virtues. As a trusted partner, the market became someone investors could get to know. Operating through the market, investment offered individuals a personal connection to their future that contrasted sharply with the faceless bureaucrats and self-absorbed politicians who administered insurance.

The Values of Insurance

Insurance highlighted the importance of community. The very idea of insurance depended on people coming together to address issues that they could not resolve individually. Insurance utilized collective action to strengthen the position of each member of an insured group. Insurance premiums represented a financial commitment to provide goods, services, and income to others in times of accident, crisis, or change, knowing that others had committed to do the same. Committing oneself to another thus ensured one's own well-being. In these ways, social insurance emphasized interconnectedness and mutual concern. Eric Kingson, a professor of social work at Syracuse University, urged policymakers not to lose sight of the moral basis of Social Security. Referencing Bill Bradley, Kingson praised Social Security as the nation's "best expression of community." Others agreed. They celebrated Social Security as a monumental legislative achievement that improved the lives of generations of Americans. Rep. Richard Neal maintained that "from generation to generation [Social Security] gives us a sense of community, and it does tie us together as members of the American family."[70] In contrast, private accounts undermined community by insisting that individuals could rely on no one but themselves for their well-being. If Social Security drew Americans together as a national family, then private accounts dissolved familial bonds.

From a national family to particular families, supporters of insurance stressed connectedness and familiarity in their defense of Social Security. Arguing on behalf of President Clinton's proposal to dedicate a portion of the budget surpluses to bolstering the finances of Social Security, Jacob Lew, director of the Office of Management and Budget, situated the plan "in a framework that most families tend to think about when considering these kinds of financial matters. If we think about a family that has an 8-year-old child, and you are beginning to plan for college, you know it is going to be expensive. The first thing you do is try to put your family's financial house in order." In seeking to put the nation's financial house in order to prepare for future college expenses—the impending retirement of the baby boomers—the president acted as a responsible parent. He demonstrated a willingness to sacrifice the immediate gratification of a new car or a vacation—tax cuts or increased spending—to ensure the well-being of his children. Also pursuing the family metaphor, Kenneth Apfel, commissioner of the Social Security Administration, urged policymakers to remember the perspective through which most Americans considered Social Security. He held that "their concerns are with kitchen table economics, and the questions of providing for a family's own big-ticket budget items: education, health care, and retirement."[71] Locating Social Security in the context of kitchen-table discussions implied that Americans relied on their familiarity with the program to project some stability into an uncertain future.

As associations with generation, nation, and home suggest, familial metaphors figured prominently when debate participants articulated the values of insurance. This contrasted dramatically with the effective absence of familial metaphors in arguments for investment, indicating that insurance and investment invited and discouraged other metaphorical connections. Insurance, community, and family resonated because these metaphors all valued connection and belonging positively. In this way, family and community enabled insurance to offer an alternative formulation of the idea that more is better—namely, *more* than one person working together to achieve a goal. The interaction of insurance and family foregrounded positive attributes of both metaphors. Insurance cast families as sources of protection (rather than sources of squabbles), and family cast insurance as a set of intimate connections (rather than a cold calculation of risk). Investment could not appeal to these associations, because doing so would acknowledge the value of connection that investment ostensibly rejected as a constraint. Instead, investment invoked familiarity by personifying the market as a partner.

Insurance pooled people's resources to promote stability and security. Henry Aaron, a senior fellow at the Brookings Institution, insisted that the "fundamental philosophy" of social insurance "is to achieve an adequate basic income." Social insurance did not promise to make retirees rich, but pledged to provide them with a secure source of income. Workers could count on social insurance in the case of serious injury or retirement. Aaron countered that investment introduced uncertainty into situations of disability or retirement: some investments might pay off handsomely, but others would lose money. He insisted that the "option to invest in something that might do better and might do worse . . . fights the fundamental objective of social insurance." Alicia Munnell, a professor of management at Boston College, argued that the defined-benefit structure of Social Security, rather than a private accounts system, offered "the best way to assure Americans an adequate retirement income."[72] Its guaranteed benefits ensured that workers would not exhaust their financial resources in retirement.

Supporters of social insurance invoked the metaphor of a three-legged stool to situate the role of Social Security in the larger context of retirement. The three-legged stool referred to the idea that an individual's retirement income should consist of a combination of Social Security, employment-based retirement benefits, and personal savings. While advocates of privatization insisted that investment criteria should be applied to Social Security itself, supporters of social insurance urged a mixture of insurance and investment within this larger context. Encouraging diversity, Wendell Primus, a policy analyst at the Center on Budget and Policy Priorities, held that "you don't need or expect each component of the system to have the same attributes." Primus contended that policymakers would be wrong to model all three legs of the stool according to a defined-benefit or a defined-contribution structure. As part of the three-legged stool, Social Security properly provided retirees with their most secure source of income. Deputy Treasury Secretary Lawrence Summers explained that "Social Security is, in a sense, the foundation, the minimum, the assurance for people, so it seems to me that uncertainties that might be tolerable with respect to someone's private savings account or their portfolio outside of their pension would certainly not be acceptable with respect to Social Security."[73] Workers could invest elsewhere in their retirement portfolio without undermining the security of insurance. Emphasizing interdependence, the three-legged stood cohered with familial metaphors: both suggested that a larger entity obtained its strength from the interrelationship of its parts. Moreover, both metaphors attributed different roles to their constituent parts. Just as the members of a family played different roles, such as parent and child, so, too, did the legs of the retirement stool.

Whereas Social Security offered stability, stocks entailed variability. For this reason, comparing average rates of return for stocks and bonds mattered less than considering returns across different historical periods. Gary Burtless, a senior fellow at the Brookings Institution, stressed the variability of stock-market returns in his appearances before congressional committees. Burtless examined 108 twenty-year periods from the late 1800s onward to calculate the real rates of return for investing in the stock market. Although the average rate of return for these periods was 6.4 percent, six periods returned less than 2 percent. For most of the 1960s and 1970s, stocks returned less than 1 percent. In dramatic fashion, stock prices fell 50 percent between 1973 and 1975. He concluded that "there is no way that someone planning to retire in 1975 could have had such a good pension as he planned on in 1973 given this change in prices."[74] Burtless and others wondered what would happen if a similar drop occurred in the future and most workers had dedicated their retirement savings to the stock market: economic crisis, political crisis, or both might ensue.

Supporters of insurance reminded policymakers that a stock-market crash created problems leading to the establishment of Social Security in the first place. David Langer, an employee-benefits consultant, observed that "people are saying, let us have a market-oriented Social Security system, but that is what caused the need for a non-market-oriented system that we have today." Burtless reminded policymakers of this, too, and he added that no one would have proposed investing in 1983 "after the stock market had 15 years of negative returns." He likened the current fascination with the stock market to "shifts in fashion." Even Alan Greenspan conceded that a "lottery principle" best explained the sky-high prices of Internet stocks. He explained that "you get a premium in that stock price which is exactly the same sort of price evaluation process that goes on in a lottery."[75] From these perspectives, privatization appeared as chasing after the latest fad, or allowing the promise of a fantastic payoff to overwhelm one's critical judgment. While retirement planning required delaying immediate gratification, supporters of privatization appeared more interested in searching for a quick fix than utilizing the varied aspects of retirement policy to form an overall strategy. In contrast, supporters of insurance displayed clearheadedness by resisting fickle trends and the false promises of the stock market. They insisted on the need for a secure and stable source of retirement income, even if it appeared unfashionable. An insurance metaphor recast supposed stodginess as sound judgment.

A primary focus on investment ignored the wide-ranging protection provided by Social Security, which benefited workers and their families throughout their lives. Social Security Commissioner Shirley Chater testified that "many young families are today receiving value from Social Security decades before they will ever receive a retirement benefit check." Chater noted that 30 percent of Social Security's beneficiaries received disability or survivors' benefits. The value of these benefits amounted to a half-million dollars worth of additional insurance for every worker. Jane Ross, a deputy commissioner in the Social Security Administration, stressed the importance of disability benefits. She explained that "an average 20-year-old stands about a 25 to 30 percent chance of becoming disabled before reaching retirement age." Moreover, Social Security offered universal protection and uniform coverage, rather than selecting among workers wishing to enroll in a private insurance program. By contrast, "Private insurers are selective, excluding those individuals at higher risk of becoming disabled. A great many people would simply not be able to buy private disability insurance at any price."[76] For some workers, the half-million-dollar price tag attached to disability and survivors' insurance understated its value. For all workers, Social Security provided peace of mind with the knowledge that serious injury or death would not put their families in a precarious financial state.

Rates of return could not adequately measure the wide-ranging protection afforded by Social Security. Stanford Ross, who served briefly as commissioner of Social Security in the late 1970s, held that because Social Security offered more than retirement benefits, providing "insurance against risks that are best covered on a wide social basis," it could not be assessed through rates of return. Instead, "The real question is the total social return—somebody 20 doesn't know whether they are going to be rich or poor, disabled or not." Considering its social returns, Social Security offered workers of all ages a terrific return. Robert Myers, who served as chief actuary of Social Security from 1947 to 1970, also dismissed the notion of rates of return as irrelevant for the program. He reminded policymakers that Social Security had served as a social-insurance program since its enactment. Myers offered the analogy of school taxes: "Everybody pays school taxes, whether they have ever had kids or ever will have kids. There is a pooling."[77] One would not object to school taxes because they did not offer a handsome monetary return, nor should one object to payroll taxes on the same grounds.

Supporters of insurance also charged that advocates of privatization overestimated anticipated returns from investments by downplaying the transition costs to a private-accounts system. Martha Phillips, executive director of the Concord Coalition, discounted advocates' "enthusiasm for privatization . . . because people haven't thought through carefully what the problems are." She highlighted the problems of transition: "At least one generation, and perhaps several generations, will be required to continue paying for the retirement of their elders while putting aside for their own retirement. This double burden can be spread out, but it cannot be avoided altogether." Advocates of privatization might wish to bill the transition costs of private accounts to the present Social Security system, but they could not ignore these costs in calculating rates of return. Wherever advocates sent the bill, workers and retirees would see the charges in their taxes and benefits. John Mueller, chief economist for the consulting firm of Lehrman, Bell, Mueller, Cannon, concluded that the transition tax would worsen benefits for everyone: "Every group now alive faces substantial loses from partial or full privatization."[78] Mueller added that advocates of privatization could not assume that the transition tax would be paid by higher returns on stock-market investments. Higher stock returns assumed higher economic growth and increased revenues for Social Security, which sustained its advantage over private accounts.

Perhaps more importantly, supporters of insurance retorted that advocates of investment could not use their preferred criteria to evaluate the history of the program because the program had been designed and administered to meet other objectives. Eric Kingson invoked the history of Social Security to substantiate this position. He noted that "if the goal were to provide only a fair rate of return, then we would have given previous retirees far smaller benefits when they began." However, the program's early administrators and policymakers decided to give full benefits to all workers covered by Social Security, even if they contributed payroll taxes for only a brief period before retirement. Previous generations did not concern themselves with "money's worth," and one could not properly ascribe this motive to them. Kingson explained that "we blanketed in the older worker. To then come back and say that rates of return are declining is assessing it from a very different perspective."[79] By characterizing Social Security as a "bad deal" for younger workers, advocates of privatization applied a misleading, anachronistic metaphor in assessing the program's treatment of successive generations. The associated metaphors of insurance collectively served to refute this approach: family and community members helped one another because they held a common bond, not because they expected a financial reward.

Through its wide-ranging protection and progressive benefit formula, Social Security helped alleviate poverty. Echoing the view of many others, Social Security commissioner Kenneth Apfel characterized Social Security as the nation's "most significant anti-poverty program." Social Security kept many seniors above the poverty line. Apfel observed that "the elderly poverty rate is just 11 percent now." This rate suggested a dramatic improvement in the lives of seniors compared to other moments in the nation's history, and Social Security deserved the credit. Without the protection of Social Security, "the elderly poverty rate would be about 48 percent."[80] Rev. Jesse Jackson highlighted this theme during his testimony, tying antipoverty efforts to support for families. He portrayed Social Security as the "difference between decency and despair" for many Americans. He noted that two-thirds of elderly Americans relied on Social Security for more than half of their retirement income. And yet, the program did not only eliminate the prospect of poverty for many retirees. Jackson called Social Security "America's most vigorous family program. With it, families are protected not just in retirement, but in tragedy, sudden death, disability or disaster. Its benefits go to workers, to spouses, to children."[81] In this way, Jackson called on advocates of privatization to reconsider their position in light of other values. Offering wide-ranging protection, Social Security stood as an important expression of family values. Privatization encouraged people to think of themselves not as members of families, but as individual investors concerned with a specific type of return. Invoking family, Jackson drew together values of community and poverty alleviation. Just as family members sought one another's well-being, they could appreciate the ways that Social Security safeguarded the well-being of other families. Further, insofar as Social Security expressed national familial bonds, it ensured that no family member went hungry.

Unlike public-assistance programs, Social Security alleviated poverty without raising the ire of middle- and upper-class Americans. Public-assistance programs isolated and stigmatized poor people; receipt of benefits marked someone as poor and raised associations of poverty with moral undeservingness. These associations raised the suspicions of nonrecipients, who often demanded that potential public-assistance recipients prove their financial need and moral worth. As a universal program,

Social Security did not create divisive distinctions between recipients and nonrecipients. Social Security required no proof of financial need or moral worth. Instead, it gave all workers a shared stake and common standing in the program, and thus garnered the support of Americans of varied socioeconomic standing. Whereas public-assistance programs marked people as poor, Social Security addressed poverty "invisibly." As Henry Aaron explained, "Social Security is the most powerful instrument for equalizing incomes in the United States by providing relatively more generous benefits to low earners than to higher earners, but financing benefits with a proportional tax on the same earnings used to compute benefits." So, while everyone paid the same payroll tax rate, low earners received a higher percentage of their income back in retirement. All of this took place under a universalist discourse: retirees had earned their benefits—no one benefited from largesse. Aaron held that private accounts would undo and even reverse the redistributive effects of Social Security. He maintained that "rates of return are likely to be higher for high earners than for low earners. Administrative costs take a larger part of the accounts of low earners than of high earners."[82] By exacerbating inequality, private accounts threatened to install a hierarchy of deservingness in old age.

Contrasts between Social Security and public assistance revealed the power of an insurance metaphor. Although both programs shared a goal of poverty alleviation, they invited decidedly different value judgments. This difference stemmed in part from the ways that assistance and insurance cast people as strangers and intimates, respectively. Assistance maintained a strict division between individuals who funded its benefits and those who received benefits. Familiarity did not reach across this division, since beneficiaries appeared as "other than" the person providing the funding. By contrast, insurance attributed a common standing to all program participants regardless of their ratio of contributions to benefits. The associated metaphors of insurance justified this attribution by suggesting that program participants did not object to poverty alleviation because they knew beneficiaries as members of their families and communities. Social Security constituted "America's most vigorous family program" not only because it provided disability and death benefits to a worker's dependents, but because its familial character overcame divisions among Americans to affirm their common bonds. Insurance thus enabled a national reconciliation.

The Social Security Trust Fund

Connecting policy goals to core values, metaphors of investment and insurance enabled understanding and evaluation of existing features of Social Security. Differing perceptions of the trust fund offered dramatic evidence of this metaphorical function, as debate participants disagreed about its very reality. Their disagreements produced contrasting projections of when the Social Security system would experience fiscal shortfalls—if not outright crisis.

Advocates of privatization insisted over and over again that the Social Security trust fund amounted to nothing more than a stack of IOUs. Sen. Alan Simpson offered a representative account when he asserted during his opening statement to a 1996 subcommittee hearing that "there is actually no trust fund." He dismissed the supposed trust fund as "a bookkeeping entry, a pile of IOUs." As mandated by law, the Social Security Administration purchased U.S. Treasury bonds with the excess revenues it collected through the payroll tax. As a consequence of the 1983 reforms, Social Security had amassed a trust fund to pay for future benefits. In depicting these Treasury bonds as IOUs, supporters of privatization transformed an ostensibly secure and sensible procedure into a shaky and suspicious activity. The image of an IOU conjured up dubious lending practices that replaced real, legitimate assets with nonexistent, illegitimate ones. IOUs suggested lending to people otherwise unable to obtain legitimate credit, or informal instances of lending that did not require a secure guarantee of payback—neither of these situations appeared appropriate for the nation's retirement system. The holders of IOUs—in this case, the American people—appeared as dupes who allowed poor judgment, naiveté, or sentimentality to obstruct sound financial decision making. Moreover, depicting Treasury bonds as IOUs implied that only a particular practice by the government could count as an acceptable treatment of surplus revenue: holding hard assets. Short of storing precious metals or like assets in bank vaults, the federal government would be guilty of spending the trust fund. Along these lines, Carolyn Weaver observed that "there are no physical assets backing up those securities in the trust funds."[83] Of course, supporters of privatization did not object to individuals or businesses purchasing bonds and other financial assets, but individuals and businesses had demonstrated their market credibility.

They could be trusted to understand issues of savings and investment for the future, whereas the federal government warranted only suspicion.

Although they did not employ familial metaphors to argue for investment, some advocates of privatization co-opted these metaphors to discredit the trust fund. Sen. Phil Gramm likened the status of the trust fund to a mother who spent her child's college savings and replaced the money with notes promising future repayment. He imagined that "you have got a young man and he is a paper boy, and he gives his mother money to put aside for him to go to college. His mother builds the money into the family budget. He gets ready to go to college. Does she have the money or does she not? Well, the test is, can she give him the money to go to college without changing the financing of the family?"[84] If Social Security affirmed family values, as the insurance metaphor suggested, then the present condition of the trust fund signaled a dereliction of parental responsibility. Citizen-children trusted their politician-parents to act on their behalf, but instead of saving their children's money, the parents spent it as their own. Rather than sacrificing their own desires by tightening the family budget, these irresponsible parents used their children as sources of income. This reformulation of the family metaphor demonstrated how metaphors invoke difference through their meaningful entailments. Some connotations may comport with articulated associations, while others may disrupt metaphorical associations. If family served as a justification for insurance, then it also invited criticism of this purpose.

Supporters of insurance defended the trust fund by comparing the practices of the Social Security Administration to the private sector, and by insisting on the good credit of the federal government. They observed that investors did not treat Treasury bonds as dubious IOUs. Henry Aaron explained that "when I think about whether the trust fund is real or not, I ask myself, would Chase Manhattan Bank, holding a portfolio of Treasury securities, regard that portfolio as real or not?"[85] Answering affirmatively, Aaron appealed to a principle of consistency: if Treasury bonds constituted a portion of a good portfolio for Chase Manhattan and other private investors, then they should count the same for the Social Security Administration. The nature of the Treasury bond did not change with its purchaser. Echoing the views of others, Jacob Lew described the bonds in the trust fund as "full faith and credit obligations of the United States government." For Lew and others, this standing offered the strongest possible assurance that the trust fund could be viewed as an asset. He maintained that "there is no full faith and credit obligation of the United States in our history that has ever not been paid, and these will not be an exception." The unblemished credit history of the federal government evidenced its creditworthiness. Treasury bonds represented a more secure investment than bonds available through the private sector. Along these lines, Rep. Lynn Rivers asked Stephen Bodurtha, a vice president at Merrill Lynch, to compare the creditworthiness of his employer to the government: "Do you think Merrill Lynch is a better credit risk than the United States government?" Bodurtha responded: "No, I wouldn't say that."[86] On these grounds, the federal government defaulting on its obligations would signal far greater economic turmoil. The centrality of the Treasury and the Federal Reserve in fiscal policy tied the fate of the economy to the fate of the federal government. To doubt its creditworthiness would be to hold such deep cynicism about government as to question its very viability.

When confronted with comparative claims of creditworthiness, advocates of privatization responded that they did not doubt the ultimate repayment of the bonds held in the trust fund, but retorted that this would require the federal government to raise additional revenues. Rep. Pat Toomey reported his objection to characterizing the trust fund as "an asset to draw upon in the way that a positive balance in a checking account is." The trust fund did not constitute cash on hand; the federal government would have to make good on its debt to the Social Security system by billing taxpayers. Addressing the full faith and credit of the U.S. government, Rep. Clay Shaw argued that "the IOUs that are backed by the full faith and credit of the Federal Government are backed by the taxpayers of tomorrow." He contended that when the Social Security system begins to draw down the trust fund, future taxpayers "are going to have to step up to the plate and put that money in there. It means more and more taxes."[87] Rather than securing retirement benefits for future generations, the trust fund pitted future generations against each other; workers would continue to pay for the benefits of retirees. Since trust-fund "assets" did not grow like an investment, talk of a trust fund only made matters worse by giving the appearance of savings and thus enabling continued fiscal irresponsibility. Advocates of privatization insisted that a day of reckoning for the Social Security system loomed sooner than its supporters wished to believe.

The most contentious issue regarding the trust fund concerned the proposal first suggested by the supporters of the MB plan on the 1994–96

Advisory Council, and adopted by President Clinton, to invest a portion of the trust fund in the stock market. When Clinton proposed trust-fund investing in his 1999 State of the Union address, he argued that doing so would comport with sound business practices followed by managers of state and private pensions. During congressional hearings on the proposal, administration officials and others reiterated this argument and noted the advantages of system versus individual investing. Lawrence Summers asserted confidently that the proposal was "in line with best practice in the management of defined-benefit pension plans in both the public and the private sector." Moreover, system-based investment actually represented a better business decision because it addressed the limits of an individual approach. Because the Social Security system would always hold its investments for the long-term, it could smooth out the market fluctuations that could worsen the position of an individual investor looking to retire in a specific period. Further, by lowering administrative costs, system-based investing better adhered to the business principle of economies of scale. Importantly, Summers and most other supporters of trust-fund investing believed that strict economic considerations should direct investment decisions. Like advocates of private accounts, they sought to protect the trust fund from "political interference." Robert Reischauer, a senior fellow at the Brookings Institution, called for the creation of an independent agency modeled after the Federal Reserve to manage the investments "solely to enhance the economic interests of future Social Security beneficiaries."[88]

While Summers, Reischauer, and others focused their recommendations on potential problems of implementation, they did not attend to a significant rhetorical problem. As the report of the 1994–96 Advisory Council demonstrated, an insurance metaphor could not safely contain values of investment. Comparing the practices of the Social Security Administration to the private sector effectively abdicated the heuristic power of an insurance metaphor by situating market norms as the appropriate evaluative framework. If investment constituted a superior approach to the trust fund, then it may have represented a superior approach to Social Security itself. The difficulty of incorporating investment values into insurance manifested in supporters' promises that trust-fund investing would proceed according to strict economic criteria, which propagated a dichotomy that represented political decisions as value-based and economic decisions as value-free. An insurance metaphor implied a contrary position—all realms of human interaction expressed value commitments. Most supporters of insurance disavowed this potentially powerful critical framework. For this reason, their proposal to invest the trust fund in the stock market appeared as an easy target.

Advocates of privatization insisted that no bulwark for trust-fund investing could withstand political pressure. Some advocates equated the proposal with socialism or fascism—the sort of thing that Mussolini supported during his dictatorial reign in Italy. In a more measured but equally unequivocal rebuke, Alan Greenspan maintained that investing the trust fund would undermine the efficiency of the stock market. He held that "even with Herculean efforts, I doubt if it would be feasible to insulate, over the long run, the trust funds from political pressures, direct and indirect, to allocate capital to less than its most productive use." Politics would get in the way of good business sense. Special interests would demand attention to their pet projects rather than the overall well-being of the market. Calculations of political strength and weakness might override legitimate economic concerns. Plainly put, the stock market and the political arena adhered to different decision-making logics. Michael Tanner feared that trust-fund investing would lead the federal government to intervene "in how corporations conduct their affairs, making those decisions on the basis of political passions, rather than on the best interests of the company, the economy, or the shareholders."[89] Passion and interest did not mix: determining the latter entailed distancing oneself from the former. Yet, the political process prevented people from doing so. Politics appeared as irrational when contrasted with the rational decision making of the marketplace. Trust-fund investing only invited trouble.

Only a few debate participants objected to the market-politics dichotomy that structured consideration of trust-fund investing. Rev. Jesse Jackson held that focusing exclusively on the highest possible monetary return risked a situation in which "we separate morality from our money interests." Jackson retorted that economic decisions, too, entailed moral decisions, and that the nation's promise lay in its ability to reconcile the two. He insisted that "we could never divorce our money interests from our moral interests and our commitment to human rights. Without that, we lose our moral authority in the world." Ways and Means Committee chair Bill Archer asked Jackson if the federal government should consider factors such as company hiring practices or goods (like tobacco) in making investment decisions. Answering affirmatively, Jackson insisted that either option—investing or not investing—would implicate policymakers in moral choices. He envisioned trust-fund investments as "a stimulus for companies as opposed to a deterrent."[90] Archer treated Jackson's answers as self-evidently damaging to the prospects for trust-fund investing. The very suggestion to limit investments proved the foolishness of the proposal. The pervasiveness of the view of the economy as value-free rendered unreasonable Jackson's effort to make manifest economic morality.

Jack Kemp, who testified on the same panel as Jackson, explicitly addressed the criticisms implied by Archer. Kemp maintained that limiting investments in any manner opened a Pandora's box. Tobacco, guns, gambling, and even apartheid represented "issues of great complexity that some people will think are moral, others immoral. . . . We should not go down that path." Instead, Kemp supported a system of private accounts because it allowed individuals to make these decisions as individuals. He held that "it should be personalized. That is the beauty of a free choice for the American worker."[91] If some people wanted to limit their investment opportunities because of a political passion, they could do so without limiting the choices of other investors. Kemp's invocation of choice recuperated the challenge in Jackson's social critique by recasting an expression of shared values in individual terms. Jackson spoke of *our* moral interests and *our* moral authority, which resonated with the value of community associated with an insurance metaphor. In contrast, Kemp intimated that citizens could not reach collective moral decisions—*some* will discern moral interests where *others* will not—so these choices rested properly with the individual worker. Kemp invoked the consonant investment values of individual and choice, whereas Jackson sought to synthesize the competing insurance and investment values of community and choice. In the context of a discussion about trust-fund investing, Jackson carried the far greater rhetorical burden—a task made more difficult by the prevailing view of economic choices as value-free.

Policy and Purpose

The power of policy metaphors lies importantly in their capacity to orient public debates. Exemplifying notions of perspective and entailment, metaphors situate specific proposals in wider contexts by associating policy purposes with underlying values and commitments. Affirming values of individualism, wealth creation, ownership, and market superiority, advocates regarded investment as a guide to restructuring a program that usurped citizens' freedom and control. Prcmising independence, insurance actually perpetuated dependence on government and facilitated a divisive politics of redistribution. Supporters of insurance disagreed, seeing their purpose as an affirmation of values of community, security, wide-ranging protection, and poverty alleviation. They rejected investment as a callous disregard for one's family. As these contrasting judgments suggest, insurance and investment invoked difference in their very articulation, frustrating the ontological claims of each metaphor and fueling debates about the proper purpose of Social Security.

Promising more for everyone, investment cast the future in optimistic terms. Envisioning greater wealth, investment implicitly contrasted its ever-expanding view of the economy with the supposedly static, pessimistic view of insurance. Investment believed in individuals, while insurance treated people "paternalistically." Further, investment comported with the changes wrought by the new economy. Its embrace of individualism fit with the flexibility of the new economy, and its capacity for wealth creation enabled workers' autonomy. Investment appeared as a trustworthy retirement plan—more so than insurance—because the market stood as a reliable partner. The market acted consistently and offered transparent justifications of its actions. Unlike the faceless bureaucrats who administered insurance, the market presented a familiar face for retirement planning.

Highlighting the associated metaphor of family, insurance stressed the virtues of connection and belonging. Moreover, family and the metaphor of the three-legged stool suggested that their constituent parts played distinct and important roles in sustaining the smooth operation of the larger entity. Insurance offered an implicit retort to the charge that it behaved paternalistically—namely, that it exhibited good judgment by adhering to a consistent course of action and resisting fads. This implicit interplay exhibited how metaphors may invoke counterclaims. For advocates of investment, the familial connotations of paternalism served as an insult: workers should not be treated as children. For supporters of insurance, the family metaphor identified a desired outcome. Insurance worked well historically because it treated citizens as intimates. Unlike public-assistance programs, insurance ascribed common standing to participants regardless of their contributions and benefits.

Policies require populations as well as purposes. In this spirit, the 1994–96 Advisory Council offered this explanation for identifying money's worth as a criterion for Social Security: "The Council feels that equity among generations is a serious issue and that it is important to improve the return on retirement saving for young people."[92] In this explanation, several populations appeared. The Advisory Council referenced young people explicitly, but its expressed concern with "equity among generations" invoked perceptions of past, present, and future workers and retirees. The Advisory Council imagined these different populations as variously served by the program, and they sought to redress imbalances. Other debate participants also explored these issues. Both advocates of investment and supporters of insurance imagined workers and retirees in different ways. I explore these different representations in the following chapter.

3

Representing Target Populations

S ocial policies ineluctably invoke target populations—people who, in the case of Social Security, would contribute to and benefit from an insurance or investment system. Whether supporting or opposing a policy proposal, debate participants address various qualities of a target population. Policymakers may assert that future retirees harbor hopes and dreams for their retirement, while retirees may expect policies to help them realize their visions. Beyond aspirations, potential beneficiaries may exhibit stated and unstated needs. Workers certainly do not plan to suffer a serious on-the-job injury or premature death, but they may need to protect their families against a tragic event. Workers also may possess particular knowledge and abilities that better prepare them for some retirement plans versus others. Shifting workplace practices may instill skills that prepare workers for an investment-based approach to retirement. In addition to these attitudinal and behavioral concerns, target populations may express greater or lesser interest in policy proposals. Privatization may appear as an intriguing idea or an urgent demand. However, none of these qualities constitute objectively discernible properties.

Just as policymakers frame their preferred policies by invoking alternative purposes, so, too, do they construct diverse target populations for their preferred policies.

Policy purposes and populations constitute a mutually informative relationship. Sometimes, advocates of a policy purpose, such as advocates of investment who begin with a principled opposition to insurance as contrary to the free operation of the market, may construct a population to advance their goals. Other times, advocates may imagine a population, such as champions of an emergent "investor class," and pursue a policy to meet its ostensible interests. In their mutual influence, purpose and population exert mutual constraint. A supporter of insurance who stresses the value of poverty alleviation would likely imagine seniors as needing benefits to sustain a decent way of life. Similarly, an advocate who imagines technology-savvy younger workers prospering in the new economy likely would regard investment as a superior purpose for retirement policy. Along these lines, purposes and populations may exhibit better and worse fits. Imagining investors as family members creates greater rhetorical dissonance than imagining family members as insurees.

Since policies and populations often change over time, good fits may deteriorate and bad fits may improve. In this spirit, advocates of investment have sought to break the original association of insurance and independence. For instance, Paul Hewitt, executive director of the National Taxpayers Union Foundation, insisted that "Social Security has indeed helped make many of today's elderly very dependent on government." He exhorted Congress to break "the cycle of dependency in old age."[1] Hewitt and others championed investment as an embrace of individualism that would return independence and control to all seniors. Hewitt's appeal utilized the shared financial basis of insurance and investment plans to insert a crucial difference. In the founding debates over Social Security, supporters of insurance invoked the dedicated financing provided by the payroll tax to associate their preferred purpose with independence and to charge assistance with fostering dependence. In the privatization debates, both insurance and investment emphasized contributions, which created an opportunity for Hewitt and others to insist that investment better fit the goal of an independent elderly population and that insurance actually inculcated the debilitating dependency of assistance.

Pursuing the populations that attend policy purposes, this chapter explores representations of past, present, and future Social Security recipients that circulated in the mid-1990s privatization debates. After a brief discussion of the conceptual connotations of representation, I begin my analysis by considering how debate participants invoked age in their representations of Social Security recipients. Many debate participants perceived young people, baby boomers, and seniors as having different—and potentially conflicting—interests in retirement policy. I next consider how debate participants invoked markers of class, race, and sex in debating whether private accounts would succeed where past government-based approaches had failed to fight discrimination. In the following section, I examine how advocates of privatization imagined an investment nation. Whereas representations based on age, class, race, and sex emphasized differences among Americans, representations based on investment promised to transcend these differences. In the final section of my analysis, I explore how policymakers viewed their roles as representatives. Although policymakers called for dialogue with their constituents about Social Security, they also expressed anxiety about dialogue as a potentially uncontrollable force and sometimes sought comfort through the familiar techniques of the pollster.

Policy and Representation

When debate participants identify target populations for public policies, they engage rhetoric's power of representation. Intimating aesthetic and political practices, representation is a polysemous term. In one sense, representation denotes crafting a likeness or reproduction of a person or thing, such as creating a work of art that portrays a landscape in a lifelike or compelling manner. In another sense, representation denotes appearing on behalf of a person with the authority to advocate for one's needs and interests, such as serving as a member of a legislative body. These meanings betray a crucial tension in representation between *presence* and *absence*, between making something present and standing for something absent. Representational art emphasizes presence; we marvel at the ability of a realistic painting to place viewers in its scene. Political representation emphasizes absence; we expect our elected officials to advance our interests against competing claims in restricted decision-making forums.

Although specific representational practices may emphasize presence or absence, the process of representation mutually implicates both presence and absence. Making something present expresses its absence, and standing for something absent invokes a presence. Landscape paintings absent the pastoral scene from the gallery, while assembly members present the needs and interests of their constituents to colleagues. As Hanna Fenichel Pitkin explains, "Representation, taken generally, means the making present *in some sense* of something which is nevertheless *not* present literally or in fact. Now, to say that something is simultaneously both present and not present is to utter a paradox, and thus a fundamental dualism is built into the meaning of representation."[2] With respect to public policy, congresspersons both advance a constituent agenda and portray their constituents in ways that comport with this agenda. Employing the terms "speaking for" and "speaking about," Linda Alcoff describes how participants in public debates ascribe needs and interests to others. She observes that "when one is speaking for others one may be describing their situation and thus also speaking about them." Similarly, "when one is speaking about others, or simply trying to describe their situation or some aspect of it, one may also be speaking in place of them, that is, speaking for them."[3] Presence and absence produce an irreducible tension in representation: the representation is and is not the person or thing represented. The independence that policymakers historically have ascribed to Social Security beneficiaries underscores this interplay of presence and absence. Independence has meant that policymakers cannot simply command retirees to adjust their behaviors to policies. Rather, independence has legitimated retirees as participants in the policymaking process. Policymakers have been concerned with their representation in the eyes of retirees even as policymakers have constructed retirees as a target population.

Associated with political and aesthetic practices, representation involves ethical and creative choices. To say that representation involves ethical choices is to say that all representation invokes values and interests.[4] Participants in public debates do not engage in neutral and transparent processes when they characterize themselves and others. Rather, debate participants make (often unacknowledged) choices regarding how people should be portrayed. As Linda Hutcheon explains, representational processes do not "*reflect* society as much as grant meaning and value within a particular society."[5] Representation does not occur outside of history and society, but works with the symbolic materials of specific cultures. Because this context includes societal inequalities, representation engages relations of power and social hierarchies. Further, representational processes produce material consequences by inviting judgments, attitudes, and treatment toward those represented. Along these lines, Richard Dyer holds that "representations delimit and enable what people can be in any given society."[6] This includes both division and unification. Representations may situate citizens as antagonists, but they also may form constituencies and express common bonds among citizens. Representations enable people to discern differences as well as similarities. Sometimes this process may produce understanding; at other times it may generate conflict. As a political-ethical process, representation involves cooperation and struggle.

Representations augment their political power through a tendency to assert themselves as natural, universal, and essential renderings of objective phenomena. The landscape painting simply captures the beauty of the countryside, while the congressperson plainly pursues the determined preferences of his or her constituents. Frank Lentricchia refers to the tendency of representations to hide their constructed character as the "coercive power" of representations. He explains that representations assert "an ontological claim, used like a hammer, that some part of the whole *really does* stand in for the whole." Created in particular sociopolitical contexts, representations may draw attention away from these contexts. In this guise, policy agendas may change, but target populations remain constant. Decontextualized representations imply that an advocate can only discover—and not construct—people's needs and interests. In these cases, the persuasive power of representation arises in important respects from its ability to appear detached from political struggles. Representing thus becomes a "cover-up" by concealing itself as "an agency of specific political power" and by obscuring "social and cultural difference and conflict."[7] Representations are at their most political when they appear to be nonpolitical.

The association of representation and aesthetic practice reveals its creative force. Just as debate participants make value choices through representation, so, too, do they make artistic decisions about how to portray populations. Some representations may provide generous details and invite strong identifications between subject and audience. Others may depict their subjects abstractly and encourage a distanced apprehension. Representations may highlight virtues like honesty and courage, or they may foreground vices like greed and jealousy. In these ways, representations may encourage a range of responses from their audiences. Representations may foster hope or instill fear. Some representations may inspire people to act selflessly, whereas others may justify selfish behavior. These possibilities betray a close connection between aesthetic and ethical choice as representations offer positive and negative moral lessons for how citizens should act. In this spirit, Michael Osborn characterizes representation (he uses the phrase "rhetorical depiction") as "allegory in miniature."[8] Whereas allegories traditionally offer directed moral lessons by comparing two different subjects, representations invite value judgments through a single portrayal, such as an image of a younger worker or retiree. In this process, a more compelling portrayal bolsters moral instruction. However, the naturalizing tendency of representation downplays its degree of artistic creativity. An eloquent representation often appears as effortlessly reported, hiding its artifice by plausibly asserting its reality.

Although debate participants make choices through representation, they do so within a field of constraint. Environmental, institutional, and social forces circumscribe the individual agency of debate participants. More money often means greater access and more publicity in our contemporary political climate. Institutionally, congressional committee chairs possess greater authority than other committee members and witnesses in setting agendas for committee hearings and potentially influencing the circulation of representations. All debate participants must negotiate prior rhetorical choices and existing social norms in advancing representations. Advocates of investment seeking to portray social-insurance recipients as dependents must contend with the longstanding societal view that Social Security promotes retirees' independence. In these ways, larger processes of representation resonate with Judith Butler's observation that gender performances constitute "improvisation within a scene of constraint." Butler notes that one's gender sometimes may appear as "something that I author." And yet gender is not freely constituted: "the terms that make up one's own gender are, from the start, outside oneself, beyond oneself in a sociality that has no single author."[9] Similarly, representation does not commence with a tabula rasa. Advocates may circulate new representations that dislodge previously accepted beliefs about people, or they may circulate representations that affirm existing perceptions of others. In both cases, context constrains the creative power of representation.

Processes of representation also intersect with issues of inclusion and exclusion. In important respects, the purposefully restrictive character of policy debates addresses a practical consideration: all citizens potentially affected by issues under debate—which, in the case of Social Security, means virtually everyone—could not assemble to consider various perspectives. This formal exclusion adds weight to the representations circulating in the hearing rooms, for they constitute an authorized practice of speaking for others. However, citizens cannot simply join the debate if they object to representations of themselves circulating in legislative forums. With varying degrees of success, citizens may force their way into policy debates (through the media, social protest, etc.). Exclusions also operate informally. Sometimes, witnesses from affected populations do appear before congressional committees, but their testimony must abide by the discursive norms and practices of the hearing room. This discourse favors propositional, "disinterested" modes of communication over personal, narrative modes that may express people's experiences more meaningfully. Witnesses also risk seeing their personal testimony reductively co-opted as anecdotes for policymakers' general policy preferences. Moreover, witnesses from affected populations must negotiate representations about them already circulating in the hearing room. A young person supporting insurance must not only present a cogent argument but also confront the perception that young people reject Social Security because it offers them a low rate of return. My analysis in the previous chapter suggested how some policymakers discounted Rev. Jesse Jackson's effort to elucidate moral implications of economic decisions because they expected Jackson, as a minister, to see morality everywhere. Appreciating the power of representation, debate participants sought to refute Jackson's representation of investors as moral agents.

The Coming Generational Wars

The most prominent characteristic of Social Security recipients appearing across various representations concerned their age. Policymakers and committee witnesses considered the situations of people of various ages, and they compared the treatment of past, present, and future generations in assessing the need for changes to Social Security. The aging of the baby boomers portended crisis in the view of some advocates of privatization. Inequitable treatment of young workers motivated the 1994–96 Advisory Council and others to highlight money's worth as an evaluative criterion.

In various ways, debate participants invoked age and generations in diagnosing problems with, and proposing solutions for, Social Security.

Advocates of investment believed that the present Social Security system necessarily pitted generations against each other. By redistributing resources rather than creating wealth, the present system created a zero-sum game in which gains obtained by one generation resulted in losses to another generation. This placed policymakers in the impossible position of trying to meet the needs of various generations while treating everyone fairly. Robert Palacios, an economist at the World Bank, urged policymakers to adopt investment or face social upheaval. Palacios worried that "the long-anticipated war between generations is becoming more and more likely." Others feared war, too. Heather Lamm, a board member of Third Millennium, an advocacy group for younger workers, foresaw "generational warfare" as the precarious financial condition of Social Security threatened the benefits of future retirees. Workers in their twenties and thirties had not yet appreciated the full extent of Social Security's future shortfalls, and their lack of knowledge may have been the only factor keeping the peace. Eventually, young workers would realize their mistreatment through the system and experience a political awakening. Although a peaceful call to action could not be ruled out entirely, Lamm feared that "it could take a much angrier approach that would then be pointed at senior citizens."[10] By raising the prospect of war, advocates of investment cast intergenerational relations in a highly contentious and potentially violent frame. War suggested that members of different generations—perhaps, in some cases, members of the same family—would regard each other as enemies rather than compatriots. War intimated potentially significant loss of life. Wars could not be contained easily, and a generational war started in the realm of retirement policy might spread to society as a whole. In this way, a generational war threatened a complete breakdown of daily life.

War loomed because older generations wrongly charged younger generations for their consumption. To assess the costs of Social Security for future generations, Laurence Kotlikoff, an economics professor at Boston University, advocated a system of "generational accounting." He explained that generational accounting functioned as a measure for determining fair fiscal treatment of current and future generations by assessing "how large a tax bill we are going to be leaving to our children." To make this determination, generational accounting compared "what current generations under current policy are slated to pay" to "all the bills that must be covered." Using this method, Kotlikoff concluded that future generations faced a "fiscal catastrophe." He held that a lifetime tax rate of 84 percent would be required to pay for the obligations contained in present policies. Such confiscatory rates likely would provoke anger among young people, if not the violence feared by Lamm. This situation could not stand. To achieve generational equity, policymakers needed to reorder federal spending priorities that disproportionately benefited the elderly. Kotlikoff held that young people suffered a "double whammy" of high taxes and low wage growth, both of which resulted from a "single policy which is taking from young savers and giving to old spenders."[11] Generational accounting promised to make plain this unjustified transfer of wealth.

As references to "young savers" and "old spenders" suggest, divergent representations appeared in discussions of intergenerational relations. Depicting seniors as spenders, Kotlikoff cast seniors as a fiscal drain on the economy. Seniors did not produce goods or services; they did not create wealth for themselves and others. Instead, seniors consumed the wealth of others. Their voraciousness made it difficult for young people to save for their own futures, and low savings rates constituted a national problem. Kotlikoff held that the "reason we are not saving is because we are consuming too much. The people who are doing the most consumption right now are the elderly." Seniors behaved as gluttons, either unwilling or unable to constrain their consumption. Their ever-increasing appetites threatened the health of the nation. Insisting that he did not wish to pit generations against each other, Kotlikoff urged Congress to confront a "fundamental reality": "We have to stop the growth of the consumption of the elderly if we want to turn this country around." Seniors betrayed selfishness through their consumption, exhibiting a live-for-today attitude that placed the immediate gratification of their desires above the well-being of their children and grandchildren. Failing to appreciate the consequences of their careless spending, seniors appeared improvident. Sen. Alan Simpson proclaimed that seniors had "hit the jackpot," while workers in their twenties, thirties, and forties "will have nothing."[12] Associating Social Security benefits with lottery winnings, Simpson furthered the notion that seniors engaged in impulsive and wasteful spending. A financial windfall obviated the need for careful budgeting practiced by less fortunate citizens. This association also invoked images of lavish lifestyles obtained at the expense of future generations.

Seniors not only spent other people's money, but they had the political power to protect their privilege. Seniors constituted a powerful political force because they followed political debates closely, asserted their interests forcefully, and voted for politicians whom they regarded as advancing their interests. Policymakers and committee witnesses tied seniors' votes directly to the outcome of the Social Security debates. They depicted seniors as a vigilant force ready to reward politicians who protected their consumption, and ready to punish politicians who dared to control their spending. Judging that his colleagues might lack the will to take the difficult but necessary steps toward private accounts, Sen. Mike Enzi observed that "none of us is quite ready to paint a target on our chest and run through the forest of senior citizens." As Enzi suggested, politicians advocating investment would garner the enmity of seniors, thereby risking their (political) lives. Using ballots as bullets, seniors would fire on these uncamouflaged prey during the next election cycle. While Enzi worried about political careers, others addressed the societal impact of seniors' hegemony. Ken Dychtwald, president of the consulting firm Age Wave, asserted that "we are becoming a gerontocracy." He explained that seniors have "become not only a large group in terms of their demographic heft, they have also become an economically formidable group. They have gone from being the poorest segment of society to the richest, and, at the same time, they now have unrivaled political might."[13] Seniors possessed numbers, money, and connections. Held down historically, they fought for a controlling position in American society. No longer beholden to others, seniors would exert their might and make everyone else do their bidding. Seniors would set the political agenda. Seniors would determine economic priorities. Seniors would even initiate cultural trends and fashions.

Compelling evidence of senior power came in the form of the American Association of Retired Persons. Politicians depicted the AARP as one of the most formidable lobbying groups in Washington, which had to be consulted, if not persuaded, for privatization to proceed. Bemoaning the relative lack of involvement by younger workers in the privatization debates, Sen. Alan Simpson complained that "all of us have to sit under the daily hammering of people from our states saying, we are from the AARP, and there are 33 million of us." Thirty-three million votes constituted a massive hammer that could flatten politicians instantaneously. Viewing himself as a forward-thinking leader in the push for privatization, Simpson depicted himself as "a wobbly-legged calf headed for slaughter in the woods by the grizzly bears of the AARP." Politicians stood defenseless against the ferociousness of the AARP. Like a calf facing an attack by a grizzly bear, Simpson could not hope to prevail in this fight. However, his contribution came in his willingness to sacrifice himself. Motivated by Simpson's selflessness, politicians and younger citizens might rise up to resist seniors. Unwilling to adopt Simpson's fatalism, other policymakers recognized the power of the AARP, but believed that the organization might be willing to negotiate. In this respect, Rep. Nick Smith stressed the need for policymakers to solicit the views of the organization. He observed that the "AARP is the leading senior organization. Their reaction to go against politicians that come up with proposals makes it so important to have them come and talk to us."[14] Although wary of the organization's practice of going against politicians, Smith held out the possibility that policymakers could obtain the approval of the AARP.

Not everyone saw seniors as a prosperous, powerful, and selfish demographic group. Many supporters of insurance portrayed seniors as economically imperiled and fearful of a baneful policy outcome. Rep. Donald Payne insisted that many seniors struggled to pay their bills each month as they dealt with the hardships of hunger and poor health. Payne portrayed seniors as hard workers who deserved a happier retirement: "After a lifetime of hard work . . . and contributing to the society and building in this country, millions of older Americans have retired and cannot afford to pay their bills." He explained that the average yearly Social Security benefit amounted to less than the minimum wage, which meant a humble existence for the two-thirds of seniors who relied on Social Security for a majority of their retirement income. Far from spending their meager funds carelessly, many seniors lived quite frugally. They did not buy new clothes or drive fancy cars, nor did they dine at fancy restaurants. Seniors clipped coupons and stretched their dollars, appreciating better than younger generations that economic fortunes could change quickly and dramatically. Rep. Richard Neal held that many seniors still operated with a Depression-era mentality. He recounted instances at constituent luncheons where elderly guests would take an extra piece of bread home with them. Neal regarded this as "a terrific lesson about how their parents saw their lives 50 years ago."[15] Anxious to secure their daily bread, seniors wielded little political power. Neal and others portrayed seniors as dependent on the policy decisions of well-connected insiders, many of whom stood to reap substantial financial windfalls from privatization.

Although debate participants offered varying assessments of the political power of seniors, they concurred in their views of the significance of the baby boomers' future retirement. Advocates of investment and supporters of insurance agreed that baby boomers would place financial strains on the system when they received their Social Security benefits. Echoing the views of others, Sen. Judd Gregg insisted that "the postwar baby boom generation creates a demographic shift of historic proportions."[16] Represented in this manner, boomers appeared not as autonomous agents, but as a structural force that compelled policymakers to reconsider retirement policy. Debate participants employed various metaphors to describe this trajectory, characterizing the baby boomers as "a demographic tidal wave," "a demographic tsunami," "a demographic time bomb."[17] In these variations, baby boomers appeared as an impending potential disaster. They constituted a massive, irrepressible force that would disrupt a steady state of affairs and threaten innocent lives. Their retirement could not be prevented—one could not reverse a tsunami—but steps could be taken to minimize the damage caused by this event. Even references to a time bomb suggested action focused not on locating and defusing the bomb, but on containing the explosion. The present time constituted a moment of opportunity. If policymakers acted decisively, they could save lives and protect property. But time was running out. Soon, the tsunami would be too far along its course, the time bomb would be too close to its detonation.

Some advocates of investment contended that the retirement of the baby boomers portended a fiscal crisis that threatened all the operations of the federal government. Sen. Bob Kerrey asserted that without a change in policy, the federal government eventually would devote 100 percent of its budget to entitlement spending and interest payments. Kerrey held that "the whole country will witness Washington, D.C., being converted into an ATM machine. That is all we will be able to do is transfer money. We are headed in that direction." If policymakers did not act when they had an opportunity, they would reach a situation that foreclosed all action. Future Congresses would be unable to make deliberate decisions about how to allocate funds. Instead, they would be reduced to machines that disbursed funds in accordance with programmed commands. Increases in entitlement spending represented a reversal of historical federal spending patterns. Mark Weinberger, a partner at the Washington law firm of Oldaker, Ryan, and Leonard, observed that "when President Kennedy was in office, for every dollar the Federal Government spent, only 30 cents was actually going out on automatic pilot, and 70 cents was for discretionary spending. By 2003, we will have completely reversed that."[18] Arrangements made for previous generations under different historical circumstances could not be sustained under changing conditions; seawalls built to withstand regular tides could not protect against tidal waves without significant reinforcement.

As consideration of the baby boomers turned from demographics to politics, debate participants asserted that they would sustain—if not augment—the political power of current retirees. Whereas world wars and depressions tempered the expectations of current retirees, boomers combined numbers with enormous expectations. Boomers would not be satisfied with maintaining current benefit levels—they would want more. Madelyn Hochstein, president of the public-opinion firm DYG, pointed to "high boomer expectations about everything in life" as contributing to their belief that Social Security "should provide more than it actually does." Unlike their parents, boomers would not be satisfied with the promise of a stable source of income in an uncertain future. Seeing themselves in control of their destiny, boomers believed that their individual skills and ambition would garner significant rewards. Hochstein explained that many boomers held the "belief that I can do better on my own. This is obviously currently fueled by a very hot Wall Street." However, boomers did not attribute their investment success to larger economic trends. They celebrated their financial savvy and believed that this would sustain them in retirement. Expressing this confidence, Ken Dychtwald asserted that "ours is a generation that does not simply migrate into the lifestyles and challenges that previous generations have configured. We transform them all, sometimes for better, sometimes for worse."[19] Boomers would transform retirement to meet their demands, and the rest of society would have to abide by their wishes.

Unlike their parents, boomers did not plan for the future, exacerbating concern among some debate participants that boomers would place increased demands on society in their retirement. Dychtwald characterized boomers as living "in a world that is very immediate. It is very now. . . . We are modular, we are mobile." Although this boomer characteristic fostered creativity and vibrancy, it did not bode well for retirement. Dychtwald diagnosed boomers as suffering from "financial illiteracy." He explained that "there are 25 million baby boomers that have not saved a cent, that have less than $1,000 in their total net household worth." At the same time, boomers had amassed staggering levels of credit-card debt. Boomers' credit-card debt totaled 1.3 trillion dollars, which exceeded the debt of their parents by a "10,000-times multiple. This is not a generation that is saving." Consistent with their immediate and mobile worldview, boomers wrongly believed that economic quick fixes could compensate for their failure to plan for retirement. Sen. Ron Wyden charged that baby boomers' "plan for their retirement is to invest massively in the Internet stocks and in the cyber economy."[20] Lacking foresight, boomers failed to recognize the inflated value of technology stocks as a stock bubble. They mistakenly viewed the soaring prices of these stocks as evidence of the new economy. Boomers believed that they had reconfigured the traditional economy, just as they had transformed other realms. Depictions of boomers as spenders seeking immediate gratification challenged prodigal representations of current retirees. They no longer worked, but current retirees saved more for, and expected less in, their retirement than their children.

According to many debate participants, the children of the boomers carried the largest burden of the present and future costs of Social Security. Holding that Social Security and other entitlement programs promised more than the nation could deliver, David Walker, a managing partner at Arthur Anderson, urged policymakers to "stop the process of mortgaging our children's future." Boomers and seniors borrowed money to pay for their consumption, offering creditors their children's earning potential as collateral. In doing so, rather than restraining their spending, boomers and seniors pursued their immediate gratification at the risk of their children's financial well-being. In the view of some debate participants, boomers appeared as particularly culpable, for they spent rather than invested the resources produced by their parents' generation. Sen. Carol Moseley-Braun held that "it is not fair for our generation to give the next generation less than we inherited from the previous generation of Americans."[21] Seniors might be excused for their consumption since they received little from their Depression-era forebears yet worked to rebuild a prosperous economy. However, in amassing debt and failing to save for retirement, boomers spent the rightful inheritance of their children.

Although they stood to suffer the most from the future costs of Social Security, young people appeared in most representations as uninvolved in the political process. Policymakers exhorted young people to make their voices heard so that their interests would be protected. Sen. Alan

Simpson urged them to "get in the game." He explained that "I personally have heard time and time again from those over 60 and over 65. I want to hear from those who are paying the bills for those over 65." Policymakers regarded seniors as a powerful constituency, because seniors voiced their interests loudly and rewarded or punished policymakers through their votes. Young people voted less, and they did not express their interests in ways that policymakers regularly heard. Faced with a choice between responding to a vocal constituency or eliciting the support of an ostensibly disengaged constituency, politicians would choose the former. Simpson warned young people that "if you do not get involved, you will get only what you deserve, which is nothing." In a different hearing, Gary Green, a board member for Third Millennium, conceded this point. He acknowledged that young people had adopted an "ignorance-is-bliss attitude."[22] Expressing his organization's dissatisfaction with such ignorance, he pledged an education campaign to raise awareness and create political power.

Although apathy may have circulated as a general characterization of young people, many of those who testified before congressional committees expressed anger over their financial prospects. Richard Thau, executive director of Third Millennium, maintained that "we love our parents and grandparents. And, indeed, my parents are approaching retirement age themselves, but we are not willing to become their indentured servants." No love could justify a loss of freedom and individual autonomy. Thau did not explicitly threaten intergenerational war, but, quoting the phrase "live free or die," he promised that "indentured servitude is not an option." Articulating her concern about the potential for generational warfare, Heather Lamm contended that "no generation in American history has been left with the tail end of so many dysfunctional systems as the generation currently graduating from college and entering the workplace."[23] Young people faced extraordinary pressures that justified potentially radical action. Of course, even representatives of Third Millennium conceded that many of their peers had not followed the privatization debates. As it stood, the 3,000-person membership of their group paled in comparison to the 33-million-person hammer of the AARP. However, in some respects, their marginal political position bolstered the self-representation of Third Millennium witnesses as members of an intellectual vanguard ready to foment revolution if necessary to achieve their vision of fair treatment for young people.

If most young people did not share the revolutionary zeal of the membership of Third Millennium, many apparently shared their cynicism about the future prospects of Social Security. Policymakers and committee witnesses repeatedly expressed the concern raised by the 1994–96 Advisory Council that young people had lost confidence in Social Security. In its report, the Advisory Council pointed to "polling data suggest[ing] that younger people have unprecedentedly low levels of confidence that Social Security benefits 'will be there' for them when they retire."[24] During the congressional debates, participants also referenced polling data, although of an unusual sort. Many debate participants, representing different ideological perspectives, referenced the putative polling result that young people held greater confidence in the existence of UFOs than in receipt of their Social Security benefits when they retired. Again and again, policymakers and witnesses cited this datum as compelling evidence of the crisis of confidence facing the present Social Security system.

The UFO poll had been commissioned by Third Millennium. Conducted in September 1994, the poll asked interviewees sixteen questions. Five questions addressed background issues such as age and sex, ten questions addressed retirement policy, and one question addressed unidentified flying objects. Question 6 asked interviewees: "Do you think Social Security will still exist by the time you retire?" Twenty-eight percent of respondents answered yes, 63 percent of respondents answered no, and 9 percent of respondents did not know. Question 14, placed between questions of party affiliation and sex, asked: "I ask you to take this seriously—Do you think UFOs exist?" Forty-six percent of respondents answered yes, 43 percent answered no, and 11 percent did not know. Comparing the responses to questions 6 and 14, pollsters Frank Luntz and Mark Siegel concluded that the "striking lack of confidence in the Social Security system is perhaps best illustrated by the fact that 18-to-34 year olds are more likely to believe in the existence of UFOs than in the future existence of Social Security."[25] This "fact" quickly became conventional wisdom during the privatization debates.

Not everyone accepted the UFO factoid, however. A few committee witnesses objected that a pollster could not properly infer a broader opinion by comparing these two distinct measures in a survey. Dallas Salisbury, president of the Employee Benefit Research Institute (EBRI), asserted that no "survey researcher would tell you [this] is a legitimate use of survey results." The EBRI had recently completed a survey asking young people to compare their faith in UFOs and Social Security directly. Its results refuted the assertions of Third Millennium: 63 percent of respondents expressed greater faith in the existence of Social Security, while only 33 percent of respondents placed their faith in aliens.[26]

This correction did not alter the larger flow of the debates. Even after Salisbury's testimony, policymakers repeated the "fact" that young people had greater confidence in UFOs than Social Security. President Clinton cited the UFO finding in his speeches. The prevalent circulation of this factoid undermined the position of supporters of social insurance who expressed confidence in the long-term viability of Social Security. Even as policymakers and committee witnesses repeated the findings of the Third Millennium survey, they implied that the existence of UFOs was a ridiculous claim—and sensible young people knew it. Through association, belief in the long-term existence of Social Security also became a ridiculous claim—even more so than the existence of UFOs. Rational people understood that Social Security faced serious financial trouble and would not survive without serious change. In this way, young people influenced their elders in spite of their low political capital. Their putative cynicism informed the privatization debates by outlining a boundary of reasonable opinion.

The UFO factoid circulated widely in the debates because it constituted an artful, even if misleading, representation. No necessary connection existed between Social Security and UFOs—unless, perhaps, one regarded alien abduction as a payable disability claim for a worker's family. Third Millennium's pollsters crafted this connection, and in doing so they created a memorable representation of skepticism among younger workers. Its invocation by advocates of investment and supporters of insurance demonstrated its appeal as well as its symbolic flexibility. The UFO factoid stressed skepticism, which motivated advocates of investment as well as supporters of insurance, without committing itself to a specific policy proposal. Moreover, this representation resisted refutation because its status as a poll finding conveyed a "rhetoric of science." As Michael Hogan observes, pollsters place "heavy emphasis on sampling, data collection, and data processing in their public discussions of methodology" to maintain the scientific character of their enterprise.[27] Pollsters contain potential problems of wording, ordering, and interpretation through the authoritative and seemingly quantifiable notion of "non-sampling error."

Any finding, so long as it undergoes rigorous methodological scrutiny, obtains the imprimatur of science.

Several policymakers and witnesses held that young people may have been cynical about the prospects for Social Security, but young people expressed confidence in their abilities to invest for their retirement. Elizabeth O'Connor, a board member for Third Millennium, argued that young people wanted to take part in the creation of a new "social contract by reforming Social Security to meet the realities of a new day and a new century." Younger workers had assumed positions of responsibility in the economy, and they stood ready to do the same in public policy. Holding up the private sector as a model, O'Connor concluded that "if Fortune 500 companies can trust my peers to do the strategic planning and to help program the chips that run their computers and their companies, surely our political leaders can trust us when it comes to investing a modest portion of our own Social Security taxes." In the realm of computers, young people had demonstrated their superiority over older generations: they had come up with the innovations that drove the new economy; they had created the wealth for boomers who reaped huge financial rewards through stock-market investing. Young people did not fear change but embraced it. Now they demanded that policymakers enable them to turn their creative energy toward retirement policy. Young people were better equipped than their elders to take on the responsibilities of investing. Melissa Hieger, also a board member for Third Millennium, explained that "younger people tend to have more experience with 401(k) plans, they like the portability, and in general see that as a more realistic option than staying with the pay-as-you-go structure. We don't see that as being such a large risk as somebody from the older generations that maybe lived through the Great Depression."[28] Although the experience of the Great Depression may have taught seniors valuable lessons, it also constrained their imagination and induced unnecessary and economically inefficient caution. Young people possessed the entrepreneurial spirit necessary to renew capitalism and refashion retirement policy.

Every young person did not program computers for large corporations or design investment strategies for their 401(k) plans, however. Some young people cleaned the offices of the computer programmers or served the fast-food lunch of the 401(k) planners. A clear but unspoken class politics informed the advocacy of Third Millennium as its spokespersons represented young people as eager to adopt private accounts.

Appearing as the prominent voice of young America, they represented the interests of young professionals seeking to expand their existing stock portfolios. Third Millennium presented young people as a homogeneous group, failing to account for the situations of young workers who lacked the money for investment or who relied on Social Security's disability benefits in cases of severe physical injury. For these young people, the economy had changed for the worse, as relatively well-paying industrial jobs had been replaced by low-paying service jobs. The class-based subtext of Third Millennium's testimony illustrated the choices entailed in representation and the interrelationship of policy purposes and populations. Third Millennium spokespeople did not seek out a population of young workers in a value-free search for a universal set of interests. Rather, they constructed a population of young workers from the diverse composition of young Americans. Their UFO "finding" constituted an artful choice in representing the attitudes of this population. Moreover, by representing young workers as important participants in the new economy, Third Millennium spokespeople invoked a population to bolster the purpose of investment.

The most precocious case of the gifted young investor appeared in the person of six-year-old Richard Anderson Jr., who testified during a Social Security Subcommittee hearing with his father, Richard Anderson Sr., an investment specialist. Addressing the perception that he might be too young to worry about Social Security, the junior Richard explained that "my father has taught me that you are never too young to begin to think about your future." Junior had considered his future, and as a six-year-old, he knew that "it is important to save and invest at an early age. If you want to retire, you must save and invest. If you don't, you might have to work all your life. No one wants that." Listing his accomplishments, the junior Richard recounted that he was "the youngest person ever to ring the bell and open the New York Stock Exchange." But Junior did not plan to rest on his laurels. He shared his dream to one day "have my own Richard's Kids Industrial Average. It would be just like the Dow Jones Industrial Average with 30 blue-chip stocks like McDonald's, Caterpillar, Microsoft, Campbell Soup, Nike, Intel, and others. If I can make this dream come true, I will never have to worry about Social Security when I am old."[29] Junior encouraged other kids to follow his example.

The Andersons presented an ambivalent message of intergenerational relations. On the one hand, father had taught son important lessons in life, and son had heeded father's instruction. The senior Richard did not wish his son harm: he instructed his son in the operations of the stock market so that Junior could achieve financial security during his working years and in retirement. For his part, Junior exhibited the qualities of an eager student, and the two Andersons related harmoniously. Indeed, written testimony listed Junior as vice president of Anderson Financial Services. On the other hand, the Andersons' testimony left the impression that each generation would have to "go it alone" in planning for retirement. Kids had to rely on themselves because they could not count on their parents to maintain the fiscal soundness of the Social Security system. Senior called for changes to elementary-school curricula so that children could understand the financial world at an early age. Adults needed to "make a conscious effort to make sure people, young people especially, understand at the earliest possible age that they are going to be responsible for most of their financial future."[30] Investment offered financial security where family ties had failed.

Privatization and Equal Opportunity

Advocates characterized investment as a market-oriented approach to equal opportunity. As such, investment would serve as an important corrective to the misguided or outdated efforts of the past. Investment would create a level economic playing field for people of various backgrounds because investment treated people as equally capable economic actors, rather than identifying some groups of people as needing special care. Advocates of investment saw money as the great equalizer that could overcome differences of race and sex.

Some advocates of investment characterized the present Social Security system as misguided in its efforts to overcome economic discrimination based on race. William Beach, a senior fellow with the Heritage Foundation, maintained that the problem facing black workers "isn't the glass ceiling of civil rights. Congress, the president, the courts have provided the tools necessary to fight the civil rights problems, plenty of racism left in this country." Claiming to appreciate the stubborn persistence of racism, Beach argued that the political war against racism had been won, since black citizens possessed the same political rights as white citizens. In the fight against lingering discrimination, the political system had exhausted its resources. Beach saw the continuing civil rights struggle as standing on the "sticky floor of economic opportunity." He regarded private accounts as an opportunity to "build capital in those communities."[31] Whereas politics had reached its limits, the market had just begun to exert its force. To overcome the "plenty of racism left in this country," blacks had to develop their economic power. If the achievement of full political citizenship had only partly realized equality, the drive to command respect as economic actors would complete the civil rights struggle.

Advocates of investment claimed that the present Social Security system actually retarded the movement for economic empowerment. Citing a Heritage Foundation study, Beach argued that black men born after 1959 received a negative rate of return from Social Security, and black women received a rate of return lower than the general population. In various ways, Social Security worsened the economic plight of people it ostensibly sought to help. Despite its explicit embrace of the idea of community, Social Security harmed actual communities by frustrating their ability to "develop their own sources of capital, their ability to save and then to transfer to the next generation a small estate." Social Security patronized black workers by treating them as a group needing special care. A lack of faith in black workers as capable economic actors imprisoned them as wards of the state, leaving whites only to benefit from the freedom and power of the marketplace. Like other discredited political institutions in the nation's past, Social Security transferred wealth created through the hard work of black people to whites. Sen. Phil Gramm contended that "Social Security is probably the only program in America that redistributes wealth from minorities to whites."[32] He and other advocates of investment wanted to ameliorate this situation so that economic opportunity would be available to all.

Supporters of insurance challenged the assessment that Social Security paid comparatively less in benefits to black workers. Alicia Munnell, a professor of management at Boston College, asserted that the Heritage Foundation study presented a misleading picture of Social Security and race. Utilizing a morbid calculus, she explained that blacks receive comparatively higher Social Security benefits than whites because "they tend to have lower-than-average incomes, and thereby profit from the benefit formula. Most studies suggest that this overwhelms the fact that they tend to have lower probabilities of surviving." Munnell also pointed out that the Heritage Foundation study neglected to calculate the value of disability and survivors' benefits. This constituted a significant omission because "take-up rates show that blacks benefit disproportionately from that portion of the program. The same thing that cuts short their probability of surviving after retirement causes them to die more frequently before retirement."[33] When one considered the wide-ranging protection offered by Social Security, black workers actually received proportionally higher benefits than whites.

Although they disagreed over the differing treatment of black and white workers under Social Security, neither Beach nor Munnell addressed the wider racial politics informing retirement policy. Like the participants in the 1935 debates who sought to neutralize race through the language of administration, Beach and Munnell amplified their disagreement through such technical means as actuarial tables and participation rates. Munnell's awkward reference to "the same thing" that explained black mortality rates exhibited their shared reluctance to discuss the larger implications of race. Plainly put, black Americans did not live as long as white Americans. Beach saw this as a reason to switch to a system of private accounts, while Munnell regarded this as evidence of the value of disability and survivors' benefits. Neither witness stated that the problem with retirement policy in America was that some Americans did not retire. To do so would have been to ask larger questions of economic and social justice and the role that public policies played in affording Americans equal opportunity. Beach and Munnell likely regarded these questions as outside of the proper scope of the hearings. However, in neglecting these concerns, their testimony exhibited crucial representational choices.

Debate participants also invoked equal opportunity in assessing the strengths and weaknesses of the Social Security system for women. Advocates of investment and supporters of insurance identified several distinct problems facing women. First, since women spent many of their prime earning years out of the paid workforce while caring for their children, they contributed less to Social Security than men and thus earned fewer retirement benefits in their own names. Second, since women worked more frequently in lower-paying jobs or received lower pay for comparable work, they contributed less toward their retirement while working. Third, since women lived longer than men, they were more likely to be poor in their retirement as spouses died and retirement savings dwindled. Debate participants agreed that retirement policy had to improve women's economic opportunities.

Advocates of investment responded by invoking the magic of compound interest. Compound interest did not recognize traditional gender roles; it did not care if its beneficiaries spent their days watching the kids or processing loan applications at the local bank. Compound interest cared only about increasing its principal. Sen. Phil Gramm viewed this as a tremendous potential benefit for women: "One of the benefits of an investment-based system is that during the 8 to 10 years that a woman is out of the work force, her investments will continue to grow." Rather than forcing women to choose between a successful career and a happy family life, compound interest enabled women to pursue both paths. Along these lines, some advocates pointed to changed social norms as a reason for switching to an investment-based retirement system. The present Social Security system assumed a single-breadwinner model of family life in which men worked and women stayed home to care for their children. Both work and marital patterns had changed—many women worked outside the home, and single-parent families had become common. Olivia Mitchell, a business professor at the University of Pennsylvania, observed that contemporary work and family life was "very different from what was in place 60 years ago when the Social Security system was founded." Choices for women had expanded, and retirement systems needed to offer expanded choices, too. Mitchell held that changes in women's lives "must be met by a flexibly adapting retirement income system."[34] Private accounts powered by compound interest provided this flexibility because they effectively ran themselves; all a busy mom and career woman had to do was plant a little seed money and watch her estate grow.

Advocates of investment charged that the present Social Security system actually penalized women for working outside the home. Existing law entitled retired married women to 50 percent of their husbands' benefits. Retired married women who had worked outside the home could receive the 50 percent spousal benefit or benefits based on their individual contributions, whichever amount was greater. Sharon Canner, a vice president for the National Association of Manufacturers, insisted that the present system "discriminates against millions of married women who work outside the home" because it denied many working women returns on their individual contributions. By compelling a choice, the present Social Security system devalued women's work outside the home. Laurence Kotlikoff held that the present system "is inequitable in terms of the incentives that people face to work. You are telling women, if you work, you lose this part of your wages and you get nothing back in return." The fact that spousal benefits might have provided higher benefits than the benefits based on one's own contributions offered working women little consolation. Darcy Olsen, an analyst at the Cato Institute, held that the present system forced women to relinquish their autonomy for higher spousal benefits. She countered that a system of private accounts treated women as equals: "If Congress would let women take their payroll taxes and deposit them into personal retirement accounts, women wouldn't need that preference, they wouldn't need that favoritism. Instead, every single dollar they earned would work toward their retirements and improve their retirement security."[35] The present system patronized women by suggesting that men who lived sixty years ago could make appropriate decisions about contemporary women's complex lives.

Supporters of insurance responded to these charges by highlighting the wide-ranging protections afforded by Social Security. What Olsen regarded as demeaning favoritism, Alicia Munnell characterized as proper compensation for women's lower wages and higher longevity. She argued that "women do very well under the current Social Security program" because of its progressive benefit formula and spousal and survivors' benefits. Further, Social Security offered inflation-adjusted annuities, which ensured that elderly women would never exhaust their retirement income nor see their standard of living decline as they aged. Supporters of insurance agreed that social norms had changed, but they asserted that women still did not enjoy the same economic privileges as men. They maintained that the present Social Security system addressed this reality. In contrast, an investment-based system assumed an environment that did not exist. Far from fostering equality, investment would exacerbate inequalities. Barbara Bovbjerg, an official with the U.S. General Accounting Office, explained that "women, who earn less than men, would contribute less to such accounts, and have lower amounts to invest, and so could expect less in retirement than men." Nor could advocates of investment point to long-term social trends as a justification for their preferred purpose. Jane Ross, a deputy commissioner in the Social Security Administration, acknowledged that "more women are working, they're earning more, they're staying in the work force longer, so that's going to change." However, women would benefit from the wide-ranging protection of Social Security well into the future: "By the middle of the next century, 40 percent of women will still be drawing some part of their

Social Security based on their husband's earnings."[36] Changing patterns of work and family life did not mandate a fundamental change in the nation's retirement policy.

Advocates of investment and supporters of insurance agreed that inequalities existed, but differed in their plans to promote equal opportunity. Citing changing social norms, advocates of investment asserted that their approach would sweep away old inequalities and create a level playing field for all economic actors. They trusted that the marketplace would function as a meritocracy that rewarded good decisions, and they believed that women could invest just as wisely as men. Supporters of insurance implied that old inequalities could not be swept away; these inequalities had to be addressed directly through a system that compensated people for past discrimination or circumscribed life opportunities. Supporters of insurance believed that a market-based approach would perpetuate, if not exacerbate, existing inequalities. Advocates of investment saw equality as a negative condition in which government removed barriers that prevented individuals from realizing their full potential. Supporters of insurance viewed equality as a positive condition in which government affirmatively redressed inequities in social and economic systems. Starting from a shared observation, debate participants constructed different representations, which reaffirmed their preferred purposes. As a negative condition, equality emphasized the associated investment values of freedom and autonomy. Represented as a positive condition, equality stressed the associated insurance values of community and poverty alleviation.

Investment Nation

Representations highlighting age, race, and sex stressed differences among Americans. In some cases, these differences portended potentially violent struggle and even war. In contrast, representations of the citizen-investor stressed commonality among Americans. Whether old or young, rich or poor, white or black, man or woman, a person could pursue one's investment goals while building connections with compatriots. Advocates believed that an investment nation held the answers to troubling questions of fragmentation and divisiveness, offering all Americans a prosperous future.

Recognizing that all Americans had not been able to utilize the market to serve their needs and interests, advocates of investment saw their plan as an opportunity to reposition all Americans as efficacious market actors. Rep. Michael Oxley praised private accounts for their ability to empower people. He expressed confidence that private accounts would "create more capitalists in our country and allow them to see the magic of compound interest and those kinds of returns." Utilizing the magic of compound interest, private accounts would generate solidarity among groups of people who had historically seen themselves at odds. Recounting a visit to a company that had recently implemented a wide-scale 401(k) plan, Rep. Nick Smith described the transformation he witnessed among factory workers. Smith recalled that he "went into the lunch room and there were three workers over there, sweaty and obviously line workers. One had tattoos and another had a pony tail. What they were reading in the lunch room was *The Wall Street Journal.*" Apparently, the factory workers had quickly mastered the practice of investing. The CEO told Smith that "the three of them over there will average having a stock-market investment of over $100,000 apiece."[37] As this vignette suggested, an investment nation enabled working-class Americans to learn the virtues already practiced by the investor class. Advocates hoped to unleash the entrepreneur in everyone.

An investment nation also offered to redress the troubling lack of savings in the country. Federal Reserve Board chair Alan Greenspan regarded the possibility for greater savings as the most compelling argument for private accounts. Greenspan stated this position clearly: "The strongest argument for privatization is that replacing the current underfunded system with a fully funded one could boost domestic savings significantly." However, private accounts would not increase savings by themselves; they might displace savings elsewhere. Greenspan bolstered his argument by representing a potential attitude change in citizen-investors. Investment would motivate people with sticks and carrots. Private accounts would underscore the idea of self-reliance for retirement income while inculcating a pride in savings, which would extend to a pride in good citizenship: "It has a very important effect on people's citizenship in society. My impression is that when you see it, and it's yours, you're going to want to make it bigger, which is one way of creating savings."[38] The hyphen linking the terms of the citizen-investor represented an arrow that moved from the economic to the political.

Advocates of investment held that poor people would benefit from private accounts most of all. Addressing his co-panelist Jesse Jackson's assertion that Social Security served an important antipoverty function, Jack Kemp retorted that the system took the wrong approach by managing people's finances for them. Instead, he urged policymakers to build a "bigger ladder that reaches down into the levels of poverty that you [Jackson] talked about and gives them access to capital. Without capital, you can't get rich." Kemp implicitly represented rich people as bystanders in the privatization debates. They possessed secure retirements, regardless of the structure of the Social Security system. Poor people occupied a much more precarious position; they did not know if their retirement would bring economic misery or financial relief. More so than any other segment of the population, poor people needed access to capital. Advocates of investment charged that the present Social Security system hindered poor people's efforts to build estates by confiscating their income through payroll taxes. William Beach held that payroll taxes "crowd out savings for low-income households and for many moderate-income households. Why else do we have 40,000,000 households in this country that are covered by Social Security without savings programs in any form?"[39] Beach saw the co-presence of the Social Security system and the lack of nationwide savings as evidence that the former caused the latter. He did not consider other potential causes, such as the co-presence of low savings and low wages, or low savings and high consumer debt. In imagining a nation of citizen-investors, Kemp, Beach, and others recast economic inequality as a problem of paternalistic public policy rather than an economic problem.

Advocates of investment shared stories of everyday millionaires to illustrate the financial potential of private accounts. Sen. Bob Kerrey told the story of Oseola McCarty of Hattiesburg, Mississippi, who spent seventy years working as a washerwoman. Even though she worked for low wages, McCarty had managed to set aside some money while working, which grew into a large estate. When she retired, McCarty donated $150,000 to the University of Southern Mississippi. Rep. Bill Archer, chair of the Ways and Means Committee, relayed the experiences of Regina Jennings, who earned only $10,000 annually as a custodian at West Virginia University. Yet Jennings invested enough money to purchase a nice car, and she recently had donated $93,000 to the university's law school. Not to be outdone, Jack Kemp told the tale of Annie Shriver. In 1944, this waitress invested $4,000 in three stocks: Merck, Coca-Cola, and IBM. Over time, her initial investment grew astronomically. Shriver had recently passed away, and her estate bequeathed $22,000,000 to Yeshiva University. Kemp regarded Shriver's success as compelling evidence of compound interest as "the most powerful force on earth to create wealth, to give people access to capital, to establish a shareholders' society."[40] As Kemp's comment implied, the representations of McCarty, Jennings, and Shriver demonstrated the power and ease with which private accounts would benefit low-wage workers. If these women, untrained in the ways of investing and possessing little formal education, could succeed, then everyone could achieve wealth.

These representations also implied a lesson about the power of money to overcome racial and sex discrimination. These women toiled in unrewarding, low-paying jobs, yet their investment success enabled them to overcome the barriers they faced in their daily lives. Each woman had amassed enough wealth to attain the honorific status of university benefactor; they had become everyday Carnegies and Vanderbilts. Yet these representations obscured as much as they illuminated. Neglecting the larger social issues that limited the opportunities of these women, neither Kerrey, Archer, nor Kemp commented on desperate circumstances that made these representations so remarkable. None of them called for legislation to redress the low wages and difficult working conditions that characterized the lives of these women. Instead, the magic of compound interest appeared to excuse these conditions through its power of wealth creation. In these cases, representation served an important function of problem identification. McCarty, Jennings, and Shriver represented successes, not failures. Their situations served as stories to emulate, not problems requiring redress.

On its own terms, the representation of the citizen-investor exhibited important tensions regarding the competency and choice of its practitioners. With respect to competency, advocates both affirmed and doubted the ability of citizen-investors to make their own investment decisions. Expressing confidence, Sen. Spencer Abraham maintained that "a very substantial number of people in this information age are demonstrating the capacity to do things for themselves, and not have to depend on Washington or on experts that they do not choose themselves to make decisions for them." New technologies gave people information that had previously been accessible only to insiders, and in various realms people had demonstrated the capacity to use this information for their benefit. Abraham urged his skeptical colleagues to "have more confidence in individuals to do things the way that is best for them." Citing the prevalence of stock ownership and 401(k) plans, 1994–96 Advisory Council member Carolyn Weaver concurred that "American workers have never been better positioned to make sound investment decisions." Only a lack of experience prevented every worker from exercising their investment savvy. Weaver maintained that "when workers are unsophisticated about investment strategies, it tends to be because they have nothing to invest. Personal accounts would change all that."[41] Abraham and Weaver suggested that changed times demanded a changed retirement system. Perhaps past eras justified a centrally administered, insurance-based system, but citizen-investors no longer viewed the stock market as a strange and dangerous place. Social change had engendered social learning—citizen-investors expressed a willingness and ability to assume the responsibilities of private accounts.

At other times, advocates of investment doubted the ability of ordinary citizen-investors to make sound financial decisions. Ric Edelman, a financial planner and best-selling author of such investment guides as *Ordinary People, Extraordinary Wealth* and *Discover the Wealth within You*, favored a shift to an investment-based retirement system, but he believed that specific investment decisions should be made by professionals. Edelman contended that "the vast majority of Americans do not know how to invest." He argued that workers typically made bad decisions with their IRAs and 401(k)s. Further, workers would act rashly, switching their investments at the first sign of bad news and increasing the instability of the stock market. Anticipating a negative response, Edelman asked: "If we weren't experiencing an 18-year bull market that we have been currently enjoying since the early eighties, would we even be talking about the idea of putting some of the money into the stock market?" The information age had given workers the wrong sort of experience. Teresa Tritch, a senior editor at *Money* magazine, amplified this point. She explained that "individuals may be fooled by the long-running bull market into believing they possess an investing prowess that has, in fact, never been tested by adverse market and economic conditions." In this way, the technology-fueled stock-market boom might have diminished investor savvy. As Tritch stated: "Investing experience that is confined to boom times can actually engender or reinforce faulty investing beliefs."[42] Champions of the citizen-investor differed in their interpretations of the significance of recent societal changes. Some saw these changes as a signal of the power of the individual to direct his or her financial future. Others viewed these changes as offering individuals a limited—if not skewed—perspective that would adversely inform their investment decisions.

A similar tension arose with regard to investor choice. On the one hand, advocates of investment identified individual choice as one of their primary values. They saw private accounts as a way of restoring workers' independence by enabling workers to determine their own futures. Sen. Bob Kerrey asserted that private accounts would send workers the message that this "is going to be your account, you can watch it grow, you can make a range of investment decisions." Sen. Alan Simpson concurred. He held that debates over the future of Social Security addressed fundamental issues of individual choice, control, and freedom. Simpson maintained that "what we are talking about is empowering Americans to have more control over their own retirement income." He believed that young workers would enthusiastically embrace this outcome. Substantiating this view, Heather Lamm shared the results of a Third Millennium survey finding that an overwhelming majority of "young people want to be given the freedom to invest part of their Social Security payments into private retirement accounts that they would own [and] control."[43] In these statements, choice reigned supreme. Citizen-investors appeared as sovereign in determining the best course of action for themselves and their families. Insurance had to be superseded because insurance concentrated decision making in a central authority. Against the dependency of insurance, investment affirmed the autonomy of the citizen.

Advocates of investment nevertheless sought to constrain individual decision making in certain ways. They did not trust citizen-investors completely. Without constraint, choice might lead citizens to ruin. Affirming the need to move away from paternalistic government-based programs, Budget Committee chair John Kasich observed that "the younger generation is distrustful of government and they have concluded that there is not a wizard behind the curtain; there is just a tired old man." Although he was tired, the old man still could not relinquish his control entirely. Kasich explained that "I would like to be able to give them their money, but my concern is then that people would put all of their money in an IPO. And Social Security is a contract that we have made in this country that is going to be a bedrock of the way our government works." For

Kasich, fulfilling the contract implied by Social Security overrode the distrust of young people in government and their desire for freedom. Rep. Bill Archer also saw limits to freedom. Responding to the suggestion of a colleague that individuals ought to be granted total investment freedom and be made to live with the consequences of their decisions, he retorted that "you have to weigh risk against gain." Archer had developed a proposal for private accounts, but his proposal limited the choices of citizen-investors: "I don't believe we can leave the workers with an account that is funded by the taxpayers, which all of these programs provide in one way or another, with the free opportunity to invest in Uncle Joe's automobile repair shop or whatever else." Not only did Archer question the potential decisions of the citizen-investor, he raised doubts about the property status of private accounts. Archer believed in ownership, but he also held that the government could compel owners to manage their property prudently. This meant mandatory conversion of private accounts to annuities upon retirement. He explained that "if you do not require conversion to an annuity at the time of retirement, you will have those people who live beyond actual life expectancy having exhausted their retirement account, and they will become a ward of the government potentially."[44] One would expect fully competent citizen-investors to anticipate this possibility and plan accordingly. Expecting anything less would signal a lack of trust and confidence, which motivated discredited bureaucrats concerned with perpetuating dependency. Advocates of investment could not shake this distrust entirely, and their lingering doubts produced an ambivalent representation of the citizen-investor.

Tensions of competency and choice also undermined the putative equalizing power of investing. The democratic power of investing supposedly lay in its ability to cast aside disabling social conventions about race, class, and gender. Compound interest did not concern itself with the identity or activities of the holder of a private account—it sought only to increase the size of the account. Private accounts thus promised to achieve economic opportunity and social equality where past government efforts had failed. However, some advocates of investment attributed different levels of competency and proposed varying degrees of choice for citizen-investors. Rep. Clay Shaw held that "lower-wage people may not have the sophistication to do investments, and those are the ones we have to be most concerned about. We have to be sure that the investments are made in a sensible way—that they are widespread, and that they are done by capable people." Policymakers had to devote extra attention to poor—disproportionately black, disproportionately female—workers. They needed the guidance of their more knowledgeable compatriots, like stockbrokers and financial planners, who could make the correct decisions for them. Along these lines, some committee witnesses called for a two-tiered system of private accounts.[45] The first tier would permit low-wage workers to invest in a limited range of index funds. The second tier would offer increased choices and control to workers with greater financial resources. Proposals to place added restrictions on low-wage workers suggested that choice required money, and money evidenced competency.

Aspiring to transform the United States into an investment nation, advocates imported an ideal from Chile. Leading other Latin American nations, Chile adopted a national public-pension system in 1924. Begun modestly, the Chilean system grew to cover three-quarters of the population by the early 1970s. However, the system also experienced significant financial difficulties during this period, and by the mid-1970s the Chilean pension system received large subsidies from the government's general revenues. These subsidies failed to improve the system, which offered only 20 percent of a worker's preretirement wages as benefits by the late 1970s. In 1981, under the dictatorial regime of General Augusto Pinochet, Chile fully privatized its pension system. Pinochet required employers to give workers an 18 percent wage increase to transfer to the new system, and workers received recognition bonds for their contributions to the old system. The new system mandated that workers contribute 10 percent of their wages to one of several approved funds. The authoritarianism of the Pinochet regime eased the country's transformation to the new system and overcame opposition to the policy change.[46]

In discussing Chile, advocates of investment championed markets as an unrivaled force for equality and democracy. Michael Tanner, an analyst at the Cato Institute, enthused that Chile had accomplished Marx's revolution, albeit in reverse order. He characterized the milieu in Chile as "a breakdown between capital and labor. . . . Now every Chilean worker is a capitalist." While Tanner praised the economic import of privatization in Chile, Mark Klugmann, director of the International Center for Pension Reform in Santiago, Chile, celebrated its contributions to Chilean democracy. The privatized pension system served as an "important anchor" and a "moderating force in historically divisive national politics." Klugmann contended that private pensions created political accountability, expressed the voice of the people, and facilitated democratic consensus. Private accounts created political accountability in Chile by forcing politicians to detach themselves from powerful special interests: "The elected officials are permanently aware that the voters . . . will instantly see and feel the verdicts of the markets, which creates an important political counterweight to interest group pressures." This same pocketbook connection enabled citizens to articulate their interests to politicians in a way that politicians would heed. Klugmann maintained that "the feedback mechanism is in place between electoral democracy and financial markets."[47] Speaking through their individual investment decisions, citizens made their voices known to their leaders. The market served as their check on government; it aggregated individual preferences to form political consensus.

The pied piper of Chilean privatization was José Piñera, who served as Chile's minister of labor and social security in the late 1970s and early 1980s, acting as the chief architect of the country's private pension system. A global advocate of pension privatization, Piñera subsequently obtained a senior fellowship at the Cato Institute and cochaired their Project on Social Security Choice. He represented Chile as an inspiring nation of investors before various congressional committees. He spoke confidently, passionately, articulately. Expressing faith in "universal ideas," Piñera held that "all men are created equal all over the world. . . . They have the same rights and they respond to the same incentives." Greeting his testimony enthusiastically, congressional advocates of investment granted Piñera as much deference as any witness, save Alan Greenspan. Rep. Philip Crane praised Piñera for transforming Chile into "the shining example . . . worldwide in this area. And you are to be heartily congratulated. You have had a major influence already, but you will continue to expand that influence."[48] Crane hoped his colleagues would heed Piñera's call.

Representing Chile as a country of everyday millionaires, Piñera claimed that investment "has really changed the psychology of my country." Contrasting Chile with communist China, Piñera explained that Chinese workers used to carry around books containing quotes from Mao Zedong. In Chile, workers carried books, too. But their books contained a different sort of wisdom: "Every worker also has a little book, but it's a pension book account." Workers maintained their passport books with pride, regarding these powerful little volumes as evidence of their financial acumen. Piñera depicted Chileans as carrying their passport books "in their back pocket," which "the worker uses to know month by month how much money he has. I have seen workers go every month to a friendly ATM and update the little passbook so that they know how much money they have accumulated. They show it around—to their neighbors, to their friends." Private accounts fostered fraternity—even the ATMs exuded friendliness. Chileans relived investment triumphs over meals and at neighborhood gatherings. They offered each other advice and encouragement, exchanging tips about potential investments. Moreover, private accounts enabled some Chileans to demand respect in situations where they might have been dismissed as unimportant. Piñera recounted that "my secretary goes [to the ATM] every month and goes to my office in the morning and tells me how rich she is, and therefore how much respect, not that only me, but everyone should show [her]."[49] Private accounts, not job titles or official positions, enabled Chileans to achieve social standing.

Private accounts especially empowered the Chilean worker. These accounts placed the worker in control: "The worker is a client. The worker is king. The worker is never a hostage of any monopoly—either government or private." As an eagerly sought client or, better yet, a sovereign, workers found powerful societal institutions at their beck and call. Private accounts thus affirmed individual agency, but this agency appeared as a particular type. Although Klugmann and others highlighted the democratic import of Chile's retirement system, Piñera represented empowerment in economic terms. He did not cast workers as citizens in depicting their agency. His reference to monarchs functioned not as an invocation of political authority, but as an appropriation of the language of customer service. These longstanding customers obtained an advantage over their socially privileged compatriots through the magic of compound interest: "With our system, when a poor person begins to work at 16, by the time he's 24, he already has a substantial capital in his account, whereas the Harvard graduate is just entering the work force and has zero." Presumably, the empowerment of the individual worker trumped inherited wealth or family privilege possessed by others. But this came at a price—the loss of a potentially radical class consciousness. Empowerment did not transform economic systems, it accommodated workers to existing systems. Piñera maintained that private accounts had transformed "the political culture of the workers. Since every worker in Chile now is a shareholder, every time shares go up, workers cheer. They are not [saying] someone else is getting rich. . . . So every time the economy goes up and wealth is rewarded, as it is being rewarded very handsomely in this country, every worker benefits."[50] If investment empowered workers, and low-wage workers especially, it benefited elites by co-opting social discontent that could engender movements for widespread political change.

Although Piñera served as a compelling advocate for investment, he, too, exhibited tensions in representing workers' investment savvy. At times, he expressed confidence in their capacity to understand financial markets and make wise investment decisions. He explained that "I have faith in the workers' ability to understand issues that are very close to their daily life." Financial well-being constituted one such issue, and the prevalence of passbooks and the frequency with which workers checked on the status of their accounts via ATMs evidenced the everyday quality of Chile's privatized retirement system. In Piñera's view, workers had welcomed markets into their daily lives; they cheered its ups, recognizing that a rising market benefited all shareholders. Piñera urged members of Congress to trust American workers. They, too, would appreciate the importance of markets and investing. At other times, Piñera advised policymakers to discuss privatization in simple terms so that workers could understand the proposed changes to retirement policy. Outlining a potential advocacy campaign to persuade American workers of the benefits to privatizing Social Security, he emphasized "extreme simplicity." Piñera held that many workers could not follow detailed discussions of public policy: "They have a 1-minute or 2-minute or 3-minute span of attention for your proposal. You must be able to explain it clearly in 1 minute or 2 minutes or 3 minutes." He advised members of Congress to leave out some issues altogether: "You mentioned trust funds in the middle of this—people do not understand. What is a trust fund? Why is there a trust fund?"[51] Apparently, workers could understand accumulated savings, but they could not understand projected savings. Policymakers had to account for these shortcomings of the supposedly savvy investor.

Debating Representation

Debate participants made *present* representations of past, present, and future recipients as they sought to discern the potential impact of retirement policy on target populations. Invoking a sense of representation as *absence*, debate participants also considered policymakers' roles as representatives of these target populations. In this way, the privatization debates exhibited a meta-quality as participants diagnosed the conduct of their debates. In this section, I discuss four themes that arose with respect to debates about representation: calls for and concerns with dialogue, partisanship versus bipartisanship, commission versus congressional decision making, and measures of public opinion.

Calls for a larger public dialogue to accompany policy debates appeared over the course of the mid-1990s privatization debates. The most prominent call came from President Clinton himself, who, during his 1998 State of the Union address, encouraged all Americans "to join in this discussion, in facing these issues squarely and forming a true consensus on how we should proceed." During subsequent committee hearings, witnesses reported that the national dialogue had been proceeding smoothly. Social Security commissioner Kenneth Apfel recounted that "I have personally participated in dozens of public forums designed to educate the public about this program and to discuss the pros and cons of options for ensuring its future. SSA's staff has conducted more than 5,000 meetings, presentations, and other public outreach events on this issue." Suggesting the promise of dialogue, Betty Knighton shared with policymakers the lessons gleaned from discussions moderated by the National Issues Forum during the previous year. In contrast to representations that divided workers by age, Knighton indicated that "while there were differences of opinion between the young and the old, sometimes marked differences, we saw in the forums no signs of an intergenerational war. Both young and old felt this was a common problem, something we must solve together." Marveling at the transformative power of dialogue, Knighton remarked that "it's incredible what you can see happen before your eyes when people have a chance to come together and talk about these competing convictions that they have, and to weigh them with the sense of fairness that most American people really bring into this discussion."[52] Whereas investment promised to transcend differences as a result of a policy change, dialogue promised to overcome differences as a starting point for policy change. Further, affirmations of dialogue implied that citizens' views on retirement policy could be discovered only by engaging them directly.

Policymakers did not explicitly deny citizens a role or discount their views, but they appeared impatient at times with the pace and potential outcome of a national dialogue. Sen. Connie Mack complained that when policymakers tried to engage Apfel and other officials about specific policy initiatives, "we get the sense that, after 5,000 meetings, that we are right where we started from." Deputy Treasury Secretary Lawrence Summers defended the pace of the policy debates. He retorted that "the very substantial need for education in this area" justified the administration's decision to refrain from presenting a specific proposal to Congress. Not satisfied, Sen. Mack held that "5,000 meetings would say to me that something should have been learned from that experience, other than the fact that there might be some angst out there." A national dialogue implied an extended period of learning about issues and adequate time to explore differences in opinion, but politics held to a different schedule. In the view of Mack and others, delay implied duplicity: they charged that the administration did not wish to take the lead on a potentially explosive issue. Others worried that unrestricted public dialogue would produce unwelcome outcomes. Sen. Judd Gregg called for clear procedures to guide the public: "My concern is that if you put in place public forums before you put in place the procedure for reaching cloture, you may end up with the public forums creating inalterable positions."[53] Rather than viewing dialogue as a transformative process, Gregg and some other policymakers expressed wariness of a national dialogue as a process beyond their control. As Gregg's reference to "cloture" demonstrated, he judged the potential efficacy of a national dialogue along senatorial norms. Without clear rules, the process would break down.

Anxiety about an uncontrollable and potentially angry public informed another aspect of policymakers' meta-discourse about representation: whether some of their peers would resort to partisan attacks, or whether all would act in a bipartisan manner. Along these lines, Sen. Charles Grassley stressed the importance of the tone in which members of Congress communicated with their constituents. He encouraged them to educate their constituents about retirement policy, which entailed honest discussion of difficult decisions and an emphasis on connections across generations rather than divisiveness. Grassley held that policymakers "ought to be thinking in terms of not demagoguing this issue." In invoking the specter of demagoguery, Grassley expressed the fear of many of his colleagues: policymakers would become the targets of powerful senior organizations that would cast them as attempting to eliminate Social Security. This fear threatened to forestall any action by Congress. Only a bipartisan effort would embolden many policymakers to address Social

Security in a forthright, and potentially unsettling, manner. Observing that "there is no issue easier to demagogue than Social Security," Rep. Thomas Barrett maintained that addressing its problems would require "Democrats and Republicans to hold . . . hands together and jump off whatever cliff there is."[54] The fate of Social Security depended partly on the quality of its political representation: to achieve a satisfactory outcome, policymakers would have to take risks in their communication with constituents.

The very publicity of Social Security appeared to frustrate efforts to achieve a bipartisan solution to the program's long-term problems. Bipartisanship required a willingness to sacrifice short-term political victories for long-term policy benefits; it required an environment in which policymakers subordinated individual gains for some larger good. However, the prominence of Social Security engendered a different set of incentives for policymakers. The attention given to the subject by their constituents and the news media created an unrivaled opportunity to prove one's political mettle. Ways and Means Committee chair Bill Archer urged his colleagues to resist this temptation. He held that "we need to move past posturing, partisanship, and politics and work together to get the job done." Archer implied that seeking a partisan effect, which required only posturing, would compromise the committee's efficacy, which required hard work. Opposed to privatization, Rep. Charles Rangel suggested that a less conspicuous context would enable policymakers to find common ground. Reiterating Archer's desire for a bipartisan approach, Rangel insisted that "it is not going to be done on C-SPAN, and it is not going to be done with these mikes in front of us."[55] Rangel's wish for a media-free environment signaled a bind facing policymakers as they debated Social Security: President Clinton called for a national dialogue on Social Security so that citizens could reach a consensus on the future of the nation's retirement policies; yet the unavoidable attention garnered by this dialogue seemed to create conditions in Congress that lent themselves to overt displays of partisanship.

Some debate participants sought to resolve this dilemma by proposing to remove decisions about Social Security from their typical congressional channels. Looking to the 1983 reforms as a guide, they favored the creation of a bipartisan commission charged with developing a plan for Social Security. Recounting his experience as a member of the 1983 commission, former Sen. Bob Dole explained that "when we got down to the nitty gritty . . . [if] we had everyone else in the room, we never would have gotten it done." Rep. Bill Archer, also a former commission member, agreed. He recalled that "Congress had been unable to come together, certainly not on a bipartisan basis, because a number of members demagogued the entire issue and poisoned the entire environment for those who did want to work together cooperatively, and made it impossible for the Congress to come together and to reach a solution." The fiscal condition of Social Security in 1983 portended a more immediate crisis than the exhaustion of its trust fund in the next century, but Archer contended that the outcome in the Congress would be the same. He did not believe that policymakers would resist partisan temptations: "I doubt that in this sensitive an issue that the Congress will come together and do something on a bipartisan basis without those trying to take political advantage of it, poisoning the entire environment."[56] Dole and Archer discerned an inverse relationship between publicity and sound policy decisions: less publicity produced better policies. Moreover, the attention given to Social Security created political risks. In this environment, as repeated associations of partisanship with demagoguery evidenced, many policymakers feared a particular form of representation: the representation of the committed reformer. Commitment to a particular reform likely would please some constituents and anger others. Some policymakers thus sought safety in bipartisanship, which would disperse accountability and potentially generate an eclectic reform that could appeal to the interests of various groups.

Other policymakers responded that creating a commission would abdicate congressional responsibility. Sen. William Cohen made this point directly. He expressed frustration that "every time we run into a tough problem, we say, let's form a commission. What are we doing? Why are we here? Why don't we just have commissions run the government? . . . Virtually every problem that involves tough choices, we're ducking our responsibility." In arguing against a commission, Cohen invoked an alternative view of representation: "It's important for us to go out and educate our constituents. We're unwilling to take the heat in terms of what it means by telling people what they have to know, rather than simply what they want to hear." Whereas Dole and Archer depicted policymakers as decision makers who worked best when they achieved a critical distance from their constituents, Cohen urged his colleagues to engage their constituents. He regarded distance not as a depoliticizing procedure, but as an evasive technique. Representation required persuasion: policymakers needed to tell constituents "what they have to know," presenting a compelling case for the cogency of their viewpoint. Cohen asserted a positive relationship between publicity and sound policy decisions: greater publicity produced better policies. Rep. Jerrold Nadler also affirmed engagement between policymakers and their constituents. He held that a commission would only "come between the American people and its elected representatives." He called on policymakers to conduct a "direct dialogue" with their constituents: "We don't need another middleman."[57] Nadler implied that a bipartisan commission might dissipate constituents' short-term anger over Social Security policy, but it would exacerbate their long-term alienation from the political process.

While dialogue constituted one method of learning constituents' views, policymakers often seemed reluctant to dispense with another, less direct method: polling data. To be sure, the use of polls as an assessment of public opinion has become standard practice in contemporary American politics: polls frequently have been treated as consubstantial with public opinion itself.[58] However, as calls for dialogue evidenced, some policymakers during the mid-1990s debates appeared to desire an alternative approach. Rather than learning of the views of their constituents as aggregated and interpreted by a professional pollster, these policymakers sought to obtain this knowledge through direct discussions. This desire for directness sometimes manifested in the field hearing: a congressional committee hearing held in the home district or state of a representative or senator. Of course, members of Congress interested in Social Security policy did not invent the field hearing, nor did they confine usage of field hearings to Social Security in the mid-1990s; but policymakers who participated in field hearings on Social Security justified these hearings through the language of direct dialogue.

Chairing a field hearing of the Senate Special Aging Committee in Baton Rouge, Louisiana, Sen. John Breaux concluded by informing his constituents in attendance that "it is very important that we take these hearings out of Washington as often as we can to meet with people who are in the programs, and not just speak Washingtonese back and forth to each other in our nation's capital." Breaux implied that the halls of Congress encouraged an insider mentality among politicians that disconnected them from constituents: indeed, politicians even spoke their own unique language when conducting their affairs in the nation's capital.

By contrast, field hearings enabled politicians to escape the privileged confines of the capital and reconnect with ordinary folk. In doing so, policymakers learned about important opinions and experiences that they otherwise would not have known. Hoping to bolster these connections, Breaux explained to his constituents that "I am going to need your help and your involvement, your suggestions, your criticism and your participation in helping us move to a solution that is going to work for everyone."[59] He urged everyone to get involved, rather than sitting as silent spectators watching the process unfold. He hoped to hear his constituents' views—their suggestions and their criticism—but he wanted his constituents to express themselves actively through their involvement and participation. By issuing this invitation, Breaux ascribed agency to citizens as full-fledged partners in a dialogue, as well as actors in the policymaking process.

However, prior to issuing this concluding invitation, Breaux sought to discern the public's opinion through the more traditional Washington method of polling data. One of the witnesses to appear at the field hearing was Al From, president of the conservative Democratic Leadership Council (DLC). From prominently featured a DLC poll on Social Security during his testimony. He reported that 72 percent of respondents "would support a two-tiered system that would provide a basic retirement plan for low- and middle-income Americans supplemented by individually controlled private savings." Piqued by this disclosure, Breaux sought confirmation of the public's sentiment. He again contrasted the narrow-minded Washington mentality with the more expansive views of his constituents. In Washington, insiders feared change: "We hear people saying, 'You must fix the program, but do not do this; Do not do that and do not do this, but, please, fix it.' But I think that when you get outside of Washington and into Louisiana . . . there is a great deal of support, because people who are on the programs know that it is not them who are going to be adversely affected, but their children and grandchildren." Breaux knew this because he had "honest discussions with them about the extent of the problem." Freed from the strictures of Washington, he engaged his constituents in direct and honest dialogue about Social Security. His constituents understood the issues, and, true to the transformative power of dialogue, they did not wish to place their own desires above the needs of future generations. And yet, Breaux did not seem entirely comfortable with what he learned through dialogue—at least not without verification. He queried:

"What you are saying is that the polling information indicates that people are willing to look at changes, even though they may be difficult; at least, changes that preserve the program for future generations are accepted by a lot of people who have been polled. Is that correct?"[60] From answered affirmatively, and Breaux appeared relieved. Neither sought confirmation from the public in attendance.

The representational power of polling justified the marginalization of the public present at the hearing through the invocation of an absent public. As Susan Herbst explains, "Polls make many political discussions superfluous, since they give the illusion that the public has already spoken in a definitive manner."[61] This absent public obtains its definitive character in part from the rhetoric of science that attends polling, as I discussed earlier. In Baton Rouge, the authoritative standing of the absent polled public trumped the physically present public of local citizens. They, too, learned of their views through the DLC poll. Definitiveness also indicates that polls ascribe a unidirectional clarity to public opinion—72 percent of respondents supported a two-tiered system—against the bidirectional messiness of dialogue. Invoking absent publics through opinion polls, Breaux attached a target population neatly to his preferred purpose. Dialogue would have enabled collaborative representation.

Purposes and Populations

By the end of the 1990s, debate participants had achieved particular fits among policy purposes and populations. Participants advocating investment associated their purpose with key values of individualism, wealth creation, ownership, and market superiority. These values bolstered their optimistic view of the future, which advocates contrasted with the putative pessimism of insurance. Casting the market as a trustworthy trading partner, advocates of investment projected indefinite economic growth, opposing their projection to the supposedly static view of the economy held by their antagonists. At first glance, this optimism in purpose may appear to conflict with the warnings of intergenerational war sounded by advocates of investment. However, insurance—not investment—threatened war. When different generations properly pursued investment, like the father and son Andersons, peace prevailed. Advocates feared war because insurance pitted generations against each other rather than enabling everyone to prosper. Although well-intentioned, supporters of insurance historically sought to redress societal inequalities by constraining people instead of allowing individuals to realize their potential. Engaging the aesthetic and ethical power of representation, advocates of investment promoted the idea of a just society in their vision of an investment nation, where the wealth-creating power of their purpose unleashed the potential of the new economy to enrich everyone in their target population.

Participants supporting insurance associated their preferred purpose with values of community, security, wide-ranging protection, and the alleviation of poverty. These values informed family metaphors stressing the significance of belonging. Because belonging ascribed a common standing to insurees, insurance succeeded in providing security and fighting poverty where assistance had failed. Social Security had enabled needy seniors to obtain a decent standard of living without sacrificing their dignity. Through their ethical and artistic choices, supporters of insurance represented different generations as harmoniously relying on each other to achieved shared goals. A collaborative social spirit suggested that citizens could not achieve equality negatively by simply leaving each other alone—for this connoted isolation and division—but through positive efforts to create opportunities for everyone. Adhering to insurance, Social Security already offered an instantiation of a just society. It brought together Americans often divided by age, class, race, and sex. By contrast, an investment nation appealed to people's worst motivations by encouraging personal wealth at the expense of familial and community well-being. An investment nation harbored a contradiction between the individual impulse of investment and the collective call of the nation.

Fits among purposes and populations formed in the 1990s coordinated with the constraints circulating in the economic and political contexts of the decade. Advocates of investment, especially, relied on sympathetic new congressional leadership and a soaring stock market. Promises of political revolution and new-economy forecasts invited a fundamental reconsideration of retirement policy. Insurance shepherded the country through a post-depression era, but an investment nation optimistically embraced the future and promised greater financial rewards. Even supporters of insurance admitted a newfound appreciation for money's worth as an evaluative criterion, as evidenced by the 1994–96 Advisory Council report and debates over trust-fund investing. However, as the

1990s ended, expected and unexpected developments unsettled the 1990s constellation of policy purposes and populations. A looming presidential election guaranteed a new occupant in the White House. And the stock market bubble burst.

4

Reconstructing a Time for Reform

Anew millennium brought a shift in the privatization debates. In the political realm, the year 2000 ended with great controversy as the winner of the November presidential election remained in doubt even after the polls had closed and the ballots had been counted. The nation focused its attention on the state of Florida, where reported problems with cast ballots placed in doubt the very outcome of the presidential election. Dramatic public statements and courtroom arguments by representatives of both campaigns ended only when the U.S. Supreme Court, in the case of *Bush v. Gore*, halted a partial recount of ballots in Florida and effectively named George W. Bush as president of the United States.[1] In the Congress, political repercussions from the contested presidential election worsened already strained party relations, raising doubts that significant bipartisan legislation, which most observers agreed was a necessary component of any Social Security privatization bill, would be passed in the short term. Bipartisanship surfaced for a time after the September 11, 2001, terrorist attacks on the World Trade Center and the Pentagon. However, the tragic deaths of thousands of innocent people reordered national priorities. Leaders of both political parties regarded national security and the war on terror as the most pressing problems confronting the nation. The Social Security crisis forecast by some advocates during the 1990s seemed minor by comparison.

Economic events also frustrated advocates of privatization. From their highs in early 2000, the Dow Jones Industrial Average and the NASDAQ Composite Index, two leading stock-market indicators, declined precipitously in value. The NASDAQ, which carried a higher proportion of technology stocks, lost over 75 percent of its value in less than two years. Appalling cases of corporate scandal, especially the high-profile bankruptcy of the Enron corporation, compounded these losses. Once a prosperous symbol of an investment-friendly new economy, Enron filed for bankruptcy in 2001 as a consequence of mismanagement and malfeasance. As employees and ordinary investors sometimes lost life savings, top corporate officers made millions through bonuses and stock sales, even in the weeks leading up to the declaration of bankruptcy. Enron and similar cases shifted prominent media portrayals of business executives. In contrast to the entrepreneurial hero of the 1990s, who displayed creativity and courage in launching groundbreaking technological ventures, Enron and other scandals produced images of greedy, short-sighted schemers who would willingly harm others to sustain undeserved, extravagant lifestyles.

On the eve of the third anniversary of the NASDAQ's peak, the *New York Times* editorialized that "Americans at the turn of the millennium, before the botched presidential election, the collapse of Enron, and the Sept. 11 attacks, viewed theirs as a moment of extravagant opportunity. So many of the old constraints—from the cold war's sense of peril to the business cycle—seemed a thing of the past. . . . We mourn the passing of that moment of extravagant opportunity."[2] A "moment of extravagant opportunity" suggested a special time for the nation and the prospects for privatization. Booming stocks and relative diplomatic tranquility fostered a belief that the nation could implement new approaches to longstanding public policies. Like no preceding period, the 1990s seemingly offered policymakers an opportunity to throw off constraints and charge confidently into the future. The *New York Times* recalled this time wistfully. A feeling of limitless possibility gave way to a sense of melancholy.

Perhaps, too, the time for privatization had passed. Testifying before the Senate Aging Special Committee, Alan Greenspan observed that "about a year or two ago, maybe three years ago, there were considerable discussions of partial privatization of Social Security." Greenspan believed that those discussions, unfortunately, had ended. He judged that "discussion has essentially come to a halt as far as I am concerned, and frankly, I regret it." Greenspan pined for the peaks of the dot-com policy era, where opportunities to restructure New Deal–era policies seemed limitless. He remained convinced of the power of the market, but Greenspan feared that policymakers had let their chance for reform slip away. Not surprisingly, some policymakers disagreed with this diagnosis. Immediately after Greenspan offered his remarks, Sen. Jim Bunning rejected this account. He asserted that the debate over private accounts had not ended: "It has come to the realization—and not to sound partisan—but this current administration is not going to allow that to happen on their watch, so we are delaying the further discussion until we have an administration that might be more friendly to some type of privatization."[3]

As this exchange suggests, different perceptions of time and opportunity informed the privatization debates in the post-boom period. Although their judgments differed, Greenspan and Bunning invoked time as a contextual element for public policy debates. Whether the time for privatization had passed or policymakers had initiated a strategic delay, policy contexts presented opportune moments for the passage of legislation. A booming market, a friendly executive branch, and other factors worked together to facilitate political agreement. In addition to this sense of situational time, a second sense of time as a constructed appeal implicitly informed this interaction. Debate participants appealed to notions of time—asserting urgency, counseling patience—in arguing for investment and insurance. These appeals constructed time, because debate participants did not invoke a commonly accepted policy calendar but sought to cast policy in different temporal frames. After the boom, the prospects of privatization depended importantly on contested notions of time.

This chapter explores advocates' efforts to maintain an urgent case for privatization in the face of social, economic, and political events that ostensibly counseled caution. I begin by explicating an understanding of time as both an element of rhetorical situations as well as an argumentative appeal. The trajectory of post-boom privatization debates began with President Bush appointing a commission on Social Security in 2001. Created to lay the groundwork for privatization, the commission connected private accounts to the longer history of Social Security and asserted

Chapter Four

an authoritative sense of time that moved outside of the vacillations of politics. However, the commission's efforts could not compete with media accounts that tied together corporate scandals and stock declines in a systemic critique of the stock market as an insider's game. Advocates of investment responded by treating these issues separately, thereby hoping to minimize their impact. Advocates also insisted that a democratization of investment information could place insiders and outsiders on equal ground. To ease concerns about market volatility, advocates shifted their focus from annual investment returns to a lifetime return. Advocates attempted to heighten concerns about Social Security's finances by insisting that the program meet a criterion of solvency over an infinite timeline.

Rhetoric and Kairos

As a practical art, rhetoric is time-bound. Skeptical about the possibility of discovering timeless truths, rhetoric speaks in specific moments. Rhetorical texts obtain meaning and significance from their contexts while reciprocally making meaning and ascribing significance to their contexts. In his foundational essay on the rhetorical situation, Lloyd Bitzer holds that rhetoric responds to exigencies, which he defines as "imperfection[s] marked by urgency."[4] Although Bitzer rightly has been criticized for construing situations in objective terms, his reference to urgency indicates the temporal character of the rhetorical situation. If audiences perceive that its moment has passed, rhetoric may lose its opportunity for redress.

Perhaps more than any other term in the rhetorical lexicon, the ancient Greek notion of *kairos* reveals rhetoric's temporality. We may define *kairos* provisionally as an opportune moment, or, as James Kinneavy succinctly expresses, an opportunity for discourse "at the right time in the right measure."[5] However, as Kinneavy acknowledges, *kairos* is a complex term with varied usages in antiquity and the present day. According to John Poulakos, the Sophists infused *kairos* with a radical particularity that emphasized newness, quickness, and flexibility: "The rhetor who operates with the awareness of *kairos* responds spontaneously to the fleeting situation at hand, speaks on the spur of the moment, and addresses each occasion in its particularity, its singularity, its uniqueness." *Kairos* enabled innovation and transformation. Speakers delivered distinct discourses that unsettled prevalent conventions, challenging audiences to reconsider their language use and reformulate their social norms. Poulakos explains that "what gets said kairotically strives to expand the frontiers of language and invites an audience to settle them. In so doing, it ignores the appropriate-inappropriate opposition and underscores the crucial roles that occasionality and temporality play in the practices of rhetoric."[6] *Kairos* did not dismiss questions of propriety, but pointed to the constructed character of convention and its susceptibility to change.

Subsequent classical rhetoricians tamed the radical quality of sophistic *kairos*. Although he shared the Sophists' stress on the particularity of rhetoric against universal systems, Isocrates held that *kairos* called on rhetors to accommodate their speech to the situation. Indeed, Isocrates judged the Sophists as ineffective because of "their inability to recognize the kairic exigencies of particular discourses. They fail to consider *the right time* or make the *appropriate* adjustments in any given rhetorical situation."[7] Isocrates extolled moderation, urging rhetors to accommodate their speech to situational exigencies. Although he did not explicitly mention the term, Aristotle invoked *kairos* in his definition of rhetoric, featuring temporality as a constitutive element of the art of rhetoric. Aristotle defined rhetoric as "an ability, in each [particular] case, to see the available means of persuasion."[8] References to a "particular case" and "available means" signaled the temporality of Aristotle's conception. Rhetoric assessed each situation on its own terms, for the opportunities of one moment may subsequently disappear.

As references to propriety suggest, *kairos*, in all its formulations, conveyed considerable ethical import. Poulakos notes that "the timeliness [of rhetoric] renders it more sensible, more rightful, and ultimately more persuasive."[9] The very same speech could express virtues at one moment and vices at the next, as policymakers in the 1930s likely would have regarded investment as representing moneyed interests. Identifying a foundational principle, Kinneavy asserts boldly that for the ancient Greeks, especially the Pythagoreans, "justice was *kairos*."[10] Kinneavy bases this statement on the "proper measure" aspect of *kairos*. He explains that justice operated by the principle of giving to each according to one's merit. For instance, those who worked more justly deserved greater rewards than those who worked less. We can discern this sort of kairotic appeal in the testimony of the representatives of Third Millennium, which I discussed in the previous chapter. Indignant, they insisted that now is the right time to provide younger workers a fair return—*a proper measure*—on their contributions. The ethical basis of this appeal manifested in their references to "indentured servitude" and complaints that older generations had saddled younger workers with higher taxes and greater debt than any previous generation.

Right time and measure also imbued *kairos* with ethical import in ancient Greece as a method for harmoniously resolving conflicts among opposing positions. In his groundbreaking mid-twentieth-century study of the Sophists, Mario Untersteiner writes that "a prerequisite for a sound decision is *kairos*, a harmony of conflicting elements. . . . When this exists, the decision, the act which involves a value-judgment, is possible." Because they did not subscribe to a doctrine of ultimate truths, the Sophists could not turn to a single standard to adjudicate conflicting positions. Needing more flexible guidelines, they asked questions of right time and measure to determine a probable truth among competing choices. In this way, Untersteiner praised *kairos* for "breaking up the cycle of antitheses and creating something new."[11] *Kairos* thus enabled action that otherwise would have been stymied by a search for ultimate truth. This ethical perspective appears especially relevant to our contemporary pluralistic society. Since there is no ultimate answer to the competing claims of insurance and investment, we have to answer these claims in terms of the values we want to affirm in our public policies. In this process, timeliness and appropriateness may serve as useful guides. Indeed, we may judge the particular constellation of contributory and noncontributory aims adopted by the framers of Social Security as a kairotic response to the exigencies they faced.

The ethical power attributed to *kairos* also has raised questions that historically have shadowed the art of rhetoric itself. From Socrates onward, critics have wondered whether rhetoric's attention to the particular over the universal replaces truth with falsehood. On this score, *kairos* has been charged with perpetuating a dangerous relativism that justifies decidedly unethical behavior. Although he distinguishes *chronos* and *kairos* and appreciates the qualities of the opportune moment, philosopher John Smith expresses some anxiety about the rhetorical view of *kairos* that tends "toward an emphasis, if not an over-emphasis on human action." Smith argues that attention to agency "must not be allowed to overshadow the ontological dimension of *kairos* as manifest in various orders of happening, such as constellations of historical events, natural processes and developments which have their own temporal frames and opportune times quite apart from human action."[12] However, contra Smith, while *kairos* may appear as a quality of a situation, its situational presence does not arise apart from human action. Along these lines, Carolyn Miller insightfully distinguishes different conceptions of *kairos* as "opportunity as discerned and opportunity as defined."[13] In both cases, a human agent discerns or defines. In contrast, by separating human action from history and nature, Smith creates a dichotomy in *kairos* between subject and object, which runs contrary to the spirit of harmonious reconciliation.

Building on Smith's work, Amélie Frost Benedikt reinforces this dichotomy by insisting on a distinction between "interpretation" and "actuality" in her account of a kairotic ethics. Benedikt asserts that "although I can change my action to fit a situation, the only part of the situation itself that I change unilaterally is that part of the moment that consists of myself; and the most significant change I can make to the moment often occurs, simply, by increasing or decreasing how much of the situation I am aware of."[14] The key word in this passage is "unilateral," which suggests that situational change must begin and end with a single person. However, in articulating and judging rhetoric, a speaker and an audience may collaboratively produce situational change. Or, larger discourses, such as competing metaphors of insurance and investment, may draw on the statements of numerous individuals to frame situations differently. In various ways, rhetoric, in kairotic moments, may induce collective shifts in interpretation that fundamentally recast situations. Advocates in the 1990s successfully instilled a sense of crisis in public perceptions of Social Security.

The problem with efforts to maintain strict objective and subjective notions of *kairos* is that these efforts ignore how *kairos* mediates temporal aspects of text and context. Contexts may offer a time for rhetorical texts, but rhetorical texts also make time in context. Rather than operating as static entities, text and context interact. Although his discussion focuses on analyzing a single text, Michael Leff's notion of "rhetorical timing" illuminates this point. According to Leff, the "timing in the text . . . determines the appearance of discourse as an intervention in historic time, but the discourse also stretches beyond its own margins to influence the appearance of the world in which it is made. The timing in the discourse mediates our perception of time in the public world."[15] Discourse may create its opportune moment. In the 1990s, even though forecasts projected solvency for Social Security into the twenty-first century, advocates of investment argued that the moment for reform rightly appeared before the retirement of the baby boomers stretched Social Security's finances. In a period of short- and mid-term financial stability, they propagated a sense of immanent crisis. Of course, since rhetoric does not proceed outside of time, contextual factors also played an important role. The soaring stock market of the 1990s contributed to the *kairos* for reform. As (some) workers' individual investment portfolios increased substantially, every day that passed under the present insurance-based structure of Social Security constituted a lost opportunity for investment riches. As portfolios shrank, supporters reasserted insurance as the future of Social Security.

The President's Commission to Strengthen Social Security

Little progress for privatization occurred between President Clinton's proposal for USA savings accounts and President Bush's appointment of a commission. President Clinton barely mentioned privatization in his 2000 State of the Union address. Indeed, he devoted only three sentences—two of which reiterated the same point—to the program. Clinton called on members of Congress to apply the savings from debt reduction toward guaranteeing the benefits of Social Security: "Tonight I ask you to work with me to make a bipartisan down payment on Social Security reform by crediting the interest savings from debt reduction to the Social Security trust fund so that it will be strong and sound for the next 50 years."[16] This brief statement, which Clinton repeated in different form subsequently in the address, deferred important decisions and yet sought to maintain Social Security as an insurance program.

The presidential-election campaign also produced a standstill in the debates. The two candidates for president, Texas Governor George Bush and Vice President Al Gore, reiterated many of the themes of the 1990s debates during their campaigns. Gore promised to protect Social Security by placing the trust fund in a "lockbox": "I will keep Social Security in a lockbox and that pays down the national debt. And the interest savings I would put right back into Social Security. That extends the life of Social Security for 55 years."[17] Stressing security, Gore repeated the term "lockbox" so often that it became comic fodder for late-night television.[18] Celebrating choice, control, and ownership, Bush depicted his proposal for private accounts as an effort to "share some of that money [payroll taxes] with you so you have more money to build and save and dream for your families. . . . It's a difference between government making decisions for you and you getting more of your money to make decisions for yourself." Private accounts would enable workers to act as owners. Bush maintained: "I want you to have your own asset that you can call your own." With Bush's ascension to the presidency, private accounts appeared as the likely policy option for Social Security. However, economic woes mitigated the installation of a friendly executive. Still, the administration worked to create the right time for legislation.

On May 2, 2001, President Bush announced the appointment of the President's Commission to Strengthen Social Security. He named as committee co-chairs Daniel Patrick Moynihan, the recently retired former senator from New York, and Richard Parsons, co-chief operating officer of AOL-Time Warner. The rest of the committee consisted of seven self-identified Republicans and Democrats, including former members of Congress, business executives, federal officials, and academics. Two months earlier, in a speech to a joint session of Congress, Bush indicated his intention to create a bipartisan commission, and he stated its guiding principles: "It must preserve the benefits of all current retirees and those nearing retirement; it must return Social Security to sound financial footing; and it must offer personal savings accounts to younger workers who want them." In this way, Bush mandated that private accounts would necessarily be a part of the commission's recommendations. In his May 2 remarks, Bush criticized the existing system, contending that "young workers who pay into Social Security might as well be saving their money in their mattresses. That's how low the return is on their contributions. And the return will only decline further—maybe even below zero—if we do not proceed with reform." Bush promised a system that would affirm values of "ownership, independence, [and] access to wealth."[19]

As the commission's principles and Bush's criticisms suggested, the President's Commission to Strengthen Social Security focused less on analysis and more on advocacy. Two factors primarily contributed to its persuasive orientation. First, as noted, Bush charged the commission with developing a system of private accounts for younger workers. This charge severely constricted the potential deliberations of the commission. Whatever else the commission decided, it had to endorse the most contested aspect of the Social Security debates: the creation of private accounts. By its charge, the commission could not recommend strengthening Social Security as a social-insurance program. Members of the administration insisted that the commission would consider a wide range of proposals. Lawrence Lindsey, the president's chief economic advisor, explained to reporters that "everything that does not contradict these principles are on the list."[20] Yet the principles ensured that the White House would regulate its openness to different approaches.

A second aspect indicating that the commission would function as an advocacy group concerned its composition and members' positions on privatization. Although the commission included an equal number of Republicans and Democrats, all members supported the creation of private accounts. Administration officials informed news reporters that "all 16 academic, political, and business leaders whom Bush named to the Commission assured White House aides ahead of time that they share the president's views."[21] Indeed, many of the commission members had previously advocated private accounts in various public forums. A commission constrained by guiding principles but consisting of members undecided about or opposed to privatization might have discovered a means of making its disagreement known. The commission as a whole could have indicated in its report that its charge did not adequately account for the range of opinions on Social Security. Or, the whole commission or a minority could have declared the principles unworkable as a foundation for substantial bipartisan agreement, or issued a dissenting report or addendum objecting to privatization of Social Security. The unanimous support for private accounts among commission members assured that they would not voice disagreement.

Perhaps the most visible member of the commission was its co-chair Daniel Patrick Moynihan. As discussed in chapter 2, Moynihan's views of private accounts changed during the 1990s. Initially, Moynihan associated private accounts with a coordinated political effort to repeal the progressive elements of mid-twentieth-century public policy. However, by the late 1990s, he came to regard private accounts as the next step in a progressive history of retirement policy. In his May 2 speech announcing the commission, President Bush praised Moynihan as widely respected as "the nation's best thinker among politicians since Lincoln and its best politician among thinkers since Jefferson. A profound mind, a compassionate heart, and a farseeing imagination have distinguished him throughout his career." Bush asserted that no one possessed better qualifications to update Social Security for a new era than "this great student of Social Security's history and stalwart champion of Social Security's principles."[22] Moynihan's longtime association with social policy provided Bush some political cover from charges that unyielding ideology would drive the commission. Moreover, Moynihan's role as co-chair intimated that the commission's recommendations, as Bush promised, would be in keeping with the legacy and accomplishments of the program.

The President's Commission to Strengthen Social Security functioned differently than the 1994–96 Advisory Council on Social Security. At an institutional level, the 1994–96 Advisory Council issued its report as part of the regular review process of Social Security. The President's Commission took shape as a special initiative. The charge of the 1994–96 Advisory Council focused on reviewing the program's short-term and long-term finances, without any constraints on considering potential policy initiatives. Its main recommendations, expressed in the MB and PSA plans, accurately reflected the state of the policy debate at the time the council issued its report: some policymakers and analysts favored traditional remedies of revenue increases and benefit cuts to sustain Social Security as a social insurance program, while others advocated private accounts to increase revenues for the system and returns for individuals, especially younger workers. By contrast, the President's Commission served to lay the groundwork for congressional action on privatization. Advocates hoped the commission's report would create an opportune moment for policy change by providing official endorsement of private accounts from an ostensibly disinterested and bipartisan source. The commission's final report, *Strengthening Social Security and Creating Personal Wealth for All Americans*, issued in December 2001, stood as an important policy document for understanding how advocates of privatization had begun to shift their case for private accounts in the wake of the social and economic changes at the turn of the millennium.

The introduction to the report, authored by co-chairs Moynihan and Parsons, constructed a history that represented private accounts as the next logical step in a laudable progression of social policy. Although the designers of Social Security viewed the stock market with suspicion, contemporary policymakers could utilize private accounts confidently because "partly as a consequence of 1929, we have learned a great deal about how a modern economy works." Moynihan and Parsons marveled at the "extraordinary" accuracy of modern economic statistics and the tremendous success of analysts and policymakers in bringing stability and predictability to the economy. Hard work and ingenuity had created a situation in which the "great swings in economic activity have been radically mitigated." Moynihan and Parsons acknowledged contingency and variability in economic performance, but they nevertheless predicted a period of long-term economic well-being: "There will continue to be ups and downs, and all manner of risks, but in the main the modern market economy appears to have settled down to impressive long-term growth."[23] From this perspective, the principle of private investment appeared not as a universally applicable guide for social policy, but as the right approach at the right time: private accounts required sophisticated economic knowledge that the nation now possessed.

Not only had the economy been demystified since the 1930s, but new investment tools had democratized the stock market. Most important among these was the development of the mutual fund: "A new form of investment, the mutual fund, was developed which enabled small savers to 'pool' their investments over a range of stocks and bonds."[24] The emergence and growth of mutual funds helped to recast the stock market as no longer just an economic arena for the privileged, but as a people's forum. Mutual funds opened the doors of investment to all workers; a potential investor no longer needed a large capital reserve to reap the rewards of stock ownership. Freed from structural constraints, ordinary workers could exercise their economic agency to build wealth. Investment bankers and the workers who cleaned their offices at night could act as equals in the stock market. By pooling the resources of small investors, mutual funds brought a measure of insurance to an investment realm.

Just as new private investment tools had emerged, the elements of the Social Security Act had developed and expanded since its passage in 1935. In this spirit, Moynihan and Parsons approvingly quoted Arthur Altmeyer's assertion that "Social Security will never be a finished thing because human aspirations are infinitely expandable." Social Security retirement benefits expanded to cover larger portions of the population in the decades after the Second World War. Congress added survivors' and disability benefits to the basic retirement benefits. Congress also increased benefit amounts regularly. Recognizing the increasing need to assist seniors with medical costs, policymakers approved Medicare in the 1960s. Private accounts constituted the next step in this laudable lineage: "By the 1990s, the time had come for Personal Retirement Accounts."[25] Moynihan and Parsons characterized private accounts as the "logical completion" of the drive for Social Security. Private accounts enabled all workers to achieve ownership and wealth—goals as fundamental for public policy in the twenty-first century as a secure source of retirement income was in the mid-twentieth century.

Representing private accounts as part of a progressive history of social policy, Moynihan and Parsons cast time as teleology. Investment did not constitute a rejection of the principles of Social Security, but their fulfillment. From this perspective, different policy purposes fit specific historical periods. Insurance offered an immediate and preliminary response to policy needs that arose in the 1930s. However, as knowledge accumulated, policymakers could implement more advanced purposes. Policymakers had finally learned enough to complete the aims of Social Security, with greater knowledge facilitating a "truer" policy objective. Moreover, short-term changes in the stock market did not affect this teleology. A cumulative understanding of time meant that market decreases offered as many lessons as increases. Similarly, corporate actions, whether good or bad, stood apart from social policy. Social Security developed according to its own schedule, regardless of how CEOs behaved.

In contrast to the historical narrative of the introduction, the body of the commission's report employed an authoritative, putatively disinterested discourse to organize its contents. The report contained four chapters: the first chapter advocated private accounts, the second chapter discussed their administration, the third chapter compared measures of solvency for Social Security, and the fourth chapter explained three different models for private accounts. At the beginning of each chapter, the report previewed the main points of the chapter as a "summary of findings." For the first three chapters, the report introduced each main point, effectively a bullet point, as a "finding." The report subdivided the contents of the fourth chapter according to the three models of private accounts it considered.

By repeatedly highlighting the term "finding" as a description of its main points, the report presented its conclusions as resulting from a process of open discovery belied by the commission's charge and composition. For example, the very first main point addressed in the body of the report appeared as follows: "Finding: It is the finding of the President's bipartisan commission that Social Security will be strengthened if modernized to include a system of voluntary personal accounts." Organizing its main points this way, the report invoked scientific and legal authority to dissociate its argument from specific political ideologies. According to the *Oxford English Dictionary*, the term "finding" denotes, among other meanings, "that which is found or discovered; . . . the action of inventing or devising; . . . the result of a judicial examination or inquiry."[26] These definitions represent different ways of generating knowledge, but they share certain qualities. Requiring thoughtful consideration, discovery, invention, and examination, all suppose that the specific outcome of an act of investigation is not known in advance. For instance, a medical researcher may hope to discover a cure for breast cancer, but this goal does not shape the investigation itself. However, the commission's finding did not constitute a finding in this sense. Indeed, the "finding" quoted above simply repeated, and yet transfigured, the commission's charge. The finding of the superiority of private accounts transformed a political objective into objective fact. In this way, the authoritative voice articulated in the report obscured its tendentious character by appearing to exist outside of political time. The changed party affiliation of the executive branch created new opportunities for legislation, but a finding did not shift with political exigencies. Whereas political time moved erratically and unpredictably, the authoritative time connoted by a finding moved only after thoughtful and disinterested inquiry.

Assessing the finances of the existing Social Security system, the commission's report insisted on a criterion of indefinite solvency while hastening the arrival of the system's deficits. With respect to the former, the commission dismissed the traditional seventy-five-year solvency measure, chiding insurance for failing to produce a perpetually solvent system. In contrast, the 1994–96 Advisory Council considered years beyond the seventy-five-year period, but framed its discussion through the traditionally employed measure of long-term balance. The Advisory Council explained that the program faced a long-term imbalance that worsened with the passage of time. This framing, through the language of balances and imbalances, cast the problems of Social Security in a particular way: the program needed to square its accounts by increasing revenues or decreasing expenses. The 2001 Commission rejected the measure of long-term balance because balancing Social Security over a specified period did not rule out future imbalances. Instead, the commission evaluated Social Security's finances through the terminology of "fiscal sustainability." The commission reported: "Finding: Action should be taken soon to place

Social Security on a fiscally sustainable course."[27] Sustainability invited questions about the viability of the system itself, implying that insurance would fail eventually. Sustainability suggested that balancing its books would not solve the problems facing Social Security, because doing so would only defer a day of reckoning. Sustainability required attention to guiding principles as well as potential sources of revenue.

Achieving sustainability meant obtaining real assets, which discounted the value of the trust fund and advanced the insolvency date for Social Security. The supposedly valuable trust fund presented a false picture of Social Security's finances. The commission asserted that "solvency could be achieved in an accounting sense by issuing new bonds to the Trust Fund or raising the interest rate on existing Trust Fund bonds. However, such an approach would not produce additional real resources needed to pay benefits. Thus, solvency could be technically consistent with requiring future generations to make large general revenue transfers that they may not desire or be able to afford." Contrasting "accounting" devices to real assets, the commission implied that the trust fund actually cost taxpayers money, since profligate politicians had spent its revenues. Pro-insurance politicians attempted to disguise their actions by presenting the trust fund as real. This created a false sense of security among citizens, wrongly suggesting that they did not have to attend to Social Security in the short term. However, once the commission examined the fragile structure erected by traditional measures of solvency, it discovered a program facing an impending financial crisis. In this way, the commission asserted an urgent need to restructure Social Security. Further, the commission held that traditional measures of solvency prejudiced the case against new approaches that offered a more accurate timeline and appropriate solution. The report contended that "the criterion of actuarial balance is biased against programs that advance fund the system through personal accounts."[28] The commission insisted that it properly discounted the value of the trust fund, yet it objected to assessments of future finances that "improperly" ignored the potential value of private accounts as a contribution to the financial well-being of the system.

Of course, a system of private accounts also generated costs. However, the report urged that policymakers and citizens view these costs in a particular light. The report stated: "Finding: Transition investments in personal accounts are not 'costs,' but investments in a fiscally sustainable Social Security system." The commission preferred the phrase "transition investment" over the phrase "transition cost" because the former rightly accounted both for costs and returns. An investment did not constitute a simple expenditure; rather, an investment entailed a dedication of resources with the expectation that an investor's initial outlay would produce increased future benefits. The commission's report compared an investment in private accounts to a homeowner paying off a mortgage early by dedicating a small additional amount each month to principal. The report characterized the additional principal payment as "an investment that brings rewards, not a cost." Likewise, the additional payments necessary for private accounts promised rewards to the account holders. The commission insisted that "if the extra savings proposed for Social Security personal accounts is a 'cost,' then any person who saves or sacrifices for the future for any reason pays a similar cost."[29] In objecting to the biases of actuarial forecasts and likening the transition investments to early mortgage payments, the body of the commission's report invoked the progressive history recounted in the introduction. Traditional measures had been adopted for an earlier period; the opportunities of the present moment called for new methods of analysis.

The structure of a new system appeared in the three reform models detailed in the commission's report. Of these, model 2 appeared as the candidate the Bush administration likely would advocate.[30] Model 2 proposed "voluntary progressive personal accounts combined with an inflation-indexed but more progressive traditional system." The commission envisioned this system taking shape by permitting workers under fifty-five years old to redirect 4 percentage points of their payroll taxes, up to a maximum of $1,000 annually, to a personal account. In exchange, workers would see their benefits reduced by the amount of their contributions plus 2 percent interest. In addition, the inflation index for traditional Social Security benefits would be switched from a wage-based to a price-based formula, which would effectively reduce traditional benefits for all workers. The report characterized these reductions as "slow[ing] the growth in future benefits."[31] However, the commission also sought benefit increases for minimum-wage workers to at least 20 percent above the poverty line, as well as increases in widows' benefits. To fund the investments in private accounts, the commission recommended general-revenue transfers to Social Security from 2025 to 2054.

As the two references to "progressive" in the report's summary description of model 2 suggested, the commission maintained that private accounts could retain—and even bolster—Social Security's historical commitment to alleviating poverty among the elderly. However, the commission cast progressiveness in market terms. The report explained that model 2 would make Social Security "more progressive than the current program."[32] Two aspects of model 2 would achieve this result. First, the contribution limit of $1,000 per worker meant that lower-wage workers could contribute a higher proportion of their payroll taxes to private accounts. Workers earning $25,000 annually could contribute 4 percent of their payroll taxes, whereas workers earning $50,000 could contribute only 2 percent of their payroll taxes. Presuming higher returns on private accounts, low-wage workers would receive a higher dollar-for-dollar return on their payroll taxes than high-wage workers. Second, model 2 guaranteed benefits to minimum-wage workers of at least 120 percent of the poverty level. The report held that this would improve the actual and relative financial situations of low-wage workers.

Yet the progressiveness of model 2 threatened to undermine investment values of ownership and control. The report's executive summary proclaimed that all three models "would permit participants to build substantial wealth . . . [and] would enhance workers' control over their retirement benefits with accounts they own."[33] From one vantage point, the commission could argue that the private accounts in model 2 upheld these values because they did not redistribute contributions from one worker to another. However, progressiveness could be made to comport with this practice only in the first aspect of the model, through the imposition of a contribution ceiling of $1,000. If private accounts genuinely affirmed ownership and control, then any contribution ceiling might appear as arbitrary and unjustified—as an infringement on the rights of ownership. Moreover, circumscribing private accounts by dollar amount or percentage implied that policymakers needed to set money aside to serve noncontributory aims—namely, to achieve progressiveness through the second aspect of the model: the guarantee that workers would receive basic benefits that exceeded the poverty line by at least 20 percent. This guarantee appeared to contravene directly claims of ownership and control. Guaranteeing poor people proportionally higher benefits reverted to an unsustainable insurance model that advantaged some participants at the relative expense of others.

Advocates of investment had hoped that the report of the President's Commission to Strengthen Social Security would help create an opportune moment for legislation. Towards this end, the commission's report recounted a history of successive advances in Social Security, and it positioned private accounts as the next step. The report also presented its views through an authoritative discourse that invoked scientific and legal objectivity, offering new analytic methods for a new policy era. Nevertheless, the endorsement offered by the report could not overcome the negative implications of stock-market losses and corporate scandal.

Stock Bubbles and Corporate Scandals in the News

News media accounts of stock bubbles and corporate scandals reflected an emergent cultural anxiety about privatizing Social Security. Dramatic declines in stock-market indexes and numerous cases of corporate fraud and mismanagement severely dampened public enthusiasm for investing and raised doubts about the veracity of corporate financial statements and the ethics of corporate executives. Some recast the late 1990s as an extravagant time, a period of heady—and ultimately unfounded—optimism in the prospects of a technology-led new economy. From this perspective, far from fostering new opportunities for policy innovation, the 1990s witnessed impaired political and economic judgment. Failure to advance privatization did not constitute a lost opportunity, but a blessing in disguise.

Negative returns gave investors good reasons to question the soundness of the stock market. By the end of 2002, the stock market had declined for three consecutive years, which had last occurred in 1941. Moreover, the average stock price declined further in 2002 than in either of the two previous years, suggesting that the bear market had not ended with the dramatic declines of technology stocks in the year after their early 2000 peak. The technology-heavy NASDAQ received significant attention, leading the chief market analyst at Standard & Poor's to conclude that "the only comparison to NASDAQ you can make is 1929." Yet the declines impacted a wide variety of publicly held companies. While AOL's stock declined 81 percent in three years, General Electric—a stalwart of the "old" economy—saw its stock decline 45 percent over the same period. All major stock indexes exhibited significant declines. In 2002, the Standard & Poor's 500 suffered its worst year since 1974. The Wilshire 5000, the broadest stock-market index, declined 43 percent between 2000 and 2002. Nor were stock losses limited to the United States. Between 2000 and 2002, Japan's Nikkei 225 declined 62 percent, Germany's DAX declined 65 percent, and the UK's FTSE 100 declined 46 percent.[34]

Instances of corporate scandal appeared to be just as widespread. Highly publicized cases of bankruptcy and scandal at Worldcom, Adelphia Communications, and Tyco International followed Enron. Worldcom, which had been the nation's second-largest long-distance telephone company, overstated its cash flow by $3.8 billion in a fifteen-month period. Successive scandals led one *Wall Street Journal* commentator to remark that "the scope and scale of the corporate transgressions of the late 1990s, now coming to light, exceed anything the U.S. has witnessed since the years preceding the Great Depression." In significant respects, this claim appeared justified. A 2001 study by Financial Executives International reported that publicly held companies revised their financial statements 464 times between 1998 and 2000, which constituted almost as many revisions as in the previous twenty years combined. A 1998 survey of 160 chief financial officers of publicly held companies found that two-thirds had been asked by other executives to misrepresent their corporations' finances—12 percent admitted that they complied. Nor did the scandals appear confined to the corporations themselves. In April 2003, prosecutors announced that they had reached an agreement with ten of the nation's largest investment firms to pay $1.4 billion in fines and restitution to settle charges of fraud and abuse in the late 1990s. Prosecutors charged that analysts had issued overly optimistic stock reports to curry favor with corporate clients. They also charged that investment firms received secret payments from companies for issuing strong buy recommendations, and underwriters offered corporate clients special prior access to highly anticipated initial public offerings.[35]

The Enron scandal received particular scrutiny. Some commentators regarded Enron as "the business world's equivalent of Watergate," threatening to engender long-term public cynicism toward corporate America.[36] At the time of its filing in December 2001, Enron constituted the largest corporate bankruptcy in U.S. history. In less than a year, the price of its stock fell from $84 to 40 cents. On January 14, 2002, the New York Stock Exchange suspended trading of Enron stock and sought to delist it from the Exchange. This represented a dramatic reversal of fortune, since Enron had impressed investors as a rapidly growing energy company in the late 1990s. However, to finance its growth, Enron assumed significant amounts of debt, which it disguised through various partnerships and dubious accounting methods. In these ways and others, Enron repeatedly overstated its profitability. Eventually, in the fall of 2001, Enron could no longer maintain these practices, and it announced massive losses. Its stock price, which already had fallen to less than half of its January high, fell rapidly to less than one dollar. Especially appalling was the fact that as ordinary employees and investors lost millions, Enron's top executives profited handsomely from their stocks. They sold off their shares during peak periods, even as they knew of the company's financial troubles and (falsely) reassured employees and investors of its future growth. Moreover, several Enron executives received large bonuses in the months before the declaration of bankruptcy.[37]

Commentators discerned an intrinsic connection between the stock-market bubble and cases of corporate scandal. The *Wall Street Journal* held that Enron's bankruptcy revealed the "underside of that [late 1990s] boom. Human nature being what it is—and capitalists being human—some will lose their moral bearings; others will make mistakes and try to cover them up." Whereas the *Journal* focused on the misdeeds of individual executives, Edward Chancellor, a journalist and author of a history of financial speculation, addressed the cultural milieu of a bubble economy. Chancellor asserted that "in its hubris and attending hype, in its focus on earnings instead of ethics, in its insistence that it is unique and unprecedented—in touting its innovative use of technology—Enron stands as the quintessential Internet company."[38] Chancellor explained that Enron benefited from the deregulation typical of bubble economies. Further, it evidenced the bubble tendency of executives to manage businesses for the short-term gratification of speculators rather than the long-term benefit of investors. In these ways and others, Enron did not represent a success story undone by too much greed; rather, its ethical failures, and the larger business culture they reflected, enabled its financial successes.

News accounts portrayed an anxious investing public whose nervousness grew with each drop in the stock market and every revelation of corporate wrongdoing. *Newsweek* likened citizens to family members coping with the serious illness of a relative: "Like a family holding a vigil around a sick relative, Americans are living through a moment of high anxiety, carefully monitoring vital signs to see if the U.S. economy will emerge from its recent funk." The magazine shared the coping strategies of investors whose stock portfolios had suffered dramatic declines. Some families stopped eating out; others turned down thermostats and warmed themselves with blankets and sweaters. Some parents regretfully spoke of delaying their children's college education. *U.S. News and World Report* relayed the assessment of prominent investment adviser Peter Bernstein, who characterized Americans as entering stage three of a psychological reaction to a bear market. In the first stage, investors' enthusiasm for the stock market wanes. In the second stage, investors exhibit increasing concern about economic warning signs they ignored during the bull market. In the third stage, investors experience "utter panic."[39]

Not surprisingly, people's anxiety about the stock market undermined their confidence in the economy more generally, which threatened to reduce consumer spending and to increase economic woes. Citing the crash of 1929 and the decline of 1973–1974, economist Robert Shiller explained that "a longtime erosion in market confidence reverberates throughout the economy." Others agreed, characterizing consumer spending as the driving force behind long-term economic stability. *Time* exhorted that it was more important for consumers to "buy socks—and shoes, and televisions and airline tickets—than stocks." Yet consumers did not appear able or willing to sustain significant spending. Perhaps buoyed by their rising stock portfolios, consumers had increased their debt during the 1990s. In 1990, total household debt amounted to 85 percent of personal disposable income. By 2000, total household debt had reached 105 percent of disposable income. Payments on this debt neared record levels. Moreover, consumer confidence had declined to a four-year low in spring 2001.[40]

News articles and feature stories reported the dashed hopes of baby boomers and others who regarded their ballooning investment accounts as a pathway toward an early and prosperous retirement. On the cover of one of its issues, *Time* asked: "Will you *ever* be able to retire?" The cover noted that "with stocks plummeting and corporations in disarray, Americans' financial futures are in peril." Inside, the cover story shared the disillusionment of workers forced to reconsider their retirement plans. Jan Thompson, a sixty-two-year-old bookkeeper, represented a typical case. She had amassed $300,000 in her company's profit-sharing plan—but the bear market reduced her assets by half. After retiring in 2000, Thompson planned to return to work in fall 2001. She regretted her decision to invest in the stock market: "If I'd put all my money in a bank account or money-market fund, I'd still have what I started out with. What does concern me is that all these scandals are making people have a lack of faith in the market and leave it." The attitude expressed in this quote contrasted sharply with the "gold-rush mentality" that had characterized many investors' approach to the stock market only a few years earlier.[41]

Shrunken stock portfolios led some commentators to reflect on the poor judgment of investors hooked by the lure of easy money. At the height of the bubble, "middle-age investors were throwing conservatism to the wind, mortgaging their homes to put more money into hot tech stocks. Fifty-something workers were making quick plans to retire early in dot.com paradise." Stock-market investing had become a kind of cultural craze; workers risked real assets to pursue trendy investments. In some cases, reflections on poor judgment assumed the tone of a confessional. *New York Times* columnist Bill Keller conceded that "we were living an economic lie." He held that "over the past decade, we have been absurdly captivated by the stock market. The Dow became our national mood ring. Investing went from a form of savings to being a kind of lottery. . . . The fact that Americans are losing faith now is no bad thing; we've been worshiping in a casino." Keller confessed the sins of investors who thought that stock-market riches could replace prudent savings and honest work. And Lester Thurow, a management professor at the Massachusetts Institute of Technology, readily identified which of the seven deadly sins investors had committed: "Greed. We all knew that these stocks were overpriced, but we all wanted to get wealthy. We knew that prices would eventually fall, but we believed that we could get out before the declines began."[42] Both Keller and Thurow used the first-person plural pronoun "we." Both confessed the sins not just of a few isolated individuals—they confessed the sins of a society swept up in a mania.

Contrition about rash behavior—chasing hot stocks, obsessing over a mood ring—expressed an implicit reaction against the temporal qualities advocates had associated with investment. Speed and flexibility, which supposedly comported investment with a new economy, actually undermined the retirement planning of individual investors. As Keller and Thurow suggested, investors sought quick riches instead of secure growth. Evidencing melancholy about acting too hastily, Jan Thompson pined for the security of a savings account. In this milieu, the supposed weaknesses of insurance revealed themselves as strengths. Contrary to the stodginess attributed to it by advocates of investment, insurance offered workers the stability and predictability they desired. Retirement planning necessitated a long-term temporal perspective that the 1990s investment mania lacked.

Some commentators feared that speculation about technology stocks had impaired the development of technology itself. They welcomed the bursting of the bubble as an opportunity for Silicon Valley to rediscover itself. These commentators pressed a distinction between innovators whose ideas drove the technology sector and others who looked to profit from their innovations. Michael Moritz, a local venture capitalist, compared the region to a vacation town after spring break: "Today Silicon Valley is akin to Fort Lauderdale, Fla., after spring break. The tourists have abandoned us. Most of the people who came here in search of a quick buck during the past few years have gone." Moritz saw this as a positive development because it allowed committed venture capitalists to return to their primary mission: cultivating young companies. Innovators, too, could regain their focus without the interference of profiteers. Another commentator noted that "while many of the M.B.A. gold diggers hightailed it back to Old Economy-ville, the people who matter in Silicon Valley—the geeks—weren't going anywhere. Back on their own, many of them . . . immediately began doing what they do best—making high-tech magic."[43] Seeking easy money, speculators did not commit themselves to Silicon Valley for the long-term; they lacked the patience required to encourage technological innovation. Speculators followed the flows of capital, leaving others to clean up their mess.

Yet bad judgment and speculation by themselves could not explain the expansion of the bubble nor justify the economic woes resulting from its bursting. Commentators insisted that overinflated stocks and corporate scandals evidenced a larger systemic failure. By February 2002, *Time* reported that since Enron declared bankruptcy three months earlier, Moody's Investor Service had requested additional financial information from four thousand companies whose accounting methods raised questions about their creditworthiness. Enron and other scandals revealed lapses by executives, accountants, bankers, analysts, regulators, and public officials. *Newsweek* held that the Enron case demonstrated that "money talks. Or, with Enron, shouts. The company put lots of money in pockets of the people and institutions that were supposed to police it." Enron purchased protection for its illicit activities. The regularity with which it defeated institutional safeguards evidenced the extent of financial privilege in the conduct of corporate activities. Along these lines, *New York Times* columnist Frank Rich asserted that "each new corporate scandal confirms the cynical but settled view that big business is conducted with two sets of mostly legal rules, one for inside investors who get in early and get out before the deluge, and another for the rest of us."[44] During the 1990s, advocates of privatization, buoyed by the bubble, celebrated a democratized stock market. No longer would stocks serve as an investment option reserved exclusively for the wealthy. Exercising their individual autonomy, assembly-line workers could invest like executives. However, for Rich and others, the old rules still applied.

If executives could protect themselves personally from financial losses, they could not protect themselves publicly from a loss of esteem. Indeed, this may have been the greatest injury they suffered from the corporate scandals. Whereas a booming stock market facilitated heroic portrayals of executives as innovators who created jobs and wealth for others, revelations of corporate wrongdoing invited negative images of executives as selfish crooks. Of course, former Enron CEO Kenneth Lay received significant negative news coverage. Numerous stories noted how he profited handsomely while some rank-and-file Enron employees lost everything. But the media coverage did not treat Lay as an isolated individual. Another figure of scorn was Dennis Kozlowski, former CEO of Tyco International, whom prosecutors charged with looting $600 million from the company. Kozlowski's conspicuous consumption became a potent symbol of the excesses of the bubble. News accounts revealed that Kozlowski used corporate funds to purchase an $18 million duplex in New York City. He also used Tyco funds to purchase artwork for the duplex, including paintings by Renoir and Monet. Yet the $2-million, six-day birthday party Kozlowski threw for his wife in Sardinia, Italy, may have received the most media attention. Guests jet-skied, sailed, golfed, and feasted. The party featured a performance by singer Jimmy Buffett, who received $250,000 for his appearance. The theme of the party was Roman luxury: gladiators and chariots greeted guests as they arrived at the door for the official celebration. Once inside, the guests could mingle with live male models dressed in togas and Speedos, while female servants dressed in tunics hand-fed grapes to partygoers.[45]

Judged from a post-boom perspective, the accomplishments of CEOs appeared less impressive. *Time* columnist Michael Elliot recalled that in the 1990s, "businessmen seemed to combine a buccaneer's spirit with a slide-rule mind. 'Washington' (the word had to be said with a sneer) was, by comparison with the world of our titans, disorganized and inefficient, quite hopeless." Now, even if subjected to the changing winds of fashion, the roles had been reversed: "Corporate titans are out. Government reforms are in." As a general statement, this claim would not withstand close scrutiny. Still, a celebration of the deeds of public actors in comparison to private actors appeared in unlikely places. In an op-ed column for the *Wall Street Journal*, Uwe Reinhardt, an economics professor at Princeton University, observed that the terrorist attacks of September 11 and the Enron scandal enabled citizens to witness "both the heroic and the pathetic in adult American society." Reinhardt recounted the powerful images of valiant police officers and firefighters risking their own lives to save others trapped in the World Trade Center. He noted, too, the sacrifices of soldiers in Afghanistan who left their homes and families to battle a worldwide terror. Reinhardt characterized these public servants as the heirs of the greatest generation, who battled fascism abroad and created economic prosperity at home. He urged the *Journal's* readers to "compare these brave folks with the morally flexible ones whose shenanigans helped fuel the recent asset bubble in what was supposed to be the most efficient and trustworthy financial market in the world." Reinhardt imagined executives, lawyers, auditors, consultants, and bankers gathered in boardrooms with one purpose in mind: to deceive shareholders. Yet the damage went beyond shareholders. Bad corporate actors devalued "one of the nation's most precious assets: an efficient, accurately informed capital market known for impeccable integrity. Can we ever trust Wall Street again?"[46] With the passing of time, seemingly heroic corporate actions appeared utterly self-interested. It would take even more time for the market to regain the public's trust.

Corporate Scandal and the "Enronization" of Political Rhetoric

In a 2002 Social Security Subcommittee hearing, Rep. J. D. Hayworth protested what he regarded as "the convenient Enronizing of political rhetoric."[47] Hayworth's complaint revealed the frustration of many advocates of privatization who saw their cause hindered by corporate scandals. Supporters of insurance used the case of Enron to reaffirm the protections offered by Social Security and to highlight the risks associated with stock-market investing. Although the news media linked corporate scandals with the stock-market bubble, policymakers tended to treat these issues separately. In this section, I examine how policymakers and committee witnesses discussed the significance of corporate scandal for Social Security. In the next section, I examine how they interpreted the significance of market losses for private accounts. I consider the implications of this separate treatment in both sections.

As Hayworth's complaint implied, "Enron" functioned as a condensation symbol within the debates. Opponents of privatization utilized the term to invoke associations of wrongdoing, mismanagement, risk, greed, and privilege, which appeared as antithetical to sound Social Security policy. Rep. Robert Matsui rebuked the administration for attempting to use payroll taxes "to pay for the $254-million tax cut for Enron." Hans Riemer, an analyst at the Institute for America's Future, charged the administration with practicing "Enron-style accounting" in using the Social Security surplus for other purposes. Joan Entmacher, a vice president of the National Women's Law Center, similarly dismissed a proposal to distribute guarantee certificates for Social Security benefits: "Such certificates . . . would be worthless except as something to hang on the wall next to the Enron stock certificate."[48] Matsui, Riemer, Entmacher, and others associated policies they opposed with the discredited practices of Enron, implying that these policies would produce similar outcomes. In this way, Enron packed larger arguments by analogy into a single name. Enron expressed both an enumeration of past acts and a judgment of the unethical quality of these acts. Enron also condensed emotions of betrayal and deceit expressed by the ordinary workers and investors who suffered from the company's bankruptcy. Enron thus offered supporters of insurance a single term to challenge competing values of wealth, ownership, and control. "Enronizing" political rhetoric meant invoking the term as a trump card in an effort to foreclose further consideration of private accounts.

As with media commentators, some debate participants asserted that Enron and other scandals revealed an insider-outsider structure that governed investments in the stock market. Chuck Leven, an AARP board member, reported a "growing sense that only corporate and market-based insiders know how companies are really doing." Insider knowledge gave these connected investors an unfair advantage in making their investment decisions: they knew the truth about a corporation's profitability; they learned about upcoming mergers or layoffs before companies announced this information to the public. The potential existence of an insider system belied characterizations of the stock market as a democratic arena where people encountered each other on equal ground and prospered by their own ingenuity and hard work alone. Instead of bracketing privilege, the stock market rewarded it—the stock market enabled people to turn connections into money. Those without connections found themselves losing out. Keith Taylor, a retiree who lost a significant portion of his investments, concluded that perseverance by the ordinary investor could not overcome insider connections: "Even doing your homework and studying hard and looking at past performance, if there is somebody out there who is flat-out lying to you with the intention of cheating you, chances are, if you are a little investor, that guy is going to get the job done."[49] Perhaps an institutional investor could uncover false information, but the ordinary investor had to rely on a corporation's public documents. Seen as an insider's game, the stock market appeared rigged. Outsiders functioned like marks in a poker game; they supplied the money from which the hustlers profited.

Although an inside-outside game constituted an explicit spatial metaphor, it also exhibited temporal qualities. Insiders and outsiders experienced the ups and downs of the market differently. Insiders obtained stock information first, which enabled them to purchase or sell stocks before prices changed with larger trends. Outsiders had to wait for public announcements of proprietary information, hoping that they did not buy a stock too late or hold a stock too long. Insiders acted more quickly and confidently than outsiders because they possessed knowledge of the future. In this way, insiders sought to control time. In sharing information with other insiders about a corporate acquisition or quarterly profits, insiders controlled the information that the market used in making putatively objective price determinations. By controlling this information, insiders could cause a stock price to rise or fall, thus staging a sequence of predictable actions and consequences. Insiders could eliminate for themselves the contingency that outsiders experienced daily as investors. Insiders acted, whereas outsiders reacted.

Scandal cast CEOs, perhaps the ultimate insiders, in a villainous light. Debate participants repeatedly contrasted the fortunes of CEOs who profited through scandal with the fate of ordinary people who lost their savings. Sen. Charles Grassley, although an advocate of private accounts, held that "it is especially tragic that, at both Enron and Global Crossing, workers lost so much while the top executives were lining their pockets with gold." Images of CEOs with gold-lined pockets suggested serious doubts about their desire to protect the public good. Far from heroic, these images represented business executives as plutocrats whose pockets bulged with their workers' savings. With seemingly insatiable appetites for greater wealth, executives steered their corporations away from sound business dealings toward surreptitious ventures that rewarded officers at the very top of the corporate hierarchy. They risked the savings of ordinary workers and investors while protecting themselves from financial loss. Having already demonstrated an abdication of their fiduciary duty to shareholders by placing personal wealth above corporate well-being, CEOs likely would treat private accounts as simply another opportunity for self-enrichment. Rep. Bob Etheridge maintained that "the recent Enron scandal clearly demonstrates that we cannot allow the retirement system and security of working people in America to become victims of unrestricted corporate greed."[50] CEOs would feel no duty toward beneficiaries; they would not maintain the promises of Social Security. Given this alternative, policymakers needed to stand firm where business executives had fallen, by upholding their duties to workers and retirees.

Debate participants feared that the betrayal and deception of thousands of ordinary investors had undermined public confidence in the stock market—if not the economy itself. Opening a Finance Committee hearing on the Enron bankruptcy, Sen. Max Baucus explained that "at the most fundamental level, this hearing, among others that the Congress will be conducting, is about confidence. All across the country, the story of Enron has shaken public confidence in our system." Investors felt themselves taken in by the overly optimistic talk of the 1990s; they were wary of further deceptions. Ironically, in the view of some policymakers and witnesses, this lack of confidence first found expression through the very people who should have been most bullish about the economy and the long-term benefits of stock-market investing: CEOs. Keith Taylor held that "I have lost two-thirds of my retirement investments because of wrongdoings by the CEOs, and because of the lack of confidence of business leaders in the market."[51] Taylor implied that executives engaged in illegal activities because they ultimately lacked confidence in the stock market as a meritocracy. Doubting both the capacities of their own corporations and the good judgment of investors, these CEOs did not believe that the stock market would reward honest corporate growth and profitability. In the end, they sought to eliminate the contingencies of genuine competition by rigging the system.

This lack of confidence stood in stark contrast to the supreme confidence of ordinary investors and employees in companies like Enron. Sen. Max Baucus maintained that "most of Enron's employees voluntarily were concentrated heavily in their company stock. . . . Many workers knew they were engaged in risky behavior but bought Enron shares anyway because they believed in their company." Enron employees trusted their employer; they believed the public statements of corporate executives regarding the financial health of the company. They saw themselves, their coworkers, and their superiors working toward a common set of goals, and their stock purchases reflected this sense of commitment. Indeed, many employees of Enron and other companies had participated in Employee Stock Ownership Plans (ESOPs) that had been designed to achieve precisely this result. By law, ESOPs required employees to invest a majority of their holdings (50 percent plus one dollar) in employer stock. David Walker, comptroller general for the General Accounting Office, explained that ESOPs "are not the optimum type of retirement plan. They are designed to achieve other objectives, for example, to try to correlate the employees' interests with the company's interest; to try to correlate the employees' interests to the shareholders' interests; to try to encourage productivity, innovation, and other types of things; and to broaden ownership."[52] Participating in ESOPs and other plans, employees and "outsider" investors pursued a long-term strategy, yet they paid a steep price for CEOs' pursuit of short-term gain.

Solutions to problems of corporate scandal involved ethical corporate executives and accurate investor information. Although the scandals received significant public attention, as some debate participants reminded their colleagues, they involved a small minority of the people and companies in corporate America. Sen. Larry Craig asserted that "we've got about 16,000 registered publicly held companies with the SEC—my guess is you're going to be able to count on maybe both hands and your toes the bad actors." Craig and others envisioned a straightforward solution to the problems at Enron and other companies: replace the dishonest executives with honest ones, who ran the overwhelming majority of American corporations. Whereas Craig supported private accounts, AARP board member Chuck Leven did not. Both supported stricter laws governing corporate responsibility. Leven also called for more ethical actors: "In the end reputable people will have to be selected to make the new system work."[53] By focusing on people, these proposed solutions drew attention away from potential problems with the system. As Craig suggested, Enron appeared as the exception, not the rule. The system functioned properly—and so, too, would companies like Enron, once the bad actors were replaced with good ones.

Investors also needed to arm themselves with good information. Sen. Evan Bayh called for stricter laws and ethical executives, but he viewed information as paramount. Bayh promised that "we are going to throw people in jail when they break the law, but as you [Leven] point out, at the end of the day there is no substitute for honesty in the management of some of these companies. . . . Really our best defense is an informed consumer." In this statement, Bayh constructed a series of fortifications that established the law as a first defense, ethical management as a second defense, and an informed investor as "our best defense." Others shared this view. Elisse Walter, an executive vice president at NASD, the principal private-sector regulator of securities in the United States, assured members of Congress that "NASD is doing everything it can to ensure that our country's financial markets remain strong." She reported that NASD had recently completed a joint investigation with the Federal Securities and Exchange Commission that resulted in a $100-million fine against an investment bank for offering its favored customers special access to stock deals. However, Walter explained that these sorts of actions would never offer investors complete assurance against fraud: "At the end of the day regulators can never eliminate risk in the markets or do the homework that we as investors all need to do for ourselves."[54] Ultimately, an investor had to rely on his or her own judgment as a protection against fraud; public policy could achieve only a limited result.

To facilitate investors' judgment, some debate participants envisioned a democratization of investment information. William Sweetnam, an official in the Treasury Department, insisted that corporations should offer rank-and-file employees the same quality of investment advice they provide for executives: "Plan provisions really must provide the same availability . . . to all the people within the plan. So you could not give, as a plan benefit, this investment advice being part of the plan benefit, greater investment advice to the executive and have lesser investment advice for the individual." In this way, the advantages attached to elevated positions in the corporate hierarchy could be attenuated. Insider information served as capital for the well-connected: an equal flow of information promised to reduce the investment gains attributable to one's social standing. As many witnesses testified, democratizing information required bolstering unbiased sources of investment information. In the case of Enron, employees relied too heavily on company sources for advice. These company sources did not provide a realistic assessment of the value and security of Enron stock. David Walker recommended that policymakers "make sure that participants get qualified investment advice, either from independent parties, or if the parties are not independent, with sufficient safeguards to avoid conflicts of interest."[55] With equally shared information presented by objective advisors, ordinary investors could exercise their judgment and defend themselves against unethical corporate executives.

Calls for better-informed investors represented an effort to realize visions of a democratic stock market. With information, ordinary investors could overcome the bad behavior of insiders, restoring public confidence in a market that had been undermined by a few unethical actors. However, the manner in which debate participants envisioned a democratization of information did not acknowledge its full force. Insiders did not control information qua information; insiders controlled the content and timing of information. Proposed reforms addressed the issue of content, but they ignored the crucial issue of timing. References to "homework," "greater" and "lesser" advice, and advice from "independent parties" all referred to elements of content. In effect, Sweetnam, Walker, and others held that advisors should not say one thing to insiders and something else to outsiders. While this constituted a good start, privilege also meant that during the boom, insiders received information sooner than outsiders and used this information to orchestrate events and force outsiders to react. Considering both the content and timing of information required going beyond the individual to systemic considerations.

Debate participants resisted this move, reiterating the overall soundness of the stock market. Some participants, like Sen. Larry Craig, attempted to minimize the damage caused by media accounts of scandal. Still, even participants who did not explicitly limit scandal to a few cases implicitly adopted an individual-based solution to a potentially systemic problem by supporting as solutions more ethical executives and better investor information. Focusing on these changes deflected attention from what some media commentators, in comparison, regarded as a failure of an entire system of checks and balances. Some media commentators discerned a system of incentives that rewarded people for overstating profits and discounting losses, and normalized misleading and inaccurate financial disclosures. Indeed, the very identification of an insider-outsider's game suggested problems that more ethical executives and better information could not solve. Whereas news media accounts suggested that a corrupt corporate culture helped produce a bubble economy, policymakers did not see scandal as enabling some of the financial "successes" that drew praise in the 1990s.

Individual-based solutions also implied that policymakers could not effectively prevent corporate scandals. They could pass laws, but laws themselves could not overcome greed or engender ethical behavior. Unscrupulous executives would discover ways of circumventing new laws. Policymakers had little control over the producer side of the stock market, but they could bolster the consumer side. Information appeared as potentially more efficacious than law because information enabled consumers (investors) to engage producers (corporations) on equal ground. In this way, policymakers upheld what Robert Kuttner identifies as a core assumption of free markets: perfect information. Kuttner explains that "in a stylized free market, consumers are said to possess 'perfect information.' This is almost never literally true, but is often close enough to be a reasonable approximation."[56] Presuming equality in content and time, perfect information (along with other core assumptions) permitted individuals to realize the freedom and control promised by markets. Both supporters of insurance and advocates of investment responded to corporate scandal by reaffirming the tenets of the market.

Stock Market Losses and Private Accounts

In the 1990s, a rising stock market heightened the appeal of private accounts. Comparing annual returns on stocks with traditional Social Security benefits, advocates argued that workers should benefit from the higher returns of the stock market.[57] The bursting of the stock-market bubble denied this line of argument—if only for a time—to advocates of investment. Supporters of insurance insisted that the bubble's bursting demonstrated the untenable risk that stocks presented for Social Security. Advocates of investment stressed a long-term view of stock-market returns, and they argued that diversified stock portfolios could guard against substantial losses.

For supporters of insurance, dramatic declines represented the down-side of a democratized stock market. Like casual gamblers who bet more than they could afford to lose, ordinary people had become overinvested in stocks. Addressing an audience at a field hearing of the Aging Special Committee in Las Vegas, Nevada, Sen. Harry Reid observed that "it used to be that the stock market was just for a certain small group of people to invest. But it appeared so easy that—I watched on TV last night, a cab driver who has lost everything he had in the stock market. He is trying to determine if he should file bankruptcy, because he thought it would be easy. It is not easy."[58] Correctly identifying rising and falling stocks pre-sented a challenge to all investors. However, wealthy investors, "a certain small group," possessed extensive financial resources that enabled them to withstand market declines. For wealthy investors, stocks represented only a portion of their overall holdings, which they could risk because they had secure financial holdings elsewhere. Like professional gamblers who had amassed a large reserve that remained distinct from their betting stakes, wealthy investors purchased in stocks what they were willing to risk. By contrast, ordinary investors appeared as desperate gamblers who had placed all of their stakes on a specific number at the roulette table—a high-risk, high-yield investment. If their number hit, they would reap a financial windfall. But if the ball landed anywhere else on the wheel, they would be tapped out.

Supporters of insurance held that losses likely would prompt inves-tors to seek relief from Congress, which would increase the financial and political costs of Social Security. Robert Greenstein, executive director of the Center on Budget and Policy Priorities, maintained that the prospect of political pressure from unsuccessful investors would undermine the entire federal budget. He encouraged policymakers to "imagine what would happen if the Commission plans were in effect already. Say they took effect two or three years ago, and the stock market plunged, as it has in recent months, wiping out a significant share of the assets in personal accounts that the public had been told were a basic part of the Social Security system." He maintained that members of Congress might view disgruntled investors as a potential political threat: "The risks are high that the political pressure on Congress to take some action to fill in the gaps and make up for those losses in the private accounts, particularly in an election year, would be tremendous." Similarly, Gary Burtless, an ana-lyst at the Brookings Institution, predicted that constituents would flood

Congress with appeals for relief: "You can imagine the flow of mail into Capitol Hill if this kind of a plan is adopted."[59] Far from removing politics from Social Security policy, private accounts would politicize benefits. Policymakers would witness a return to the days before automatic, inflation-adjusted benefit increases, where politicians regularly raised benefits in election years to curry favor with their elderly constituents. Other citizens, whom politicians regarded as less of an electoral threat, would suffer as politicians diverted money from other areas of the budget to make up for investment losses.

Advocates of investment responded to the bursting of the stock bubble by stressing the long-term performance of stocks. Several advocates identified twenty-year periods, which had never produced a negative rate of return, as an appropriate measure of stock performance. In an exchange with Treasury Secretary Paul O'Neill, Sen. John Breaux pursued this line of argument. Recounting the concerns of others, he noted that "some said, look, the market is going down the last couple of days, it is a terrible idea, although over a 20-year-period, which is a normal period that people invest in retirement, we have never had a negative rate of return in the market." O'Neill concurred, holding that one could look back only three or four years to find that "equity investments always win." In O'Neill's view, the future for young investors shone even brighter: "When one is planning a retirement account . . . say at age 20 or 21, and looks forward for 40 or 45 years, there is no question, at least not in recorded history, that one would be better off invested in the general equities of the United States than in risk-free returns."[60] From the perspective of Breaux, O'Neill, and others, critics of private accounts reacted like skittish novices who regarded every movement in the market—however slight— as indicative of a portentous trend. Lacking the level-headedness of the regular investor, these critics misjudged the market and failed to recognize the effective returns on private accounts.

Supporters of insurance retorted that policymakers should consider long-term returns alongside stock-market variability. Workers would not hold stocks indefinitely, and their Social Security benefits would depend in part on the status of the stock market at the time of their retirement. On this score, the stable benefits of insurance outperformed the uncertain returns from private accounts. Larry Winawer, representing the Alliance for Retired Americans, observed that "Social Security benefits do not change with ups and downs in the economy or the stock market. The value of individual accounts invested in private investment markets can vary substantially from year to year and the value of a worker's account benefits at retirement can be far different from what the worker expected." Winawer held that the variability of the stock market would frustrate workers' attempts to plan a secure retirement. Recent market downturns had forced some workers to reconsider retirement plans: "Sharp declines in the stock market have forced workers to delay retirement and forced some retirees to return to work." Social Security offered workers a source of stability in planning their retirement. Rep. Jerrold Nadler reminded his colleagues that with the "dramatic fall of stock prices in the past year, Social Security never lost a dime."[61] Although investment advisors could project long-term returns, they could not eliminate the variability of the stock market. Stability could be achieved only by maintaining the social-insurance structure of Social Security.

Advocates of investment upheld diversification as a guard against stock-market declines and variability. A diversified stock portfolio would attenuate swings in share prices among companies and across sectors, and diversification would offer investors a reliable rate of return. Social Security deputy commissioner James Lockhart maintained that the "volatility of stock market returns is overcome with regular investing and long-term diversified index funds, which have done much better than Treasury bonds even at the bottom of the last bear market, and certainly after last year's recovery." Lockhart reiterated the importance of investing in stocks for the long term, but in the short term, diversification appeared to offer investors a steady source of income. Investors who had suffered extensive losses in the bear market invested too heavily in particular corporations or sectors, such as high-tech stocks. David Walker contended that "in the case of what happened in Enron, it was clearly a violation of one of the fundamental tenets of investment, and that is the tenet of diversification. You should not put all your eggs in one basket."[62] Although Walker connected Enron to the bursting of the stock bubble, he did not draw this connection in the same way as some media commentators. Discerning a dysfunctional system of checks and balances, these commentators regarded Enron's soaring stock price as a product of its illegal actions. By contrast, Walker saw Enron as an instance of overexuberant investors looking to make a quick profit and, in the process, ignoring the principles of sound investing. As with calls for better information, affirmations of diversification drew upon individual rather than systemic explanations for stock-market downturns.

Although debate participants did not completely dissociate market declines from corporate scandal, as Walker's connection of Enron and diversification evidenced, they treated these economic developments as separately solvable issues. In doing so, their discourse minimized the extent of corporate scandal and restored the stock market as a naturally rising (albeit with downturns along the way) arena. Viewed on its own, corporate scandal emerged as an aggregation of uncoordinated episodes that influenced the specific corporations involved rather than the market as a whole. As a distinct issue, corporate scandal assumed the quality of a theft rather than an effort to control the market. Similarly, seen in isolation, market declines reflected the belief that the stock market diffused decision making: individual investors, and not corporate titans, determined the value of stocks. Moreover, stock prices always reflected their worth, since they always indicated a price that investors willingly paid. If a particular stock or sector seemed overinflated, the fault lay with these individual investors.

While separating stock declines from scandal may have reaffirmed a belief in the stock market as a self-regulating realm beyond the control of nefarious actors, it did not fully address the argument that caution ought to attend any reform of Social Security in the wake of the bubble's bursting. To refute this argument, advocates of investment represented the long-term growth of the stock market through a plotted trajectory that smoothed out the variability of annual returns. Whereas advocates in the 1990s emphasized annual returns, post-boom advocates referenced twenty- and forty-year periods to shift focus to a "lifetime" return. Breaux, for instance, identified twenty years as a "normal period" of investment. Diversification served as the tool enabling this temporal shift. Because sound investing mandated a diverse portfolio that balanced the risks of individual stocks, investors could de-emphasize temporary annual declines. Even if one stock—like a high-tech venture—did not pan out, the other holdings in an investor's portfolio would sustain a lifetime growth rate.

Urgency of Reform and Sustainable Solvency

Besides reframing appropriate temporal judgments of the stock market, advocates of investment also sought to shift perceptions of Social Security's future. The need for this shift arose because, beginning in the late

1990s, Social Security's long-term financial condition slowly but steadily improved. The 1997 trustees' report projected that Social Security's expenditures would exceed its revenue in 2012. To continue to meet its obligations, Social Security would have to draw on the interest and principal from the trust fund, which would be exhausted in 2029. The following year, the trustees' report postponed the first date to 2013 and the exhaustion date to 2032. The 1999 trustees' report again postponed both dates to 2014 and 2034, respectively. By 2003, the trustees' report projected that expenditures would exceed income in 2018 and the trust fund would be exhausted in 2042.[63] With each passing year, the long-term financial condition of Social Security appeared to improve.

Advocates of investment attempted to create a sense of urgency for reform by emphasizing the earlier set of dates (the revenue-expenditure dates) and adopting the criterion of sustainable solvency, which the President's Commission proposed in 2001. Some advocates expressed frustration at the attention given to receding insolvency dates. Sen. Charles Grassley complained about "banner headlines, that is what is talked about. You will see it in every publication and rag and everything else." He asked David Walker if "we can really afford to feel secure about the fact that the solvency date appears to be receding slightly." Walker replied that a looming negative cash flow for Social Security in 2017 portended financial strains. In subsequent testimony, he reiterated that "[2017] is really the key date. . . . The sense of urgency is a lot more immediate than many people realize." Walker and other advocates stressed cash flow because they insisted that a negative cash flow in Social Security would have a deleterious effect on other areas of government. Sen. John Breaux urged his colleagues not to seek comfort in the resources of the trust fund. He held that when the Social Security Administration seeks to redeem its Treasury bonds, "the rest of the government has to find the cash. . . . The only way we are going to continue to pay those benefits is by taking money from some other function of government."[64] In this statement, Breaux discounted the view of Social Security, in its current form, as a self-funded program. Social Security made claims on government resources just like any other program: when its expenditures exceeded payroll-tax revenues, the government would have to find those resources elsewhere.

Creating a sense of urgency for reform drew on claims circulated by advocates in the 1990s, President Bush, and the President's Commission that the Social Security trust fund lacked real assets. In this spirit, Rep.

Clay Shaw reiterated his longstanding characterization of the trust fund as "nothing more than an IOU from the government to the government." Without the trust fund as a resource, Social Security faced a looming crisis. Shaw asserted that the system would go bankrupt in 2016. Anticipating a charge from supporters of insurance that he sought to frighten workers and retirees, Shaw substantiated his position by referencing a legal definition of bankruptcy: "I would like to submit for the record the definition of bankruptcy as it appears in Black's Law Dictionary: The state or condition of one who is unable to pay his debts as they become due."[65] In Shaw's view, Social Security would go bankrupt in fifteen years because its only legitimate source of revenues lay in the payroll tax, which would not meet expenditures in 2016. Yet the use of the term "bankruptcy" to characterize Social Security's financial condition also connoted vernacular meanings of the term that heightened a state of crisis. In popular usage, bankruptcy also connotes a condition of "being broke," or penniless. In this sense, forecasting the bankruptcy of Social Security implied that the program would exhaust its resources and thus be unable to pay benefits after 2016. This suggested a far more urgent situation than the Social Security Administration redeeming some of its Treasury bonds. Advocates of investment insisted on restructuring Social Security because they believed that traditional methods would not fund the program indefinitely. Following the lead of the President's Commission, some advocates rejected standard measures for assessing the long-term finances of Social Security, pressing for a criterion of sustainable solvency instead. Along these lines, David Walker contended that "our current system, I mean, even if you can make it work for 75 [years], it is pre-programmed that it doesn't work beyond that." The present system was "pre-programmed" to fail because its relative costs would continue to increase, and policymakers, so long as they maintained its existing structure, would be powerless to prevent these increases. An ever-expanding entitlement program would usurp policymakers' decision-making authority. Former commission member Olivia Mitchell maintained that trust-fund solvency represented only a portion of this underlying problem. One could achieve trust-fund solvency by raising taxes or reducing benefits: "The problem with such a proposal is that there is no guarantee that the money would actually be saved in the trust fund." Policymakers might continue to use the trust fund as a cover for profligacy elsewhere in the federal budget. Only sustainable solvency could secure the financial future of Social Security. And private accounts would allow this goal to be realized: "Money would have to be taken off the table and put in the individual accounts in order to ensure that the money would be there for retirement."[66] Mitchell maintained that private accounts would permit Social Security to return to the original model that FDR had envisioned for the program: to live within its means.

According to its deputy commissioner, the Social Security Administration understood the importance of sustainable solvency. James Lockhart reported that "Commissioner Jo Anne Barnhart has made achieving sustainable solvency a major goal of the agency." Lockhart praised sustainable solvency because this measure did not construct an arbitrary time period to judge Social Security's finances: "It is important to strengthen Social Security not just for a short-term period or some arbitrary period, but for the long term, for our children and grandchildren." Only sustainable solvency could maintain the promise of Social Security for successive generations. The traditional seventy-five-year actuarial measure, which ostensibly gauged the long-term finances of the system, actually left an enormous bill for future generations: "If you don't have sustainable solvency, you are going to fall off the cliff, just like they are falling off the cliff in 2042."[67] Even if one accepted as real the balances in the trust fund, its exhaustion would leave an immediate negative financial impact. By contrast, sustainable solvency would create a positive annual cash flow for Social Security. Lockhart promised that the Social Security Administration would undertake a program of "solvency education" to inform citizens of the urgency of this change to system financing.

The invocation of the phrase "sustainable solvency" represented an effort to shift the burden of proof in the debates. Advocates of investment attempted to persuade policymakers and citizens that private accounts constituted a greater improvement in the finances of Social Security than the traditional remedies of payroll-tax increases and benefit cuts. The Greenspan Commission had used these traditional remedies in 1983 to avert an immediate fiscal crisis, suggesting a possible response to the crisis that advocates of private accounts discerned twenty years later. By identifying sustainable solvency as a goal, advocates sought to compel defenders of insurance to prove the indefinite viability of their preferred remedies. Yet sustainable solvency placed an additional burden on supporters of insurance insofar as it entailed a shift from intergenerational financing (whether by a strict pay-as-you-go approach or a trust-fund approach) to individual financing. Calling for a positive annual cash flow meant that the retirement accounts of every worker had to generate income every year. Sustainable solvency discredited intergenerational payments as drawing on insufficient funds. Further, sustainable solvency suggested that policymakers could fix Social Security's finances once and for all, promising that they could transform Social Security from a system "pre-programmed" to fail to one programmed to succeed. This implied the ability to foresee and control an indefinite future. No unexpected events—a baby boom, a world war, an economic depression—would undermine a sustainably solvent system.

Advocates also followed the lead of the President's Commission in referring to the costs of private accounts as an investment. James Lockhart explained that the Social Security Administration regarded the funding required for private accounts "not [as] a transition cost. It is a transition investment. The return on investment is excellent." Given his agency's commitment to sustainable solvency, this return appeared as the very preservation of Social Security itself. Others adopted this language, too. Jeffrey Brown, a finance professor at the University of Illinois, maintained that people frequently misunderstood the concept of transition costs. He held that people wrongly understood the concept to reference additional costs beyond those already entailed by the system. Rather, "What we are really talking about here is a re-timing of costs. The transition costs will rise because of the fact that we have made benefit promises to current workers and retirees, and if we fulfill those promises and simultaneously want to fund the accounts, that certainly requires that we put more money aside today."[68] Whereas supporters of insurance characterized this dynamic as "paying twice" for private accounts, Brown suggested that privatization merely meant paying future debts today. Presumably, "re-timing" costs would generate long-term savings. In this way, debt payment constituted an investment, which served the purpose of constructing a sense of urgency for reform by addressing a potential concern with private accounts.

Testing Faith in Market Democracy

The new millennium brought a changed sociopolitical context for the privatization debates. A contested presidential election exacerbated partisan tensions in the Congress. The stock market stopped rising. While ostensibly innovative and prosperous new-economy companies betrayed their weak foundations, seemingly savvy CEOs revealed themselves as crooks and schemers. As a cultural unease with investing and distrust of corporate America emerged, the long-term finances of Social Security slowly but steadily improved. These changes converged to suggest a cautious time for retirement policy. Any change to Social Security, especially a fundamental restructuring of the system, required careful examination. Under the circumstances, the best change for Social Security appeared as no change at all.

The Bush administration's effort to transform this situational sense of wariness into a propitious appeal began with the appointment of the President's Commission to Strengthen Social Security, co-chaired by former senator and eminent social-welfare expert Daniel Patrick Moynihan. The commission report ascribed a telos to Social Security with private accounts constituting the completion of the 1935 Act. According to this teleology, policymakers could justify the opportune moment for private accounts as a policy for a new era, rather than a short-term response to the bubble's bursting. The body of the commission's report reinforced this sense of inevitability by asserting an authoritative sense of time that proceeded independently of political time.

This reframing of the policy context for privatization confronted a difficult challenge from media accounts that tied together stock declines and corporate scandal in a systemic critique of the stock market. Media accounts depicted an insider-outsider game that benefited individuals with money and connections at the expense of ordinary investors. Advocates of investment attempted to respond to this critique by treating scandal and decline as separately solvable issues. With respect to scandal, advocates proposed a democratization of information to overcome differences between insiders and outsiders. However, their proposal did not fully address insiders' manipulation to orchestrate events to their advantage. Responses to declines sought to shift focus from annual to lifetime returns, using diversification as a means of accomplishing this temporal shift.

Advocates of investment desperately needed to respond to public perceptions of an insiders' market, for their case relied crucially on a view of the stock market as a democratic realm. Advocates had drawn on this notion repeatedly in arguing for private accounts, holding that the market disregarded sexist and racist stereotypes. They insisted that the stock market would allow low-wage workers to overcome the disadvantages of their class position. Whatever their background, investors could succeed in the stock market by relying on their skills and motivation. A housekeeper could prove herself the equal—if not superior—of her executive employer. But declines and scandal revealed that privilege and power still mattered on Wall Street. Insiders controlled the content and timing of information, selling their stocks before prices declined sharply. By setting the rules and controlling the enforcement mechanisms, insiders eliminated contingency for themselves and increased uncertainty for outsiders. Outsiders served insiders as resources for exploitation.

To the extent that citizens regarded these suspicions as true, the case for private accounts was lost. Ordinary investors would not support sacrificing their retirement for the benefit of a privileged few. Advocates of investment would have to rebuild public trust in the market over time. Yet at least one prominent citizen appeared unfazed by the events of the new millennium, remaining convinced of the democratic basis of the stock market, and hoping to achieve for the nation what private accounts promised to retirees. In his 2004 reelection campaign, President Bush shared with audiences his vision of an "ownership society." At the start of his second term, Bush set out on a barnstorming campaign to make private accounts the policy centerpiece of an ownership society. I examine this campaign in the next chapter.

5

Going Public with Privatization

In a press conference two days after his election to a second term, President Bush assessed the import of his victory: "I earned capital in the campaign, political capital, and now I intend to spend it." President Bush interpreted the election results as a clear expression of public opinion. Through their votes, citizens indicated their support for his policy agenda: "After hundreds of speeches and three debates and interviews and the whole process, where you keep basically saying the same thing over and over again, that—when you win, there is a feeling that the people have spoken and embraced your point of view." Innumerable times through various forums, the campaign offered Americans a choice between two views of the nation's future. Americans considered these views and decided that they preferred the president's vision, which included a new approach to retirement policy. Americans chose the principle of investment. Bush asserted that "we'll start on Social Security now. We'll start bringing together those in Congress who agree with my assessment that we need to work together. . . . Reforming Social Security will be a priority of my administration."[1]

President Bush had good reasons to call confidently for quick legislative action on his policy priorities. In a presidential election in which more
people cast ballots than in any other in American history, George Bush
received three million more votes than his challenger, Sen. John Kerry.
This represented a dramatic turnaround from 2000, when Bush actually
lost the popular vote to Vice President Al Gore by more than one-half
million votes. Moreover, although reports of voting irregularities surfaced
in Ohio, which proved to be the decisive state in terms of the electoral college, John Kerry conceded the day after the election, avoiding the court
battles and protracted controversies of the 2000 presidential election.[2]
Further, Republicans increased their majorities in the House and Senate.
The combination of single-party control, a reelected president, and increased congressional majorities suggested that Bush could expect success
in achieving his legislative priorities. Long-time advocates of investment
appeared giddy at the prospect of fundamental change. Recounting his
twenty-four years as champion of Chile's retirement system, José Piñera
asserted that "there is now an opportunity for a bipartisan agreement in
the United States in this crucial area of public policy." Stephen Moore,
cofounder of the Club for Growth, praised the years of hard work by
conservative think tanks and advocacy groups to circulate market-based
approaches to public policy. Moore reported "extremely high expectations
among conservatives that real change is going to take place. Conservatives
have waited 20 years for this alignment."[3]

Perhaps, too, confidence arose from the crucial role that private accounts played in Bush's vision for the nation's future, which he portrayed
as an "ownership society." With increasing frequency during his first term,
peaking during the 2004 election campaign, President Bush expressed
his desire to achieve an "ownership society" in America.[4] Accepting his
party's nomination for president, Bush held that a "priority for a new
term is to build an ownership society, because ownership brings security
and dignity and independence." Ownership did not refer exclusively to
material possessions. Rather, ownership signaled a general orientation to
public policy and social goods. Bush explained that "in an ownership society, more people will own their health care plans and have the confidence
of owning a piece of their retirement. . . . We must strengthen Social
Security by allowing younger workers to save some of their taxes in a
personal account, a nest egg you can call your own and Government
can never take away." In its present form, Social Security affirmed values

antithetical to ownership. Its guiding principle of insurance promoted collectivism and interdependence, compelling workers and retirees to rely on one another for their well-being. Insurance removed individual control, leaving workers and retirees at the mercy of capricious government bureaucrats.

Ensuring change required bold action. In the winter of 2005, President Bush launched a barnstorming tour to promote private accounts for Social Security. Holding town-hall meetings in more than twenty states, Bush sought to urge the public to increase pressure on reluctant members of Congress.[5] Towards this end, Bush utilized his most valuable rhetorical asset: his highly cultivated image as a likable, regular guy. Perhaps no single datum encapsulated this image more than a 2004 Zogby poll finding that more voters would prefer to have a beer with George Bush than his challenger John Kerry.[6] Portrayed in the news media as a "stuffy" New Englander, Kerry served as the perfect foil for Bush. Whereas typical politicians presumably exuded pretentiousness, Bush was down-to-earth. While typical politicians thumbed their noses at regular folk, Bush shared the interests of ordinary Americans. He liked baseball. He called his co-workers by funny nicknames. He got dirty, relaxing at his Crawford ranch by clearing brush. Bush did not speak eloquently, often fumbling his words, but many Americans shared his unease with public speaking. As a regular guy, Bush could explain the complexities of Social Security in the framework of ordinary needs and interests. He could relate to Americans as a peer—or at least the White House hoped so.

Although he possessed the power of the bully pulpit, Bush did not campaign alone. Groups supporting and opposing private accounts joined the debate, circulating various media advertisements (television, print, Internet) to convey their message. Along these lines, *USA Today* reported that "just days after Bush unveiled part of his proposal [during the State of the Union speech], tens of millions of dollars are being raised and spent on ads, including some that begin today." The newspaper noted pro-privatization ad campaigns planned by Progress for America and the Club for Growth, as well as opposition ads planned by the AARP, the Campaign for America's Future, and MoveOn.org. The article quoted Derrick Max, director of the pro-privatization group the Alliance for Worker Retirement Security, who predicted that "people are going to be surprised at the level of organization on both sides."[7] With the intense publicity attending the privatization debates in the winter and spring of 2005, previous debates seemed almost obscure by comparison. To be sure, in the 1990s, congressional committees held hearings, and various witnesses supported or opposed private accounts, but debate participants largely restricted their communication to policymakers and interested others. In 2005, President Bush and other debate participants directly engaged members of the public.

With President Bush's barnstorming tour serving as my focal point, I explore in this chapter these processes of public engagement. To orient my analysis, I examine how scholars have conceptualized the relationship between the state and the public sphere, situating Bush's barnstorming tour as a case of a prominent state actor engaging wider publics. I then discuss some of the challenges Bush faced, including his need to refocus public attention on domestic issues amid the ongoing "War on Terrorism." On this point, Bush's apocalyptic war rhetoric threatened to drain public energy from all other policy issues. To elucidate the larger debates surrounding Bush's tour, I turn to the coordinated campaign for private accounts. Various advocacy groups produced advertisements supporting the president, using fear appeals and invoking history to characterize private accounts as the fulfillment of FDR's original vision. However, supporters of insurance responded with a campaign of their own. The AARP weighed in prominently, using humor in one advertisement to argue that President Bush had exaggerated Social Security's problems. The remaining two main sections of this chapter focus on Bush's barnstorming tour. Affecting his regular-guy image, Bush used the terms "broke" and "bust" to represent Social Security's finances. When discussing the trust fund, which he dismissed as IOUs, Bush presented himself as the eyes of his audience in verifying its paltry resources. Bush's tone shifted dramatically when he discussed private accounts as the centerpiece of an ownership society. Although Bush, unlike "elitist" politicians, believed that every American possessed the skills for ownership, he articulated a passive mode of citizenship that left the practice of democracy to others.

Policy Debate in the Public Sphere

As a historical and critical concept, the "public sphere" refers to the emergence and development of deliberative forums in Western democracies and serves as a normative framework for investigating public discourse (including deliberation and other modes) in diverse contemporary societies. Its most famous chronicler is Jürgen Habermas, who recounted the rise of the bourgeois public sphere in Western Europe in his germinal 1962 book *The Structural Transformation of the Public Sphere*.[8] Attention to the public sphere has only increased in the decades since the publication of this book, as scholars invoking alternative intellectual traditions in rhetoric, philosophy, and elsewhere have employed a public-sphere framework to address important issues in complex, pluralist contemporary societies.

Towards this end, contemporary scholars have promoted the perspective of a "multiple public sphere," which indicates that *the* public sphere actually refers to a *multitude* of overlapping, intersecting, collaborating, and contesting sites of discourse. Scholars often invoke metaphors of networks and webs to give shape to this amorphous realm. Gerard Hauser writes that the public sphere "has become a web of discursive arenas, spread across society and even in some cases across national boundaries."[9] As a web metaphor suggests, direct and indirect linkages associate the sites and participants in a multiple public sphere. An individual may know only a fraction of the other participants in a societal discussion, but a person's direct conversations contribute to innumerable indirect interactions to sustain what Seyla Benhabib has termed an "anonymous public conversation."[10] In this process, discourse may occur in a wide range of sites, but specific locales do not bear an intrinsic meaning or function: specific locales may host forums, but these forums may not be reduced to their locales per se. For example, a town square, office cafeteria, or grocery checkout line may serve as a site in the public sphere where people discuss common concerns. In his more recent work, Habermas defines the public sphere as the *"social space* generated in communicative action."[11] Instantiating a public sphere, individuals enact roles that produce a qualitatively different space from their interactions as family members, friends, coworkers, or residents of a community.

Participants in discussions utilize the constitutive power of discourse to draw lines between public and private. Sometimes, people may agree about the public standing of an issue; other times, judgments may differ. Alternative judgments invite struggle, disclosing the politics of line drawing. Marking an issue as public or private may benefit or harm important interests—advocates may win or lose arguments by admitting or preventing issues from reaching public agendas. Indeed, the most contested aspect of public debates sometimes concerns the question of whether an issue merits the attention of others. In any case, the network structure of the public sphere means that no single agenda exists, and various sites may draw lines of public and private differently. Further, no distinction of public and private exists indefinitely. Issues regarded by various sites as private in one historical period may emerge as public in another era. For instance, Nancy Fraser recounts the work of feminist activists to bring issues like sexual harassment to public agendas. Activists succeeded in transforming ostensibly private workplace issues into matters of public import.[12]

Qualities of relationality, power, and temporality condition the circulation of discourse in the public sphere. Multiplicity intimates that relations among sites inform the conduct of discourse as much as interactions within specific sites. Debates may activate particular nodes in the network while bypassing others. Much to the chagrin of advocates of investment, seniors have participated in the privatization debates more extensively than younger workers. Power suggests that social hierarchies ascribe meaning and significance to individuals' contributions. Social standing may increase the salience of one person's position while dismissing someone else's. Policymakers paid special attention to seniors and the AARP—some policymakers feared the political power of this group. Power also indicates that the discourse norms and practices of one group may circulate uncritically as the appropriate evaluative criteria for others. In this vein, representatives of Third Millennium repeatedly demanded choice in retirement planning commensurate with their work experience in the New Economy, obscuring a class subtext that offered "freedom" to some workers and constraint to others. Temporality signals that discourse moves through the nodes of the network at different speeds. Some issues may take years to reach the agendas of multiple public forums, whereas other issues may emerge across forums seemingly instantaneously. In launching his barnstorming tour, President Bush quickly focused media and public attention on privatization, generating more publicity in a brief period than the numerous committee hearings held during the 1990s.

Yet the status of the hearings and barnstorming tour themselves may raise questions for scholars who disagree about the relationship between the public sphere and the state. On the one hand, theorists like Habermas strictly separate the public sphere and the state. In his model of deliberative democracy, Habermas distinguishes between contexts of justification and contexts of discovery. He characterizes state institutions as contexts of justification, where deliberations have "less to do with becoming sensitive to new ways of looking at problems than with justifying the selection of a problem and the choice among competing proposals for solving it." Habermas discerns contexts of discovery in the public sphere, whose "open and inclusive network" enables more sensitive perception of "new problem situations."[13] On the other hand, theorists like Michael Schudson regard the public sphere as "a set of activities that constitute a democratic society's self-reflection and self-governance."[14] Schudson locates the deliberative forums of the state in the public sphere, viewing legislative bodies as privileged public spheres. The stakes in this scholarly debate consist of the relative analytic value of emphasizing the autonomy of the public sphere from governing institutions, versus highlighting how some publics combine deliberation and institutionally sanctioned decision making.

Rather than placing the public sphere inside or outside of the state, this chapter considers how state actors may engage wider publics. With respect to deliberations in Congress, policymakers undoubtedly seek solutions to perceived public problems by debating legislation, but congressional deliberation also frames issues and (albeit without the bully pulpit of a presidential tour) calls public attention to issues. Members of Congress may hold hearings to build public support for an issue that holds little support among their colleagues, and they may attempt to persuade citizens from within the institutions of government, as evidenced by large visual aids displayed during House and Senate floor debates, with the hope of making the evening news. When state actors engage citizens outside of the institutions of government, they may betray different levels of commitment to civic-minded engagement. Sometimes, policymakers may engage their constituents to gather more information or persuade them to support a policy proposal. However, policymakers also may manipulate their constituents or engage them in an effort to squelch dissent. Critics leveled both of these charges at President Bush, arguing that his town-hall meetings excluded opponents of privatization and created a false sense of open debate. In cases of both low- and high-mindedness, state actors often stand as more powerful participants than their interlocutors. Regardless of his motives, as president of the United States, Bush could not simply participate as one of several attendees at a town-hall meeting. His very presence informed the conduct of the discourse and referred back to institutional settings. In this respect, Bush explicitly announced his desire to use the barnstorming tour to pressure members of Congress to support private accounts.

In taking his case directly to the people, President Bush confronted a different set of discourse norms and practices than those guiding policymakers in the committee hearing room. In a widely cited essay, G. Thomas Goodnight characterizes this movement as a distinction between technical and public spheres of argument. He defines spheres as "branches of activity—the grounds upon which arguments are built and the authorities to which arguers appeal."[15] Goodnight's reference to "activity" indicates that *spheres* actually signify discursive *processes* guided by established norms (i.e., "grounds" and "authorities"). The comparatively technical sphere of the hearing room facilitates a more formal argumentative practice emphasizing rank and procedure. This normative framework informs the participation of policymakers and witnesses alike. Along these lines, Daniel Brouwer has examined the congressional testimony of ACT UP, an AIDS activist group. In the 1980s, ACT UP built its reputation by staging highly provocative street demonstrations and acts of civil disobedience. However, during the late 1980s and early 1990s, some members of ACT UP also testified before congressional committees. Although concerned that their participation might lead to co-optation, ACT UP witnesses nevertheless abided by the norms of the hearing room, providing a stark contrast to their extra-institutional discourse. Yet, as Brouwer notes, they did so under conditions of constraint: "Witnesses do not have the power to dictate the overarching course of the hearing, to challenge the rules or norms of the setting, to engage in excessively non-normative modes of expression without the threat of expulsion, or to engage in extended cross-examination with other witnesses or with representatives."[16] The spirit of these rules applies to policymakers, too. More senior members of Congress and members with more influential positions possess a greater ability to control the flow of the debates.

When engaging publics directly, as in a town-hall meeting, policymakers accustomed to having their way often must attempt to sustain their privilege while appearing to facilitate unrestricted debate. This predicament arises because even though normative frameworks guide debates in the public sphere, they operate less conspicuously, comporting with the self-presentation of the public sphere as an informal, egalitarian discursive network. Of course, power still matters. Social hierarchies contribute to the relative influence of all participants—not just presidents. However, while the committee hearing room announces its inequities loudly, the public sphere perpetuates inequity under the guise of equality. President Bush negotiated this tension deftly, playing on his reputation as a regular guy to speak plainly with citizens about the challenges facing Social Security and the benefits of private accounts.

Challenges and Opportunity

Although President Bush insisted that the election results constituted a strong endorsement of his policy priorities, he still confronted rhetorical challenges in advocating private accounts. With the nation engaged in a "War on Terrorism" and American soldiers battling an elusive enemy in Iraq, Bush needed to refocus public attention on domestic issues. Adopting a campaign-style strategy for private accounts, he also needed to negotiate the tensions of ongoing policy debates to craft a coherent and accessible message. This involved tailoring his message to different audiences without alienating any particular audience. On this score, an urgent appeal designed to capture the attention of younger workers might raise anxiety among baby boomers about private accounts. Further, the election results—mandate or not—did not stop competing discourses. Opponents of private accounts did not refrain from argument simply because Bush received a majority of ballots cast. The barnstorming tour occurred amid a constellation of discourses.

The question of a mandate itself generated media debates. For example, editorialists for the *Rocky Mountain News* insisted that Bush possessed a clear mandate. They wrote that "Bush is the first president to garner more than 50 percent of the popular vote since his father in 1988. Republicans bolstered majorities in both the Senate and the House. How could all of this be taken as anything other than a mandate for the president's policies?" The *Rocky Mountain News* treated the election results as self-evident. They implied, too, that any objections to the president's policies made prior to the election no longer warranted attention now that a mandate had been achieved. Others rejected the idea of a mandate, cautioning against interpreting the election results as indicating support for a particular policy, especially one as significant as Social Security. The *St. Louis Post-Dispatch* editorialized that "even voters who supported Mr.

Bush probably didn't think they were voting for privatization."[17] Supporters of the president may have voted for him for any number of reasons, and their support may have come in spite of hesitation about some of Bush's positions.

Although connecting issues to voting decisions is tricky, the War on Terrorism and the military operations in Iraq stood as the two issues that dominated the campaign rhetoric. George Bush and John Kerry discussed these issues far more extensively than Social Security. Indeed, Bush framed the War on Terrorism—which, in his view, included Iraq—in apocalyptic terms. Christian Spielvogel holds that "Bush relied upon a framing of the war as part of an ongoing struggle between 'good and evil.'" Cast as a fundamental moral struggle, the war required leaders with strong moral standing. In his stump speech, Bush emphasized his steadfast character, drawing "a causal relationship between morality and failure or success in the war on terrorism."[18] In this crusade, Bush's regular-guy image bolstered his case. Regular guys understood the difference between right and wrong. Regular guys spoke plainly, unconstrained by political correctness and unafraid to renounce sin. By contrast, elites suffered from self-doubt, habitually viewing the transgressions of others as self-provoked. Elites cared more about diplomatic niceties than the right course of action. Unlike secular elites, Bush possessed the certainty of faith. And this message of moral strength (apart from any specific issue) apparently influenced voters. Analyzing NES survey data, Herbert Weisberg and Dino Christenson maintain that Bush invoked the War on Terrorism to bolster his image as a "strong and decisive" leader.[19] Weisberg and Christenson conclude that this image garnered more than enough support to overcome some voters' doubts about the conduct of military operations in Iraq.

Bush's challenge to refocus public attention on domestic issues arose importantly as a consequence of his war rhetoric. An apocalyptic struggle between good and evil required a total and unyielding national commitment. Although citizens could live normally, using their purchasing power to support the troops, policymakers, and the president most of all, had to focus intently on winning the war. If the United States lost this battle, then the nation itself would perish. Not even the most ardent advocates of investment could make this claim about Social Security. Advocates of investment insisted that an insurance-based retirement system harmed the nation's financial future, but insurance did not pose the same immediate danger as terrorism. In this way, the president's apocalyptic rhetoric threatened to consume the energy of all other policy discourses, inviting audiences to regard all other policy issues as off the agenda until the nation defeated the terrorists.

In the months after the election, ordinary Americans did not place the same priority on Social Security as the president. A December Gallup poll found that only 2 percent of respondents identified Social Security as "the most important problem facing the country today," whereas 23 percent cited the war in Iraq. This finding demonstrated the necessity of a determined presidential effort to move Social Security from its comparatively marginal position on the national agenda, even if, under the circumstances, it appeared unlikely that Social Security could displace the war as the public's top priority. However, simply raising the profile of Social Security would not suffice—President Bush also had to stress the urgency of reform. According to a February *Washington Post* poll, only a minority of citizens believed that policymakers needed to act soon to repair Social Security's finances; the *Post* reported that "barely one in four Americans believes that a crisis exists" for Social Security.[20] Without a sense of crisis, fundamental change would not occur. For this reason, key policymakers highlighted the need for a shift in public perception. In a February interview with the *Chicago Tribune*, Speaker of the House Dennis Hastert insisted that Congress could not pass a privatization bill against public objections: "I have said to the president, I've said it to all of his advisers, and I've said it to all of our folks, 'Look, you can't jam change down the American people's throat unless they perceive there really is a problem.'"[21] Still, Hastert remained convinced that Americans would support change once they appreciated the magnitude of the problem facing Social Security.

On this topic, newspaper accounts portrayed skeptical audiences greeting legislators in their home states and districts. The *Washington Post*, for example, relayed the response to a "listening tour" conducted by Rep. Paul Ryan of Wisconsin, one of the youngest members of the House and an ardent supporter of private accounts. Launching a thirty-five-session, twelve-day tour that included PowerPoint presentations, Rep. Ryan drew only five people, with an average age of sixty-nine, to his first session. The audience remained unconvinced by Ryan's presentation, which included a quote from Albert Einstein extolling the powerful force of compound interest. Similarly, Sen. Charles Grassley, chair of the Finance Committee, noted little demand for change from constituents in the town-hall meetings he held across Iowa. Grassley stated: "What I need to hear people say is, 'We expect you to fix this.' I'm not hearing that."[22] Grassley and others needed to hear this because Congress would not cross the powerful supporters of insurance without clear evidence of a shift in public opinion. While citizens expressed concerns about the future of Social Security, they remained unconvinced that private accounts would strengthen the program's finances.

The challenge of coherent messaging confronted an obstacle in the term "privatization" itself. Advocates of investment increasingly realized that "privatization" connoted a contrasting objective to the administration's expressed desire to "strengthen Social Security," as the name of the 2001 presidential commission suggested. In an op-ed essay, former Rep. Timothy Penny, a Democrat who supported private accounts and appeared with President Bush at some town-hall meetings, bemoaned the practice of many of his party members who "have fallen into the temptation of simply hurling the dreaded 'privatization' word at anyone who mentions Bush's plan to allow younger workers to put a small percentage of their Social Security payroll taxes into private accounts." Penny rebuked his colleagues for their cynicism. Opponents used the word "privatization" because they "know that the word carries connotations of tearing apart the publicly administered Social Security system, something the public would never tolerate. They are placing a bet that perception will win out over reality." Penny and other advocates saw reality as an effort to spread the values of investment across society. Rather than discuss this proposal directly, opponents sought refuge in the coloration of language, playing on people's fears as a substitute for sound policy debate. Penny exhorted against the use of misleading language: "This warping of language is dangerous. At a time when we sorely need to begin funding our future obligations, it demonizes efforts to do precisely that."[23] Penny insisted that honest debate meant foreswearing the use of privatization.

Appreciating the challenges of reluctant publics and coherent messaging, advocates of investment nevertheless praised Bush's campaign for private accounts as a momentous effort to realign national politics. Grover Norquist, president of Americans for Tax Reform and a key figure in national conservative politics, held that Bush's plan for Social Security "dwarfs everything else the Bush administration is talking about doing." Norquist maintained that private accounts would transform "America from being a country of workers to being a country of workers and owners." Characterizing ownership as "revolutionary," Norquist predicted that an ownership society would "change the national psyche: increasing the political constituency for lower taxes, stronger property rights, and greater personal responsibility and self-reliance." He insisted that subsequent observers would come to regard Bush's second term as a profoundly transformative moment in the nation's history: "Fifty years from now the move to an Ownership Society will be recognized as a change to America's political landscape as dramatic as the move from farms to factories."[24] Ownership constituted the completion of the nation's earlier transition from an agricultural to an industrial society.

A Coordinated Campaign

The Bush administration developed a campaign strategy for private accounts in the months after the election. Peter Wehner, the president's director of strategic initiatives, drafted a confidential memo explaining this strategy for a limited audience of legislators and influential conservative activists. The first line of the memo, which became known as the "Wehner memo," contained the directive "Not for attribution." However, the *Wall Street Journal* obtained a copy of the memo and printed the document in full. Almost immediately, electronic copies of the memo circulated across liberal and conservative political websites. The *Journal* characterized the memo as part of the "White House's behind-the-scenes efforts to avert a split in Republican ranks over the politically charged Social Security issue."[25]

Echoing Norquist and other conservative activists, Wehner discerned unrivaled opportunity in the current context. He maintained that "for the first time in six decades, the Social Security battle is one we can win—and in doing so, we can help transform the political and philosophical landscape of the country." Wehner's reference to "six decades" and a "battle" suggested conservative opposition to Social Security since its inception. Chastened by Alf Landon's 1936 defeat, some conservatives may have muted their criticisms, but they did not disavow their opposition. Social Security still constituted a "cruel hoax." Persistent opposition also intimated fundamental contempt toward the principle of insurance. For many conservatives, Social Security did not appear as a good program that had encountered financial difficulties. Rather, it affirmed unacceptable principles that undermined core conservative values. Wehner held that "we have it within our grasp to move away from dependency on government and toward giving greater power and responsibility to the individual." Private accounts would engender an irrevocable break with the paternalistic welfare state and a decisive move towards an owner-ship society. Wehner proclaimed that "if we succeed in reforming Social Security, it will rank as one of the most significant conservative governing achievements ever. The scope and scale of this endeavor are hard to over-estimate." [26] The creation of private accounts would stand as a watershed moment in conservative social policy.

Since a momentous opportunity necessitated a well-conceived and coordinated campaign, the memo outlined the administration's basic plan "in terms of sequencing and political strategy." Affirming the judgment of congressional leaders, Wehner held that the first step required advocates of investment to foster doubt about the current program. He anticipated presidential speeches that would insist on a basic premise: "The current system is heading for an iceberg." If the administration could not establish this claim as the first premise of the ensuing debates, then reform would not occur. Wehner underscored this point: "We need to establish in the public mind a key fiscal fact: right now we are on an unsustainable course. That reality needs to be seared into the public consciousness; it is the pre-condition to authentic reform." Still, Wehner did not foresee a smooth road to reform. Quite the contrary: he acknowledged that "the debate about Social Security is going to be a monumental clash of ideas—and it's important for the conservative movement that we win both the battle of ideas and the legislation that will give those ideas life." [27] A conserva-tive defeat might bolster Social Security against future efforts at reform, thereby sacrificing decades of hard work by activists in the movement.

Congressional Republicans prepared for the impending campaign with the aid of a reform guide issued by Rep. Deborah Pryce and Sen. Rick Santorum, chairs of the House and Senate Republican Conferences. The guide included a series of talking points prepared by the White House Office of Communications. These talking points affirmed the importance of Social Security for current retirees, but stressed the need for changes for the program to serve future generations. Citing an "unfunded obliga-tion" of more than $10 trillion, the talking points identified a decreasing worker-to-retiree ratio—from 15 to 1 in 1950, to 3 to 1 presently—as a source of Social Security's financial troubles. The guide highlighted two key dates: 2018, when the program would begin to pay more in benefits than it collected in payroll taxes, and 2042, when the program would be "bankrupt."[28]

Cautioning against complacency, the guide stressed the need for immediate reform. In only one year, the first of the baby boomers would turn sixty, and their impending retirement would place significant pressures on the system. Further, the longer legislators postponed action, the more expensive and difficult the solutions would be. The guide maintained that a present-day thirty-year-old worker faced a 27 percent benefit cut at retirement under the current system. This cut illustrated the costs of "doing nothing" in the short term. Just as important, the present context called on legislators to work with the president in acting boldly and fulfilling their duties as public officials. The guide declared that "one of the tests of leadership is to confront problems before they become a crisis. President Bush came to Washington to solve problems, not pass them on to future presidents and future generations."[29] In subsequent speeches, President Bush would liken his courageous actions to those of FDR, who acted boldly in the 1930s to save the country from an earlier financial crisis.

Concerned with messaging, the guide stressed "'personalization' not 'privatization.'" The guide explained to legislators that "personalization suggests increased personal ownership and control. Privatization connotes total corporate takeover of Social Security; this is inaccurate and thoroughly turns off listeners, who are very concerned about corporate wrongdoing." Although Enron no longer dominated news headlines, memories withstood the passage of time, as ordinary investors remembered their mistreatment at the hands of greedy CEOs. Armed with focus-group data, Pryce and Santorum hoped that personalization would signal a retirement policy developed specifically for ordinary folk. Just as consumers could personalize various retail goods, so too could workers personalize their investments. The guide emphasized communicating three general messages to constituents: they "must realize what is at stake, why reform is necessary in the very near future, and how they and their grandchildren will benefit from Personal Retirement Accounts." Following this advice, the sample speeches included for legislators eschewed the word "private," referring instead to "personal accounts." Further, the guide stressed the important role of personal accounts for an ownership society. Personal accounts promised to expand access to markets for many Americans who did not have the opportunity to experience the independence and control of ownership. Personal accounts would enable workers to build "a nest egg that they can call their own, [that] government cannot take away, and [that] they can pass on to their children."[30] By affecting a personal relationship, advocates of investment sought to reestablish the connection between values of individualism and ownership weakened by the misdeeds at the new millennium.

Interest groups advocating private accounts prepared for a massive media and lobbying campaign. Trade associations, led by the National Association of Manufacturers, and advocacy organizations, like the Club for Growth, initiated a fundraising drive to finance an intense campaign. Stephen Moore predicted that "it could easily be a $50 million to $100 million cost to convince people that this legislation needs to be enacted. It's going to be expensive because it's the most important public policy fight in 25 years."[31] Reports indicated that funds would cover a diverse range of campaign activities, including lobbying, television advertising, letter-writing, phone-calling, and grassroots activity. Although its financing and sponsorship suggested a top-down campaign, activists hoped to generate popular participation. Wall Street firms also participated in the campaign. In the weeks after the election, the Securities Industry Association released a self-serving report claiming that private investment firms would benefit only modestly from managing private accounts. Investment firms like Charles Schwab and Wachovia participated in business coalitions promoting private accounts.[32]

An unusual case of interest-group participation appeared in the form of USA Next, an advocacy group seeking to position itself as the conservative alternative to the powerful American Association of Retired Persons (AARP). Founded in 1991 by activist Richard Viguerie, the organization had raised millions of dollars for conservative causes through direct-mail solicitations. More recently, the organization had switched to a mass-media approach. Explaining their current campaign, USA Next president Charlie Jarvis characterized the AARP as "the boulder in the middle of the highway to personal savings accounts. We will be the dynamite that removes them."[33] Seeking this goal, USA Next gained notoriety for an advertisement that ran briefly on the website of the conservative magazine *The American Spectator.* Purporting to disclose the "real AARP agenda," the ad contained two photographs placed next to each other: the first photograph showed the profile of a male U.S. soldier dressed in desert combat fatigues; the second photograph showed two young men dressed in tuxedos and holding bouquets—apparently just married—kissing.[34] At first, the ad showed the two pictures side-by-side, the banner headline "The Real AARP Agenda," and a side-bar note encouraging viewers to click on the ad for more information. After a few seconds, a red X appeared over the photo of the soldier. A few seconds later, a green checkmark appeared over the photo of the newlyweds. Apparently, the AARP agenda consisted of opposition to the military and support for same-sex marriage. Clicking on the ad redirected viewers to the USA Next web site. Given its content and placement, the advertisement more likely constituted an effort to attract media attention than to persuade seniors that their familiar source for aging information and travel discounts opposed the military. However, in attracting attention, the advertisement implicitly asserted that the AARP represented only one of many senior groups rather than *the* voice for seniors so feared by legislators.

Other groups pursued a more traditional route in their advertising campaigns, emphasizing the themes articulated in strategy documents. The advocacy organization Progress for America ran a series of television advertisements supporting Bush's plan for private accounts. One ad recalled the iceberg metaphor of the Wehner memo.[35] The ad began with a shot of an iceberg, which grew larger and larger in the visual frame. As a ship's horn blew, a deep-voiced male announcer stated: "Some people say Social Security is not in trouble, just like some thought the *Titanic* was unsinkable." The screen then shifted to a graph, and the announcer explained that the worker-to-retiree ratio would decrease from 16 to 1 in 1950, to 2 to 1 when today's younger workers retired. If nothing is done, the announcer maintained, the system would go bankrupt. At this point, the mood of the advertisement shifted, with the ominous music turning hopeful. An image of Bush delivering his State of the Union speech appeared, and the announcer explained: "President Bush wants to rescue Social Security now, before we hit the iceberg." As the announcer moved from "now" to "before," the visual frame returned to the image of the iceberg. The frame shifted once again, as the announcer introduced Bush's plan for personal retirement accounts. Images of people of different generations—grandparents, parents, children—appeared on the screen (sometimes alone, sometimes together) as the announcer extolled the benefits of the plan. Moreover, he noted, nothing would change for people fifty-five and older. The visual frame then returned to Bush during the State of the Union challenging legislators "to move ahead with courage and honesty." Then the image of the iceberg returned for a final time, as the announcer promised: "We don't have to hit the iceberg."

This iceberg advertisement utilized an explicit fear appeal, invoking a partially known and visible threat that signaled a far greater unknown danger lurking invisibly beneath the water. The image of the iceberg played on audiences' capacity to amplify exponentially a visible threat (like the fleeting image of a knife blade in a horror movie) into an unseen yet terrifyingly catastrophic event. Only a small fraction of the iceberg floated above the water; its awesome destructive force, which could tear through a steel hull, resided in the depths. As passengers on a ship heading toward an iceberg, we knew that our current course would precipitate an icy death, but we could not know the exact moment of impact. Would our ship collide with the iceberg at twenty-five yards from its tip? At fifty yards? This uncertainty added to the intensity of our imagined death. Moreover, this advertisement followed what Douglas Walton has termed the dichotomous structure of many fear appeals: "Either take the recommended action [personal retirement accounts] or the fearful outcome will occur." As Walton suggests, "dichotomization . . . leav[es] no room for potential rationalization or equivocation."[36] So long as we stayed on an insurance path, we would collide with the iceberg—no outcome existed but death. Survival lay in taking an entirely different path, announced by the dramatic shift to a hopeful tone when we encounter the course President Bush charted with personal accounts. Like other fear appeals, this advertisement offered a solution—the *only* solution—to the fear it stoked. And, just in case its hopeful message lulled audiences into a false sense of security, the advertisement closed with a final glimpse of the image of horror.

Another Progress for America television advertisement linked Bush's plan for private accounts to FDR's original plan for Social Security. The advertisement stressed the courage of both men in pressing for important legislation.[37] The ad began with footage from the signing ceremony for the 1935 Social Security Act. As viewers watched FDR signing the legislation, with notables like Frances Perkins in the background, an announcer (the same one from the "Iceberg" advertisement) proclaimed: "It took courage to create Social Security." As the visuals remained the same, the audio shifted from the voice of the announcer to the voice of FDR himself, who began, "This Social Security measure . . ." Just as FDR finished this phrase, the audio switched back to the announcer, and the visual frame shifted to Bush signing a piece of legislation. The announcer asserted: "It'll take courage and leadership to protect it." The advertisement then used the same audio and video from the "Iceberg" ad to discuss the decreasing worker-to-retiree ratio. When the subject shifted to personal accounts, pictures of different generations accompanied the voice of the announcer. He assured audiences that nothing would change for retirees or workers nearing retirement, but "younger workers should have the option of a personal savings account." The advertisement ended by urging audiences to call Congress and voice their support for the president's plan.

Visually and orally, the advertisement represented Bush's plan for private accounts as the fulfillment of the 1935 Social Security Act. Visually, the contiguous footage of FDR and Bush at signing ceremonies associated the two presidents and their policies. Although they lived in different eras, FDR and George Bush contributed to the same tradition of progressive public policy. Both men appreciated that good policies accounted for the exigencies of their eras—anachronistic policies benefited no one. Orally, the announcer connected the two leaders as courageous: both men confronted vocal opposition, yet both men possessed the strength of character to pursue justice over expediency. Just as FDR fought to establish Social Security, Bush would fight to save it. More subtly, the advertisement linked Bush's plan with the original legislation by switching immediately from FDR's reference to "this Social Security measure" to Bush signing legislation. *This* Social Security measure seemingly referred to Bush's proposal for personal accounts. In this way, FDR, recognizing the provisional character of his legislation, discerned in the future a more mature retirement system that better met the needs of workers and retirees. Implicitly, the advertisement invoked FDR as speaking from the past to endorse Bush's plan. Indeed, the advertisement depicted President Bush as signing Social Security legislation—this *Social Security* measure— even though he had not yet put forward a specific plan and Congress had not passed a bill.

Like the congressional guide and pro-media campaigns, the White House sought to deliver a coherent message during the barnstorming tour. To achieve this goal, administration staff carefully orchestrated the discussion in the town-hall meetings. Staffers did not open the meetings to anyone wishing to attend, and they did not permit spontaneous participation by the laypeople on discussion panels. In a March article, the *Washington Post* reported that the "White House follows a practiced formula for each of the meetings. First it picks a state in which generally it can pressure a lawmaker or two, and then it lines up panelists who will sing the praises of the president's plan. Finally, it loads the audience with Republicans and other supporters." As this summary suggested, the administration did not treat the town-hall meetings as genuinely deliberative forums, but as elaborately staged events designed to pressure members of Congress to accept private accounts. To illustrate the orchestrated character of these town-hall meetings, the *Post* interviewed Mark Darr, a thirty-one-year-old insurance agent who served on a discussion panel in Little Rock, Arkansas. A representative from the governor's office who knew Darr had called to inquire about his participation in the event. Before offering a definite invitation, the representative asked about Darr's views of the president's plan. During the conversation, Darr suggested that his mother also appear on the panel. The representative seemed eager to use her, but she failed the screening. Darr recounted: "She wasn't really for the private accounts, so they didn't decide to use her."[38]

After passing a screening, chosen participants gathered the night before the town-hall meeting to practice their discussion. An administration staff person acted as the president and questioned the panelists. Darr recalled that "we ran through it five times before the president got there." Some panelists denied that the White House scripted the meetings. Erma Fingers Hendrix, a seventy-four-year-old retiree, described the practice session as "a matter of learning." She maintained that "we just really talked about what was going on, what the president was proposing and what did we think about it. . . . They didn't prompt me what to say or how to say it." Still, the carefully planned meetings drew the ire of some editorialists. Noting "disturbing reports" of people being shut out of meetings, the *St. Petersburg Times* concluded that "it is apparent that Bush and his handlers are afraid to allow even an inkling of dissent in the audience." The *Times* dismissed the town-hall meetings as photo-ops: "By avoiding legitimate questions, sticking with those that are staged and scripted, and filtering out anyone who isn't willing to cheer the president, the administration creates the illusion that the American people are fully behind the president."[39] In rebuking the barnstorming tour, the *Times* intimated a process of deliberation in which citizens would express their doubts and the president would address them. Of course, opponents of private accounts also dismissed the meetings.

A Determined Response

In spite of this campaign, congressional opponents of private accounts held firm in their views. Just a few days after the president's State of the Union speech, every Democratic senator but one signed a letter indicating that they would oppose any Social Security bill that would increase the federal deficit, which included Bush's plan. Senate Democrats unveiled their letter at a staged event at the Franklin Delano Roosevelt Memorial in Washington. Some of these senators represented states targeted by the president for his barnstorming tour—Arkansas, Florida, Montana, and North Dakota—all of which the president had won in the November election. In March, forty-two senators signed a letter expressing direct opposition to Bush's plan. Calling the plan "unacceptable," the letter exhorted the president "to unambiguously announce that you reject privatized accounts funded with Social Security dollars."[40] Unified opposition from Senate Democrats played both a surprising and crucial role in undoing the prospects of any legislation creating private accounts. This opposition arose surprisingly because for most of President Bush's first term, Senate Democrats, perhaps intimidated by the overwhelming public support for the president in the aftermath of the 9/11 terrorist attacks, had appeared unwilling to present unified opposition to any of Bush's major policy initiatives. This opposition played a crucial role because as long as forty-one of the forty-four Democrats (plus an additional independent) opposed the plan, senators could use the parliamentary tactic of the filibuster to prevent any Social Security bill from coming to a vote. Ending a filibuster by invoking a rule known as cloture required the support of sixty senators.

Although Democrats in the House could not employ these parliamentary tactics, they also found ways to oppose the administration's plan. The minority staff of the Government Reform Committee prepared a report that detailed what committee Democrats regarded as the "politicization" of the Social Security Administration. The report contended that "the Social Security Administration has markedly changed its communications to the public over the last four years. . . . [These changes] call into question the agency's independence." Along these lines, the SSA's press releases did not reflect the ostensibly improved long-term finances of Social Security. The report asserted that "as the Trustees' projections of the solvency of Social Security have improved over the last four years, the agency's press releases have grown more dire." Even more revealing, the SSA appeared to change its strategic goals to comport with Bush administration priorities. During the 1990s, the SSA identified "strengthen[ing] public understanding of Social Security" as a strategic goal. However, in March 2003, the SSA eliminated this goal in a revised strategic plan. Instead, "the 2003 plan established a new objective to 'support reforms' that 'ensure sustainable solvency and more responsive retirement and disability programs.'"[41] The minority staff report concluded that policymakers could no longer trust the SSA as an objective source of information for policy debates. Rather, the SSA had become an active participant in these debates. Democrats also rebuked SSA deputy commissioner James Lockhart for appearing with Republicans at public events designed to promote private accounts.[42] In challenging the objectivity and independence of the SSA, Democrats implied that the administration had to rely on exaggeration and misinformation to raise doubts about an otherwise sound program.

Led by the powerful AARP, interest groups also expressed opposition. In the week after the presidential election, the AARP announced that it would oppose any effort to incorporate private accounts into Social Security. AARP president Marie Smith asserted that her organization "adamantly opposes replacing any part of Social Security with individual accounts." In the December 2004 issue of the *AARP Bulletin*, in an open letter to its members, the AARP praised Social Security as "the most successful program in our nation's history" and cautioned against drastic change. The AARP objected that "taking some of the money that workers pay into the system and diverting it into newly created private accounts would weaken Social Security and put benefits for future generations at risk." The AARP promised to "fight to ensure that Social Security's guaranteed and inflation-protected lifetime benefits stay in place for generations to come." As with other issues concerning seniors, the organization's position attracted the attention of members of Congress. One year earlier, the AARP crucially supported a new Medicare prescription-drug benefit, which gave political cover to policymakers fearful of angering seniors. As the *New York Times* reported, some legislators believed that the Congress likely would not "make major changes in Social Security over the organization's objections."[43] If so, then the adamancy of its opposition portended great difficulties for the president's plan as early as November 2004.

In January 2005, the AARP ran a series of full-page advertisements in national newspapers like the *New York Times* and the *Washington Post*. The advertisements all followed the same visual layout. The graphics from a Social Security card framed each advertisement. Classical columns bordered the sides of the page, leading to an arch at the top. Across the top of the page, in bold capital letters, were the words "SOCIAL SECURITY." The first advertisement bore the headline "Winners & Losers" and a picture of the trading floor of a commodities exchange. At the center of the page, it explained: "Winners & Losers are stock market terms. Do you really want them to become retirement terms?" In smaller print, the text continued: "Let's not turn Social Security into Social Insecurity. While the program needs to be strengthened, private accounts that take money out of Social Security are not the answer and will hurt all generations. There are places in your retirement planning for risk, but Social Security isn't one of them." The second advertisement contained the picture of a young couple, declaring: "If we feel like gambling, we'll play the slots." The smaller print repeated the message of the first ad. The third advertisement contained a picture of three smiling children and declared in large print in the center of the page: "Passing the buck is one thing. Passing 2 trillion bucks is another." The smaller print began the same as the first two ads, but after noting that private accounts "will hurt all generations," the text continued, "and could add up to two trillion dollars in more debt. Let's not stick our kids with the bill."[44]

This series of advertisements highlighted themes of security/insecurity and connections among generations. All three repeated the phrase "Let's not turn Social Security into Social Insecurity." The first and second installments compared private accounts to explicitly risky activities of futures trading and casino gambling. In contrast to the insecurities associated with private accounts, the advertisements represented the security of the present system by visually reproducing the image of a Social Security card, as sturdy, stable columns encapsulated the risky realms of futures and casinos. In "Winners & Losers" especially, the picture of frenzied traders trying desperately to sell or purchase the right commodity at the right price presented a negative image against the strength of the columns and arch surrounding it. Addressing intergenerational connections most directly, the third installment contrasted the picture of smiling children with the idea of indebting future generations by trillions of dollars. All three advertisements claimed that private accounts "will hurt all generations."

Moreover, they urged their disproportionately middle-aged and older readers (given their placement in national newspapers) to consider the needs of future generations as well as their own needs.

In one television advertisement, the AARP used humor to argue that private accounts constituted an overreaction to a manageable financial shortfall.[45] Titled "Kitchen Sink," the advertisement began with a repairman and a female homeowner standing in a kitchen. The repairman observed: "Yep, looks like the drain is clogged. Only one way to fix it. We're going to have to tear down the entire house." Surprised, the homeowner asked: "What?" As she queried, the repairman spoke into his radio, instructing his coworkers to "go ahead." "Yeah," he responded, "we got to tear down the house." The homeowner queried once more: "To fix my drain?" The repairman reiterated: "Yeah, it won't take long." At this point, a bulldozer plowed through the rear French doors. As the visuals remained on the demolition crew and the startled homeowner, the audio—while retaining the sounds of smashed glass, falling bricks, and broken timber—switched to the voice of an announcer. The announcer affirmed that if the viewers had a problem with their kitchen sink, they wouldn't tear down their house. He asked: "So why dismantle the Social Security system with private accounts when it can be fixed with moderate changes?" The announcer dismissed private accounts as "too drastic, too expensive, and way too risky." He explained that private accounts would create two trillion dollars in debt and lead to large benefit cuts. The advertisement repeated the slogan of the AARP's ad campaign: "Let's not turn Social Security into Social Insecurity."

This advertisement used hyperbole to argue that the Bush administration had created an unwarranted sense of crisis about Social Security. By playing on audience recognition of the destruction of the house as wildly disproportionate to its damage, the advertisement minimized the financial deficit confronting Social Security. Although audiences may not have known the exact finances of Social Security, they could infer from the equation of the two solutions—demolition and private accounts—that a similarly minimal problem existed. Further, the comic appeal invited what some scholars have called a tension-relieving function of humor.[46] By all accounts, Social Security constituted a very serious issue. "Kitchen Sink" affirmed the need to fix Social Security, but it suggested that audiences could "exhale" and consider less drastic remedies. In this way, it worked to reopen a critical space closed by the "Iceberg" advertisement.

Although, as Michael Pfau explains,[47] some fear appeals may serve a civic function by enabling deliberation, "Iceberg" and similar invocations of crisis sought to foreclose debate by insisting that no other option existed and no time remained to linger over our present course. "Kitchen Sink" deflated this sense of crisis.

"Kitchen Sink" also enacted a humorous appeal to the locus of the irreparable. As J. Robert Cox observes, "Claims that a decision cannot be repeated or that its consequences may cause an irreplaceable loss are invoked at strategic moments in almost every aspect of our personal and public lives." Once demolished, the house would never reappear. The property owners could build a new house on the site, but it would never possess the history and character of the original. Once privatized, Social Security would cease to exist. Policymakers could adopt a new retirement policy, but it would never offer the protection and security of the original. Cox explains that an appeal to irreparability "calls attention to the *unique* and *precarious* nature of some object or state of affairs, and stresses the *timeliness* of our relationship to it."[48] Social Security occupied a unique position in American life by safeguarding families and building community. Efforts to privatize the system placed Social Security in a precarious state, and only a timely public response could stop privatization from demolishing Social Security.

Two days before President Bush's State of the Union speech, the progressive advocacy organization MoveOn.org announced a media campaign of its own. The group planned targeted broadcasts of a television advertisement titled "Working Retirement," and a full-page advertisement in the *New York Times* on the day of Bush's speech. Showing seniors in their seventies and eighties performing exhausting physical labor (lifting boxes, mopping floors, shoveling dirt, doing laundry), "Working Retirement" also appealed to irreparability. As the images appeared, an announcer spoke: "First, someone thought up the working lunch. Then, we discovered the working vacation. And now, thanks to George Bush's planned Social Security benefit cuts of up to 46 percent to pay for private accounts, it won't be long before America introduces the world to the working retirement."[49] MoveOn.org asserted that private accounts would transform retirement from a comfortable and joyous period of life to a time of uncertainty and struggle—retirement effectively would end.

In its *New York Times* advertisement, MoveOn.org compared Social Security's finances to the prewar threat posed by Iraq to argue that Bush

had misled Americans in both cases. In large capital letters, Social Security cards spelled out the acronym "WMD." Below this image, in smaller
print, the advertisement read: "Now George Bush is misleading us about
Social Security." In still smaller print, the ad continued: "First George Bush
said Saddam Hussein had weapons of mass destruction and a 'mushroom
cloud' was imminent. Now, he's claiming something equally outrageous;
a phony Social Security 'crisis.'"[50] Clearly, the advertisement challenged
Bush's credibility. MoveOn.org purported to identify a modus operandi
for the president: create crises to advance unnecessary, unwise, and un-
wanted policy agendas. Further, the advertisement implied that Bush's
interests in Social Security lay with the wealthy, just as some progressive
groups charged that Bush's interests in Iraq rested with the oil industry
and well-placed contractors.

The organization announced that "Working Retirement" would
initially run in three congressional districts—two Republican, one Democrat—whose representatives either won close races for reelection or,
in the case of the Democrat, announced support for private accounts.
Describing the ad campaign directed toward Pennsylvania representative
Jim Gerlach, the *Pittsburgh Post-Gazette* noted that the "fact that Gerlach
won his seat in 2002 and 2004 by just a 2 percentage point margin made
him a more likely target to oppose the president's Social Security plan." In
a press release announcing the campaign, Eli Pariser, executive director of
MoveOn.org, asserted: "We are committed to this effort for the long haul.
We will make sure that members of Congress who consider supporting a
plan that reduces benefits for future retirees know that their constituents
will hear from us—and they will hear from their constituents."[51] Just as
Bush hoped to leverage public opinion to motivate Congress to enact his
plan, advocacy groups hoped to use this same leverage against it.

Imminent Bankruptcy and a Pile of IOUs

Bush likened his campaign to create personal accounts to FDR's original push for Social Security. He praised FDR for acting boldly in 1935
to establish Social Security even as critics doubted the appropriateness
and feasibility of the program. Critics did not intimidate FDR—and FDR
proved critics wrong. Bush maintained that "Franklin Roosevelt did a
good thing when he created the Social Security system, and it has worked

for a lot of folks. Social Security has provided an important safety net for many, many senior citizens." Just as FDR spurned critics to pursue a greater societal goal, Bush had decided to confront powerful interests to preserve Social Security for future generations. Bush called attention to the risks he undertook in doing so: "I understand that for years, Social Security was the third rail of American politics. That meant that if you grabbed ahold of it, you weren't going to do well politically." Demonstrating his steadfastness, the president explained that threats would not frighten him: "You'll hear me describe the fact that I believe the system needs to be reformed, and I'll tell you why. And I believe political people, when they see a problem, have a duty to address that problem and not to pass that problem on to future Presidents and future Congresses. I ran for office to solve problems."[52] A concern for the nation's future, rather than an interest in his political fortunes, motivated Bush's call to reform Social Security.

In this effort, Bush sought to enlist citizens to persuade a reluctant, politically cautious Congress to enact legislation, assuring audiences that they could raise an efficacious voice on this important issue. Although Congress would not lead, it could not resist an assertive public indefinitely. Bush explained that he decided to travel around the country "because I think the American people actually have a lot to do with how Congress responds. You may not think that, but having been up there long enough to tell you how it works, you can make a difference in how people [members of Congress] respond." President Bush intimated that citizens shared his preference for bold and decisive action. Together, they would form an irresistible political force. Members of Congress would accede when they discerned a shift in the political landscape. Bush explained that politicians "calculate there's a political cost when dealing with a tough issue." An engaged citizenry would increase the costs of maintaining the status quo. On this score, Bush predicted that "those who obstruct reform, no matter what party they're in, will pay a political price."[53] President Bush portrayed himself as the right politician to form an alliance with citizens against Congress, since the president and the people both disliked the waffling, weak-kneed behavior of most politicians. Sharing a common policy agenda, the president and the people would force congressional action.

Invoking FDR's courage, Bush argued that changed times required changes to the program. Policymakers designed the original Social Security Act for the America they knew. In his various appearances, Bush pointed to the same trends to explain the challenges facing Social Security. First, the ratio of workers to retirees had decreased substantially in the years since the creation of the program. Bush maintained that the "system works well when you got a bunch of workers paying in for a few beneficiaries. That's the way it was when Franklin Roosevelt designed the system. . . . What's changed is there is a bulge of people fixing to retire called the baby boomers." Second, average life expectancies had increased since the 1930s. This created a situation in which "you've got people who have been made promises by the government receiving checks for a longer period of time than was initially envisioned under Social Security."[54] Third, benefit amounts had increased in real terms since Social Security began paying annuities. Irregular increases became standardized in the early 1970s, when Congress established a formula causing benefits to grow at a faster rate than inflation. President Bush contended that Social Security would face serious financial difficulties as soon as 2018, when benefits paid to retirees exceeded the revenue generated by the payroll tax.

In describing these challenges, Bush regularly cast the situation as a "mathematical problem." As he summarized: "More people living longer, getting greater benefits with fewer people paying into the system. The math just doesn't work anymore." A mathematical framing of the problem created an inevitable outcome: the system required restructuring. Highlighting the "math" of Social Security, President Bush suggested that the relevant debate did not concern policy preferences. The present system simply—numerically, objectively—would not last. The numbers did not add up. Additional revenue might postpone the day of reckoning, but revenue would not alter the basic formula: "You can put all the money in you want, but because of the demographics and the math, there's not going to be anything left." A mathematical frame served as an implicit rebuke of charges that the president had propagated a false sense of crisis. As the president observed: "These numbers are real; they're justifiable. You can ask the experts." His administration did not fabricate a crisis; it merely analyzed the numbers produced by experts. Further, a mathematical problem demanded the assent of opponents of personal accounts. The "math says, 'We've got a problem.'" The math left no room for debate: "When you see people who say, 'Well, there's really not a problem,' just— the facts speak for themselves."[55]

In this explanation, Bush distanced himself from the experts. If audiences had questions about the math, the experts—and not Bush—could provide answers. President Bush did not pursue the path of his predecessor, who often conveyed an aura of expertise regarding his policy priorities. Had he done so, Bush could have offered particular insight combining his study of the issue with his role as chief advocate for private accounts. Yet, associating himself with experts would have distanced Bush from his audiences and reaffirmed the very status hierarchies that he wished to deemphasize. Still, by intimating that he possessed no more information about Social Security's finances than his audience, Bush professed a disingenuous ignorance. As a president dedicated to establishing private accounts, Bush knew the facts and their contexts better than the primary and secondary audiences participating in and watching the town-hall meetings to learn more about Social Security's future.

Still, from Bush's perspective, the math portended a trajectory toward bankruptcy, which would occur when today's younger workers reached retirement age. In discussing the system's future, Bush suggested that bankruptcy entailed a complete lack of funds. To various audiences, he asserted that "in 2042, it's bust." To other audiences, he held that "in 2042, the system will be broke." Oftentimes, Bush modified "bust" and "broke" with "flat." He insisted to some audiences that "in 2042, it is flat bust" and "in 2042, the system is flat broke." Bust and broke—especially "flat bust" and "flat broke"—connoted an especially severe form of bankruptcy. Whereas the latter denotes an inability to pay all of one's creditors, bust and broke connote a condition of being penniless, of complete financial ruin. Bush used these terms interchangeably, treating them as equivalent signifiers. So, for example, he contended that in "2042, it's bust; it's bankrupt." Equating these terms, Bush implied that Social Security would pay no benefits at all in 2042. In perhaps his most explicit expression of this view, Bush told an audience in Westfield, New Jersey, that "in 2042, it goes broke, for good. It not only goes in the red, but whatever paper is available in the form of IOUs is gone. I mean, it's just—it's a fact."[56] Bush's colloquialisms functioned as rhetorical intensifiers. If dates like 2018 and 2042 suggested an abstract and distant problem, then depicting Social Security as going "broke" and "bust" conveyed an unambiguous message of impending financial doom.

However, this representation of the system's bankruptcy contrasted with the reports of the Social Security trustees. The trustees' 2004 annual report characterized the long-term finances of Social Security in a less drastic manner: "Present tax rates would be sufficient to pay 73 percent of scheduled benefits after trust fund exhaustion in 2042 and 68 percent of scheduled benefits in 2078." The trustees did not release their 2005 report until April, by which time Bush had held many of his town-hall meetings, but it expressed a similarly mixed message: "Present tax rates would be sufficient to pay 74 percent of scheduled benefits after trust fund exhaustion in 2041 and 68 percent of scheduled benefits in 2079."[57] President Bush did not mention either set of percentages during his town-hall meetings. Nor did he acknowledge that Social Security would continue to pay a large majority of scheduled benefits after 2042 if no changes were made to the program. Rather than clarifying matters, Bush's regular-guy character misrepresented the finances of Social Security. Paying three-quarters of scheduled benefits constituted a dramatically less severe crisis than the pennilessness connoted by "flat broke."

President Bush asserted that Social Security would experience financial difficulties long before 2042 because policymakers could not rely on the Social Security trust fund to provide benefits. Like other advocates of private accounts, the president dismissed the trust fund as "a pile of IOUs." He repeated this characterization to virtually every audience he addressed. As a pile of IOUs, the trust fund amounted to potentially worthless paper: "There is no Social Security savings account. There's paper in a file cabinet." Bush contrasted this paper with the "solid asset[s]" of an individual's investment account. Whereas an investment account conveyed strength and stability, the trust fund connoted weakness and insecurity. Printed on flimsy paper that risked workers' retirements, the bonds in the trust fund tied their worth to the capricious decision making of a spendthrift Congress. Bush told audiences that "we're spending your money and left behind some paper that can only be good if the government decides to redeem the paper." The same body that issued the IOUs would decide whether it wished to honor them. In vouching for this characterization of the trust fund, Bush presented himself as a witness. As he told several audiences, he saw firsthand the "file cabinet with IOUs in West Virginia. I actually went and saw the file cabinet."[58]

Drawing on his unaffected demeanor, Bush cut through the layers of discourse to determine the truth of Social Security's finances. Able to discern pertinent information, Bush possessed a common sense lacking in most politicians. As members of the Washington elite, most politicians spoke the obfuscating language of Treasury bonds and actuarial tables, creating realities where none existed. By contrast, Bush did not succumb to talk of certificates and accrued interest. He sought verification in the most unimpeachable manner possible: direct sensory perception. Bush knew what he knew because he saw it. The sureness of sense counteracted the distortions of elite discourse. No matter what the elites said, Bush saw the supposed trust fund, and it amounted to "paper in a file cabinet." In this way, Bush acted as the eyes of his audiences. They could trust his assessment because he simply reported what he saw.

In presenting his criticism of the trust fund, President Bush raised an implicit contrasting image of a proper trust fund. During one meeting, Bush maintained that "some of you probably think there is a kind of—a bank, a Social Security trust bank. But that's not what's happened over time. . . . There are empty promises, but there's no pile of money that you thought was there when you retired." To another audience, he explained that "there is no vault holding your cash, waiting for you to retire." Criticizing the trust fund, Bush raised the alternative image of a bank vault, perhaps located at Fort Knox, overflowing with stacks of gold bullion or mountains of large-denomination bills. Armed guards watched this bounty and kept it safe from pilfering. No one entered or exited the vault without passing through several layers of security. No one—not even the president himself—obtained unlimited access to the vault. When contrasted to this real, non-abstract, awe-inspiring, non-interest-bearing alternative, the Treasury bonds constituting the trust fund appeared as ephemeral IOUs. The present trust fund lacked weight; its physicality seemed inconsequential when considering its putative financial significance. After visiting the Bureau of Public Debt in Parkersburg, West Virginia, President Bush remarked: "There is no trust fund, just IOUs that I saw firsthand. . . . The office here in Parkersburg stores those IOUs. They're stacked in a file cabinet. Imagine, the retirement security for future generations is sitting in a file cabinet."[59] As a Texan, Bush valued size in trust funds; he expected something more substantial than papers in a file cabinet. The material compactness of the trust fund made it seem unreal. The president criticized the trust fund as an abstract financial instrument by raising the implicit standard of an actual physical place.

Whereas the math assured safety for older workers and retirees, bankruptcy and an unreliable trust fund created danger for younger workers. Along these lines, in his town-hall meetings, Bush conveyed different messages to different generations. He repeatedly assured older audiences that they need not worry, insisting that Social Security "is not a problem for people who have retired or near-retired. This is not a problem for people who are now on Social Security [or] who were born before 1950. It is not a problem. I don't care what they tell you. I don't care what the brochures say." The "they" who produced "brochures" consisted of entrenched interests benefiting from the status quo. *They* preferred the current arrangement, even if it portended long-term woes, and *they* would pit generations against each other to maintain the status quo. *They* practiced a scare politics by leveraging the political engagement of older citizens for their self-serving purposes. President Bush encouraged older workers and retirees to resist these tactics. He assured older audiences that they need not fear change: "The Social Security trust is sound and solvent for people who are counting on the checks today and people who are going to be counting on the checks who are near retired. It's just the way it is."[60] Any other message constituted a craven turn to politics.

However, President Bush offered no reassurances to younger audiences. Instead, he warned of financial insecurity, holding that "the problem exists for younger workers. And that's why in my State of the Union I put this issue in a generational context." A generational context better accounted for societal trends and the shaky status of the trust fund than a uniform approach. Moreover, since the value of the IOUs in the trust fund depended on the federal government's ability and willingness to pay, those workers whose retirement benefits depended on the trust fund risked more than older workers who would receive benefits through the payroll tax. And this caused the president great concern. He disclosed that "what really makes me worried is I understand that we have made promises for younger Americans that we can't keep." So long as Congress filled the trust fund with IOUs instead of real assets, it could continue to profess a commitment to future generations, even if this constituted an empty promise. And yet, while President Bush qualified his message in discussing the likelihood of benefits for older and younger workers, his message to the latter—like his discussion of the system's bankruptcy—suggested an all-or-nothing outcome. For instance, in one conversation with a young worker, President Bush asserted that "I'm not so sure you're going to have a check." The worker responded: "And that's something, as a 23-year-old person who's paying into Social Security now, really scares me." The president replied: "I hope so."[61] In this exchange and others, the president represented a future without benefits for younger workers. No check—not even a reduced check—would appear unless policymakers fundamentally restructured the system. Although President Bush criticized fear appeals as cynical when directed toward older audiences, he invoked fear to motivate younger audiences.

Social Security and Ownership

Harnessing the power of compound interest, personal accounts offered investors a safe and substantial rate of return. President Bush explained that "there's something called the compounding rate of interest. In other words, if you set aside dollars over time, they will grow with interest, and it compounds. It gets bigger and bigger and bigger." Whereas Treasury bonds sat diminutively in an obscure filing cabinet in West Virginia, compound interest enabled personal accounts to grow before investors' eyes. Moreover, its "bigness" better comported with the magnitude of retirement than the seemingly inconsequential file cabinet. Only compound interest, with its substantial bulk, could refigure the present, gloomy math of Social Security, so much so that it would create wealth for all owners of personal accounts. Bush offered the example of a worker earning $35,000 annually who contributed 4 percent of payroll taxes to a personal account. Upon retirement, this person would have amassed a quarter of a million dollars. By contrast, insurance did not possess sufficient resources to save Social Security. Bush asserted that "the government can't possibly pay the promises we have made, as you've seen from the charts. It's just impossible to do so. So my idea is to let you take some of your own money, set it aside, let it earn interest over time, let it compound." Bush wanted to enlarge everyone's assets: "We can give every American the chance to tap into the power of compound interest."[62] As a power, compound interest worked its magic on all assets, large or small. Over time, compound interest would create wealth for everyone who used it.

This wealth accrued to the owners of the personal accounts, which constituted the primary virtue of privatization. Above all else, personal accounts enabled ownership. Utilizing the near-universality of Social Security, personal accounts would permit workers to possess capital. With individuals owning the accounts, the spirit of ownership would pervade society as a whole. Bush embraced ownership as an organizing societal goal, declaring: "I strongly believe in an ownership society. I want more people owning their home, owning their own business, owning and managing their own health care account, and owning and managing their retirement account. I think it makes America a better place."⁶³ Exemplifying the qualities that the president admired in individuals and the nation, ownership promised to ameliorate various aspects of life as it spread across the country. Building an ownership society would accentuate admirable American qualities and improve an already enviable way of life.

Making his case, President Bush enumerated several qualities of an ownership society. As he spoke, his tone shifted from his somber discussion of math and bankruptcy. The president spoke enthusiastically, sketching a bright future of prosperity and goodwill. He stressed that "personal accounts are critical to building an ownership society, a more optimistic and more hopeful America." He observed that "there is something incredibly vital about a society in which people own something." He maintained that "helping people build up an asset base . . . is a vital part of a stable future." Similarly, he contended that "there's nothing healthier for a society in which they see an asset base grow."⁶⁴ Optimism, hope, vitality, stability, health—these qualities appeared as reasons for President Bush's commitment to achieving an ownership society. Optimistic and hopeful, an ownership society looked confidently toward the future, setting goals and working purposefully towards their achievement. An ownership society could move ahead with assurance because it possessed the energy and strength—vitality and health—to achieve its goals. An ownership society did not sit about wistfully, wishing for unseen and unknown forces to move it along. Proceeding energetically and confidently, an ownership society cultivated stable progress and growth. An ownership society exhibited care to build on its strength, rather than risking its accomplishments to achieve a further goal. In this way, an ownership society exhibited the unflappable confidence of past success, rather than the nervous excitement of present speculation.

In its essence, an ownership society represented the aggregated power of individuals, for individual—and not collective—ownership motivated Bush's vision. Ownership and individuals constituted a mutually informative relationship. Individuals could utilize the power of ownership to benefit themselves and society, while ownership, in turn, could transform individuals. Bush demanded that "Congress ought to consider personal accounts . . . because [they] empower the individual." This promised a significant reversal of decades of government policies, which actually disempowered individuals and placed the federal government in a position of paternalistic control. Insurance propagated this injustice by leaving retirees dependent on others for their retirement security; workers provided the funding, and bureaucrats made the decisions.

Personal accounts promised to transform dependency into independence. Assessing the comments of a worker who had discussed managing her 401(k) accounts, President Bush judged: "You listen to Betty's language. She's talking about her assets. She's not relying upon the government. She says, 'These are my assets, and I own these assets.' And that's important."[65] Positioning himself as a peer, Bush beamed with pride in Betty's accomplishments. He cheered her success as if he were a friend or coworker—someone who knew her personally and appreciated the newfound confidence and energy in her bearing. Bush wanted to revel in the successes of others, too. Ownership would instill pride and dignity in everyone who experienced it. As Betty's case demonstrated, an increasing account represented a tremendous personal accomplishment. The assets in the account reflected the resourcefulness and self-reliance of the investor, who sought information and made sound decisions. Further, since ownership conferred autonomy and control, it restored the dignity of human agency to people who had looked to others for assistance. Retirees no longer would have to act as supplicants beseeching Congress for increased retirement benefits. They would decide for themselves.

The independence and self-control of ownership appeared especially important when contrasted with the uncertainty of promised Social Security benefits. President Bush asserted that personal accounts would "give our children and grandchildren a chance to replace a burden of uncertainty with a new opportunity. Instead of leaving their full retirement in the hands of future politicians, younger workers will be able to take part of their retirement into their own hands." Self-control engendered peace of mind, since individuals could count on themselves to make the right decisions for their retirement. After all, concern for one's retirement constituted a proper self-interest. Politicians also acted self-interestedly, but their self-interest did not necessarily coincide with the interests of their constituents—either individually or collectively. Politicians considered a range of factors in determining their self-interests, and they responded to a range of appeals in making their decisions, many of which lay outside the reach of citizens. Unlike politics, ownership did not trade in promises. Stressing the differences between the present Social Security system and personal accounts, President Bush explained: "Your Social Security benefit is simply a promise. You don't own it; the government will decide. If the government can't pay for it, the government says, 'Well, we're going to reduce your benefits.' When you have your own personal account, it's yours. The government cannot take it away."[66] A secure retirement lay in possession, not promises.

Because ownership entailed control, President Bush promised that account owners could leave accumulated assets to heirs. He maintained that "in a personal account, if you had one of those and your assets were growing and you passed away, you could leave it to whomever you want." Since a personal account represented the property of its owner, its owner could distribute the assets in the account as desired. For Bush, this promised feature of personal accounts compared favorably with the present system, which confiscated workers' money. With the present system, he held, "somebody works hard, doesn't live long enough to get the benefits, dies earlier than the national average, and that money that they put in the system—unless you've got younger kids—just is gone, goes to help somebody else." Insurance constituted a coercive income-transfer system. Money distributed to "somebody else," even if helping to secure someone else's retirement, amounted to money lost for the contributor and his/her family. Bush likened this lack of property rights to a disappearance: "Somebody has worked all their life, contributed to the system, dies early, and the money just disappears." Bush declared that the present system "doesn't seem fair to me." Personal accounts promised to restore fairness and extend an important national legacy. Bush maintained that personal accounts would enable "a lot of people to transfer assets from one generation to the next. That's what America is about."[67] Control offered material benefits to owners and their heirs.

Individuals properly controlled personal accounts because they provided the funds for the present Social Security system. President Bush insisted to audiences that "when you pay in payroll taxes, it's your money, it's not the government's money; it's your money—you ought to be allowed to take some of your own money and set it aside in a personal savings account that you can call your own." Politicians traditionally demanded that individuals relinquish their money, but they stripped individuals of the authority of capital. For the president, this represented a basic question of trust: "It's your money. I trust you with your own money. To me that's an attitude that Congress ought to take: We trust you with your own money." Bush's invocation of trust comported with his unassuming self-presentation. Representing himself as familiar, Bush also asserted familiarity with the needs and interests of ordinary Americans. He trusted people because he knew them. He understood their desire to act as agents capable of making competent decisions about their futures; in short, he trusted people as owners. Elite politicians resisted this bond. Unwilling to relinquish the power of ownership, elites exhibited far greater comfort with the standard practice of paternalistic social policy. Lacking trust, elites had no recourse but paternalism, thus betraying a central democratic principle. Recognizing this contradiction, the president hoped to align retirement policy with a longer American tradition of self-determination. He declared that the "strength of our country is trusting the people."[68] In this way, ownership exemplified political values of freedom and liberty.

In addition to empowering people as individuals, ownership fostered political engagement. Ownership promised to turn disaffected and disinterested persons into concerned citizens. President Bush asserted that "the more people watch their assets grow, they're going to be saying, 'I better pay attention to fiscal policy in Washington, D.C.' There's nothing that causes more participation in government than if your wealth is directly associated with the decisions of government." This statement implied that wealthy people participated more in government because wealthy people invested more in government policies. They possessed real, substantial assets that policymakers could adversely impact with bad decisions. The assertion that wealth served as the primary motivator for political participation also dismissed other possible motivations as unimportant or improper. Bush's primary emphasis on wealth suggested that the status of citizen itself—with its legal and social rights and privileges—did not sufficiently motivate political participation. Indeed, at times he indicated that ownership would compel otherwise inattentive individuals to assume their roles as citizens: "It's a notion of getting people to understand that they've got to pay attention to the future of the country when you, on a monthly basis, in some cases on a daily basis if you want to get on the Internet and look at your asset base."[69] Where appeals to civic obligations had failed, ownership would succeed in reviving the body politic.

Yet ownership encouraged a specific form of political participation that emphasized spectatorship and shareholding. President Bush warned that "politicians will be—their actions will be a lot more scrutinized when somebody is watching whether or not the decisions made in

Washington is affecting their work on a daily or quarterly basis."[70] This explanation did not indicate clearly whether the "somebody" (presumably, a citizen-owner) watching politicians would undertake the critical inquiry denoted by scrutiny, or whether the person's charge would end with watching alone. Implying the latter, Bush repeatedly cast political participation as "pay[ing] attention" or exhibiting "more interest" in government policies.[71] These phrases suggested that citizen-owners acted like individual shareholders in a corporation: they observed the proceedings in Washington, and they held authority over these proceedings in the form of the vote, but citizen-owners did not participate in governance themselves. In this way, President Bush circumscribed the agency of participants, constructing a passive mode of citizenship. This passivity did not arise from Bush's use of visual metaphors, but from his separation of seeing from knowing and doing. Scrutiny held the possibility of depicting citizenship as active vision, but Bush reverted to forms of "watching" alone. "Paying attention" indicated increased awareness, but it did not denote the cognition or standing signified in a visual term like "recognizing." Nor did "paying attention" connote the creative, forward-thinking qualities of a visual term like "envisioning." President Bush asked citizens to pay attention, but he did not invite citizens to recognize or envision vibrant democratic practices. Envisioning, for instance, would have encouraged citizens to imagine democratic possibilities. By contrast, watching placed citizens in a reactive mode, leaving the practice of democracy to others.

Nevertheless, President Bush asserted that watching initiated inquiry, arguing that people who lacked investment knowledge and experience would learn to function competently in the financial arena. Bush declared that "there's nothing like solving financial illiteracy when you're watching—when you're making decisions for your own money. You start asking questions; there's advisers, there's people around to help you make a rational decision what to do with your own money. And a good way to learn is when you're watching your own money grow."[72] This formulation constituted a weak recovery of agency. Bush ascribed learning to citizen-investors, but such learning consisted of surrounding oneself with trustworthy advisors who possessed specialized knowledge of money management. Reason modified good decisions, but citizen-investors did not possess the quality of reason per se. At best, they required the help of others to make a "rational decision." Watching taught citizen-investors to ask questions of others, but watching did not enable citizen-investors to discover the answers themselves. Transposed to democracy, this formulation still placed citizen-investors in a passive state.

For Bush, the pedagogical power of ownership promised to grant independence to individuals and groups. He bemoaned that "there are some neighborhoods in which financial literacy has not been passed on from one generation to the next. And we've got to break that cycle." Financial illiteracy made people vulnerable to elite control. Elites spoke about empowerment while propagating paternalistic policies to maintain power, leaving residents of targeted communities to languish as dependents forced to rely on the productivity of others to survive. Disavowing this disappointing path, Bush shifted referents from breaking a "cycle of dependency" to breaking a "cycle of financial illiteracy." He exhorted that "the way to tackle the issue is not to deny people the great aspect of ownership but to reach out to faith organizations, community-based organizations, and help people become financially literate." Bush insisted that "we shouldn't run away from ownership. We ought to provide the means to encourage ownership."[73] In running away from ownership, elites ran away from poor local communities, which they regarded with suspicion. Unimpressed with hierarchy, Bush saw ownership as a direct, tangible means of ameliorating everyday life in poor communities.

For all its potential virtues, an ownership society exhibited a crucial tension between inclusion and exclusion, between owners and nonowners. Ownership offered an exclusive perspective on political issues that Bush hoped would eventually include all Americans. With respect to its exclusive dimension, an ownership society not only engendered political participation, but it established ownership as a necessary condition for political participation. As Bush asserted repeatedly: "When a person owns something, they have a vital stake in the future of the country."[74] By itself, this statement did not limit stake-holding to owners. As a hypothetical statement, this formulation allowed for the possibility that other attributes besides ownership could enable someone to obtain a stake in the future of the country. However, Bush emphasized ownership as the central concept that cultivated values of independence, control, and stake-holding. He committed his administration to achieving an ownership society—not a stake-holder society. Valuing personal accounts as key policy exemplars of ownership, he extolled the virtues of ownership during his town-hall meetings.

Read in the context of his barnstorming tour, Bush's linkage of ownership and stake-holding transformed ownership from a sufficient to a
necessary condition of stake-holding. As such, ownership granted citizens
exclusive standing and voice in determining the future of the nation.
Only owners could participate in policy debates, for only they possessed
the judgment necessary to make informed policy decisions. Since government decisions threatened to impact owners directly (thus their political
supervision), only they could properly offer opinions on government policies. By implication, nonowners did not possess the qualities necessary for
political participation. Lacking property, nonowners failed to demonstrate
substantial implication in government actions, and they did not exhibit
the independence of ownership.

Bush expressed dissatisfaction with the current extent of ownership
in America, however. So long as ownership remained an exclusive possession, the nation would not realize its true democratic potential. Bush
hoped to extend ownership to all Americans, and he regarded personal
accounts as an excellent vehicle for doing so. Bush insisted that "every
citizen—every citizen—has got the capacity to manage his or her own
money. And if they don't, we help them understand how to. . . . I believe
the so-called investor class ought to be every American, regardless of his
or her background."[75] Proclaiming his belief in the abilities of ordinary
Americans, Bush demystified investing and confidently invoked the
equality of the market. To suggest that every citizen possessed investment
competency—or could learn such competency—implied that successful
investing did not require a highly specialized set of skills. Investing did
not require years of education and training, nor did it require mastery of
an esoteric vocabulary. Instead, successful investing drew on judgment
and honest effort. Moreover, investors could rest assured that these qualities would produce success, because the market treated everyone equally.
The market did not distinguish between large and small investors, and it
paid no attention to social markers of gender, race, and class. The market
served as the weapon of ordinary folks and the enemy of elites. Although
participation in the market required ownership standing—whether one
purchased stocks, bonds, or some other financial instrument—personal
accounts promised to make ownership universal.

President Bush chided opponents of personal accounts for what he
regarded as an effort to disqualify certain groups of people as capable
investors. He observed that "there's a certain notion in America that the

investor class is only a certain type of person. I just don't believe that. I don't subscribe to that. I don't think that's what America is about." Bush believed in an America without class divisions. The notion of an intrinsic investor class betrayed a hereditary-based understanding of social order more appropriate to European monarchies than American democracy. An intrinsic view of investment savvy attached personal virtues to socioeconomic standing and denied the possibility of social mobility. Moreover, in American history, class discrimination often implicated race, and Bush discerned this linkage in the position against personal accounts. The very phrase "investor class" appeared racially coded: "The investor class—it kind of sounds like to me, you know, a certain race of people living in a certain area. I believe everybody's got the capability of being in the investor class."[76]

In this way, objections to personal accounts enabled President Bush to display his solidarity with ordinary Americans and to contrast his cultivated image of genuineness with a snobbery that he attributed to most politicians. By opposing personal accounts, defenders of insurance actually perpetuated racism by treating low-income, urban, black citizens as incapable of providing independently for their retirement. Revealing their elitist character, defenders of insurance kept black Americans dependent on Social Security because they lacked confidence in black Americans. By contrast, President Bush expressed confidence in all Americans regardless of race and socioeconomic standing. Personal accounts thus represented a more American approach to retirement—manifesting equality and opportunity—than insurance.

Social trends provided solid evidence against viewing investment savvy as an intrinsic trait. Rejecting the notion of an "investor class," President Bush argued that the growth of 401(k)s had spurred the emergence of "an investor society." This represented a dramatic change from the era when Social Security was established. Bush observed that "when our folks were coming up, there wasn't anything like a 401(k)." The workplace pensions of the boomers' parents mirrored the insurance basis of Social Security, so they accepted a system in which politicians and bureaucrats assumed responsibility for their retirement. However, familiarity with 401(k)s had changed the expectations of the boomers and their children. Feeling constrained by insurance, these postwar generations associated retirement with choice and control. Bush remarked that "401(k)s have become a part of how people think." Contemporary workers planned their retirements in light of the investment accounts they earned from employers, because they could not trust government promises about Social Security. Whereas 401(k)s appeared familiar, Social Security, with its doubtful future finances, remained mysterious and uncertain. Workers knew the balances in their 401(k)s, and they could invest their assets as they desired. Workers did not know how much—if anything—they would receive in Social Security benefits, and they did not control the trust fund. Along these lines, Bush identified a gap in understanding between members of Congress and their constituents. He held that "there's a cultural change in America. Congress is lagging behind the cultural change, but there's a lot of folks who are comfortable about watching their own money grow, a whole lot of folks."[77] According to Bush, Congress did not wish to relinquish the power it had acquired over the years. By comparison, the president, a man of the people, saw his own hopes and dreams represented in the people's desire for self-determination. Aligning himself with the American people against a recalcitrant Congress, Bush hoped that their combined will would spur change.

Mediating State-Public Interactions

The 109th Congress concluded without passing Social Security legislation. In the 2006 congressional elections, Democrats regained majorities in the Senate and House, recapturing the lower chamber for the first time since the Republicans fomented revolution in 1994. With the change in congressional leadership and a public increasingly dissatisfied with the conduct and policies of the administration, the electoral mandate of 2004 morphed into decidedly lame-duck status. The portentous moment anticipated by Piñera, Moore, and other advocates of investment had departed. Cruelly, the president's regular-guy image did not succeed in selling private accounts to skeptical citizens. By mid-March, 2005, the *Washington Post* reported that only one in three Americans "approves of the way President Bush is dealing with Social Security." Indeed, the same poll discovered that 58 percent of respondents "say they are more inclined to oppose the administration's reform plans as they learn more about [the plans]."[78] Poll respondents may have regarded the president as a potentially entertaining drinking buddy, but they did not share his vision for retirement policy.

Although unsuccessful, the Bush administration crafted contextual and discursive elements of the barnstorming tour to mediate tensions of state/public-sphere interaction. Rather than fostering open deliberation, the town-hall meetings exhibited a highly constructed sense of equality among the president and the other participants. The screening of potential attendees and the rehearsing of questions and answers effectively granted Bush control of the meetings while he appeared to interact in an informal, unstructured setting. Moreover, excluding opponents of private accounts permitted Bush to perform the image of a likable guy among constituents who already liked him. Bush did not have to worry about troublesome questions or awkward moments that might have prompted a defensive or peevish presidential response. No one tested Bush's likeability by pressing him to articulate a position that might have alienated some viewers.

In his discourse, President Bush distinguished himself from other politicians to maintain common standing with the other meeting participants. Bush could not deny his authority as president, but he did represent himself as a nonpolitician who stood with the people against the Washington elite. Because he knew them, Bush trusted citizens as owners who could make competent decisions regarding their financial futures. Elites preferred the standard policy practice of paternalism, which enabled elites to retain control over people's lives. The president appreciated that payroll taxes constituted the people's money, whereas elites spent the revenue from the payroll tax as their own. Bush believed that all Americans would learn investment skills, while elites subscribed to a hierarchical and racist notion of an investor class. Further, the president spoke the people's language, calling situations as he saw them, like the "flat-broke" future of insurance-based Social Security. Elites enunciated an obfuscatory idiom of trust funds, confusing people and hiding their financial machinations.

No president campaigned as hard against Social Security as George W. Bush. He may not have created private accounts, but Bush exacerbated public concern about Social Security. In the wake of the barnstorming tour, Americans may doubt Social Security more than at any moment since the program's inception. After two decades of privatization debates, insurance no longer reigns supreme as the guiding principle of retirement policy. Debate participants have contested Social Security's fundamental values as much as its finances.

Securing a Vibrant Democracy

FDR understood the dynamics of politics and public policy. Defending the dedicated financing of Social Security, he recounted that "we put those payroll contributions there so as to give the contributors a legal, moral, and political right to collect their pensions and their unemployment benefits. With those taxes in there, no damn politician can ever scrap my social security program."[1] And he was right. Dedicated financing distinguished Old-Age Insurance from most other social policies and provided the program with a compelling basis for support. Old-Age Insurance ostensibly operated independently, and its conspicuous character enabled Americans to develop a proprietary view of the program. Supporters invoked its contributory basis to demonstrate the superiority of insurance over assistance in building public support for the program. Of course, taxes financed both insurance and assistance programs for the elderly, and early recipients of both programs received more in benefits than they paid in taxes. However, the idea of paying for one's benefits (through the payroll tax) helped assure the symbolic priority of insurance, sparing Social Security from the attacks on "welfare" that have attended debates over social policy in the United States.

Although FDR's decision demonstrated his political prowess, he could not control the meanings that people would associate with Social Security, neither in its founding debates nor as participants have debated changes to Social Security over its history. From the beginning, policymakers, committee witnesses, and Americans more generally have understood Social Security variously, and the very qualities that ensured Social Security's existence have served as sites of polysemy enabling different policy trajectories. The idea of paying for one's benefits applies just as well to an investment-based program, since investments also may draw on a dedicated funding source that returns benefits to individuals. The perception that Social Security is unlike other social policies has provided advocates of privatization with a symbolic means of arguing for a fundamental restructuring of the program. Advocates of privatization have pressed the contributory logic of the program, insisting that workers and retirees should be free to make decisions about, and seek better returns on, their money. Advocates have contended that doing so would create a more direct link between program participants and their money. Neither advocates of privatization nor supporters of social insurance have proposed eliminating Social Security—and, as FDR anticipated, it is unlikely that many politicians will. However, even after the unsuccessful conclusion of President Bush's barnstorming tour, Social Security may persist in the future as an insurance or investment program.

By identifying meaning and, in turn, rhetoric as central to policymaking, I risk complicating and confusing our ethical judgments about arguments over public policy. If we could discern a stable "reality" to serve as a standard for measuring competing claims, we could judge better and worse arguments incontrovertibly. We could determine "right" by measuring the comparative distance between claims and an independent ground. However, a rhetoric-free reality must forever elude us, because any policy objective, as my introductory example of "providing retirement benefits" demonstrates, necessarily implicates our understanding of its key terms. Further, in this context, "reality" does not serve as a heuristic term. To be sure, we should determine as best we can the truth or falsity of factual claims about Social Security, such as the percentage of workers whose income exceeds the cap on payroll taxes, or the comparative cost of public and private retirement annuities. But these issues do not constitute the heart of the debates, which involve weighing potentially competing values like security and individualism as well as, of course, purposes of insurance and investment. To decide among these claims, we require an alternative ethical framework that recognizes value pluralism and accounts for the unavoidable contingency of human affairs. Put differently, we need to resist the tendency to treat Social Security as a technical issue for experts, and instead appreciate it as a matter of public debate for all citizens. Doing so demands passionate, informed arguments about the values, principles, and goals we wish to pursue through public policy.

In this conclusion, I address the issue of ethical policy debate directly, considering how participants may debate changes to Social Security as well as what I regard as an appropriate ethics of democracy for judging Social Security. First, I identify five characteristics of vibrant policy debate—honesty, context, openness, better selves, and vigor—to assess what went wrong in the privatization debates and to suggest how we may deliberate about Social Security in the future. Second, embracing an alternative to a market-based approach to social policy, I argue that a democracy-based approach will help us achieve far more important goals than those identified by advocates of investment—namely, providing the material and symbolic resources that people need to enact their primary roles as engaged citizens.

Fostering Vibrant Policy Debate

Attending to the rhetorical force of policymaking does not grant debate participants license to say whatever they please, since we still should hold people accountable for their claims. Towards this end, I explicate five characteristics of potentially vibrant policy debate: participants should speak honestly, contextualize their claims, exhibit openness to contrary evidence, appeal to audiences' better selves, and engage each other vigorously. I draw on examples from the previous chapters to demonstrate problems in the privatization debates and to imagine how we can do better.

At a basic level, participants in policy debates ought to engage each other honestly. In the contemporary period, we have learned through many painful national and global policy failures that a call for honesty does not represent a naive attempt to cling to a quaint relic of an earlier age—a call for honesty does not betray a hopeless desire for an ideal mode of communication free of human passion and interest.[2] Quite the contrary, honesty serves a decidedly pragmatic function, since debate loses its coherence when we cannot believe our interlocutors. Further, honesty is a complex term that signals various responsibilities and commitments from debate participants, such as expressing one's motives and position explicitly so that audiences may judge the relative worth of policy positions. In this sense, honesty requires a participant to advocate a case confidently, with the express goal of persuading an audience to adopt one's position. From this perspective, libertarian critics of Social Security ought to state their principled objections explicitly.

With respect to honesty, the privatization debates frequently proceeded under false pretenses, as the Wehner memo dramatically evidenced. Exhibiting a harmful skepticism toward public debate, the memo identified a principled rationale for opposing Social Security, but envisioned a public campaign conducted by other means. In seeking to "move [Social Security] away from dependency on government and toward giving greater power and responsibility to the individual,"[3] the memo expressed fundamental opposition to an insurance-based approach to retirement policy. However, Wehner recommended that the administration seek its objectives by stoking public concerns about the financial condition of Social Security, referring to this tactic as the "pre-condition to authentic reform." In this light, we can reasonably conclude that Wehner—and, by extension, others in the administration—lacked confidence that the public shared its view of Social Security as perpetuating a dangerous dependency. Otherwise, the memo would not have encouraged the president to base his arguments on finances rather than purposes. Wehner anticipated the forthcoming debates as a "monumental clash of ideas," but his proposed strategy evidenced a fear of debate.

Honesty also entails acknowledging one's role in policymaking and representing events accurately according to one's knowledge of a situation. President Bush failed to uphold these responsibilities during his barnstorming tour, presenting himself as a bystander to events that he actively influenced, and misrepresenting Social Security's financial future to suit his agenda. Discussing the challenges confronting Social Security, Bush depicted the situation as a "mathematical problem," thereby denying his agency and asserting that "the facts speak for themselves."[4] But facts do not speak, and policy trajectories do not develop independently of human intervention. Whether Bush and other policymakers committed themselves to addressing Social Security's finances through an insurance or investment approach, they would have to make a decision. Bush may have disavowed agency because he wanted to escape blame if citizens rejected privatization, but evasiveness does not produce vibrant debate.

In terms of his representation of events, Bush repeatedly cast the future of Social Security in terms more dire than those warranted by Social Security Administration assessments. Bush depicted Social Security as going "flat bust" and "flat broke," asserting to one audience that "in 2042, it goes broke, for good. It not only goes in the red, but whatever paper is available in the form of IOUs is gone."[5] Bush issued these pronouncements even as he knew (or, at least, should have known) that the Social Security trustees reported that the program, without any changes, would continue to pay the large majority of benefits well into the twenty-first century. If questioned, Bush may have followed the lead of Rep. Clay Shaw and appealed to a legal definition of bankruptcy, but this would have constituted a weak defense of his position, since "flat bust," "flat broke," and "gone" strongly suggested that Social Security would pay no benefits whatsoever in three decades. In recasting Social Security's future from paying a majority of benefits to paying no benefits, President Bush advanced a deeply inaccurate representation of events.

Ethical policy debates obligate participants to place statements in context, since the same story, quotation, or statistic can convey very different meanings when understood in different contexts. An objection may appear as an endorsement if one neglects qualifiers, or an isolated instance may appear as a trend if one discounts contrary cases. Although debate participants cannot possess perfect knowledge, nor should they provide an extensive history of every particular point, participants should consider the contexts of their claim-making. Scholars, in turn, should analyze policy debates with an eye towards discrepancies between the context of the hearing room and the other social worlds inhabited by participants and others absent from the debates. For instance, in demanding an investment-based approach to retirement, representatives of Third Millennium compared Social Security to their work experiences. Insisting on change, Elizabeth O'Connor maintained that "if Fortune 500 companies can trust my peers to do the strategic planning and to help program the chips that run their computers and their companies, surely our political leaders can trust us when it comes to investing a modest portion of our own Social Security taxes."[6] Expressing assurance, O'Connor represented a generation eager to adopt a new approach to retirement. But her reference to "peers" and her use of plural pronouns—"us" and "our"—betrayed the particular context of her claim. O'Connor and other Third Millennium representatives did not speak for all young workers— they spoke for a well-paid professional class. A young person employed in a low-paying, no-benefits retail cashier job likely would not recognize him- or herself in O'Connor's account. Instead of highlighting "strategic planning," this young worker might characterize employment as anxious and alienating. Moreover, this person would have different needs than O'Connor and her "peers." Although representatives of Third Millennium might willingly forsake insurance and its associated benefits like disability, others would regard insurance as an irreplaceable source of security.

Of course, people can triumph under difficult circumstances, but context importantly illuminates their achievements. To illustrate the virtues of private accounts, advocates sometimes celebrated the efforts of low-paid workers who somehow managed to save considerable sums of money by the end of their lives. In this spirit, Sen. Bob Kerrey shared the story of Oseola McCarty, who had worked for seventy years as a washerwoman. Living an austere lifestyle, she had built a significant estate. Upon retirement, McCarty donated $150,000 to the University of Southern Mississippi, located in her hometown of Hattiesburg. Sen. Kerrey held that her story demonstrated "the magic of compounding interest rates."[7] True, but McCarty's story also demonstrated how pervasive structural inequities shape people's lives. And no one in the hearing room pursued this context. No one asked why McCarty had worked so long under such low-wage, exhausting conditions. No one noted that she left school in the sixth grade to care for a sick aunt. No one mentioned that had McCarty wished to attend Southern Mississippi when she was eighteen, she would have been barred because she was black. Nor did anyone mention that for much of her working life McCarty had been unable to contribute to Social Security, or that her earnings would have produced meager returns through private accounts.[8] In short, debate participants celebrated her triumph, but largely ignored the conditions over which she triumphed. Yet this context holds important lessons about the limits of insurance and investment approaches absent a wider policy commitment to tackle larger issues of inequality.

Honesty and context imply a basic attitude of openness toward debate, which involves a willingness to reflect critically on one's assumptions and to reconsider claims in light of contrary evidence. Openness should not produce an impartial or ambivalent attachment to one's position. Quite the opposite: participants ought to debate each other with passion and commitment even as an awareness of human limitations makes salient our capacity to learn from others, including learning that sometimes we are wrong.[9] From this perspective, citizens and scholars should join with the editorialists who rebuked President Bush for holding pro-privatization, invitation-only "town-hall meetings." In these venues, rather than engaging others with an openness toward debate, Bush cynically implicated his interlocutors in a large-scale public-relations campaign. Citizens in a democracy should demand that presidents advocate for their policy priorities among diverse audiences, rather than meeting only with people who share their viewpoints. Further, Bush's barnstorming tour insulted his supporters, treating attendees as props rather than citizens with reflective views about Social Security.

While the "town-hall meetings" evidenced a resistance to openness by orchestrating venues to exclude diverse positions, some debate participants displayed a lack of openness in their responses to corporate scandals and market declines. Convinced of the market's virtues, some participants, like Sen. Larry Craig, insisted that only a few wrongdoers impugned an otherwise trustworthy market. Others, including opponents of privatization, upheld the "informed consumer" as the "best defense" against corporate fraud. Reaffirming the market assumption of "perfect information," this response proposed a remedy that unscrupulous market actors had already contravened in manipulating the content and timing of stock information. Addressing this problem required shifting one's perspective from an individual to a systemic focus, which policymakers, in contrast to media commentators, resisted. Similarly, prescriptions for diversified investing as a remedy for stock declines individualized a potentially systemic problem. As an isolated prescription, diversification placed the burden on investors, who presumably erred in concentrating their portfolios too narrowly. From this perspective, declining prices proved the market's superiority. But the bursting of the dot-com bubble suggested a market-wide problem of stock valuation that undermined individual judgment. In these ways, advocates of investment displayed an imperviousness to actual market conditions in their recommendations for Social Security, as their position remained the same in good and bad times.

Citizens may support policies for any number of reasons, whether driven by fear, hope, spite, solidarity, antipathy, compassion, or innumerable other motives. They may insist on a narrow interpretation of self-interest, even if their actions harm others, or citizens may view their interests in light of others. As experienced advocates who understand that arguments must resonate with audiences to garner support, most debate participants make choices about how to craft their arguments to appeal to audiences' values and beliefs.[10] They may pull people together or push people apart. Participants may challenge audiences to develop their capabilities and widen their imaginations, or participants may remind people of their limits and narrow their horizons. From these possibilities, we can identify a quality of ethical policy debate as urging participants to appeal to their audiences' "better selves." By this, I mean our capacity to see ourselves and others as capable agents who participate in a shared project of ameliorating our common worlds, even as we (vociferously) disagree about policy issues.

The present structure of Social Security underscores the importance of this ethical quality, since the contributions of current workers pay for the benefits of current retirees. However, advocates of investment too often placed generations in competition with each other, going so far as to predict a "generational war." If we pursue the implications of a war metaphor, we discover that generations waging war may treat each other as "enemies," forestalling collaboration and foreclosing the opportunity for members of different generations to learn from one another. Further, war frames retirement policy as a zero-sum game: if seniors experience gains, then young workers lose. War also treats interests as unalterable, preventing the possibility for an intergenerational interest to arise. Even in the absence of war metaphors, advocates of investment sometimes portrayed seniors as malicious actors. Economics professor Laurence Kotlikoff charged seniors with "consuming too much," invoking an image of seniors as gluttons who did not care for their children or grandchildren. Raising the specter of servitude, Richard Thau, executive director of Third Millennium, vowed that "we are not willing to become [our parents' and grandparents'] indentured servants."[11] At first glance, one might dismiss Thau's declaration as a "dramatic flourish." Yet, as I have argued throughout this book, language matters. Thau's vow established an antagonistic relationship between generations that invited young workers to regard their interests as opposed to the interests of seniors.

Failing to encourage audiences to develop their capabilities and widen their imaginations, President Bush conspicuously put forward a limited and narrow view of the democratic potential of an ownership society. Bush asserted that "there's nothing that causes more participation in government than if your wealth is directly associated with the decisions of government."[12] In this assertion, Bush equated wealth with participation, and, by implication, he held that greater wealth equaled greater participation. Doing so cast participation in sharply self-interested terms. Since people participated to protect their possessions, other people stood only as threats to one's wealth. A sense of civic duty as well as a notion of a greater good remained entirely absent from this rationale. Participation ostensibly driven by a concern for others appeared foolhardy, as Bush's position resonated with Adam Smith's claim that individuals should address fellow citizens "not to their humanity but to their self-love."[13]

Constructing a passive mode of citizenship, Bush did not challenge citizens to extend themselves. Bush encouraged people to "pay attention," but he did not urge participants to involve themselves in local and national communities, nor did he invite citizens to imagine the future shape of their polity. Indeed, the learning that Bush associated with "paying attention" subordinated citizenship to expertise. In an ownership society where wealth constituted the primary motive for participation, the best that citizens could do was to surround themselves with capable advisors who could "help you make a rational decision."[14] If citizens could not make decisions about how to "grow" their wealth, then how could they make decisions about which government policies would best protect their wealth? Of course, expertise plays an important role in investing and governing, but financial advisors typically ask their clients about their investment goals. So, too, should a president encourage citizens to articulate their policy goals.

Some readers may regard my ethical prescriptions as a call for "nice" and "civil" policy debate, where participants keep their emotions in check and examine issues in the most "objective" way possible. As my generous use of quotations suggests, I hope to dispel this impression, since I fully appreciate that my quoted terms may serve as code words for refraining from debate or means of excluding people from debate. Exclusions may operate in discursive forums directly and indirectly. Direct exclusions expressly prevent people from participating in public debates, such as nineteenth-century prohibitions in the United States against women speaking in public. Indirect exclusions offer people entry into previously restricted forums, but compel participants to conform to established modes of address that negate the alternative insights offered through people's diverse experiences. Calls for "nice," "civil," and "objective" debate often have functioned as indirect exclusions, upholding culturally specific modes of address as universal.[15] Against this disabling history, I support passionate, partisan, challenging, and confrontational policy debate. Policymakers and others must have faith in citizens' abilities to make good judgments when presented with compelling alternatives. Too often during the privatization debates, participants resisted this move. They appeared unwilling to involve citizens in policymaking, seeking instead the numerical strength of masses of citizens standing by participants' positions.[16]

To see how participants may avoid or engage in vigorous debate, I turn to the founding debates over Social Security, because George Haynes and Charles Houston's arguments about the racial implications of Old-Age Insurance hold valuable lessons for us today. However, to appreciate their intervention, we first need to consider how their contemporaries invoked the language of administration to avoid discussions of race. Noted social-insurance expert Abraham Epstein initially appealed to efficiency in objecting to the inclusion of farm workers and domestics under Old-Age Insurance. Epstein held that "you are going to have to spend more money in administering the act than you will ever collect." Race ostensibly appeared as a nonfactor in Epstein's thinking, as he assessed the issue from the "disinterested" perspective of the administrative expert seeking to make Old-Age Insurance cost-effective. However, Epstein quickly shifted ground in his testimony to reveal a more pressing concern: "I do not want the farmers to come in here and fight us. . . . Do not let us undertake a fight that will defeat us."[17] This plea betrayed the avoidance strategy of Epstein and other participants, demonstrating how efficiency served as political cover. To be clear, Epstein's assessment of the comparative strength of farmers and supporters of social insurance may have been accurate, but his rhetorical approach retreated from debate.

In contrast, Haynes and Houston addressed the issue of race directly. They explained that the Social Security Act would exclude a majority of black workers from Old-Age Insurance, and they illustrated how the absence of explicit language prohibiting discrimination in federal policy actually enabled unequal outcomes. Moreover, Haynes and Houston demystified the symbolic politics that informed the Social Security Act.

They recognized that language and symbols matter, and that black elderly receiving assistance would not garner the same respect as white elderly receiving insurance benefits. Charles Houston explained that "the old-age annuity is a direct Federal right with the worker receiving his old-age annuity direct from the Federal Social Insurance Board."[18] Old-Age Assistance did not invoke the language of rights, and it permitted differential treatment across states and localities. Although Haynes and Houston did not prevail, they advanced an important critique of the debates. In shifting the issue of race from unspoken to spoken, Haynes and Houston held policymakers accountable for their actions. Even though policymakers refused to engage the substance of their testimony, Haynes and Houston made explicit an important problem with the original legislation.

We, too, may not solve all of the problems that citizens identify with the contemporary Social Security system. We, too, may encounter recalcitrance when attempting to publicize important issues. We may not achieve agreement among advocates of investment and supporters of insurance over the proper future for Social Security. But we can never hope to obtain an understanding of people's interests and ideas if we avoid vigorous debate of these topics. In our contemporary era, appreciating the different purposes and populations that people associate with Social Security would constitute a considerable achievement.

A Democracy-Based Alternative

Ever a champion of democracy, John Dewey remained open throughout his long and distinguished career to new ideas for realizing democracy's promise. In a 1939 address written for a banquet honoring his eightieth birthday, John Dewey sketched a vision for "creative democracy" as an ongoing moral project. Just as FDR had observed a few years earlier, Dewey held that since Americans no longer faced a physical frontier, they needed to focus on values and proposals that would enable citizens to live fuller lives. Calling this a "moral frontier," he urged Americans to resist the tendency to see democracy as a self-sustaining mechanism, and instead view democracy as something citizens actively created. Dewey defined democracy as "a *personal* way of individual life . . . [that] signifies the possession and continual use of certain attitudes, forming personal character and determining desire and purpose in all the relations of life."

In Dewey's view, democracy's pulse traveled along non-institutional channels: rather than citizens accommodating themselves to institutions, institutions had to express citizens' values. Dewey accordingly located the spirit of democracy in the interactions of ordinary folk: "The heart and final guarantee of democracy is in free gatherings of neighbors on the street corner to discuss back and forth what is read in uncensored news of the day, and in gatherings of friends in the living rooms of houses and apartments to converse freely with one another."[19]

Referencing personal attitudes and public meetings, Dewey situated democratic practice in the interactions of individuals and their communities. Given the contingency of these interactions, democracy rested on a faith in human potential, regardless of "race, color, sex, birth and family, of material or cultural wealth." Dewey was not naive, and he insisted that people needed sufficient material resources to realize their potential. Moreover, he discerned in history compelling evidence of "the capacity of human beings for intelligent judgment and action if proper conditions are furnished." Nor could differences undermine this democratic faith. Quite the opposite, Dewey insisted that "the expression of difference is not only a right of other persons but is a means of enriching one's own life-experience."[20]

I have referenced Dewey because his vision of democracy offers a compelling alternative for Social Security to the market-based approach that oriented the privatization debates. His emphasis on democracy as an activity serves as an important reminder that public policy should not proceed independently of citizen involvement. Of course, citizens cannot participate in the details of drafting legislation—that is the task of Congress—but citizens ought to assert the values they want to inform public policy, and policymakers have an obligation to comport policy and public values. Imagining democracy as an orientation toward action indicates that policymakers should not circumscribe its province to certain aspects of governance—like the vote—and proceed in an authoritarian or exclusionary manner in policymaking. President Bush may have perceived a mandate in the results of the 2004 election, but he had a responsibility to listen to the millions of citizens who did not vote for him or support privatization. Further, Dewey's faith in human potentiality illustrates how citizens in a democracy ought to treat each other—namely, as equals, fairly, with a vision of justice. Finally, Dewey's insistence that discussion constituted the "heart and final guarantee of democracy" underscores the importance of debates over public policy, in both the hearing rooms of Congress and the diverse forums of the wider public sphere.

If we approach Social Security from the perspective of democracy as an ongoing moral project, then we ought to foreground values as a primary aspect of policy debate. My analysis has done so, but debate participants mostly foregrounded issues like rates of return, solvency dates, and investment procedures. In this way, debate participants privileged a technical perspective over a public perspective, which not only obscured the values associated with insurance and investment but also dampened public engagement. The flow of the debates sent a message to citizens that if they could not compare solvency dates according to different assumptions of economic growth, then they could not speak intelligently about Social Security. However, the comparative benefits of insurance and investment do not raise a technical question—they prompt questions about the values citizens want their policies to affirm. Rather than requiring training in public policy, answering these questions articulates a sense of what citizens want to achieve, and this applies equally to all citizens. In contemporary American political culture, we have witnessed the rise of the phrase "values voter," which typically refers to conservative Christian voters who pay particular attention to issues like abortion and same-sex marriage. In the wake of the 2004 presidential election, some media commentators claimed that "values voters" carried Bush to victory.[21] Besides the methodological problems entailed in this assessment, the very phrase "values voters" implies that only a subset of citizens vote their values. But Social Security (and politics more generally) cannot escape values, since values inform the positions of all policymakers and citizens.

Approaching Social Security this way requires reframing the rhetoric we use to justify the program. As I have suggested throughout this book, I oppose market-based approaches to social policy because the latter serves nonmarket ends. I find Social Security's enactment of community especially compelling, since it brings together Americans of different backgrounds more than any other public policy. When pressed during the privatization debates, supporters of insurance invoked the value of community, but their typical justification of Social Security as an insurance program undermines this value. The logic of the contributory right grounds Social Security benefits in the individual rather than the individual's connection to others. This justification disguises insurance as investment. A justificatory rhetoric resonating with the values of insurance would champion Social Security's intergenerational compact and explain its finances as citizens pooling together individual contributions to ensure everyone's protection.

In a rare instance, political-science professor Benjamin Barber offered a democracy-based defense of Social Security in a January 2005 op-ed column in the *Los Angeles Times*.[22] Barber argued that "the most profound cost of privatization" lay in its "irreplaceable harm to our democratic 'common ground.'" Stressing that Social Security promised benefits to citizens regardless of race, class, and gender, Barber held that "you cannot simply take justice out of the public realm and put it into the private realm without fundamentally weakening the democracy on which the very possibility of justice depends." A healthy democracy sustained a strong sense of public good, while fostering empathy and shared understandings among citizens. In contrast, "Dollars don't deliberate. They don't seek common ground." Privatization constituted a "reverse social contract" by dissolving the bonds that tie people together as citizens. As insurance, Social Security stood as "an emblem of civic membership and a reflection of the benefits that come with the responsibilities of citizenship." Whatever its shortcomings on "technical grounds," privatization represented a "disaster" on the ground of citizenship.

Advancing this argument, Barber did not reinvent Social Security. Instead, Barber amplified the democratic potential of the existing program to make explicit, and affirm the link between, important public values and an insurance-based retirement system. Barber crafted an argument available to all supporters of insurance, yet his op-ed column appeared as a refreshingly different entry into the privatization debates. Successfully reframing the rhetorical justification for Social Security in the spirit of democracy would entail turning Barber's exceptional op-ed column into a common theme in future policy debates. Although his professional background may have inclined him to seek out democratic potential in public policies, Barber did not invoke the specialized academic language of a political scientist. Rather, his key terms—common ground, justice, public, deliberation, membership, and citizenship—circulate prominently in vernacular discourses. These terms voice a public language that citizens as citizens may articulate. Future debate participants, too, may adopt this language with confidence that their arguments will resonate with audiences' experiences and beliefs about the nation.

In the short term, any attempt at democratic transformation may appear counterintuitive to many audiences, since advocates of privatization have participated in a thirty-five-year-plus movement to ascribe to the market the status of a common sense. Democratic discourses resonate in American political culture, but too often policymakers have subordinated these discourses to the dictates of market talk. From this perspective, a citizen might say: "Of course we should focus primarily on 'money's worth.' How else could we evaluate retirement benefits?" Even in this environment, justice retains its rhetorical power, recalling a longer history of struggles for inclusion and fair treatment in American democracy. Attending to the nation's celebration of these struggles as positively transformative, a democracy-based appeal could draw on this proud history to situate Social Security as an enactment of an inclusive nation. Moreover, as Barber suggests, a democratic approach values deliberation, which creates opportunities for citizens to forge collective interests and goals. Describing deliberations moderated by the National Issues Forum, Betty Knighton recalled how participants adjudicated their interests during their interactions: "It's incredible what you can see happen before your eyes when people have a chance to come together and talk about these competing convictions that they have, and to weigh them with the sense of fairness that most American people really bring into this discussion."[23] Rather than fighting, younger workers and seniors shared perspectives and reconsidered their own interests with regard to the interests of others.

As Dewey recognized, faith in human potentiality without a commitment to achieving the material conditions necessary for citizens to realize their potential would constitute a dangerously quietistic form of wishful thinking. People need solid material and symbolic bases to engage fully as citizens. These bases work together to foster efficacious human agency, providing individuals with resources for action and recognizing individuals as capable actors. From this perspective, Social Security—as an insurance system—represents a tremendous success story. Social Security's monetary benefits have kept millions of seniors out of poverty, while its celebrated social standing has bolstered retirees' reputations as senior *citizens*. In a study of the political implications of Social Security, Andrea Campbell reports that seniors' involvement in traditional political activities has increased since the expansion of the program from the 1950s onward.[24] By the 1980s, seniors established their civic prowess, voting and volunteering at higher rates than the rest of the population.

Significantly, senior participation has overcome traditional barriers of lower education and income levels. Of course, as Dewey would remind us, trends in traditional activities provide only a partial picture of active citizenship, which must secure itself through vibrant deliberation. But the trends identified by Campbell bode well for democracy as an ongoing moral project.

Social Security's successful mediation of material and rhetorical elements is increasingly important in the wake of the widening gulf of income inequality in the United States. Wiping out the gains of a prosperous post–World War II economy, economic and political trends over the past three decades have pushed inequality to its worst point since the 1920s. Between 1979 and 2000, real income for the lowest quintile of households grew at a modest rate of 6.4 percent. The middle quintile of households saw their income grow at a moderately higher rate of 12.4 percent during this period. Meanwhile, households in the 95th to 99th percentiles experienced an impressive 53.6 percent growth rate in income, while the top 1 percent of households witnessed an astonishing 184.3 percent growth rate in real income. Further, a lack of class mobility exacerbated these inequalities, since families overwhelmingly ended this period in the income quintile in which they began. Nor did stock ownership improve this situation, since the top 10 percent of households owned over three-quarters of all stocks in 2001.[25]

In light of these developments, we need to consider whether the United States may be approaching a threshold beyond which citizens cannot engage in the kind of perspective-taking necessary for meaningful deliberation across differences. If inequality continues unabated, will citizens' life experiences become so distinct that they cannot imagine each other as compatriots? Will debate participants lose the idea of a better self to which they can appeal? Moreover, we must not allow these statistics to lull us into thinking that inequality has appeared as a "natural" market outcome. Human decisions produced these results. Among other choices, policymakers reformulated the tax code to reduce the obligations of wealthy Americans while increasing the burden on the middle class, and corporations increased returns to stockholders at the expense of their workers. Only a dedicated policy commitment can redress inequality.

Social Security shows us the way toward tackling this troubling issue by offering a model of what policymakers and citizens can achieve. Far from shackling the nation as it develops over the course of the twenty-first century, Social Security will serve as an irreplaceable element of a just and prosperous polity. Rather than applying the norms of the market to Social Security, debate participants ought to apply the norms of Social Security to other areas of public policy. As a guide for public policy, Social Security's significant features do not lie in its technical details, since specifics like retirement ages should change over time, but in the very principle of insurance and its associated values. In our own time, just as in FDR and Dewey's time, renewing the spirit of democracy constitutes our most urgent national task. Social Security stands as a shining model of democracy in action.

Notes

INTRODUCTION. THE MARKET REACHES
FOR SOCIAL SECURITY

1. Adam Smith, *An Inquiry into the Nature and Causes of the Wealth of Nations*, ed. Edwin Cannan (Chicago: University of Chicago Press, 1976), IV.2.9.

2. Smith, *Wealth of Nations*, I.2.2. Noting the frequency with which policymakers and political theorists appeal to self-interest as a guide for public policies, David Gore argues that efforts to ground these appeals in Smith's writings constitute a partial interpretation of his work. Gore retorts that Smith's invocation of self-interest should be understood in conjunction with his appeals to sympathy in *The Theory of Moral Sentiments*. Gore maintains that "self-interest as it applies to policy, in Smith's system, always accompanies sympathy." David Charles Gore, "Between Sympathy and Self-Interest: A Reframing of Adam Smith's Economic Rhetoric," in *Rhetorical Democracy: Discursive Practices of Civic Engagement*, ed. Gerard A. Hauser and Amy Grim (Mahwah, NJ: Lawrence Erlbaum Associates, 2004), 161. Jerry Muller argues that Smith's reference to "the benevolence of the butcher" was not meant to denigrate benevolence, but to assert that "an economic system cannot be *based* on benevolence." Jerry Z. Muller, *The Mind*

and the Market: Capitalism and Western Thought (New York: Anchor, 2002), 62. See also Stephen Darwall, "Sympathetic Liberalism: Recent Work on Adam Smith," *Philosophy & Public Affairs* 28 (1999): 139–64.

3. Franklin D. Roosevelt, *The Public Papers and Addresses of Franklin D. Roosevelt*, vol. 4, *The Court Disapproves* (New York: Random House, 1938), 17.

4. For insightful discussions of privatization, see Joel F. Handler, *Down from Bureaucracy: The Ambiguity of Privatization and Empowerment* (Princeton, NJ: Princeton University Press, 1996); Martha Minow, *Partners Not Rivals: Privatization and the Public Good* (Boston: Beacon Press, 2002); Elliott D. Sclar, *You Don't Always Get What You Pay For: The Economics of Privatization* (Ithaca, NY: Cornell University Press, 2000).

   In the realm of social insurance, political scientist Jacob Hacker identifies a large-scale "privatization of risk." To privatize risk is "to fragment and undermine collective insurance pools that offer reduced-cost protection to higher-risk and lower-income citizens in favor of arrangements that leave individuals and families responsible for coping with social risks largely on their own" (249). Jacob S. Hacker, "Privatizing Risk without Privatizing the Welfare State: The Hidden Politics of Social Policy Retrenchment in the United States," *American Political Science Review* 98 (2004): 243–60.

5. John Dewey, *The Public and Its Problems* (1927; Athens, OH: Swallow Press, 1954), 208.

6. Ron Suskind, "Without a Doubt," *New York Times Magazine*, 17 October 2004, 51.

7. Bob Herbert, "Bush's Blinkers," *New York Times*, 22 October 2004, late edition, A23.

8. Maria Cancian, "Rhetoric and Reality of Work-Based Welfare Reform," *Social Work* 46 (2001): 309, 310.

9. A lively debate among rhetorical scholars has explored the relationship of rhetoric and its material conditions. One position in this debate, noting rhetoric's constitutive power and its pervasive influence in our nonlinguistic environment, construes rhetoric as a material practice. Another position argues for a distinction between rhetoric and materiality, expressing a concern that equating the two terms would elide important political and economic forces informing rhetorical practice. As my approach to public policy suggests, I see critical value in sustaining a conceptual distinction between rhetoric and material conditions, even as I reject the view that material conditions independently direct rhetorical practice. In this way, I regard this relationship as mutually informative. A fuller consideration of this debate is beyond the scope of my book. For a sense of the

development of this debate, see Michael Calvin McGee, "A Materialist's Conception of Rhetoric," in *Explorations in Rhetoric: Studies in Honor of Douglas Ehninger,* ed. Raymie E. McKerrow (Glenview, IL: Scott, Foresman, 1982), 23–48; Raymie E. McKerrow, "Critical Rhetoric: Theory and Praxis," *Communication Monographs* 56 (1989): 91–111; Dana L. Cloud, "The Materiality of Discourse as Oxymoron: A Challenge to Critical Rhetoric," *Western Journal of Communication* 58 (1994): 141–63; Ronald Walter Greene, "Another Materialist Rhetoric," *Critical Studies in Mass Communication* 15 (1998): 21–41; Carole Blair, "Reflections on Criticism and Bodies: Parables from Public Places," *Western Journal of Communication* 65 (2001): 271–94; Ronald Walter Greene, "Rhetoric and Capitalism: Rhetorical Agency as Communicative Labor," *Philosophy and Rhetoric* 37 (2004): 188–206; Dana L. Cloud, "The Matrix and Critical Theory's Desertion of the Real," *Communication and Critical/Cultural Studies* 3 (2006): 329–54.

10. Frank Fischer, *Reframing Public Policy: Discursive Politics and Deliberative Practices* (New York: Oxford University Press, 2003), 60.

11. See my previous book, *Visions of Poverty: Welfare Policy and Political Imagination* (East Lansing: Michigan State University Press, 2002); Nancy Fraser, "Women, Welfare, and the Politics of Needs Interpretation," in *Unruly Practices: Power, Discourse, and Gender in Contemporary Social Theory* (Minneapolis: University of Minnesota Press, 1989), 144–60.

12. James T. Patterson, *America's Struggle against Poverty, 1900–1994* (Cambridge, MA: Harvard University Press, 1994), 179.

13. Jürgen Habermas, *Between Facts and Norms: Contributions to a Discourse Theory of Law and Democracy,* trans. William Rehg (Cambridge: Massachusetts Institute of Technology Press, 1996), 307.

14. Robert Kuttner, *Everything for Sale: The Virtues and Limits of Markets* (Chicago: University of Chicago Press, 1996), 4.

15. Eckehard F. Rosenbaum, "What Is a Market? On the Methodology of a Contested Concept," *Review of Social Economy* 58 (2000): 463; Edward Schiappa, *Defining Reality: Definitions and the Politics of Meaning* (Carbondale: Southern Illinois University Press, 2003), 32. For a concise discussion of various disciplinary efforts to conceptualize markets, see Karin Knorr Cetina, "The Market," *Theory, Culture & Society* 23 (2006): 551–56.

16. What count as benefits and costs are also determined through the framework of market talk. As Pierre Bourdieu notes, this approach to policy analysis does not "take account of what are called social costs." Pierre Bourdieu, *Acts of Resistance: Against the Tyranny of the Market,* trans. Richard Nice (New York: New Press, 1998), 39.

254 *Notes*

17. James Arnt Aune, *Selling the Free Market: The Rhetoric of Economic Correctness* (New York: Guilford Press, 2001), 40. Aune draws on the work of Robert Hariman, who has written an instructive book on political style. Robert Hariman, *Political Style: The Artistry of Power* (Chicago: University of Chicago Press, 1995).

18. Deirdre N. McCloskey, *The Rhetoric of Economics*, 2d ed. (Madison: University of Wisconsin Press, 1998), 9. See also Willie Henderson, Tony Dudley-Evans, and Roger Backhouse, eds., *Economics and Language* (New York: Routledge, 1993); Arjo Klamer, Donald N. McCloskey, and Robert M. Solow, eds., *The Consequences of Economic Rhetoric* (New York: Cambridge University Press, 1988).

19. Thomas Frank, *One Market Under God: Extreme Capitalism, Market Populism, and the End of Economic Democracy* (New York: Doubleday, 2000), 29, xiii.

20. George Cheney, "Arguing about the Place of Values and Ethics in Market-Oriented Discourses of Today," in *New Approaches to Rhetoric*, ed. Patricia A. Sullivan and Steven R. Goldzwig (Thousand Oaks, CA: Sage, 2004), 74.

21. Roger Thompson, "*Kairos* Revisited: An Interview with James Kinneavy," *Rhetoric Review* 19 (2000): 76.

CHAPTER 1. POLICY POLYSEMY AND THE 1935 SOCIAL SECURITY DEBATES

1. Celeste Michelle Condit, "The Rhetorical Limits of Polysemy," *Critical Studies in Mass Communication* 6 (1989): 106.

2. Leah Ceccarelli, "Polysemy: Multiple Meanings in Rhetorical Criticism," *Quarterly Journal of Speech* 84 (1998): 395–415.

3. Ibid., 408.

4. For detailed discussions of the economic status of the elderly in preindustrial and industrial America, see Carole Haber and Brian Gratton, *Old Age and the Search for Security: An American Social History* (Bloomington: Indiana University Press, 1994); David Hackett Fischer, *Growing Old in America* (New York: Oxford University Press, 1977); William Graebner, *A History of Retirement: The Meaning and Function of an American Institution, 1885–1978* (New Haven, CT: Yale University Press, 1980); Dora L. Costa, *The Evolution of Retirement: An American Economic History* (Chicago: University of Chicago Press, 1998).

5. Michael B. Katz, *In the Shadow of the Poorhouse: A Social History of Welfare in America* (New York: Basic Books, 1986), 179.

6. Olivier Zunz, *Making America Corporate, 1870–1920* (Chicago: University of Chicago Press, 1990), 14.

7. Haber and Gratton, *Old Age and the Search for Security*, 80.

8. Industrial responses to security for the elderly came initially as part of a movement known as welfare capitalism. Stuart Brandes defines welfare capitalism as "any service provided for the comfort or improvement of employees which was neither a necessity of the industry nor required by law." Stuart D. Brandes, *American Welfare Capitalism, 1880–1940* (Chicago: University of Chicago Press, 1976), 5–6, 22–25. See also Daniel Nelson, *Managers and Workers: Origins of the Twentieth-Century Factory System in the United States, 1880–1920,* 2d ed. (Madison: University of Wisconsin Press, 1995), 99–118; G. John Ikenberry and Theda Skocpol, "Expanding Social Benefits: The Role of Social Security," *Political Science Quarterly* 102 (1987): 389–416; David Brody, *Workers in Industrial America: Essays on the Twentieth Century Struggle* (New York: Oxford University Press, 1980), 48–81.

9. Murray Webb Latimer, *Industrial Pension Systems in the United States and Canada,* vol. 1 (New York: Industrial Relations Counselors, 1932), 42, 55.

10. Jacob S. Hacker, *The Divided Welfare State: The Battle over Public and Private Social Benefits in the United States* (New York: Cambridge University Press, 2002), 89.

11. Abraham Epstein, *Insecurity: A Challenge to America,* 2d rev. ed. (New York: Random House, 1938), 144. See also Luther Conant Jr., *A Critical Analysis of Industrial Pension Systems* (New York: Macmillan, 1922), 80–81.

12. Theda Skocpol, *Protecting Soldiers and Mothers: The Political Origins of Social Policy in the United States* (Cambridge, MA: Harvard University Press, 1992), 102–3, 109. See also Jill Quadagno, *The Transformation of Old Age Security: Class and Politics in the American Welfare State* (Chicago: University of Chicago Press, 1988), 36–47.

13. Isaac M. Rubinow, *Social Insurance, with Special Reference to American Conditions* (1913; reprint, New York: Arno Press, 1969), 406, 408.

14. Massachusetts Commission on Old Age Pensions, Annuities and Insurance, *Report of the Commission on Old Age Pensions, Annuities and Insurance* (Boston: White and Potter Printing, 1910), 300.

15. Ibid., 314.

16. Roy Lubove, *The Struggle for Social Security, 1900–1935* (Cambridge, MA: Harvard University Press, 1968), 114–16, 137–43.

17. David M. Kennedy, *Freedom from Fear: The American People in Depression and War, 1929–1945* (New York: Oxford University Press, 1999), 163; Katz, *In the Shadow of the Poorhouse,* 207; W. Andrew Achenbaum, *Social Security: Visions and Revisions* (Cambridge: Cambridge University Press, 1986), 16.

18. James T. Patterson, *America's Struggle against Poverty, 1900–1994* (Cambridge, MA: Harvard University Press, 1994), 38–39.

19. Kennedy, *Freedom from Fear,* 87.

20. This is the title of chapter 26 of Epstein, *Insecurity: A Challenge to America.*

21. Epstein, *Insecurity,* 493.

22. Ibid., 506.

23. Walter I. Trattner, *From Poor Law to Welfare State: A History of Social Welfare in America,* 5th ed. (New York: Free Press, 1994), 274.

24. Blanche D. Coll, *Safety Net: Welfare and Social Security, 1929–1979* (New Brunswick, NJ: Rutgers University Press, 1995), 8–10.

25. For detailed discussions of the movements of Senator Huey Long and Father Charles Coughlin, see Alan Brinkley, *Voices of Protest: Huey Long, Father Coughlin, and the Great Depression* (New York: Vintage Books, 1983); Kennedy, *Freedom from Fear,* 227–42.

26. Abraham Holtzman, *The Townsend Movement: A Political Study* (New York: Bookman, 1963). On the relationship between Townsend and Roosevelt, see Daniel J. B. Mitchell, "Townsend and Roosevelt: Lessons from the Struggle for Elderly Income Support," *Labor History* 42 (2001): 255–76. Arthur Altmeyer recalls that Roosevelt exhibited greater concern about Long's "share the wealth" movement than the Townsend plan. Arthur J. Altmeyer, *The Formative Years of Social Security* (Madison: University of Wisconsin Press, 1966), 10. This may have been true, but in the case of the members of the Ways and Means Committee and the Finance Committee, the Townsend movement elicited far greater scrutiny. Long did not testify before either committee, and his name surfaced only a few times during the committee hearings. In contrast, Townsend and several associates testified extensively before both committees, and his name was mentioned by several committee members and witnesses.

27. Edwin E. Witte, *The Development of the Social Security Act* (Madison: University of Wisconsin Press, 1963), 86.

28. Franklin D. Roosevelt, *The Public Papers and Addresses of Franklin D. Roosevelt,* vol. 3, *The Advance and Recovery of Reform* (New York: Random House, 1938), 291.

29. Quoted in Frances Perkins, *The Roosevelt I Knew* (New York: Viking Press, 1946), 281.

30. Committee on Economic Security, *Report to the President of the Committee on Economic Security* (Washington, DC: Government Printing Office, 1935), 25.

31. Committee on Economic Security, *Social Security in America: The Factual Background of the Social Security Act as Summarized from Staff Reports to the Committee on Economic Security* (Washington, DC: Government Printing Office, 1937), 198. The "old-age security" portion of this volume drew from the reports of Armstrong, Latimer, Brown, and other staff members.

32. Arthur M. Schlesinger Jr., *The Politics of Upheaval* (Boston: Houghton Mifflin, 1960), 392.

33. Quoted in William E. Leuchtenburg, *The Supreme Court Reborn: The Constitutional Revolution in the Age of Roosevelt* (New York: Oxford University Press, 1995), 90. The Court held that Congress had improperly delegated its legislative authority to the Executive Branch and its National Recovery Administration. Further, the Court ruled that even though Schechter Poultry purchased its chickens from out-of-state vendors, its slaughter operations only indirectly contributed to interstate commerce, and thus its activities lay beyond the jurisdiction of Congress. See Richard A. Maidment, *The Judicial Response to the New Deal* (Manchester, UK: Manchester University Press, 1991), 82–103.

34. Thomas H. Eliot, *Recollections of the New Deal: When the People Mattered* (Boston: Northeastern University Press, 1992), 96, 97.

35. Jacob Hacker notes that if business exemptions had survived, "it would have been nearly impossible for old-age insurance program to redistribute across income and age groups without prompting an exodus of higher-income and younger employment groups from the public program into private plans." Hacker, *Divided Welfare State*, 101.

36. Eliot, *Recollections of the New Deal*, 119.

37. Hacker, *Divided Welfare State*, 103.

38. House Ways and Means Committee, *The Social Security Act of 1935*, 74th Cong., 1st sess., 1935, H. Rept. 615, 43.

39. Ibid., 44.

40. *Social Security Act of 1935, U.S. Statutes at Large* 49 (1935): 622–25, 636–39.

41. Roosevelt, *Advance of Recovery and Reform*, 288, 292.

42. Ibid., 288.

43. Ibid., 288. Yet, in his other statements, FDR sought a spatial balance that matched his temporal balance: some government functions, such as relief, could be handled more effectively in local communities. In a speech on September 28, 1934, Roosevelt characterized the relationship between local and national government as supplementary. He told his audience that "with the enormous growth of population we have had, with the complexities of the past generation, community efforts have now been supplemented by the formation of great national organizations." This called for a response from the federal government. Roosevelt explained that "the Federal Government has been compelled to undertake the task of supplementing the more normal methods which have been in use during all the preceding generations" (411).

44. Roosevelt, *Advance of Recovery and Reform*, 291.

45. Ibid. 291.

46. Ibid., 316–17.

47. Ibid., 292.

48. Arthur M. Schlesinger Jr., *The Coming of the New Deal* (Boston: Houghton Mifflin, 1958), 308–9.

49. Roosevelt, *Advance of Recovery and Reform*, 453.

50. Franklin D. Roosevelt, *The Public Papers and Addresses of Franklin D. Roosevelt*, vol. 4, *The Court Disapproves* (New York: Random House, 1938), 19.

51. Roosevelt, *Court Disapproves*, 20.

52. Ibid., 20–21.

53. Ibid., 44.

54. House Ways and Means Committee, *Economic Security Act: Committee on Ways and Means*, 74th Cong., 1st sess., 1935, 484–85.

55. Senate Finance Committee, *Economic Security Act: Hearings before the Committee on Finance*, 74th Cong., 1st sess., 1935, 554.

56. Ways and Means, *Economic Security Act*, 221.

57. Ways and Means Committee, *Economic Security Act*, 88; Finance, *Economic Security Act*, 57.

58. Finance, *Economic Security Act*, 305.

59. Ways and Means, *Economic Security Act*, 173–74, 177.

60. Ibid., 240.

61. Ibid., 108.

62. Finance, *Economic Security Act*, 132–33.

63. Ibid., 285.

64. Ways and Means, *Economic Security Act*, 102.

65. Finance, *Economic Security Act*, 7.

66. Ibid., 288.

67. Ibid., 110, 108.

68. Ways and Means, *Economic Security Act*, 899–900. See also Perkins, *The Roosevelt I Knew*, 293–94; Eliot, *Recollections of the New Deal*, 101–4.

69. Finance, *Economic Security Act*, 943, 889.

70. Ways and Means, *Economic Security Act*, 200.

71. Ibid., 751–52.

72. Finance, *Economic Security Act*, 1019, 1022.

73. Ways and Means, *Economic Security Act*, 108.

74. Finance, *Economic Security Act*, 256.

75. This point has been noted widely in scholarship on the Social Security Act, although disagreement exists as to the relative influence of racial and economic

considerations driving policymakers' support of this exclusion. See, for example, Quadagno, *Transformation of Old Age Security*, 115–16; Michael K. Brown, *Race, Money, and the American Welfare State* (Ithaca, NY: Cornell University Press, 1999); Robert C. Lieberman, *Shifting the Color Line: Race and the American Welfare State* (Cambridge, MA: Harvard University Press, 1998).

What has not been examined, however, is how the discourse of the committee hearings diffused the potentially explosive issue of race. Andrew Achenbaum, for instance, writes that the exclusion of "most of the poorest workers—such as Southern blacks" from OAI "suggests that policymakers were willing to make politically expedient compromises" (*Social Security: Visions and Revisions*, 23). Missing from this account, however, are the ways that policymakers enacted these compromises while appearing to concern themselves with sound policy-making. Plainly put, policymakers did not appeal to race as a basis for excluding certain categories of workers. Indeed, when confronted with charges of racial discrimination, policymakers explicitly denied this motive. Instead, the issue of race was neutralized by highlighting the administrative and tax-collecting difficulties attending certain populations. The insidious way in which race informed the hearings may have bolstered the efficacy of racial appeals.

76. Ways and Means, *Economic Security Act*, 113.

77. Finance, *Economic Security Act*, 15; Ways and Means, *Economic Security Act*, 902.

78. Ways and Means, *Economic Security Act*, 559, 560.

79. Finance, *Economic Security Act*, 644. Haynes made the same point to the committee. He maintained that the "facts make clear that about three-fifths of all Negroes gainfully employed in the United States will be excluded by the very terms of this bill from its unemployment and old-age benefits." Finance, *Economic Security Act*, 487.

80. Ibid., 480.

81. Ways and Means, *Economic Security Act*, 601.

82. Finance, *Economic Security Act*, 644. For a detailed discussion of the racial politics of Old-Age Assistance, see Quadagno, *Transformation of Old Age Security*, 132–42.

83. See T. H. Marshall's justly famous "Citizenship and Social Class," especially his discussion of social rights in the twentieth century. Marshall included in the social elements of citizenship "the whole range from the right to a modicum of economic welfare and security to the right to share to the full in the social heritage and to live the life of a civilised being according to the standards prevailing in the society." T. H. Marshall and Tom Bottomore, *Citizenship and Social Class* (London: Pluto Press, 1992), 8. Marshall published his essay in 1950, fifteen years after the passage of the Social Security Act, and he wrote it from the

perspective of a British scholar with application to the United Kingdom, which developed a more extensive social-welfare state in the mid-twentieth century than the United States. Still, it is fair to note that the Social Security Act—and discussions attending this Act—represented an incipient discussion of the suitability of social citizenship in the United States.

84. Ways and Means, *Economic Security Act*, 600.

85. Ibid., 598, 977; Finance, *Economic Security Act*, 492.

86. Coll, *Safety Net*, 82.

87. Alfred M. Landon, "Text of Gov. Landon's Milwaukee Address on Economic Security," *New York Times*, 27 September 1936, late city edition, 31.

88. Advisory Council on Social Security, *Final Report*, 76th Cong., 1st sess., 1939, S. Doc. 4, 11, 22.

89. House Ways and Means Committee, *Hearings Relative to the Social Security Act Amendments of 1939*, vol. 2, 67th Cong., 1st sess., 1939, 1133.

90. Ibid., 3:2113.

91. Ibid., 2:1542, 1107.

92. Advisory Council on Social Security, *Old-Age and Survivors Insurance*, 80th Cong., 2d sess., 1948, S. Doc. 149, 2.

93. Senate Finance Committee, *Social Security Revision*, pt. 1, 81st Cong., 2d sess., 1950, 488; House Ways and Means Committee, *Social Security Act Amendments of 1949*, pt. 2, 81st Cong., 1st sess., 1949, 1545. For some additional statements along these lines, see Finance, *Social Security*, 2:2043, 2088, 2138, 2243, 2251.

94. Ways and Means, *Social Security*, 2:1213, 1216.

95. Ibid., 2:1582.

96. Ibid., 2:2185.

97. Martha Derthick, *Policymaking for Social Security* (Washington, DC: Brookings Institution, 1979), 346. See also Edward D. Berkowitz, *Robert Ball and the Politics of Social Security* (Madison: University of Wisconsin Press, 2003), 183–90.

98. See *Congressional Record*, 92d Cong., 2d sess., 1972, vol. 118, pt. 5:5229, pt. 11:13669.

99. Ibid., pt. 18:23289, 23317, 23295.

100. Ibid., pt. 5:5270.

101. Ibid., pt. 18:23298, 23290, 23509, 23318.

102. Social Security Administration, Board of Trustees, Federal Old-Age and Survivors Insurance and Disability Insurance Trust Funds, *2005 Annual Report of the Board of Trustees of the Federal Old-Age and Survivors Insurance and Disability Insurance Trust Funds*, Washington, DC, April 2005, 47.

103. Paul Krugman, *The Age of Diminished Expectations* (Cambridge: Massachusetts Institute of Technology Press, 1992), 3; "Real Income Down 5.5% in 1980 in a Record Drop," *New York Times,* 21 August 1981, late city edition, A1.

104. Social Security Administration, Board of Trustees, Federal Old-Age and Survivors Insurance and Disability Insurance Trust Funds, *1982 Annual Report of the Board of Trustees of the Federal Old-Age and Survivors Insurance and Disability Insurance Trust Funds,* Washington, DC, April 1982, 2.

105. Dan Balz, "Public Increasingly Doubts Survival of Social Security," *Washington Post,* 13 February 1982, final edition, A1.

106. National Commission on Social Security Reform, *Report of the National Commission on Social Security Reform,* Washington, DC, January 1983, 2-2.

107. For further discussions of the 1983 Amendments, see Daniel Béland, *Social Security: History and Politics from the New Deal to the Privatization Debate* (Lawrence: University Press of Kansas, 2005), 150–62; Wilbur J. Cohen, "The Future Impact of the Social Security Amendments of 1983," *Journal of the Institute for Socioeconomic Studies* 8 (1983): 1–16; Peter J. Ferrara, "Social Security: The Reforms Have Just Begun," *Journal of the Institute for Socioeconomic Studies* 8 (1983): 17–29; Robert J. Myers, "Social Security Amendments of 1983: Did They Solve the Financing Problem?" *CLU Journal* 38 (1984): 22–31; Martha N. Ozawa, "The 1983 Amendments to the Social Security Act: The Issue of Intergenerational Equity," *Social Work* 29 (1984): 131–37.

108. G. Thomas Goodnight, "Controversy," in *Argument in Controversy: Proceedings of the Seventh SCA/AFA Conference on Argumentation,* ed. Donn W. Parson (Annandale, VA: Speech Communication Association, 1991), 2.

109. Milton Friedman, *Capitalism and Freedom* (Chicago: University of Chicago Press, 1962), 182–89.

CHAPTER 2. COMPETING METAPHORS OF INSURANCE AND INVESTMENT

1. Joseph E. Stiglitz, *The Roaring Nineties: A New History of the World's Most Prosperous Decade* (New York: W. W. Norton, 2003), 59.

2. Aristotle, *Poetics,* trans. Ingram Bywater (1920; New York: Oxford University Press, 1990), chap. 22; Aristotle, *On Rhetoric: A Theory of Civic Discourse,* 2d ed., trans. George Kennedy (New York: Oxford University Press, 2007), 1404b. On the suitability of metaphor to prose style, Aristotle writes: "A word in its prevailing and native meaning and metaphor are alone useful in the *lexis* of prose."

3. John Kirby objects to this interpretation of Aristotle's understanding of metaphor, which had been advanced by such twentieth-century theorists as I. A. Richards. Kirby retorts that Aristotle effectively adopts a semiotic model of metaphor. He argues that this approach avoids debates between substitutive and interactive theories of metaphor and "highlight[s] the quintessentially cognitive nature of the Aristotelian formulation." John T. Kirby, "Aristotle on Metaphor," *American Journal of Philology* 118 (1997): 540.

4. I. A. Richards, *The Philosophy of Rhetoric* (1936; New York: Oxford University Press, 1965), 90.

5. Arjo Klamer and Thomas C. Leonard, "So What's an Economic Metaphor?" in *Natural Images in Economic Thought*, ed. Philip Mirowski (Cambridge: Cambridge University Press, 1994), 40. Deirdre McCloskey holds that metaphor is central to economic thought: "Each step in economic reasoning, even the reasoning of the official rhetoric, is metaphoric." Deirdre N. McCloskey, *The Rhetoric of Economics*, 2d ed. (Madison: University of Wisconsin Press, 1998), 40.

6. Kenneth Burke, "Four Master Tropes," in *A Grammar of Motives* (Berkeley: University of California Press, 1969), 504. Although I value the association of metaphor and perspective, I believe that his conception retains a substitution view of metaphor in which meaning flows in one direction from A to B.

7. Lakoff and Johnson write: "Metaphorical entailments can characterize a coherent system of metaphorical concepts and a corresponding coherent system of metaphorical expressions for those concepts." George Lakoff and Mark Johnson, *Metaphors We Live By* (1980; Chicago: University of Chicago Press, 2003), 9.

8. Ruth E. Malone, "Policy as Product: Morality and Metaphor in Health Policy Discourse," *Hastings Center Report*, May–June 1999, 20.

9. Richards, *Philosophy of Rhetoric*, 100.

10. Paul Ricoeur, *The Rule of Metaphor: Multidisciplinary Studies of the Creation of Meaning in Language*, trans. Robert Czerny (Toronto: University of Toronto Press, 1977), 125. Although he regards Richards' theory as "pioneering," Ricoeur maintains that Richards wrongly locates metaphor in the single word.

11. Klamer and Leonard, "What's an Economic Metaphor?" 36.

12. Ricoeur, *Rule of Metaphor*, 255.

13. Philip Eubanks, "Conceptual Metaphor as Rhetorical Response: A Reconsideration of Metaphor," *Written Communication* 16 (1999): 186.

14. Louis F. Powell Jr., "Attack of the American Free Enterprise System," *Media Transparency*, 23 August 1971, http://www.mediatransparency.org/storyprinter-friendly.php?storyID=22 (accessed 24 August 2005).

15. William E. Simon, *A Time for Truth* (New York: McGraw-Hill, 1978), 234.

16. Ibid., 229. Olin and other foundations have provided substantial funding to conservative think tanks. See National Committee for Responsive Philanthropy, *Axis of Ideology: Conservative Foundations and Public Policy*, Washington, DC, March 2004.

17. See James Allen Smith, *The Idea Brokers: Think Tanks and the Rise of the New Policy Elite* (New York: Free Press, 1991); David M. Ricci, *The Transformation of American Politics: The New Washington and the Rise of Think Tanks* (New Haven, CT: Yale University Press, 1993); Jean Stefancic and Richard Delgado, *No Mercy: How Conservative Think Tanks and Foundations Have Changed America's Social Agenda* (Philadelphia: Temple University Press, 1996).

18. Charles L. Heatherly, ed., *Mandate for Leadership: Policy Management in a Conservative Administration* (Washington, DC: Heritage Foundation, 1981), viii.

19. Quoted in Ricci, *Transformation of American Politics*, 171.

20. Eugene J. McAllister, ed., *Agenda for Progress: Examining Federal Spending* (Washington, DC: Heritage Foundation, 1981), 275.

21. Peter J. Ferrara, "The Prospect of Real Reform," *Cato Journal* 3 (1983): 620.

22. Stuart Butler and Peter Germanis, "Achieving a 'Leninist' Strategy," *Cato Journal* 3 (1983): 554.

23. Gerald F. Seib and John Harwood, "Shift in Power: Big Republican Gains Bring the Party Close to Control of Congress," *Wall Street Journal*, 9 November 1994, eastern edition, A1; Thomas B. Rosenstiel and Edith Stanley, "Gingrich Tames Rhetoric, Savors 'Speaker,'" *Los Angeles Times*, 9 November 1994, home edition, A14; David S. Broder, "Vote May Signal GOP Return as Dominant Party," *Washington Post*, 10 November 1994, final edition, A1.

24. Quoted in Kenneth J. Cooper, "Gingrich: 'Cooperation, Yes. Compromise, No,'" *Washington Post*, 12 November 1994, final edition, A1, A10.

25. Ed Gillespie and Bob Schellhas, eds., *Contract with America* (New York: Times Books, 1994), 7.

26. Dave Kaplan, "This Year, Republicans Gamble That All Politics Is Local," *CQ Weekly*, 22 October 1994, 3008.

27. Charles O. Jones, *Clinton and Congress, 1993–1996: Risk, Restoration, and Reelection* (Norman: University of Oklahoma Press, 1999), 108.

28. John J. Fialka, "Cato Institute's Influence Grows in Washington as Republican-Dominated Congress Sets Up Shop," *Wall Street Journal*, 14 December 1994, eastern edition, A16.

29. William J. Clinton, *Public Papers of the Presidents of the United States: William J. Clinton, 1995* (Washington, D.C.: Government Printing Office, 1996), 1:547.

30. See David G. Levasseur, "The Rhetorical Construction of Economic Policy: Political Judgment and the 1995 Budget Debate," *Rhetoric & Public Affairs* 3 (2000): 183–209.

31. For evaluations of the claims of new-economy proponents, see Doug Henwood, *After the New Economy* (New York: New Press, 2003); Robert J. Shiller, *Irrational Exuberance* (New York: Broadway, 2001).

32. Michael J. Mandel, "The Triumph of the New Economy: A Powerful Payoff from Globalization and the Info Revolution," *Business Week*, 30 December 1996, 68.

33. James K. Glassman and Kevin A. Hassett, *Dow 36,000: The New Strategy for Profiting from the Coming Rise in the Stock Market* (New York: Times Books, 1999), 4, 22.

34. Thomas Frank, *One Market Under God: Extreme Capitalism, Market Populism, and the End of Economic Democracy* (New York: Doubleday, 2000), xiv.

35. Ibid., 89–91.

36. Thomas L. Friedman, *The Lexus and the Olive Tree*, rev. ed. (New York: Anchor Books, 2000), 72.

37. For excellent histories of private pensions, see Steven A. Sass, *The Promise of Private Pensions: The First Hundred Years* (Cambridge, MA: Harvard University Press, 1997); Robin Blackburn, *Banking on Death, or, Investing in Life: The History and Future of Pensions* (London: Verso, 2002).

38. Leora Friedberg and Anthony Webb, "Retirement and the Evolution of Pension Structure," *Journal of Human Resources* 40 (2005): 281. See also Richard A. Ippolito, "Toward Explaining the Growth of Defined Contribution Plans," *Industrial Relations* 34 (1995): 1–20; Emily S. Andrews, "The Growth and Distribution of 401(k) Plans," in *Trends in Pensions, 1992*, ed. John A. Turner and Daniel J. Beller (Washington, DC: Government Printing Office, 1992), 149–76.

39. Quoted in Bob Woodward, *The Agenda: Inside the Clinton White House* (New York: Simon & Schuster, 1993), 165. Quoted in Robert Reich, *Locked in the Cabinet* (New York: Knopf, 1997), 105.

40. Reich, *Locked in the Cabinet*, 64; Joseph E. Stiglitz, *The Roaring Nineties*, 70, 66.

41. Robert Pollin, *Contours of Descent: U.S. Economic Fractures and the Landscape of Global Austerity* (New York: Verso, 2003), 43–44; Heather Boushey and Christian E. Weller, "What the Numbers Tell Us," in *Inequality Matters: The Growing Economic Divide in America and Its Poisonous Consequences*, ed. James Lardner and David A. Smith (New York: New Press, 2005), 30–32; Dwight D. Murphy, "An Economic Paradox? Displacement and Polarization in a Booming Economy," *Journal of Social, Political, and Economic Studies* 24 (1998): 349–71.

42. Advisory Council on Social Security, *Report of the 1994–1996 Advisory Council on Social Security* (Washington, DC, 1997), 25.

43. Ibid., 30. Supporters of the PSA plan acknowledged that "there is a cost of transition to the new system." They explained that "in moving toward a system in which each generation pays for its own benefits rather than those of its elders, some workers have to pay for the benefits that come due under the old system to earlier generations as well to prefund their own retirement" (30). In other words, one generation of workers would have to pay twice—once for benefits of current retirees, and a second time for their retirement benefits. To pay for this transition cost, the PSA plan proposed additional borrowing by the federal government for the next forty years (by issuing bonds) and a 72-year payroll tax increase of 1.52 percent.

44. Advisory Council, *Social Security*, 12.

45. Ibid., 61.

46. William J. Clinton, *Public Papers of the Presidents of the United States: William J. Clinton, 1998* (Washington, DC: Government Printing Office, 1999), 1:113.

47. William J. Clinton, *Public Papers of the Presidents of the United States: William J. Clinton, 1999* (Washington, DC: Government Printing Office, 2000), 1:62, 63.

48. Ibid., 1:63.

49. John M. Murphy, "Cunning, Rhetoric, and the Presidency of William Jefferson Clinton," in *The Presidency and Rhetorical Leadership*, ed. Leroy G. Dorsey (College Station: Texas A&M University Press, 2002), 244.

50. Craig Allen Smith, "Bill Clinton in Rhetorical Crisis: The Six Stages of Scandal and Impeachment," in *Images, Scandal, and Communication Strategies of the Clinton Presidency*, ed. Robert E. Denton Jr. and Rachel L. Holloway (Westport, CT: Praeger, 2003), 191.

51. House Budget Committee, *Addressing Our Long-Term Budget Challenges*, 105th Cong., 1st sess., 1997, 3; Senate Special Committee on Aging, *Women and Social Security Reform: Are Individual Accounts the Answer?* 106th Cong., 1st sess., 1999, 32. For another example associating Social Security benefits with dependence, see the testimony of Louis Enoff, who served briefly as acting commissioner of Social Security in the early 1990s. Senate Special Committee on Aging, *The Stock Market and Social Security: The Risks and the Rewards*, 105th Cong., 2d sess., 1998, 121.

52. House Social Security Subcommittee, *Impacts of the Current Social Security System*, 106th Cong., 1st sess., 1999, 26.

53. Senate Finance Committee, *Retirement Security Policy: Proposals to Preserve and Protect Social Security*, 105th Cong., 2d sess., 1998, 7; House Ways and Means Committee, *Preserving and Strengthening Social Security*, 106th Cong., 1st sess., 1999, 5.

54. Senate Special Committee on Aging, *Preserving America's Future Today*, 105th Cong., 2d sess., 1998, 30; Senate Budget Committee, *Concurrent Resolution on the Budget for the Fiscal Year 2000*, 106th Cong., 1st sess., 1999, 6.

55. Senate Social Security and Family Policy Subcommittee, *Social Security Advisory Council Report*, 104th Cong., 2d sess., 1996, 27, 28; Senate Aging Subcommittee, *Confronting the Challenges Presented by an Aging Population*, 104th Cong., 2d sess., 1996, 22.

56. Senate Social Security and Family Policy Subcommittee, *Privatization of the Social Security Old Age and Survivors Insurance Program*, 104th Cong., 1st sess., 1995, 7, 25; House Social Security Task Force, *Social Security Reform*, 106th Cong., 1st sess., 1999, 69, 71.

57. House Ways and Means Committee, *Social Security Reform Lessons Learned in Other Countries*, 106th Cong., 1st sess., 1999, 75.

58. House Social Security Subcommittee, *The Future of Social Security for this Generation and the Next: Current State of Public Opinion on the Future of Social Security*, 105th Cong., 1st sess., 1997, 42, 43; Senate Budget Committee, *Social Security Reform*, 105th Cong., 2d sess., 1998, 34.

59. Senate Health Care, Social Security and Family Policy, and Securities Subcommittees, *Investment-Based Alternatives to Financing Social Security and Medicare*, 105th Cong., 1st sess., 1997, 17; Senate Budget Committee, *Social Security Reform*, 47.

60. Senate Finance Committee, *Personal Retirement Accounts*, 106th Cong., 1st sess., 1999, 40; Senate Budget Committee, *Concurrent Resolution*, 76.

61. House Ways and Means Committee, *Strengthening Social Security*, 48.

62. Lakoff and Johnson, *Metaphors We Live By*, 16.

63. House Ways and Means Committee, *Use of an Expert Panel to Design Long-Range Social Security Reform*, 105th Cong., 2d sess., 1998, 34.

64. Moynihan appeared as a surprising advocate because he had staunchly defended social insurance in the past and warned of privatization at the outset of the mid-1990s debates. During a March 1996 Senate subcommittee hearing, Moynihan asserted that Frances Perkins "would be appalled that we would not trust our own government's securities better than the market's securities. I fear this is coming." Senate Social Security and Family Policy Subcommittee, *Social Security and Future Retirees*, 104th Cong., 2d sess., 1996, 19. In August 1996, on the Senate floor, as his colleagues approved a highly publicized welfare-reform bill that repealed Title IV of the Social Security Act, the Aid to Families with Dependent Children program, Moynihan predicted that "it is the first step in dismantling the social contract that has been in place in the United States since at least the 1930s. Do not doubt that Social Security itself, which is to say insured

retirement benefits, will be next." *Congressional Record*, 104th Cong., 2d sess., 1996, vol. 142, pt. 116:S9329.

During the same period, he seemed to come to terms with the Advisory Council report, and he expressed "delight" that the Advisory Council unanimously agreed that "some portion of the federal national retirement system should go into private investment," even if they disagreed over the primacy of insurance versus investment. Senate Social Security and Family Policy Subcommittee, *Social Security Advisory Council Report*, 30. In a 1997 *New York Times* op-ed essay, Moynihan again touched on the issue of agreement among the members of the Advisory Council. He noted that their report contained three plans, "with the 13 members divided every which way, and no majority for anything." However, a comparison of the plans revealed "a striking accord among the three factions. . . . If the council has its way, all of the reserves, or much of the reserves, would be invested in the stock market." Daniel Patrick Moynihan, "Social Security, as We Knew It," *New York Times*, 5 January 1997, late edition, sec. 4, 13.

65. Senate Finance Committee, *New Directions in Retirement Security Policy: Social Security, Pensions, Personal Savings and Work*, 105th Cong., 2d sess., 1998, 2; Senate Finance Committee, *Personal Retirement Accounts*, 2, 38.

66. Senate Finance Committee, *Retirement Security Policy*, 5; House Social Security Subcommittee, *Investing in the Private Market*, 106th Cong., 1st sess., 1999, 43; House Ways and Means Committee, *Proposals Certified to Save Social Security*, 106th Cong., 1st sess., 1999, 109.

67. House Social Security Subcommittee, *The Future of Social Security for this Generation and the Next: Personal Savings Accounts and Individual-Owned Investments*, 105th Cong., 2d sess., 1998, 45; House Social Security Subcommittee, *Investing*, 21.

68. House Social Security Task Force, *Social Security Reform*, 426; House Social Security Subcommittee, *Individual-Owned Investments*, 70.

69. House Budget Committee, *Budget Challenges*, 55, 56.

70. House Social Security Subcommittee, *The Future of Social Security for this Generation and the Next*, 105th Cong., 1st sess., 1997, 14; House Social Security Subcommittee, *The Future of Social Security for this Generation and the Next: The Implications of Raising the Retirement Age*, 105th Cong., 2d sess., 1998, 52.

71. House Ways and Means Committee, *The President's Social Security Framework*, 106th Cong., 1st sess., 1999, 9, 17.

72. Senate Budget Committee, *Social Security Reform*, 82; Senate Finance Committee, *Retirement Security Policy*, 29.

73. House Ways and Means Committee, *Use of an Expert Panel*, 92; Senate Finance Committee, *New Directions*, 33.

74. Senate Budget Committee, *Concurrent Resolution*, 44.

75. Senate Special Committee on Aging, *Preserving America's Future*, 56; Senate Budget Committee, *Concurrent Resolution*, 64, 130.

76. Senate Social Security and Family Policy Subcommittee, *Social Security and Future Retirees*, 6; House Social Security Task Force, *Social Security Reform*, 264.

77. Senate Finance Committee, *Proposals to Create Personal Savings Accounts under Social Security*, 104th Cong., 2d sess., 1996, 21, 24.

78. Senate Special Committee on Aging, *Social Security Reform Options: Preparing for the 21st Century*, 104th Cong., 2d sess., 1996, 75; House Social Security Subcommittee, *Investing in the Private Market*, 88.

79. House Subcommittee on Social Security, *Future of Social Security for this Generation and the Next*, 48.

80. Senate Special Committee on Aging, *A Starting Point for Reform: Identifying the Goals of Social Security*, 105th Cong, 2d sess., 1998, 6. Kenneth Apfel succeeded Shirley Chater as commissioner of Social Security in 1997.

81. House Ways and Means Committee, *Strengthening Social Security*, 23.

82. Senate Budget Committee, *Concurrent Resolution*, 28.

83. Senate Social Security and Family Policy Subcommittee, *Future Retirees*, 2; Senate Finance Committee, *Retirement Security Policy*, 44.

84. Senate Finance Committee, *Retirement Security Policy*, 44.

85. Senate Social Security and Family Policy Subcommittee, *Social Security Advisory Council Report*, 13.

86. House Ways and Means Committee, *Social Security Framework*, 55; House Social Security Task Force, *Social Security Reform*, 247.

87. House Social Security Task Force, *Social Security Reform*, 214; House Ways and Means Committee, *Social Security Framework*, 24.

88. House Finance and Hazardous Materials Subcommittee, *The Market Impact of the President's Social Security Proposal*, 106th Cong., 1st sess., 1999, 22, 129.

89. Senate Budget Committee, *Concurrent Resolution*, 118; House Social Security Subcommittee, *Investing in the Private Market*, 42.

90. House Ways and Means Committee, *Strengthening Social Security*, 33, 36.

91. Ibid., 35.

92. Advisory Council, *Social Security*, 12.

CHAPTER 3. REPRESENTING TARGET POPULATIONS

1. Senate Aging Special Committee, *Social Security Reform Options: Preparing for the 21st Century*, 104th Cong., 2d sess., 1996, 44.

2. Hanna Fenichel Pitkin, *The Concept of Representation* (Berkeley: University of California Press, 1967), 8–9. In *Keywords*, Raymond Williams makes the same observation. He writes that representation involves "the sense (a) of making present to the mind and the sense (b) of standing for something that is not present." Raymond Williams, *Keywords: A Vocabulary of Culture and Society*, rev. ed. (New York: Oxford University Press, 1985), 267. See also Jacques Derrida, "Sending: On Representation," *Social Research* 49 (1982): 294–326.

3. Linda Alcoff, "The Problem of Speaking for Others," *Cultural Critique* 20 (1991–92): 9.

4. This argument is drawn from my article "Imagining in the Public Sphere." See Robert Asen, "Imagining in the Public Sphere," *Philosophy and Rhetoric* 35 (2002): 345–67.

5. Linda Hutcheon, "The Politics of Representation," *Signature: A Journal of Theory and Canadian Literature* 1 (1989): 24–25.

6. Richard Dyer, *The Matter of Images: Essays on Representation* (New York: Routledge, 1993), 3.

7. Frank Lentricchia, *Criticism and Social Change* (Chicago: University of Chicago Press, 1983), 153.

8. Michael Osborn, "Rhetorical Depiction," in *Form, Genre, and the Study of Political Discourse*, ed. Herbert W. Simons and Aram A. Aghazarian (Columbia: University of South Carolina Press, 1986), 80. Osborn adopts George Campbell's terminology.

9. Judith Butler, *Undoing Gender* (New York: Routledge, 2004), 1.

10. Senate Aging Subcommittee, *Confronting the Challenges Presented by an Aging Population*, 104th Cong., 2d sess., 1996, 53; Senate Social Security and Family Policy Subcommittee, *Solvency of the Social Security Trust Funds*, 104th Cong., 1st sess., 1995, 25, 37.

11. Senate Aging Subcommittee, *Is Working America Preparing for Retirement?* 104th Cong., 2d sess., 1996, 5–7.

12. Senate Aging Subcommittee, *Working America*, 16, 20; Senate Social Security and Family Policy Subcommittee, *1995 Annual Report of the Social Security and Disability Trust Funds*, 104th Cong., 1st sess., 1995, 40.

13. Senate Aging Special Committee, *Retiring Baby Boomers: Meeting the Challenges*, 105th Cong., 1st sess., 1997, 79; Senate Aging Special Committee, *The Boomers Are Coming: Challenges of Aging in the New Millennium*, 106th Cong., 1st sess., 1999, 18.

14. Senate Social Security and Family Policy Subcommittee, *Social Security and Future Retirees*, 104th Cong., 2d sess., 1996, 31; Senate Social Security and Family

Policy Subcommittee, *Solvency of the Social Security Trust Funds*, 7; House Social Security Task Force, *Social Security Reform*, 106th Cong., 1st sess., 1999, 213.

15. House Employer-Employee Relations Subcommittee, *Hearing on Defusing the Retirement Time Bomb: Encouraging Pension Savings*, 105th Cong., 1st sess., 1997, 4; House Social Security Subcommittee, *The Future of Social Security for this Generation and the Next*, 105th Cong., 1st sess., 1997, 45.

16. House Social Security Subcommittee, *The Future of Social Security for this Generation and the Next*, 4.

17. Senate Aging Special Committee, *Retiring Baby Boomers*, 28; Senate Finance Committee, *Retirement Security Policy: Proposals to Preserve and Protect Social Security*, 105th Cong., 2d sess., 1998, 18; Senate Social Security and Family Policy Subcommittee, *1995 Annual Report*, 12.

18. Senate Social Security and Family Policy Subcommittee, *Solvency of the Social Security Trust Funds*, 5, 21.

19. Senate Aging Special Committee, *Retiring Baby Boomers*, 139, 87; Senate Aging Special Committee, *The Boomers Are Coming*, 19.

20. Senate Aging Special Committee, *The Boomers Are Coming*, 63, 20; Senate Budget Committee, *Concurrent Resolution on the Budget for the Fiscal Year 2000*, 106th Cong., 1st sess., 1999, 129.

21. Senate Social Security and Family Policy Subcommittee, *1995 Annual Report*, 22; Senate Aging Special Committee, *Retiring Baby Boomers*, 6.

22. Senate Social Security and Family Policy Subcommittee, *Social Security and Future Retirees*, 3, 4; House Social Security Subcommittee, *The Future of Social Security for this Generation and the Next*, 80.

23. Senate Social Security Task Force, *Education, International Affairs, and Social Security Task Forces*, 105th Cong., 2d sess., 1998, 463; Senate Social Security and Family Policy Subcommittee, *Solvency of the Social Security Trust Funds*, 27.

24. Advisory Council on Social Security, *Report of the 1994–1996 Advisory Council on Social Security* (Washington, DC, 1997), 12.

25. Third Millennium, "Survey: Social Security: The Credibility Gap," *Third Millennium*, September 1994, http://www.thirdmil.org/publications/surveys/surv7.html (accessed 7 December 2002); Frank Luntz and Mark Siegel, "Analysis of Third Millennium Survey," *Third Millennium*, September 1994, http://www.thirdmil.org/publications/surveys/surv5.html (accessed 7 December 2002).

26. House Social Security Subcommittee, *The Future of Social Security for this Generation and the Next: Current State of Public Opinion on the Future of Social Security*, 105th Cong., 1st sess., 1997, 24. Explaining these divergent findings in a *New Republic* essay, political scientists Lawrence Jacobs and Robert Shapiro observed

that "people generally approach survey questions with different 'metrics.'" Jacobs and Shapiro suspected that respondents to the Third Millennium poll likely treated the UFO question as a thought experiment. In contrast, people consider Social Security policy "in concrete, real-life terms." They explained that directly comparing the two possibilities, as the EBRI poll did, would "produce a more telling result." Lawrence R. Jacobs and Robert Y. Shapiro, "UFO Stories," *New Republic*, 10 August 1998, 13.

27. J. Michael Hogan, "George Gallup and the Rhetoric of Scientific Democracy," *Communication Monographs* 64 (1997): 172.

28. Senate Budget Committee, *Concurrent Resolution*, 89; House Ways and Means Committee, *Use of an Expert Panel to Design Long-Range Social Security Reform*, 105th Cong., 2d sess., 1998, 33.

29. House Social Security Subcommittee, *Impacts of the Current Social Security System*, 106th Cong., 1st sess., 1999, 8–9.

30. Ibid., 17.

31. House Social Security Task Force, *Social Security Reform*, 429.

32. Senate Social Security Task Force, *Education, International Affairs, and Social Security Task Forces*, 411; House Ways and Means Committee, *Proposals Certified to Save Social Security*, 106th Cong., 1st sess., 1999, 77.

33. Senate Social Security Task Force, *Education, International Affairs, and Social Security Task Forces*, 422.

34. House Ways and Means Committee, *Ideas for Advancing the Upcoming Debate on Saving the Social Security System*, 105th Cong., 2d sess., 1998, 14; Senate Aging Special Committee, *Women and Social Security Reform: Are Individual Accounts the Answer?* 106th Cong., 1st sess., 1999, 9.

35. House Social Security Subcommittee, *Impacts of the Current Social Security System*, 103; House Social Security Task Force, *Social Security Reform*, 39–40, 17.

36. Senate Aging Special Committee, *Women and Social Security Reform*, 17; House Social Security Subcommittee, *Impacts of the Current Social Security System*, 67; Senate Aging Special Committee, *The Impact of Social Security Reform on Women*, 106th Cong., 1st sess., 1999, 19.

37. House Finance and Hazardous Materials Subcommittee, *The Market Impact of the President's Social Security Proposal*, 106th Cong., 1st sess., 1999, 121; House Social Security Task Force, *Social Security Reform*, 71.

38. House Budget Committee, *Addressing Our Long-Term Budget Challenges*, 105th Cong., 1st sess., 1997, 9, 41, 50.

39. House Ways and Means Committee, *Preserving and Strengthening Social Security,* 106th Cong., 1st sess., 1999, 44; House Social Security Subcommittee, *Impacts of the Current Social Security System,* 182.

40. Senate Finance Committee, *Retirement Security Policy,* 10; House Ways and Means Committee, *Preserving and Strengthening Social Security,* 5, 11.

41. Senate Budget Committee, *Concurrent Resolution,* 109, 110; Senate Finance Committee, *Retirement Security Policy,* 37.

42. House Social Security Subcommittee, *The Future of Social Security for this Generation and the Next: Personal Savings Accounts and Individual-Owned Investments,* 105th Cong., 2d sess., 1998, 82, 83, 87.

43. Senate Social Security and Family Policy Subcommittee, *1995 Annual Report,* 12; Senate Social Security and Family Policy Subcommittee, *Privatization of the Social Security Old Age and Survivors Insurance Program,* 104th Cong., 1st sess., 1995, 2; Senate Social Security and Family Policy Subcommittee, *Solvency of the Social Security Trust Funds,* 26.

44. House Social Security Task Force, *Social Security Reform,* 339, 323–24.

45. Ibid., 325. For an example of a two-tiered private-accounts proposal, see Senate Budget Committee, *Social Security Reform,* 105th Cong., 2d sess., 1998, 12–15.

46. For detailed discussions of Chile's retirement system, see Rossana Castiglioni, "The Politics of Retrenchment: The Quandaries of Social Protection under Military Rule in Chile," *Latin American Politics and Society* 43 (2001): 37–66; Barbara E. Kritzer, "Social Security Privatization in Latin America," *Social Security Bulletin* 63 (2000): 17–37; Carmelo Mesa-Lago, "Myth and Reality of Pension Reform: The Latin American Evidence," *World Development* 30 (2002): 1309–21; John B. Williamson, "Privatizing Public Pension Systems: Lessons from Latin America," *Journal of Aging Studies* 15 (2001): 285–302.

47. Senate Securities Subcommittee, *Social Security Investment in the Securities Markets,* 105th Cong., 1st sess., 1997, 30, 77.

48. House Budget Committee, *Protecting the Future of Social Security,* 105th Cong., 1st sess., 1997, 42; House Ways and Means Committee, *Social Security Reform Lessons Learned in Other Countries,* 106th Cong., 1st sess., 1999, 17.

49. Senate Securities Subcommittee, *Social Security Investment in the Securities Markets,* 70; House Ways and Means Committee, *Lessons Learned in Other Countries,* 17.

50. Senate Securities Subcommittee, *Social Security Investment in the Securities Markets,* 74, 69; House Budget Committee, *Protecting the Future of Social Security,* 7.

51. House Budget Committee, *Protecting the Future of Social Security,* 28, 52.

52. William J. Clinton, *Public Papers of the Presidents of the United States: William J. Clinton, 1998* (Washington, DC: Government Printing Office, 1999), 1:113; Senate

Finance Committee, *New Directions in Retirement Security Policy: Social Security, Pensions, Personal Savings and Work*, 105th Cong., 2d sess., 1998, 9; House Social Security Subcommittee, *Current State of Public Opinion on the Future of Social Security*, 32, 46.

53. Senate Finance Committee, *Social Security, Pensions, Personal Savings and Work*, 25, 26; Senate Social Security Task Force, *Education, International Affairs, and Social Security Task Forces*, 517.

54. Senate Finance Committee, *Social Security, Pensions, Personal Savings and Work*, 28; House Finance and Hazardous Materials Subcommittee, *Market Impact*, 73.

55. House Ways and Means Committee, *Proposals Certified to Save Social Security*, 4, 7.

56. House Ways and Means Committee, *Use of an Expert Panel*, 44, 67.

57. Senate Aging Special Committee, *Preparing for the 21st Century*, 133; Ways and Means Committee, *Use of an Expert Panel*, 57.

58. On the pervasiveness of polling in contemporary American politics and its historical significance, see Philip E. Converse, "Changing Conceptions of Public Opinion in the Political Process," *Public Opinion Quarterly* 51 (1987): S12–S24; Susan Herbst, *Numbered Voices: How Opinion Polling Has Shaped American Politics* (Chicago: University of Chicago Press, 1993); John Durham Peters, "Historical Tensions in the Concept of Public Opinion," in *Public Opinion and the Communication of Consent*, ed. Theodore L. Glasser and Charles T. Salmon (New York: Guilford Press, 1995), 3–32.

59. Senate Aging Special Committee, *Preparing for the Retirement of the Baby Boom Generation*, 105th Cong., 2d sess., 1998, 73.

60. Senate Aging Special Committee, *Retirement of the Baby Boom Generation*, 62, 66–67.

61. Herbst, *Numbered Voices*, 166.

CHAPTER 4. RECONSTRUCTING A TIME FOR REFORM

1. On the Supreme Court case and its implications, see Cass R. Sunstein and Richard A. Epstein, *The Vote: Bush, Gore, and the Supreme Court* (Chicago: University of Chicago Press, 2001); James T. Patterson, *Restless Giant: The United States from Watergate to Bush v. Gore* (New York: Oxford University Press, 2005).

2. Editorial, "Pop Went the Bubble," *New York Times*, 9 March 2005, late edition, sec. 4, p. 12.

3. Senate Aging Special Committee, *Income Taxes: The Solution to the Social Security and Medicare Crisis?* 106th Cong., 2d sess., 2000, 21.

4. Lloyd F. Bitzer, "The Rhetorical Situation," *Philosophy and Rhetoric* 1 (1968): 6.

5. Roger Thompson, "*Kairos* Revisited: An Interview with James Kinneavy," *Rhetoric Review* 19 (2000): 76.

6. John Poulakos, *Sophistical Rhetoric in Classical Greece* (Columbia: University of South Carolina Press, 1995), 61, 62. Eric Charles White also emphasizes particularity. He writes that Gorgias viewed *kairos* as "a radical principle of occasionality which implies a conception of the production of meaning in language as a process of continuous adjustment to and creation of the present occasion." Eric Charles White, *Kaironomia: On the Will-to-Invent* (Ithaca, NY: Cornell University Press, 1987), 14.

7. Phillip Sipiora, "Introduction: The Ancient Concept of *Kairos*," in *Rhetoric and Kairos: Essays in History, Theory, and Praxis*, ed. Phillip Sipiora and James S. Baumlin (Albany: State University of New York Press, 2002), 9.

8. Aristotle, *On Rhetoric: A Theory of Civic Discourse*, 2d ed., trans. George Kennedy (New York: Oxford University Press, 2007), 1356a. As Kinneavy and Eskin maintain, although he did not use the term explicitly in his definition, "Aristotle's art is to be applied at a particular *kairos*." James Kinneavy and Catherine R. Eskin, "*Kairos* in Aristotle's *Rhetoric*," *Written Communication* 17 (2000): 434.

9. John Poulakos, "Toward a Sophistic Definition of Rhetoric," *Philosophy and Rhetoric* 16 (1983): 40.

10. James L. Kinneavy, "*Kairos*: A Neglected Concept in Classical Rhetoric," in *Rhetoric and Praxis: The Contribution of Classical Rhetoric to Practical Reasoning*, ed. Jean Dietz Moss (Washington, DC: Catholic University of America Press, 1986), 87.

11. Mario Untersteiner, *The Sophists*, trans. Kathleen Freeman (Oxford: Blackwell, 1954), 72, 161. I was made aware of Untersteiner's views on *kairos* and ethics by Michael Carter's excellent explication of the topic. See Michael Carter, "*Stasis* and *Kairos*: Principles of Social Construction in Classical Rhetoric," *Rhetoric Review* 7 (1988): 101–6.

12. John E. Smith, "Time and Qualitative Time," *Review of Metaphysics* 40 (1986): 5.

13. Carolyn R. Miller, "*Kairos* in the Rhetoric of Science," in *A Rhetoric of Doing*, ed. Stephen P. White, Neil Nakadate, and Roger D. Cherry (Carbondale: Southern Illinois University Press, 1992), 312.

14. Amélie Frost Benedikt, "On Doing the Right Thing at the Right Time: Toward an Ethics of *Kairos*," in *Rhetoric and Kairos: Essays in History, Theory, and Praxis*, ed. Phillip Sipiora and James S. Baumlin (Albany: State University of New York Press, 2002), 229–30.

15. Michael Leff, "Textual Criticism: The Legacy of G. P. Mohrmann," *Quarterly Journal of Speech* 72 (1986): 385.

16. William J. Clinton, *Public Papers of the Presidents of the United States: William J. Clinton, 2000* (Washington, DC: Government Printing Office, 2001), 1:131–32.

17. Al Gore and George W. Bush, "The First Gore-Bush Presidential Debate," 3 October 2000, *Commission on Presidential Debates*, http://www.debates.org/pages/trans2000a.html (accessed 24 February 2006). All subsequent quotes of this debate are taken from the transcript posted on the commission's website.

18. See Chris Smith and Ben Voth, "The Role of Humor in Political Argument: How 'Strategery' and 'Lockboxes' Changed a Political Campaign," *Argumentation and Advocacy* 39 (2002): 110–29.

19. George W. Bush, *Public Papers of the Presidents of the United States: George W. Bush, 2001* (Washington, DC: Government Printing Office, 2003), 1:146, 477–78.

20. Amy Goldstein, "Social Security Panel Gears Up for Revamp," *Washington Post*, 3 May 2001, final edition, A1.

21. Ibid., A1. See also Mimi Hall, "Social Security Review Being Rigged, Critics Say," *USA Today*, 3 May 2001, final edition, 6A; "Social Security Commission Is Tilted toward Privatization," *St. Louis Post-Dispatch*, 2 May 2001, three-star edition, A7.

22. Bush, *Public Papers*, 478.

23. President's Commission to Strengthen Social Security, *Strengthening Social Security and Creating Personal Wealth for All Americans*, Washington, DC, 21 December 2001, 4–5.

24. Ibid., 5.

25. Ibid., 6.

26. Ibid., 21; www.dictionary.oed.com/entrance.dtl (accessed 11 April 2006).

27. President's Commission, *Strengthening Social Security*, 61.

28. Ibid., 63–65.

29. Ibid., 67.

30. Of the three proposals, model 2 adhered most closely to President Bush's campaign promise to ensure the benefits promised by Social Security while permitting younger workers to devote a portion of their payroll taxes to private accounts. Model 1 called for private accounts, with workers' traditional benefits to be reduced by the amount of their contribution plus a 3.5 percent interest rate, but made no changes to the existing system. Model 3 proposed private accounts, but required workers to contribute an additional 1 percent to their payroll taxes to be eligible to participate in these accounts. In subsequent congressional committee hearings, policymakers and witnesses treated model 2 as the administration's proposal, even though the administration did not submit a specific plan to Congress.

31. President's Commission, *Strengthening Social Security*, 109. In subsequent congressional testimony, commission member Olivia Mitchell acknowledged that model 2 would cut traditional Social Security benefits by half: "Model 2 of the Commission proposes reducing revenue needs by about 45 or 50 percent." Senate Finance Committee, *Final Report Produced by the President's Commission to Strengthen Social Security*, 107th Cong., 2d sess., 2002, 11.

32. President's Commission, *Strengthening Social Security*, 111.

33. Ibid., 10.

34. Alex Berenson, "Wall St. Down a 3rd Year, Leaving Fewer Optimists," *New York Times*, 1 January 2003, national edition, C1; Carol Emert, "Point of No Returns," *San Francisco Chronicle*, 3 July 2002, final edition, B1; Floyd Norris, "3 Years Later, Investors Crave Safety," *New York Times*, 10 March 2003, late edition, C1.

35. Simon Romero and Alex Berenson, "Worldcom Says It Hid Expenses, Inflating Cash Flow $3.8 Billion," *New York Times*, 26 June 2002, late edition, A1; David Wessel, "Why the Bad Guys of the Boardroom Emerged En Masse," *Wall Street Journal*, 20 June 2002, eastern edition, A1; Alex Berenson, "The Biggest Casualty of Enron's Collapse: Confidence," *New York Times*, 10 February 2002, late edition, sec. 4, p. 1; Randall Smith, Susanne Craig, and Deborah Solomon, "Wall Street Firms to Pay $1.4 Billion to End Inquiry—Record Payment Settles Conflict-of-Interest Charges," *Wall Street Journal*, 29 April 2003, eastern edition, A1; Stephen Labaton, "10 Wall St. Firms Reach Settlement in Analyst Inquiry," *New York Times*, 29 April 2003, late edition, A1.

36. "Reformers All, in Enron's Wake," *New York Times*, 2 February 2002, national edition, A28.

37. For detailed accounts of the Enron bankruptcy and its aftermath, see Robert Bryce, *Pipe Dreams: Greed, Ego, and the Death of Enron* (New York: PublicAffairs, 2002); Kurt Eichenwald, *Conspiracy of Fools: A True Story* (New York: Broadway Books, 2005); Bethany McLean and Peter Elkind, *The Smartest Guys in the Room: The Amazing Rise and Scandalous Fall of Enron* (New York: Portfolio, 2003).

38. "Enron's Sins," *Wall Street Journal*, 18 January 2002, eastern edition, A10; Edward Chancellor, "The Trouble with Bubbles," *New York Times*, 27 January 2002, national edition, sec. 4, p. 13. For Chancellor's history of speculation, see Edward Chancellor, *Devil Take the Hindmost: A History of Financial Speculation* (New York: Farrar, Straus, Giroux, 1999).

39. Daniel McGinn, "Weathering the Storm," *Newsweek*, 26 March 2001, 23–25; Ann Kates Smith, "What Kind of Bear?" *U.S. News and World Report*, 26 March 2001, 39.

40. Robert J. Shiller, "The Market's Future: You Won't Hear a Pop," *Plain Dealer*, 16 May 2000, final edition, 9B; Daniel Kadlec, "Zap!" *Time*, 26 March 2001, 28; Robert J. Samuelson, "What If Washington's Tool Kit Won't Work?" *Newsweek*, 26 March 2001, 29.

41. Daniel Kadlec, "Everyone, Back in the Labor Pool," *Time*, 29 July 2002, 25; Peter Grier, "Stocks' Gilded Age Finally Closes," *Christian Science Monitor*, 2 January 2001, 1.

42. Teresa Dixon Murray, "Market's Fairy Tale Had Bitter Ending," *Plain Dealer*, 9 March 2002, final edition, C9; Bill Keller, "The Sunny Side of the Street," *New York Times*, 27 July 2002, late edition, A11; Lester C. Thurow, "Market Crash Born of Greed," *Boston Globe*, 17 April 2001, third edition, C4.

43. Michael Moritz, "Spring Comes Early to Silicon Valley," *Time*, 26 March 2001, 32; Steven Levy, "Silicon Valley Reboots," *Newsweek*, 25 March 2002, 44.

44. Daniel Kadlec, "Under the Microscope," *Time*, 4 February 2002, 29; Howard Fineman and Michael Isikoff, "Lights Out: Enron's Failed Power Play," *Newsweek*, 21 January 2002, 20; Frank Rich, "Sacrifice Is for Losers," *New York Times*, 22 June 2002, late edition, A11.

45. Daniel Eisenberg, "Dennis the Menace," *Time*, 17 June 2002, 47; Kevin McCoy, "A Birthday Party for the Ages," *USA Today*, 28 October 2003, final edition, 3B.

46. Michael Elliott, "The Incredible Shrinking Businessman," *Time*, 4 February 2002, 26; Uwe Reinhardt, "Can't Executives Be as Honorable as Our Soldiers?" *Wall Street Journal*, 12 March 2002, eastern edition, A26.

47. House Social Security Subcommittee, *Social Security Improvements for Women, Seniors, and Working Americans*, 107th Cong., 2d sess., 2002, 70.

48. Ibid., 7, 55, 112.

49. Senate Aging Special Committee, *Retirement Security and Corporate Responsibility*, 107th Cong., 2d sess., 2002, 25, 20.

50. Senate Finance Committee, *Retirement Security: Picking Up the Enron Pieces*, 107th Cong., 2d sess., 2002, 4; House Social Security Subcommittee, *Social Security Improvements*, 144.

51. Senate Finance Committee, *Enron Pieces*, 1; Senate Aging Special Committee, *Corporate Responsibility*, 5.

52. Ibid., 32, 18.

53. Senate Aging Special Committee, *Planning for Retirement: Promoting Security and Dignity of American Retirement*, 107th Cong., 2d sess., 2002, 19; Senate Aging Special Committee, *Corporate Responsibility*, 25.

54. Senate Aging Special Committee, *Corporate Responsibility*, 23, 34.

55. Senate Finance Committee, *Enron Pieces*, 35, 19.

56. Robert Kuttner, *Everything for Sale: The Virtues and Limits of Markets* (Chicago: University of Chicago Press, 1996), 16.

57. As I explain in chapter 3, the concept of "money's worth return" was introduced by the 1994–96 Advisory Council.

58. Senate Aging Special Committee, *Modernization of Social Security and Medicare*, 107th Cong., 1st sess., 2001, 11.

59. Senate Finance Committee, *Final Report Produced*, 23; House Social Security Subcommittee, *Social Security and Pension Reform: Lessons from Other Countries*, 107th Cong., 1st sess., 2001, 77.

60. House Ways and Means Committee and Senate Finance Committee, *Social Security and Medicare Trustees' 2001 Annual Reports*, 107th Cong., 1st sess., 2001, 30–31.

61. House Social Security Subcommittee, *Social Security's Future*, 108th Cong., 2d sess., 2004, 44; House Ways and Means Committee and Senate Finance Committee, *Social Security and Medicare*, 133.

62. House Social Security Subcommittee, *Social Security's Future*, 22; Senate Finance Committee, *Enron Pieces*, 20.

63. The dates for 2000 were 2015 and 2037; for 2001, 2016 and 2038; for 2002, 2017 and 2041. See Board of Trustees, Federal Old-Age and Survivors Insurance and Disability Insurance Trust Funds, *1997 Annual Report of the Board of Trustees of the Federal Old-Age and Survivors Insurance and Disability Insurance Trust Funds*, Washington, DC, April 1997, 6, 19–25; Board of Trustees, Federal Old-Age and Survivors Insurance and Disability Insurance Trust Funds, *1998 Annual Report of the Board of Trustees of the Federal Old-Age and Survivors Insurance and Disability Insurance Trust Funds*, Washington, DC, April 1998, 4, 18–24; Board of Trustees, Federal Old-Age and Survivors Insurance and Disability Insurance Trust Funds, *1999 Annual Report of the Board of Trustees of the Federal Old-Age and Survivors Insurance and Disability Insurance Trust Funds*, Washington, DC, March 1999, 4, 18–24; Board of Trustees, Federal Old-Age and Survivors Insurance and Disability Insurance Trust Funds, *2000 Annual Report of the Board of Trustees of the Federal Old-Age and Survivors Insurance and Disability Insurance Trust Funds*, Washington, DC, March 2000, 3–4, 19–25; Board of Trustees, Federal Old-Age and Survivors Insurance and Disability Insurance Trust Funds, *2001 Annual Report of the Board of Trustees of the Federal Old-Age and Survivors Insurance and Disability Insurance Trust Funds*, Washington, DC, March 2001, 2, 8–13; Board of Trustees, Federal Old-Age and Survivors Insurance and Disability Insurance Trust Funds, *2002 Annual Report of the Board of Trustees of the Federal Old-Age and Survivors Insurance and Disability Insurance Trust Funds*, Washington, DC, March 2002, 3, 11–17; Board

of Trustees, Federal Old-Age and Survivors Insurance and Disability Insurance Trust Funds, *2003 Annual Report of the Board of Trustees of the Federal Old-Age and Survivors Insurance and Disability Insurance Trust Funds,* Washington, DC, March 2003, 2, 7–12.

64. House Budget Committee, *Social Security: The Long-Term Budget Implications,* 107th Cong., 2d sess., 2002, 21–22; Senate Aging Special Committee, *Analyzing Social Security: GAO Weighs the President's Commission's Proposals,* 108th Cong., 1st sess., 2003, 5–6; Senate Aging Special Committee, *Straight Shooting on Social Security: The Trade-offs of Reform,* 107th Cong., 1st sess., 2001, 155.

65. House Ways and Means Committee and Senate Finance Committee, *Social Security and Medicare,* 22.

66. Senate Aging Special Committee, *Analyzing Social Security,* 26; Senate Finance Committee, *Final Report Produced,* 13.

67. Senate Aging Special Committee, *Social Security: Whose Trust Will Be Broken?* 108th Cong., 1st sess., 2003, 31, 51–52.

68. Senate Aging Special Committee, *Whose Trust,* 51; Senate Aging Special Committee, *Strengthening Social Security: What Can Personal Retirement Accounts Do for Low-Income Workers?* 108th Cong., 2d sess., 2004, 111.

CHAPTER 5. GOING PUBLIC WITH PRIVATIZATION

1. George W. Bush, *Weekly Compilation of Presidential Documents,* vol. 40 (Washington, DC: Government Printing Office, 2004), 2789–90.

2. See Darryl Fears, "DNC to Investigate Ohio Voting Irregularities," *Washington Post,* 7 December 2004, final edition, A10; Mark Crispin Miller, "None Dare Call It Stolen," *Harper's,* August 2005, 39–46.

3. José Piñera, "Retiring in Chile," *New York Times,* 1 December 2004, late edition, A31; Janet Hook, "They Invested Years in Private Accounts," *Los Angeles Times,* 30 January 2005, home edition, A29.

4. A keyword search for the phrase "ownership society" in the online edition of *Weekly Compilation of Presidential Documents* reveals that Bush mentioned the phrase with greater frequency annually over the course of his first term. The phrase did not appear in Bush's public statements and speeches in 2001. In 2002, the phrase appeared in his public speeches and statements four times. In 2003, this number increased to fifty-six. The number increased again in 2004 to eighty-one.

5. At almost every stop, Bush moderated a panel discussion and a question-and-answer session involving attendees. The panel discussions typically included

an expert on retirement policy and laypeople from various walks of life: children, parents, grandparents, young workers, older workers, retirees, farmers, firefighters, small-business owners, warehouse workers, students, single parents, new parents. The panelists uniformly voiced concern for the future of Social Security and support for the president's proposed reforms. Retirees expressed confidence that their benefits would not be jeopardized by private accounts, and younger workers expressed relief that they and their children could anticipate a more secure retirement. President Bush began each meeting with a short speech; then he discussed issues of work and retirement with the panelists. Less often, Bush solicited questions from audience members. Like the panelists, questioners supported his policies.

6. "Who Would You Rather Have a Beer With?" *Zogby's Real America*, October 2004, 5. http://www.zogby.com/ZRA/backissues (accessed 15 August 2007).

7. Qtd. in Oren Dorell, "Lobbying War Hits Airwaves Today," *USA Today*, 7 February 2005, final edition, 1.

8. Jürgen Habermas, *The Structural Transformation of the Public Sphere: An Inquiry into a Category of Bourgeois Society*, trans. Thomas Burger (Cambridge: Massachusetts Institute of Technology Press, 1989).

9. Gerard A. Hauser, *Vernacular Voices: The Rhetoric of Publics and Public Spheres* (Columbia: University of South Carolina Press, 1999), 71.

10. Seyla Benhabib, "Toward a Deliberative Model of Democratic Legitimacy," in *Democracy and Difference: Contesting the Boundaries of the Political*, ed. Seyla Benhabib (Princeton, NJ: Princeton University Press, 1996), 74.

11. Jürgen Habermas, *Between Facts and Norms: Contributions to a Discourse Theory of Law and Democracy*, trans. William Rehg (Cambridge: Massachusetts Institute of Technology Press, 1996), 360.

12. Nancy Fraser, "Rethinking the Public Sphere: A Contribution to the Critique of Actually Existing Democracy," in *Habermas and the Public Sphere*, ed. Craig Calhoun (Cambridge: Massachusetts Institute of Technology Press, 1992), 123.

13. Habermas, *Facts and Norms*, 307–8.

14. Michael Schudson, "The 'Public Sphere' and Its Problems: Bringing the State (Back) In," *Notre Dame Journal of Law, Ethics & Public Policy* 8 (1994): 530.

15. G. Thomas Goodnight, "The Personal, Technical, and Public Spheres of Argument: A Speculative Inquiry into the Art of Public Deliberation," *Journal of the American Forensic Association* 18 (1982): 216.

16. Daniel C. Brouwer, "ACT-ing UP in Congressional Hearings," in *Counterpublics and the State*, ed. Robert Asen and Daniel C. Brouwer (Albany: State University of New York Press, 2001), 93.

17. "Bush Stood By Agenda; Why Ignore a Mandate?" *Rocky Mountain News*, 7 November 2004, final edition, 7E; "Spending Political Capital," *St. Louis Post-Dispatch*, 5 November 2004, Five-star edition, B06.

18. Christian Spielvogel, "'You Know Where I Stand': Moral Framing of the War on Terrorism and the Iraq War in the 2004 Presidential Campaign," *Rhetoric & Public Affairs* 8 (2005): 552, 559.

19. Herbert F. Weisberg and Dino P. Christenson, "Changing Horses in Wartime? The 2004 Presidential Election," *Political Behavior* 29 (2007): 298.

20. Liz Marlantes, "How Far Will Bush's Domestic Mandate Go?" *Christian Science Monitor*, 16 December 2004, 2; Richard Morin and Dale Russakoff, "Social Security Problems Not a Crisis, Most Say," *Washington Post*, 10 February 2005, final edition, A01.

21. Qtd. in Jill Zuckman, "Hastert: Public Not Sold on Social Security Plans," *Chicago Tribune*, 11 February 2005, final edition, 1.

22. Mike Allen, "At Home, a Hard Sell on Social Security," *Washington Post*, 22 February 2005, final edition, A01; qtd. in "Social Security Bill a Tough Sell in Iowa," *Kansascity.com*, 27 March 2005, http://www.kansascity.com/mld/kansascitystar/news/politics/11239666.htm (accessed 27 March 2005).

23. Timothy J. Penny, "Privatization Foes Lose Grip on Reality," *Atlanta Journal-Constitution*, 21 November 2004, home edition, 7D.

24. Qtd. in Carolyn Lochhead, "Bush Readies Ambitious 2nd-Term Domestic Agenda," *San Francisco Chronicle*, 22 November 2004, final edition, A1; Grover Norquist, "Ownership Can Be Revolutionary," *American Enterprise*, March 2005, 50.

25. Jackie Calmes, "White House Memo Argues for Social Security Cuts," *Wall Street Journal*, 6 January 2005, eastern edition, A1.

26. Peter H. Wehner, "Memo on Social Security," *Wall Street Journal Online*, 5 January 2005, http://online.wsj.com/article/0,,SB110496995612018199,00.html (accessed 15 May 2006).

27. Ibid.

28. Deborah Pryce and Rick Santorum, *Saving Social Security: A Guide to Social Security Reform*, Washington, DC, 27 January 2005, 1.

29. Ibid., 1.

30. Ibid., 3, 9.

31. Qtd. in Jim VandeHei, "A Big Push on Social Security," *Washington Post*, 1 January 2005, final edition, A1.

32. Landon Thomas Jr., "Wall St. Lobby Quietly Tackles Social Security," *New York Times*, 21 December 2004, late edition, C1; Thomas B. Edsall, "Conservatives

Join Forces for Bush Plans," *Washington Post*, 13 February 2005, final edition, A4.

33. Qtd. in Glen Justice, "A New Battle for Advisers to Swift Vets," *New York Times*, 21 February 2005, late edition, A1.

34. USA Next, "The Real AARP Agenda," *American Spectator*, http://www.spectator.org (accessed 21 February 2005).

35. "Iceberg," *Progress for America*, 8 March 2005, http://pfavoterfund.com/docs/audiovideo/ (accessed 15 March 2005).

36. Douglas Walton, *Scare Tactics: Arguments That Appeal to Fear and Threats* (Dordrecht, Netherlands: Kluwer Academic, 2000), 20.

37. "Courage," *Progress for America*, 15 January 2005, http://pfavoterfund.com/docs/audiovideo/ (accessed 15 February 2005).

38. Qtd. in Jim VandeHei and Peter Baker, "On with the Show; President's 'Conversations' on Issue Are Carefully Orchestrated, Rehearsed," *Washington Post*, 12 March 2005, final edition, A03.

39. Ibid.; "Bush's Believers-Only Speeches," *St. Petersburg Times*, 9 April 2005, South Pinellas edition, 18A.

40. Sheryl Gay Stolberg and Carl Hulse, "Cool Reception on Capitol Hill to Social Security Plan," *New York Times*, 4 February 2005, late edition, A1; "6 Key Democratic Senators Oppose Bush Plan on Benefits," *New York Times*, 1 February 2005, late edition, A14; Charles Babington and Jim VandeHei, "Senators May Block Social Security Vote," *Washington Post*, 11 March 2005, final edition, A01.

41. Minority Staff, House Oversight and Government Reform Committee, *The Politicization of the Social Security Administration*, February 2005, i, ii, 1.

42. Anne E. Kornblut, "Democrats Criticize Social Security Official," *New York Times*, 25 February 2005, late edition, A16.

43. "Social Security: Where We Stand," *AARP Bulletin*, December 2004, 15; Robert Pear, "AARP Opposes Plan to Replace Social Security with Private Accounts," *New York Times*, 12 November 2004, late edition, A1.

44. "Winners & Losers," *New York Times*, 4 January 2005, late edition, A9; "We'll Play the Slots," *New York Times*, 9 January 2005, late edition, sec. 1, p. 18; "Passing 2 Trillion Bucks Is Another," *New York Times*, 16 January 2005, late edition, sec. 1, p. 13.

45. "Kitchen Sink," *AARP.org*, 21 March 2005, http://aarp.typepad.com/socialsecurity/2005/03/aarps_social_se.html (accessed 15 April 2005).

46. See John C. Meyer, "Humor as a Double-Edged Sword: Four Functions of Humor in Communication," *Communication Theory* 10 (2000): 310–31; David L. Paletz,

"Political Humor and Authority: From Support to Subversion," *International Political Science Review* 11 (1990): 483–93.

47. Michael William Pfau, "Who's Afraid of Fear Appeals? Contingency, Courage, and Deliberation in Rhetorical Theory and Practice," *Philosophy and Rhetoric* 40 (2007): 216–37.

48. J. Robert Cox, "The Die Is Cast: Topical and Ontological Dimensions of the *Locus* of the Irreparable," *Quarterly Journal of Speech* 68 (1982): 227, 229.

49. "Working Retirement," *MoveOn.org*, 31 January 2005, http://cdn.MoveOn.org/content/video/SS_ad.wmv (accessed 1 February 2005).

50. "WMD," *New York Times*, 2 February 2005, late edition, A7.

51. Maeve Reston, "Activists Targeting Lawmakers over Social Security; Pa. Congressman in Close District Faces Ad Campaign," *Pittsburgh Post-Gazette*, 1 February 2005, region edition, A6; "MoveOn Launches Ad Campaign Highlighting Benefit Cuts in President's Social Security Plan," *MoveOn.org*, 31 January 2005, http://www.MoveOn.org/press/pdfs/pr13105.pdf (accessed 1 February 2005).

52. George W. Bush, *Weekly Compilation of Presidential Documents*, vol. 41 (Washington, DC: Government Printing Office, 2004), 501, 416.

53. Ibid., 175, 623, 871.

54. Ibid., 461, 156.

55. Ibid., 372, 366, 168, 400, 219.

56. Ibid., 175, 146, 157, 373, 474, 365.

57. Board of Trustees, Federal Old-Age and Survivors Insurance and Disability Insurance Trust Funds, *2004 Annual Report of the Board of Trustees of the Federal Old-Age and Survivors Insurance and Disability Insurance Trust Funds*, Washington, DC, March 2004, 8; Board of Trustees, Federal Old-Age and Survivors Insurance and Disability Insurance Trust Funds, *2005 Annual Report of the Board of Trustees of the Federal Old-Age and Survivors Insurance and Disability Insurance Trust Funds*, Washington, DC, April 2005, 8.

58. Bush, *Weekly Compilation*, 222, 675, 832, 1053.

59. Ibid., 210, 622, 561.

60. Ibid., 175.

61. Ibid., 158, 473, 1058.

62. Ibid., 373, 374, 624.

63. Ibid., 142.

64. Ibid., 626, 223, 364, 244.

65. Ibid., 477, 613.

66. Ibid., 626, 149.

67. Ibid., 464, 167, 834.

68. Ibid., 373, 532, 929.
69. Ibid., 412, 874.
70. Ibid., 612.
71. See, for example, Bush, *Weekly Compilation*, 430, 495.
72. Bush, *Weekly Compilation*, 839.
73. Ibid., 432.
74. Ibid., 430.
75. Ibid., 242.
76. Ibid., 363, 401.
77. Ibid., 242, 142, 725.
78. Jonathan Weisman, "Skepticism of Bush's Social Security Plan Is Growing," *Washington Post*, 15 March 2005, final edition, A01.

CONCLUSION: SECURING A VIBRANT DEMOCRACY

1. Qtd. in Arthur M. Schlesinger Jr., *The Coming of the New Deal* (Boston: Houghton Mifflin, 1958), 308–9.
2. I should qualify this claim to say that my call for honesty does not betray a search for such an ideal. Scholars have, in my view, rightly questioned Jürgen Habermas's theory of communicative action in these terms. Habermas's difficulties stem significantly from his distinction between communicative and strategic action, which runs contrary to the spirit of a rhetorical approach to public policy. See Jürgen Habermas, *The Theory of Communicative Action*, vol. 1, *Reason and the Rationalization of Society*, trans. Thomas McCarthy (Boston: Beacon Press, 1984), 285–337.
3. Jackie Calmes, "White House Memo Argues for Social Security Cuts," *Wall Street Journal*, 6 January 2005, eastern edition, A1.
4. George W. Bush, *Weekly Compilation of Presidential Documents*, vol. 41 (Washington, DC: Government Printing Office, 2004), 219.
5. Bush, *Weekly Compilation*, 365.
6. Senate Budget Committee, *Concurrent Resolution on the Budget for Fiscal Year 2000*, 106th Cong., 1st sess., 1999, 89.
7. Senate Finance Committee, *Retirement Security Policy: Proposals to Preserve and Protect Social Security*, 105th Cong., 2d sess., 1998, 10.
8. The University of Southern Mississippi maintains a website dedicated to the life and philanthropy of Oseola McCarty. Emblematic of the larger conditions in which McCarty lived and worked was the fact that she had for many years done the laundry of the attorney who helped her prepare the gift for the university.

"Oseola McCarty Donates $150,000 to Southern Miss.," *Oseola McCarty: A Very Special Lady*, 8 July 2003, http://www.usm.edu/pr/oolamain.htm (accessed 15 August 2006).

9. Elsewhere, I discuss this issue more generally as a tension between risk and commitment. See Robert Asen, "A Discourse Theory of Citizenship," *Quarterly Journal of Speech* 90 (2004): 200–201.

10. Occasionally, ordinary citizens testify before congressional committees to relay personal experiences, like investors who testified about losing money in the corporate scandals and dot-com bust, and their testimony may constitute a singular event in their lives. However, most committee witnesses possess a record of prior testimony, or they work with organizations that regularly operate in the political domain. Of course, policymakers themselves are experienced advocates.

11. Senate Aging Subcommittee, *Is Working America Preparing for Retirement?* 104th Cong., 2d sess., 1996, 16; Senate Social Security Task Force, *Education, International Affairs, and Social Security Task Forces*, 105th Cong., 2d sess., 1998, 463.

12. Bush, *Weekly Compilation*, 412.

13. Adam Smith, *An Inquiry into the Nature and Causes of the Wealth of Nations*, ed. Edwin Cannan (Chicago: University of Chicago Press, 1976), I.2.2.

14. Bush, *Weekly Compilation*, 839.

15. For a fuller discussion of the operation of direct and indirect exclusions, see my "Imagining in the Public Sphere," *Philosophy and Rhetoric* 35 (2002): 345–67.

16. In *The Phantom Public*, Walter Lippmann argues that this is the citizen's proper role as an uninformed observer. See Walter Lippmann, *The Phantom Public* (1927; New Brunswick, NJ: Transaction, 1993), 58–59. As I argue in the next section, I find John Dewey's approach to democratic engagement far more inspiring.

17. House Committee on Ways and Means, *Economic Security Act: Committee on Ways and Means*, 74th Cong., 1st sess., 1935, 559, 560.

18. Senate Finance Committee, *Economic Security Act: Hearings before the Committee on Finance*, 74th Cong., 1st sess., 1935, 644. For a detailed discussion of the racial politics of Old Age Assistance, see Jill Quadagno, *The Transformation of Old Age Security: Class and Politics in the American Welfare State* (Chicago: University of Chicago Press, 1988), 132–42.

19. John Dewey, "Creative Democracy—The Task before Us," in *John Dewey: The Later Works, 1925–1953*, vol. 14, *1939–1941*, ed. Jo Ann Boydston (Carbondale: Southern Illinois University Press, 1991), 226, 227.

20. Ibid., 226–27, 228.

21. See, for example, John F. Harris, "Victory Bears Out Emphasis on Values," *Washington Post*, 4 November 2004, final edition, A35; Maggie Gallagher, "The Rise

of the Values Voters," *National Review Online*, 23 November 2004, http://www.nationalreview.com/comment/gallagher200411230852.asp (accessed 10 December 2007).

22. Benjamin R. Barber, "Privatizing Social Security: 'Me' over 'We,'" *Los Angeles Times*, 27 January 2005, home edition, B13.

23. House Social Security Subcommittee, *The Future of Social Security for this Generation and the Next: Current State of Public Opinion on the Future of Social Security*, 105th Cong., 1st sess., 1997, 46.

24. Andrea Louise Campbell, *How Policies Make Citizens: Senior Political Activism and the American Welfare State* (Princeton, N.J: Princeton University Press, 2003), 25–32, 40–55.

25. Lawrence Mishel, Jared Bernstein, and Sylvia Allegretto, *The State of Working America 2004/2005* (Ithaca, NY: Cornell University Press, 2005), 62, 75, 290; Timothy M. Smeeding, "Public Policy, Economic Inequality, and Poverty: The United States in Comparative Perspective," *Social Science Quarterly* 86 (2005): 955–83. See also James Lardner and David A. Smith, eds., *Inequality Matters: The Growing Economic Divide in America and Its Poisonous Consequences* (New York: New Press, 2005).

Bibliography

Achenbaum, W. Andrew. *Social Security: Visions and Revisions*. Cambridge: Cambridge University Press, 1986.

Alcoff, Linda. "The Problem of Speaking for Others." *Cultural Critique* 20 (1991–92): 5–32.

Allen, Mike. "At Home, a Hard Sell on Social Security." *Washington Post*, 22 February 2005, final edition.

Altmeyer, Arthur J. *The Formative Years of Social Security*. Madison: University of Wisconsin Press, 1966.

Andrews, Emily S. "The Growth and Distribution of 401(k) Plans." In *Trends in Pensions, 1992*, edited by John A. Turner and Daniel J. Beller, 149–76. Washington, DC: Government Printing Office, 1992.

Aristotle. *On Rhetoric: A Theory of Civic Discourse*. 2d ed. Translated by George Kennedy. New York: Oxford University Press, 2007.

———. *Poetics*. Translated by Ingram Bywater. 1920. Reprint, New York: Oxford University Press, 1990.

Asen, Robert. "A Discourse Theory of Citizenship." *Quarterly Journal of Speech* 90 (2004): 189–211.

———. "Imagining in the Public Sphere." *Philosophy and Rhetoric* 35 (2002): 345–67.

———. *Visions of Poverty: Welfare Policy and Political Imagination.* East Lansing: Michigan State University Press, 2002 .

Aune, James Arnt. *Selling the Free Market: The Rhetoric of Economic Correctness.* New York: Guilford Press, 2001.

Babington, Charles, and Jim VandeHei. "Senators May Block Social Security Vote." *Washington Post,* 11 March 2005, final edition.

Balz, Dan. "Public Increasingly Doubts Survival of Social Security." *Washington Post,* 13 February 1982, final edition.

Barber, Benjamin R. "Privatizing Social Security: 'Me' over 'We.'" *Los Angeles Times,* 27 January 2005, home edition.

Béland, Daniel. *Social Security: History and Politics from the New Deal to the Privatization Debate.* Lawrence: University Press of Kansas, 2005.

Benedikt, Amélie Frost. "On Doing the Right Thing at the Right Time: Toward an Ethics of *Kairos.*" In *Rhetoric and* Kairos*: Essays in History, Theory, and Praxis,* edited by Phillip Sipiora and James S. Baumlin, 226–36. Albany: State University of New York Press, 2002.

Benhabib, Seyla. "Toward a Deliberative Model of Democratic Legitimacy." In *Democracy and Difference: Contesting the Boundaries of the Political,* edited by Seyla Benhabib, 67–94. Princeton, NJ: Princeton University Press, 1996.

Berenson, Alex. "The Biggest Casualty of Enron's Collapse: Confidence." *New York Times,* 10 February 2002, late edition.

———. "Wall St. Down a 3rd Year, Leaving Fewer Optimists." *New York Times,* 1 January 2003, national edition.

Berkowitz, Edward D. *Robert Ball and the Politics of Social Security.* Madison: University of Wisconsin Press, 2003.

Bitzer, Lloyd F. "The Rhetorical Situation." *Philosophy and Rhetoric* 1 (1968): 1–14.

Blackburn, Robin. *Banking on Death, or, Investing in Life: The History and Future of Pensions.* London: Verso, 2002.

Blair, Carole. "Reflections on Criticism and Bodies: Parables from Public Places." *Western Journal of Communication* 65 (2001): 271–94.

Bourdieu, Pierre. *Acts of Resistance: Against the Tyranny of the Market.* Translated by Richard Nice. New York: New Press, 1998.

Boushey, Heather, and Christian E. Weller. "What the Numbers Tell Us." In *Inequality Matters: The Growing Economic Divide in America and Its Poisonous Consequences,* edited by James Lardner and David A. Smith, 27–40. New York: New Press, 2005.

Brandes, Stuart D. *American Welfare Capitalism, 1880–1940.* Chicago: University of Chicago Press, 1976.

Brinkley, Alan. *Voices of Protest: Huey Long, Father Coughlin, and the Great Depression.* New York: Vintage Books, 1983.

Broder, David S. "Vote May Signal GOP Return as Dominant Party." *Washington Post*, 10 November 1994, final edition.

Brody, David. *Workers in Industrial America: Essays on the Twentieth Century Struggle.* New York: Oxford University Press, 1980.

Brouwer, Daniel C. "ACT-ing UP in Congressional Hearings." In *Counterpublics and the State*, edited by Robert Asen and Daniel C. Brouwer, 87–109. Albany: State University of New York Press, 2001.

Brown, Michael K. *Race, Money, and the American Welfare State.* Ithaca, NY: Cornell University Press, 1999.

Bryce, Robert. *Pipe Dreams: Greed, Ego, and the Death of Enron.* New York: PublicAffairs, 2002.

Burke, Kenneth. "Four Master Tropes." In *A Grammar of Motives.* Berkeley: University of California Press, 1969.

Bush, George W. *Public Papers of the Presidents of the United States: George W. Bush, 2001.* 2 vols. Washington, DC: Government Printing Office, 2001.

———. *Weekly Compilation of Presidential Documents.* Vols. 40–41. Washington, DC: Government Printing Office, 2004.

"Bush's Believers-Only Speeches." *St. Petersburg Times*, 9 April 2005, South Pinellas edition.

"Bush Stood By Agenda; Why Ignore a Mandate?" *Rocky Mountain News*, 7 November 2004, final edition.

Butler, Judith. *Undoing Gender.* New York: Routledge, 2004.

Butler, Stuart, and Peter Germanis. "Achieving a 'Leninist' Strategy." *Cato Journal* 3 (1983): 547–61.

Calmes, Jackie. "White House Memo Argues for Social Security Cuts." *Wall Street Journal*, 6 January 2005, eastern edition.

Campbell, Andrea Louise. *How Policies Make Citizens: Senior Political Activism and the American Welfare State.* Princeton, NJ: Princeton University Press, 2003.

Cancian, Maria. "Rhetoric and Reality of Work-Based Welfare Reform." *Social Work* 46 (2001): 309–14.

Carter, Michael. "*Stasis* and *Kairos*: Principles of Social Construction in Classical Rhetoric." *Rhetoric Review* 7 (1988): 97–112.

Castiglioni, Rossana. "The Politics of Retrenchment: The Quandaries of Social Protection under Military Rule in Chile." *Latin American Politics and Society* 43 (2001): 37–66.

Ceccarelli, Leah. "Polysemy: Multiple Meanings in Rhetorical Criticism." *Quarterly Journal of Speech* 84 (1998): 395–415.

Cetina, Karin Knorr. "The Market." *Theory, Culture & Society* 23 (2006): 551–56.

Chancellor, Edward. *Devil Take the Hindmost: A History of Financial Speculation.* New York: Farrar, Straus, Giroux, 1999.

———. "The Trouble with Bubbles." *New York Times*, 27 January 2002, national edition.

Cheney, George. "Arguing about the Place of Values and Ethics in Market-Oriented Discourses of Today." In *New Approaches to Rhetoric*, edited by Patricia A. Sullivan and Steven R. Goldzwig, 61–88. Thousand Oaks, CA: Sage, 2004.

Clinton, William J. *Public Papers of the Presidents of the United States: William J. Clinton, 1995.* 2 vols. Washington, DC: Government Printing Office, 1996.

———. *Public Papers of the Presidents of the United States: William J. Clinton, 1998.* 2 vols. Washington, DC: Government Printing Office, 1999.

———. *Public Papers of the Presidents of the United States: William J. Clinton, 1999.* 2 vols. Washington, DC: Government Printing Office, 2000.

———. *Public Papers of the Presidents of the United States: William J. Clinton, 2000.* 2 vols. Washington, DC: Government Printing Office, 2001.

Cloud, Dana L. "The Materiality of Discourse as Oxymoron: A Challenge to Critical Rhetoric." *Western Journal of Communication* 58 (1994): 141–63.

———. "The Matrix and Critical Theory's Desertion of the Real." *Communication and Critical/Cultural Studies* 3 (2006): 329–54.

Cohen, Wilber J. "The Future Impact of the Social Security Amendments of 1983." *Journal of the Institute for Socioeconomic Studies* 8 (1983): 1–16.

Coll, Blanche D. *Safety Net: Welfare and Social Security, 1929–1979.* New Brunswick, NJ: Rutgers University Press, 1995.

Conant Jr., Luther. *A Critical Analysis of Industrial Pension Systems.* New York: Macmillan, 1922.

Condit, Celeste Michelle. "The Rhetorical Limits of Polysemy." *Critical Studies in Mass Communication* 6 (1989): 103–22.

Congressional Record. 92d Cong., 2d sess., 1972. Vol. 118, pts. 5, 11, 18.

Congressional Record. 104th Cong., 2d sess., 1996. Vol. 142, pt. 116.

Converse, Philip E. "Changing Conceptions of Public Opinion in the Political Process." *Public Opinion Quarterly* 51 (1987): S12–S24.

Cooper, Kenneth J. "Gingrich: 'Cooperation, Yes. Compromise, No.'" *Washington Post*, 12 November 1994, final edition.

Costa, Dora L. *The Evolution of Retirement: An American Economic History.* Chicago: University of Chicago Press, 1998.

"Courage." *Progress for America*, 15 January 2005, http://pfavoterfund.com/docs/audio-video/ (accessed 15 February 2005).

Cox, J. Robert. "The Die Is Cast: Topical and Ontological Dimensions of the *Locus* of the Irreparable." *Quarterly Journal of Speech* 68 (1982): 227–39.

Darwall, Stephen. "Sympathetic Liberalism: Recent Work on Adam Smith." *Philosophy & Public Affairs* 28 (1999): 139–64.

Derrida, Jacques. "Sending: On Representation." *Social Research* 49 (1982): 294–326.

Derthick, Martha. *Policymaking for Social Security.* Washington, DC: Brookings Institution, 1979.

Dewey, John. "Creative Democracy—The Task before Us." In *John Dewey: The Later Works, 1925–1953*, vol. 14, *1939–1941*, edited by Jo Ann Boydston, 224–30. Carbondale: Southern Illinois University Press, 1991.

———. *The Public and Its Problems.* 1927. Reprint, Athens, OH: Swallow Press, 1954.

Dorell, Oren. "Lobbying War Hits Airwaves Today." *USA Today*, 7 February 2005, final edition.

Dyer, Richard. *The Matter of Images: Essays on Representation.* New York: Routledge, 1993.

Edsall, Thomas B. "Conservatives Join Forces for Bush Plans." *Washington Post*, 13 February 2005, final edition.

Eichenwald, Kurt. *Conspiracy of Fools: A True Story.* New York: Broadway Books, 2005.

Eisenberg, Daniel. "Dennis the Menace." *Time*, 17 June 2002.

Eliot, Thomas H. *Recollections of the New Deal: When the People Mattered.* Boston: Northeastern University Press, 1992.

Elliott, Michael. "The Incredible Shrinking Businessman." *Time*, 4 February 2002.

Emert, Carol. "Point of No Returns." *San Francisco Chronicle*, 3 July 2002, final edition.

"Enron's Sins." *Wall Street Journal*, 18 January 2002, eastern edition.

Epstein, Abraham. *Insecurity: A Challenge to America.* 2d rev. ed. New York: Random House, 1938.

Eubanks, Philip. "Conceptual Metaphor as Rhetorical Response: A Reconsideration of Metaphor." *Written Communication* 16 (1999): 171–99.

Fears, Darryl. "DNC to Investigate Ohio Voting Irregularities." *Washington Post*, 7 December 2004, final edition.

Ferrara, Peter J. "The Prospect of Real Reform." *Cato Journal* 3 (1983): 609–21.

———. "Social Security: The Reforms Have Just Begun." *Journal of the Institute for Socioeconomic Studies* 8 (1983): 17–29.

Fialka, John J. "Cato Institute's Influence Grows in Washington as Republican-Dominated Congress Sets Up Shop." *Wall Street Journal*, 14 December 1994, eastern edition.

Fineman, Howard, and Michael Isikoff. "Lights Out: Enron's Failed Power Play." *Newsweek*, 21 January 2002.

Fischer, David Hackett. *Growing Old in America*. New York: Oxford University Press, 1977.

Fischer, Frank. *Reframing Public Policy: Discursive Politics and Deliberative Practices*. New York: Oxford University Press, 2003.

Frank, Thomas. *One Market Under God: Extreme Capitalism, Market Populism, and the End of Economic Democracy*. New York: Doubleday, 2000.

Fraser, Nancy. "Rethinking the Public Sphere: A Contribution to the Critique of Actually Existing Democracy." In *Habermas and the Public Sphere*, edited by Craig Calhoun, 109–42. Cambridge: Massachusetts Institute of Technology Press, 1992.

———. "Women, Welfare, and the Politics of Needs Interpretation." In *Unruly Practices: Power, Discourse, and Gender in Contemporary Social Theory*. Minneapolis: University of Minnesota Press, 1989.

Friedberg, Leora, and Anthony Webb. "Retirement and the Evolution of Pension Structure." *Journal of Human Resources* 40 (2005): 281–301.

Friedman, Milton. *Capitalism and Freedom*. Chicago: University of Chicago Press, 1962.

Friedman, Thomas L. *The Lexus and the Olive Tree*. Rev. ed. New York: Anchor Books, 2000.

Gallagher, Maggie. "The Rise of the Values Voters." *National Review Online*, 23 November 2004, http://www.nationalreview.com/comment/gallagher200411230852.asp (accessed 10 December 2007).

Gillespie, Ed, and Bob Schellhas, eds. *Contract with America*. New York: Times Books, 1994.

Glassman, James K., and Kevin A. Hassett. *Dow 36,000: The New Strategy for Profiting from the Coming Rise in the Stock Market*. New York: Times Books, 1999.

Goldstein, Amy. "Social Security Panel Gears Up for Revamp." *Washington Post*, 3 May 2001, final edition.

Goodnight, G. Thomas. "Controversy." In *Argument in Controversy: Proceedings of the Seventh SCA/AFA Conference on Argumentation*, edited by Donn W. Parson, 1–13. Annandale, VA: Speech Communication Association, 1991.

———. "The Personal, Technical, and Public Spheres of Argument: A Speculative Inquiry into the Art of Public Deliberation." *Journal of the American Forensic Association* 18 (1982): 214–27.

Gore, Al, and George W. Bush. "The First Gore-Bush Presidential Debate." 3 October 2000, *Commission on Presidential Debates*, http://www.debates.org/pages/trans2000a.html (accessed 24 February 2006).

Gore, David Charles. "Between Sympathy and Self-Interest: A Reframing of Adam Smith's Economic Rhetoric." In *Rhetorical Democracy: Discursive Practices of Civic Engagement*, edited by Gerard A. Hauser and Amy Grim, 159–64. Mahwah, NJ: Lawrence Erlbaum Associates, 2004.

Graebner, William. *A History of Retirement: The Meaning and Function of an American Institution, 1885–1978*. New Haven, CT: Yale University Press, 1980.

Greene, Ronald Walter. "Another Materialist Rhetoric." *Critical Studies in Mass Communication* 15 (1998): 21–41.

———. "Rhetoric and Capitalism: Rhetorical Agency as Communicative Labor." *Philosophy and Rhetoric* 37 (2004): 188–206.

Grier, Peter. "Stocks' Gilded Age Finally Closes." *Christian Science Monitor*, 2 January 2001.

Haber, Carole, and Brian Gratton. *Old Age and the Search for Security: An American Social History*. Bloomington: Indiana University Press, 1994.

Habermas, Jürgen. *Between Facts and Norms: Contributions to a Discourse Theory of Law and Democracy*. Translated by William Rehg. Cambridge: Massachusetts Institute of Technology Press, 1996.

———. *The Structural Transformation of the Public Sphere: An Inquiry into a Category of Bourgeois Society*. Translated by Thomas Burger. Cambridge: Massachusetts Institute of Technology Press, 1989.

———. *The Theory of Communicative Action*. Vol. 1, *Reason and the Rationalization of Society*. Translated by Thomas McCarthy. Boston: Beacon Press, 1984.

Hacker, Jacob S. *The Divided Welfare State: The Battle over Public and Private Social Benefits in the United States*. New York: Cambridge University Press, 2002.

———. "Privatizing Risk without Privatizing the Welfare State: The Hidden Politics of Social Policy Retrenchment in the United States." *American Political Science Review* 98 (2004): 243–60.

Hall, Mimi. "Social Security Review Being Rigged, Critics Say." *USA Today*, 3 May 2001, final edition.

Handler, Joel F. *Down from Bureaucracy: The Ambiguity of Privatization and Empowerment*. Princeton, NJ: Princeton University Press, 1996.

Hariman, Robert. *Political Style: The Artistry of Power*. Chicago: University of Chicago Press, 1995.

Harris, John F. "Victory Bears Out Emphasis on Values." *Washington Post*, 4 November 2004, final edition.

Hauser, Gerard A. *Vernacular Voices: The Rhetoric of Publics and Public Spheres*. Columbia: University of South Carolina Press, 1999.

Heatherly, Charles L., ed. *Mandate for Leadership: Policy Management in a Conservative Administration.* Washington, DC: Heritage Foundation, 1981.

Henderson, Willie, Tony Dudley-Evans, and Roger Backhouse, eds. *Economics and Language.* New York: Routledge, 1993.

Henwood, Doug. *After the New Economy.* New York: New Press, 2003.

Herbert, Bob. "Bush's Blinkers." *New York Times,* 22 October 2004, late edition.

Herbst, Susan. *Numbered Voices: How Opinion Polling Has Shaped American Politics.* Chicago: University of Chicago Press, 1993.

Hogan, J. Michael. "George Gallup and the Rhetoric of Scientific Democracy." *Communication Monographs* 64 (1997): 161–79.

Holtzman, Abraham. *The Townsend Movement: A Political Study.* New York: Bookman, 1963.

Hook, Janet. "They Invested Years in Private Accounts." *Los Angeles Times,* 30 January 2005, home edition.

Hutcheon, Linda. "The Politics of Representation." *Signature: A Journal of Theory and Canadian Literature* 1 (1989): 23–44.

"Iceberg." *Progress for America,* 8 March 2005, http://pfavoterfund.com/docs/audio-video/ (accessed 15 March 2005).

Ikenberry, G. John, and Theda Skocpol. "Expanding Social Benefits: The Role of Social Security." *Political Science Quarterly* 102 (1987): 389–416.

Ippolito, Richard A. "Toward Explaining the Growth of Defined Contribution Plans." *Industrial Relations* 34 (1995): 1–20.

Jacobs, Lawrence R., and Robert Y. Shapiro. "UFO Stories." *New Republic,* 10 August 1998.

Jones, Charles O. *Clinton and Congress, 1993–1996: Risk, Restoration, and Reelection.* Norman: University of Oklahoma Press, 1999.

Justice, Glen. "A New Battle for Advisers to Swift Vets." *New York Times,* 21 February 2005, late edition.

Kadlec, Daniel. "Everyone, Back in the Labor Pool." *Time,* 29 July 2002.

———. "Under the Microscope." *Time,* 4 February 2002.

———. "Zap!" *Time,* 26 March 2001.

Kaplan, Dave. "This Year, Republicans Gamble That All Politics Is Local." *CQ Weekly,* 22 October 1994.

Katz, Michael B. *In the Shadow of the Poorhouse: A Social History of Welfare in America.* New York: Basic Books, 1986.

Keller, Bill. "The Sunny Side of the Street." *New York Times,* 27 July 2002, late edition.

Kennedy, David M. *Freedom from Fear: The American People in Depression and War, 1929–1945.* New York: Oxford University Press, 1999.

Kinneavy, James L. *"Kairos:* A Neglected Concept in Classical Rhetoric." In *Rhetoric and Praxis: The Contribution of Classical Rhetoric to Practical Reasoning,* edited by Jean Dietz Moss, 79–105. Washington, DC: Catholic University of America Press, 1986.

Kinneavy, James, and Catherine R. Eskin. *"Kairos* in Aristotle's *Rhetoric."* *Written Communication* 17 (2000): 432–44.

Kirby, John T. "Aristotle on Metaphor." *American Journal of Philology* 118 (1997): 517–54.

"Kitchen Sink." *AARP.org,* 21 March 2005, http://aarp.typepad.com/socialsecurity/2005/03/aarps_social_se.html (accessed 15 April 2005).

Klamer, Arjo, and Thomas C. Leonard. "So What's an Economic Metaphor?" In *Natural Images in Economic Thought,* edited by Philip Mirowski, 20–54. Cambridge: Cambridge University Press, 1994.

Klamer, Arjo, Donald N. McCloskey, and Robert M. Solow, eds. *The Consequences of Economic Rhetoric.* New York: Cambridge University Press, 1988.

Kornblut, Anne E. "Democrats Criticize Social Security Official." *New York Times,* 25 February 2005, late edition.

Kritzer, Barbara E. "Social Security Privatization in Latin America." *Social Security Bulletin* 63 (2000): 17–37.

Krugman, Paul. *The Age of Diminished Expectations.* Cambridge: Massachusetts Institute of Technology Press, 1992.

Kuttner, Robert. *Everything for Sale: The Virtues and Limits of Markets.* Chicago: University of Chicago Press, 1996.

Labaton, Stephen. "10 Wall St. Firms Reach Settlement in Analyst Inquiry." *New York Times,* 29 April 2003, late edition.

Lakoff, George, and Mark Johnson. *Metaphors We Live By.* 1980. Reprint, Chicago: University of Chicago Press, 2003.

Landon, Alfred M. "Text of Gov. Landon's Milwaukee Address on Economic Security." *New York Times,* 27 September 1936, late city edition.

Lardner, James, and David A. Smith, eds. *Inequality Matters: The Growing Economic Divide in America and Its Poisonous Consequences.* New York: New Press, 2005.

Latimer, Murray Webb. *Industrial Pension Systems in the United States and Canada.* New York: Industrial Relations Counselors, 1932.

Leff, Michael. "Textual Criticism: The Legacy of G. P. Mohrmann." *Quarterly Journal of Speech* 72 (1986): 377–89.

Lentricchia, Frank. *Criticism and Social Change*. Chicago: University of Chicago Press, 1983.

Leuchtenburg, William E. *The Supreme Court Reborn: The Constitutional Revolution in the Age of Roosevelt*. New York: Oxford University Press, 1995.

Levasseur, David G. "The Rhetorical Construction of Economic Policy: Political Judgment and the 1995 Budget Debate." *Rhetoric & Public Affairs* 3 (2000): 183–209.

Levy, Steven. "Silicon Valley Reboots." *Newsweek*, 25 March 2002.

Lieberman, Robert C. *Shifting the Color Line: Race and the American Welfare State*. Cambridge, MA: Harvard University Press, 1998.

Lippmann, Walter. *The Phantom Public*. 1927. Reprint, New Brunswick, NJ: Transaction, 1993.

Lochhead, Carolyn. "Bush Readies Ambitious 2nd-Term Domestic Agenda." *San Francisco Chronicle*, 22 November 2004, final edition.

Lubove, Roy. *The Struggle for Social Security, 1900–1935*. Cambridge, MA: Harvard University Press, 1968.

Luntz, Frank, and Mark Siegel. "Analysis of Third Millennium Survey." *Third Millennium*, September 1994, http://www.thirdmil.org/publications/surveys/surv5.html (accessed 7 December 2002).

Maidment, Richard A. *The Judicial Response to the New Deal*. Manchester, UK: Manchester University Press, 1991.

Malone, Ruth E. "Policy as Product: Morality and Metaphor in Health Policy Discourse." *Hastings Center Report*, May–June 1999, 16–22.

Mandel, Michael J. "The Triumph of the New Economy: A Powerful Payoff from Globalization and the Info Revolution." *Business Week*, 30 December 1996.

Marlantes, Liz. "How Far Will Bush's Domestic Mandate Go?" *Christian Science Monitor*, 16 December 2004.

Marshall, T. H., and Tom Bottomore. *Citizenship and Social Class*. London: Pluto Press, 1992.

Massachusetts Commission on Old Age Pensions, Annuities and Insurance. *Report of the Commission on Old Age Pensions, Annuities and Insurance*. Boston: White and Potter Printing, 1910.

McAllister, Eugene J., ed. *Agenda for Progress: Examining Federal Spending*. Washington, DC: Heritage Foundation, 1981.

McCloskey, Deirdre N. *The Rhetoric of Economics*. 2d ed. Madison: University of Wisconsin Press, 1998.

McCoy, Kevin. "A Birthday Party for the Ages." *USA Today*, 28 October 2003, final edition.

McGee, Michael Calvin. "A Materialist's Conception of Rhetoric." In *Explorations in Rhetoric: Studies in Honor of Douglas Ehninger*, edited by Raymie E. McKerrow, 23–48. Glenview, IL: Scott, Foresman, 1982.

McGinn, Daniel. "Weathering the Storm." *Newsweek*, 26 March 2001.

McKerrow, Raymie E. "Critical Rhetoric: Theory and Praxis." *Communication Monographs* 56 (1989): 91–111.

McLean, Bethany, and Peter Elkind. *The Smartest Guys in the Room: The Amazing Rise and Scandalous Fall of Enron*. New York: Portfolio, 2003.

Mesa-Lago, Carmelo. "Myth and Reality of Pension Reform: The Latin American Evidence." *World Development* 30 (2002): 1309–21.

Meyer, John C. "Humor as a Double-Edged Sword: Four Functions of Humor in Communication." *Communication Theory* 10 (2000): 310–31.

Miller, Mark Crispin. "None Dare Call It Stolen." *Harper's*, August 2005.

Miller, Carolyn R. "*Kairos* in the Rhetoric of Science." In *A Rhetoric of Doing*, edited by Stephen P. White, Neil Nakadate, and Roger D. Cherry, 310–27. Carbondale: Southern Illinois University Press, 1992.

Minow, Martha. *Partners Not Rivals: Privatization and the Public Good*. Boston: Beacon Press, 2002.

Mishel, Lawrence, Jared Bernstein, and Sylvia Allegretto, *The State of Working America, 2004/2005*. Ithaca, NY: Cornell University Press, 2005.

Mitchell, Daniel J. B. "Townsend and Roosevelt: Lessons from the Struggle for Elderly Income Support." *Labor History* 42 (2001): 255–76.

Morin, Richard, and Dale Russakoff. "Social Security Problems Not a Crisis, Most Say." *Washington Post*, 10 February 2005, final edition.

Moritz, Michael. "Spring Comes Early to Silicon Valley." *Time*, 26 March 2001.

"MoveOn Launches Ad Campaign Highlighting Benefit Cuts in President's Social Security Plan." *MoveOn.org*, 31 January 2005, http://www.MoveOn.org/press/pdfs/pr13105.pdf (accessed 1 February 2005).

Moynihan, Daniel Patrick. "Social Security, as We Knew It." *New York Times*, 5 January 1997, late edition.

Muller, Jerry Z. *The Mind and the Market: Capitalism and Western Thought*. New York: Anchor, 2002.

Murphy, Dwight D. "An Economic Paradox? Displacement and Polarization in a Booming Economy." *Journal of Social, Political, and Economic Studies* 24 (1998): 349–71.

Murphy, John M. "Cunning, Rhetoric, and the Presidency of William Jefferson Clinton." In *The Presidency and Rhetorical Leadership*, edited by Leroy G. Dorsey, 231–51. College Station: Texas A&M University Press, 2002.

Murray, Teresa Dixon. "Market's Fairy Tale Had Bitter Ending." *Plain Dealer*, 9 March 2002, final edition.

Myers, Robert J. "Social Security Amendments of 1983: Did They Solve the Financing Problem?" *CLU Journal* 38 (1984): 22–31.

National Commission on Social Security Reform. *Report of the National Commission on Social Security Reform*. Washington, DC, January 1983.

National Committee for Responsive Philanthropy. *Axis of Ideology: Conservative Foundations and Public Policy*. Washington, DC, March 2004.

Nelson, Daniel. *Managers and Workers: Origins of the Twentieth-Century Factory System in the United States, 1880–1920*. 2d ed. Madison: University of Wisconsin Press, 1995.

Norquist, Grover. "Ownership Can Be Revolutionary." *American Enterprise*, March 2005.

Norris, Floyd. "3 Years Later, Investors Crave Safety." *New York Times*, 10 March 2003, late edition.

Osborn, Michael. "Rhetorical Depiction." In *Form, Genre, and the Study of Political Discourse*, edited by Herbert W. Simons and Aram A. Aghazarian, 79–107. Columbia: University of South Carolina Press, 1986.

"Oseola McCarty Donates $150,000 to Southern Miss." *Oseola McCarty: A Very Special Lady*, 8 July 2003, http://www.usm.edu/pr/oolamain.htm (accessed 15 August 2006).

Ozawa, Martha N. "The 1983 Amendments to the Social Security Act: The Issue of Intergenerational Equity." *Social Work* 29 (1984): 131–37.

Paletz, David L. "Political Humor and Authority: From Support to Subversion." *International Political Science Review* 11 (1990): 483–93.

"Passing 2 Trillion Bucks Is Another." *New York Times*, 16 January 2005, late edition.

Patterson, James T. *America's Struggle against Poverty, 1900–1994*. Cambridge, MA: Harvard University Press, 1994.

———. *Restless Giant: The United States from Watergate to Bush v. Gore*. New York: Oxford University Press, 2005.

Pear, Robert. "AARP Opposes Plan to Replace Social Security with Private Accounts." *New York Times*, 12 November 2004, late edition.

Penny, Timothy J. "Privatization Foes Lose Grip on Reality." *Atlanta Journal-Constitution*, 21 November 2004, home edition.

Perkins, Frances. *The Roosevelt I Knew*. New York: Viking Press, 1946.

Peters, John Durham. "Historical Tensions in the Concept of Public Opinion." In *Public Opinion and the Communication of Consent*, edited by Theodore L. Glasser and Charles T. Salmon, 3–32. New York: Guilford Press, 1995.

Pfau, Michael William. "Who's Afraid of Fear Appeals? Contingency, Courage, and Deliberation in Rhetorical Theory and Practice." *Philosophy and Rhetoric* 40 (2007): 216–37.

Piñera, José. "Retiring in Chile." *New York Times*, 1 December 2004, late edition.

Pitkin, Hanna Fenichel. *The Concept of Representation*. Berkeley: University of California Press, 1967.

Pollin, Robert. *Contours of Descent: U.S. Economic Fractures and the Landscape of Global Austerity*. New York: Verso, 2003.

"Pop Went the Bubble." *New York Times*, 9 March 2005, late edition.

Poulakos, John. *Sophistical Rhetoric in Classical Greece*. Columbia: University of South Carolina Press, 1995.

———. "Toward a Sophistic Definition of Rhetoric." *Philosophy and Rhetoric* 16 (1983): 35–48.

Powell Jr., Louis F. "Attack of the American Free Enterprise System." *Media Transparency*, 23 August 1971, http://www.mediatransparency.org/storyprinterfriendly. php?storyID=22 (accessed 24 August 2005).

President's Commission to Strengthen Social Security. *Strengthening Social Security and Creating Personal Wealth for All Americans*. Washington, DC, 21 December 2001.

Pryce, Deborah, and Rick Santorum. *Saving Social Security: A Guide to Social Security Reform*. Washington, DC, 27 January 2005.

Quadagno, Jill. *The Transformation of Old Age Security: Class and Politics in the American Welfare State*. Chicago: University of Chicago Press, 1988.

"Real Income Down 5.5% in 1980 in a Record Drop." *New York Times*, 21 August 1981, late city edition.

"Reformers All, in Enron's Wake." *New York Times*, 2 February 2002, national edition.

Reich, Robert. *Locked in the Cabinet*. New York: Knopf, 1997.

Reinhardt, Uwe. "Can't Executives Be as Honorable as Our Soldiers?" *Wall Street Journal*, 12 March 2002, eastern edition.

Reston, Maeve. "Activists Targeting Lawmakers over Social Security; Pa. Congressman in Close District Faces Ad Campaign." *Pittsburgh Post-Gazette*, 1 February 2005, region edition.

Ricci, David M. *The Transformation of American Politics: The New Washington and the Rise of Think Tanks*. New Haven, CT: Yale University Press, 1993.

Rich, Frank. "Sacrifice Is for Losers." *New York Times*, 22 June 2002, late edition.

Richards, I. A. *The Philosophy of Rhetoric*. 1936. Reprint, New York: Oxford University Press, 1965.

Ricoeur, Paul. *The Rule of Metaphor: Multidisciplinary Studies of the Creation of Meaning in Language.* Translated by Robert Czerny. Toronto: University of Toronto Press, 1977.

Romero, Simon, and Alex Berenson. "Worldcom Says It Hid Expenses, Inflating Cash Flow $3.8 Billion." *New York Times*, 26 June 2002, late edition.

Roosevelt, Franklin D. *The Public Papers and Addresses of Franklin D. Roosevelt*, vol. 3, *The Advance and Recovery of Reform.* New York: Random House, 1938.

———. *The Public Papers and Addresses of Franklin D. Roosevelt*, vol. 4, *The Court Disapproves.* New York: Random House, 1938.

Rosenbaum, Eckehard F. "What Is a Market? On the Methodology of a Contested Concept." *Review of Social Economy* 58 (2000): 455–82.

Rosenstiel, Thomas B., and Edith Stanley. "Gingrich Tames Rhetoric, Savors 'Speaker.'" *Los Angeles Times*, 9 November 1994, home edition.

Rubinow, Isaac M. *Social Insurance, with Special Reference to American Conditions.* 1913. Reprint, New York: Arno Press, 1969.

Samuelson, Robert J. "What If Washington's Tool Kit Won't Work?" *Newsweek*, 26 March 2001.

Sass, Steven A. *The Promise of Private Pensions: The First Hundred Years.* Cambridge, MA: Harvard University Press, 1997.

Schiappa, Edward. *Defining Reality: Definitions and the Politics of Meaning.* Carbondale: Southern Illinois University Press, 2003.

Schlesinger Jr., Arthur M. *The Coming of the New Deal.* Boston: Houghton Mifflin, 1958.

———. *The Politics of Upheaval.* Boston: Houghton Mifflin, 1960.

Schudson, Michael. "The 'Public Sphere' and Its Problems: Bringing the State (Back) In." *Notre Dame Journal of Law, Ethics & Public Policy* 8 (1994): 529–46.

Sclar, Elliot D. *You Don't Always Get What You Pay For: The Economics of Privatization.* Ithaca, NY: Cornell University Press, 2000.

Seib, Gerald F., and John Harwood. "Shift in Power: Big Republican Gains Bring the Party Close to Control of Congress." *Wall Street Journal*, 9 November 1994, eastern edition.

Shiller, Robert J. *Irrational Exuberance.* New York: Broadway, 2001.

———. "The Market's Future: You Won't Hear a Pop." *Plain Dealer*, 16 May 2000, final edition.

Simon, William E. *A Time for Truth.* New York: McGraw-Hill, 1978.

Sipiora, Phillip. "Introduction: The Ancient Concept of *Kairos*." In *Rhetoric and Kairos: Essays in History, Theory, and Praxis*, edited by Phillip Sipiora and James S. Baumlin, 1–22. Albany: State University of New York Press, 2002.

"6 Key Democratic Senators Oppose Bush Plan on Benefits." *New York Times*, 1 February 2005, late edition.

Skocpol, Theda. *Protecting Soldiers and Mothers: The Political Origins of Social Policy in the United States*. Cambridge, MA: Harvard University Press, 1992.

Smeeding, Timothy M. "Public Policy, Economic Inequality, and Poverty: The United States in Comparative Perspective." *Social Science Quarterly* 86 (2005): 955–83.

Smith, Adam. *An Inquiry into the Nature and Causes of the Wealth of Nations*. Edited by Edwin Cannan. Chicago: University of Chicago Press, 1976.

Smith, Ann Kates. "What Kind of Bear?" *U.S. News and World Report*, 26 March 2001.

Smith, Chris, and Ben Voth. "The Role of Humor in Political Argument: How 'Strategery' and 'Lockboxes' Changed a Political Campaign." *Argumentation and Advocacy* 39 (2002): 110–29.

Smith, Craig Allen. "Bill Clinton in Rhetorical Crisis: The Six Stages of Scandal and Impeachment." In *Images, Scandal, and Communication Strategies of the Clinton Presidency*, edited by Robert E. Denton Jr. and Rachel L. Holloway, 173–94. Westport, CT: Praeger, 2003.

Smith, James Allen. *The Idea Brokers: Think Tanks and the Rise of the New Policy Elite*. New York: Free Press, 1991.

Smith, John E. "Time and Qualitative Time." *Review of Metaphysics* 40 (1986): 3–16.

Smith, Randall, Susanne Craig, and Deborah Solomon. "Wall Street Firms to Pay $1.4 Billion to End Inquiry—Record Payment Settles Conflict-of-Interest Charges." *Wall Street Journal*, 29 April 2003, eastern edition.

Social Security Act of 1935, U.S. Statutes at Large 49 (1935): 620–48.

"Social Security Bill a Tough Sell in Iowa." *Kansascity.com*, 27 March 2005, http://www.kansascity.com/mld/kansascitystar/news/politics/11239666.htm (accessed 27 March 2005).

"Social Security Commission Is Tilted toward Privatization." *St. Louis Post-Dispatch*, 2 May 2001, three-star edition.

"Social Security: Where We Stand." *AARP Bulletin*, December 2004.

"Spending Political Capital," *St. Louis Post-Dispatch*, 5 November 2004, five-star edition.

Spielvogel, Christian. "'You Know Where I Stand': Moral Framing of the War on Terrorism and the Iraq War in the 2004 Presidential Campaign." *Rhetoric & Public Affairs* 8 (2005): 549–69.

Stefancic, Jean, and Richard Delgado. *No Mercy: How Conservative Think Tanks and Foundations Have Changed America's Social Agenda*. Philadelphia: Temple University Press, 1996.

Stiglitz, Joseph E. *The Roaring Nineties: A New History of the World's Most Prosperous Decade.* New York: W. W. Norton, 2003.

Stolberg, Sheryl Gay, and Carl Hulse. "Cool Reception on Capitol Hill to Social Security Plan." *New York Times,* 4 February 2005, late edition.

Sunstein, Cass R., and Richard A. Epstein. *The Vote: Bush, Gore, and the Supreme Court.* Chicago: University of Chicago Press, 2001.

Suskind, Ron. "Without a Doubt," *New York Times Magazine,* 17 October 2004.

Third Millennium. "Survey: Social Security: The Credibility Gap." *Third Millennium,* September 1994, http://www.thirdmil.org/publications/surveys/surv7.html (accessed 7 December 2002).

Thomas Jr., Landon. "Wall St. Lobby Quietly Tackles Social Security." *New York Times,* 21 December 2004, late edition.

Thompson, Roger. "*Kairos* Revisited: An Interview with James Kinneavy." *Rhetoric Review* 19 (2000): 73–88.

Thurow, Lester C. "Market Crash Born of Greed." *Boston Globe,* 17 April 2001, third edition.

Trattner, Walter I. *From Poor Law to Welfare State: A History of Social Welfare in America.* 5th ed. New York: Free Press, 1994.

Untersteiner, Mario. *The Sophists.* Translated by Kathleen Freeman. Oxford: Blackwell, 1954.

U.S. Advisory Council on Social Security. *Final Report.* 76th Cong., 1st sess., 1939. S. Doc. 4.

———. *Old-Age and Survivors Insurance.* 80th Cong., 2d sess., 1948. S. Doc. 149.

———. *Report of the 1994–1996 Advisory Council on Social Security.* Washington, DC, 1997.

U.S. Committee on Economic Security. *Report to the President of the Committee on Economic Security.* Washington, DC: Government Printing Office, 1935.

———. *Social Security in America: The Factual Background of the Social Security Act as Summarized from Staff Reports to the Committee on Economic Security.* Washington, DC: Government Printing Office, 1937.

U.S. House Committee on the Budget. *Addressing Our Long-Term Budget Challenges.* 105th Cong., 1st sess., 1997.

———. *Protecting the Future of Social Security.* 105th Cong., 1st sess., 1997.

———. *Social Security: The Long-Term Budget Implications.* 107th Cong., 2d sess., 2002.

U.S. House Committee on Oversight and Government Reform, Minority Staff. *The Politicization of the Social Security Administration.* February 2005.

U.S. House Committee on Ways and Means. *Economic Security Act: Committee on Ways and Means.* 74th Cong., 1st sess., 1935.

———. *Hearings Relative to the Social Security Act Amendments of 1939.* 67th Cong., 1st sess., 1939.

———. *Ideas for Advancing the Upcoming Debate on Saving the Social Security System.* 105th Cong., 2d sess., 1998.

———. *Preserving and Strengthening Social Security.* 106th Cong., 1st sess., 1999.

———. *The President's Social Security Framework.* 106th Cong., 1st sess., 1999.

———. *Proposals Certified to Save Social Security.* 106th Cong., 1st sess., 1999.

———. *Social Security Act Amendments of 1949.* 81st Cong., 1st sess., 1949.

———. *The Social Security Act of 1935.* 74th Cong., 1st sess., 1935. H. Rept. 615.

———. *Social Security Reform Lessons Learned in Other Countries.* 106th Cong., 1st sess., 1999.

———. *Use of an Expert Panel to Design Long-Range Social Security Reform.* 105th Cong., 2d sess., 1998.

U.S. House Committee on Ways and Means and Senate Committee on Finance. *Social Security and Medicare Trustees' 2001 Annual Reports.* 107th Cong., 1st sess., 2001.

U.S. House Subcommittee on Employer-Employee Relations of the Committee on Education and the Workforce. *Hearing on Defusing the Retirement Time Bomb: Encouraging Pension Savings.* 105th Cong., 1st sess., 1997.

U.S. House Subcommittee on Finance and Hazardous Materials of the Committee on Commerce. *The Market Impact of the President's Social Security Proposal.* 106th Cong., 1st sess., 1999.

U.S. House Subcommittee on Social Security of the Committee on Ways and Means. *The Future of Social Security for this Generation and the Next.* 105th Cong., 1st sess., 1997.

———. *The Future of Social Security for this Generation and the Next: Current State of Public Opinion on the Future of Social Security.* 105th Cong., 1st sess., 1997.

———. *The Future of Social Security for this Generation and the Next: The Implications of Raising the Retirement Age.* 105th Cong., 2d sess., 1998.

———. *The Future of Social Security for this Generation and the Next: Members of Congress and Business Labor Groups.* 105th Cong., 1st sess., 1997.

———. *The Future of Social Security for this Generation and the Next: Personal Savings Accounts and Individual-Owned Investments.* 105th Cong., 2d sess., 1998.

———. *Impacts of the Current Social Security System.* 106th Cong., 1st sess., 1999.

———. *Investing in the Private Market.* 106th Cong., 1st sess., 1999.

———. *Social Security and Pension Reform: Lessons from Other Countries.* 107th Cong., 1st sess., 2001.

———. *Social Security Improvements for Women, Seniors, and Working Americans.* 107th Cong., 2d sess., 2002.

————. *Social Security's Future*. 108th Cong., 2d sess., 2004.

U.S. House Task Force on Social Security of the Committee on the Budget. *Social Security Reform*. 106th Cong., 1st sess., 1999.

U.S. Senate Committee on the Budget. *Concurrent Resolution on the Budget for the Fiscal Year 2000*. 106th Cong., 1st sess., 1999.

————. *Social Security Reform*. 105th Cong., 2d sess., 1998.

U.S. Senate Committee on Finance. *Economic Security Act: Hearings before the Committee on Finance*. 74th Cong., 1st sess., 1935.

————. *Final Report Produced by the President's Commission to Strengthen Social Security*. 107th Cong., 2d sess., 2002.

————. *New Directions in Retirement Security Policy: Social Security, Pensions, Personal Savings and Work*. 105th Cong., 2d sess., 1998.

————. *Personal Retirement Accounts*. 106th Cong., 1st sess., 1999.

————. *Proposals to Create Personal Savings Accounts under Social Security*. 104th Cong., 2d sess., 1996.

————. *Retirement Security: Picking Up the Enron Pieces*. 107th Cong., 2d sess., 2002.

————. *Retirement Security Policy: Proposals to Preserve and Protect Social Security*. 105th Cong., 2d sess., 1998.

————. *Social Security Revision*. 81st Cong., 2d sess., 1950.

U.S. Senate Special Committee on Aging. *A Starting Point for Reform: Identifying the Goals of Social Security*. 105th Cong, 2d sess., 1998.

————. *Analyzing Social Security: GAO Weighs the President's Commission's Proposals*. 108th Cong., 1st sess., 2003.

————. *The Boomers Are Coming: Challenges of Aging in the New Millennium*. 106th Cong., 1st sess., 1999.

————. *The Impact of Social Security Reform on Women*. 106th Cong., 1st sess., 1999.

————. *Income Taxes: The Solution to the Social Security and Medicare Crisis?* 106th Cong., 2d sess., 2000.

————. *Modernization of Social Security and Medicare*. 107th Cong., 1st sess., 2001.

————. *Planning for Retirement: Promoting Security and Dignity of American Retirement*. 107th Cong., 2d sess., 2002.

————. *Preparing for the Retirement of the Baby Boom Generation*. 105th Cong., 2d sess., 1998.

————. *Preserving America's Future Today*. 105th Cong., 2d sess., 1998.

————. *Retirement Security and Corporate Responsibility*. 107th Cong., 2d sess., 2002.

————. *Retiring Baby Boomers: Meeting the Challenges*. 105th Cong., 1st sess., 1997.

————. *Social Security: Whose Trust Will Be Broken?* 108th Cong., 1st sess., 2003.

————. *Social Security Reform Options: Preparing for the 21st Century.* 104th Cong., 2d sess., 1996.

————. *The Stock Market and Social Security: The Risks and the Rewards.* 105th Cong., 2d sess., 1998.

————. *Straight Shooting on Social Security: The Trade-offs of Reform.* 107th Cong., 1st sess., 2001.

————. *Strengthening Social Security: What Can Personal Retirement Accounts Do for Low-Income Workers?* 108th Cong., 2d sess., 2004.

————. *Women and Social Security Reform: Are Individual Accounts the Answer?* 106th Cong., 1st sess., 1999.

U.S. Senate Subcommittee on Aging of the Committee on Labor and Human Resources. *Confronting the Challenges Presented by an Aging Population,* 104th Cong., 2d sess., 1996.

————. *Is Working America Preparing for Retirement?* 104th Cong., 2d sess., 1996.

U.S. Senate Subcommittee on Health Care, and Subcommittee on Social Security and Family Policy of the Committee on Finance, and the Subcommittee on Securities of the Committee on Banking, Housing, and Urban Affairs. *Investment-Based Alternatives to Financing Social Security and Medicare.* 105th Cong., 1st sess., 1997.

U.S. Senate Subcommittee on Securities of the Committee on Banking, Housing, and Urban Affairs. *Social Security Investment in the Securities Markets.* 105th Cong., 1st sess., 1997.

U.S. Senate Subcommittee on Social Security and Family Policy of the Committee on Finance. *1995 Annual Report of the Social Security and Disability Trust Funds.* 104th Cong., 1st sess., 1995.

————. *Privatization of the Social Security Old Age and Survivors Insurance Program.* 104th Cong., 1st sess., 1995.

————. *Social Security Advisory Council Report.* 104th Cong., 2d sess., 1996.

————. *Social Security and Future Retirees.* 104th Cong., 2d sess., 1996.

————. *Solvency of the Social Security Trust Funds,* 104th Cong., 1st sess., 1995.

U.S. Senate Task Force on Social Security of the Committee on the Budget. *Education, International Affairs, and Social Security Task Forces.* 105th Cong., 2d sess., 1998.

U.S. Social Security Administration, Board of Trustees, Federal Old-Age and Survivors Insurance and Disability Insurance Trust Funds. *1982 Annual Report of the Board of Trustees of the Federal Old-Age and Survivors Insurance and Disability Insurance Trust Funds.* Washington, DC, April 1982.

————. *1997 Annual Report of the Board of Trustees of the Federal Old-Age and Survivors Insurance and Disability Insurance Trust Funds.* Washington, DC, April 1997.

———. *1998 Annual Report of the Board of Trustees of the Federal Old-Age and Survivors Insurance and Disability Insurance Trust Funds.* Washington, DC, April 1998.

———. *1999 Annual Report of the Board of Trustees of the Federal Old-Age and Survivors Insurance and Disability Insurance Trust Funds.* Washington, DC, March 1999.

———. *2000 Annual Report of the Board of Trustees of the Federal Old-Age and Survivors Insurance and Disability Insurance Trust Funds.* Washington, DC, March 2000.

———. *2001 Annual Report of the Board of Trustees of the Federal Old-Age and Survivors Insurance and Disability Insurance Trust Funds.* Washington, DC, March 2001.

———. *2002 Annual Report of the Board of Trustees of the Federal Old-Age and Survivors Insurance and Disability Insurance Trust Funds.* Washington, DC, March 2002.

———. *2003 Annual Report of the Board of Trustees of the Federal Old-Age and Survivors Insurance and Disability Insurance Trust Funds.* Washington, DC, March 2003.

———. *2004 Annual Report of the Board of Trustees of the Federal Old-Age and Survivors Insurance and Disability Insurance Trust Funds.* Washington, DC, March 2004.

———. *2005 Annual Report of the Board of Trustees of the Federal Old-Age and Survivors Insurance and Disability Insurance Trust Funds.* Washington, DC, April 2005.

USA Next. "The Real AARP Agenda." *American Spectator,* http://www.spectator.org (accessed 21 February 2005).

VandeHei, Jim. "A Big Push on Social Security." *Washington Post,* 1 January 2005, final edition.

VandeHei, Jim, and Peter Baker. "On with the Show; President's 'Conversations' on Issue Are Carefully Orchestrated, Rehearsed." *Washington Post,* 12 March 2005, final edition.

Walton, Douglas. *Scare Tactics: Arguments That Appeal to Fear and Threats.* Dordrecht, Netherlands: Kluwer Academic, 2000.

Wehner, Peter H. "Memo on Social Security." *Wall Street Journal Online,* 5 January 2005, http://online.wsj.com/article/0,,SB110496995612018199,00.html (accessed 15 May 2006).

Weisberg, Herbert F., and Dino P. Christenson. "Changing Horses in Wartime? The 2004 Presidential Election." *Political Behavior* 29 (2007): 279–304.

Weisman, Jonathan. "Skepticism of Bush's Social Security Plan Is Growing." *Washington Post,* 15 March 2005, final edition.

"We'll Play the Slots," *New York Times,* 9 January 2005, late edition.

Wessel, David. "Why the Bad Guys of the Boardroom Emerged En Masse." *Wall Street Journal,* 20 June 2002, eastern edition.

White, Eric Charles. *Kaironomia: On the Will-to-Invent.* Ithaca, NY: Cornell University Press, 1987.

"Who Would You Rather Have a Beer With?" *Zogby's Real America*, October 2004, http://www.zogby.com/ZRA/backissues (accessed 15 August 2007).

Williams, Raymond. *Keywords: A Vocabulary of Culture and Society*. Rev. ed. New York: Oxford University Press, 1985.

Williamson, John B. "Privatizing Public Pension Systems: Lessons from Latin America." *Journal of Aging Studies* 15 (2001) 285–302.

"Winners & Losers." *New York Times*, 4 January 2005, late edition.

Witte, Edwin E. *The Development of the Social Security Act*. Madison: University of Wisconsin Press, 1963.

"WMD." *New York Times*, 2 February 2005, late edition.

Woodward, Bob. *The Agenda: Inside the Clinton White House*. New York: Simon & Schuster, 1993.

"Working Retirement." *MoveOn.org*, 31 January 2005, http://cdn.MoveOn.org/content/video/SS_ad.wmv (accessed 1 February 2005).

Zuckman, Jill. "Hastert: Public Not Sold on Social Security Plans." *Chicago Tribune*, 11 February 2005, final edition.

Zunz, Olivier. *Making America Corporate, 1870–1920*. Chicago: University of Chicago Press, 1990.

Index

representation, 137–139; rhetorical nature of, 7, 26–27; as symbolic resource, 22; and time, 149; value of, 5, 14, 139, 194–196; vision of, 244, 245, 247. *See also* Debate, policy

Debt, 79, 116, 167

Defined-benefit fund, 73, 89

Defined-contribution fund, 73, 74, 89

Deliberation, public: and democracy, 38, 239–241, 247; necessity of, 235, 239–241, 247; and policy making, 195; and public sphere, 193–195; and rhetoric, 7, 213; and townhall meetings, 208, 231. *See also* Debate, public

Demagogue, 140, 141

Democracy: as act, 248; creative, 243–249; deliberative, 10; reduction of, 192, 226, 227; value of, 5, 14, 15. *See also* Citizenship

Dependence: and assistance, 8, 25, 34, 104; and economy, 31; and elderly, 36; and financial illiteracy, 227; and government, 66, 101, 236; and insurance, 66, 101, 132, 133; and personal accounts, 223; and privatization, 77. *See also* Independence

Dewey, John, 5, 243

Difference, 104–107, 127, 244. *See also* Representation

Discourse: constellation of, 197;

constitutive power of, 2, 11–14, 192–194; cultural, 66; democratic, 247; kairotic nature of, 150, 153; legitimating, 20, 61, 164, 192; norms in, 109, 196; vernacular, 246. *See also* Rhetoric

Diversification, 178, 179, 181, 182. *See also* Risk

Dole, Bob, 140, 141

Domenici, Pete, 81

Doughton, Robert, 28

Dyer, Richard, 107

E

Economic revolution, 69, 71

Economics: moral implication of, 99, 100; principles of, 62, 65, 66, 157, 158

Efficiency, rhetorical nature of, 13, 44–46, 242

Electoral mandate, 70, 197, 230, 244

Elderly people: dependence of, 36, 37, 93, 104; increase in, 36, 37, 76; provision for, 38, 42, 43

Eliot, Thomas, 28, 29

Employee Stock Ownership Plans, 175

Empowerment: economic, 123, 128–132, 135–137; political, 222–225, 227

Enron, 148, 165, 166, 169–177, 181, 182

Entin, Stephen, 79, 80

Epstein, Abraham, 23, 25, 46, 49, 242

Gore, Al, 154, 190
Gore, Thomas P., 38
Graham, Frank, 36
Gramm, Phil, 78, 81, 96, 123, 125
Grassley, Charles, 139, 173, 183, 199, 200
Great Depression, 2, 24, 25, 35, 47
Greenspan, Alan, 57, 73, 86, 90, 99, 128, 135, 148, 149
Greenspan Commission, 57, 185
Greenstein, Robert, 179
Gregg, Judd, 84, 114, 139

H
Habermas, Jürgen, 10, 193, 194
Harrison, Byron, 28
Hastings, Daniel, 40, 45
Hauser, Gerard, 193
Haworth, J. D., 171, 172
Haynes, George, 46–49, 54, 59, 242
Herbst, Susan, 144
Heritage Foundation, 68, 123
Hewitt, Paul, 104
Hill, Samuel, 49
Honesty, 235, 236, 238
Hopkins, Harry, 27
Houston, Charles, 46, 48, 49, 54, 59, 242, 243
Hutcheon, Linda, 106

I
Ibbetson, Robert, 79, 80
Independence: and insurance, 8, 50, 76, 77, 84, 85, 101, 104; opposed to relief, 34; and ownership, 155, 190, 223, 227, 228; and policy making,

106; and private accounts, 132. *See also* Dependence
Individual investment accounts, 10, 74–76
Individualism: and investment, 104; problem of, 235; values of, 8, 63, 84, 101, 144, 204
Inflation, 54, 55, 56
Information: democratization of, 150, 176–178, 187, 188; and privatization, 239; and stocks, 173, 176, 177; and technology, 130, 131
Information age, 83, 130
Inheritance, 116
Insider system, 172, 173, 176–178, 187, 188. *See also* Time
Insurance: and assistance, 8, 9, 16, 22, 27, 47–49, 233; benefits, 52, 53, 91, 92, 123, 124, 126, 127; and change, 163; and contributory rights, 22, 33, 37–40, 45–48; coverage, 43–50; founding principle of, 4, 57, 231; framing of, 27, 66, 82–84, 94, 233; as metaphor, 62, 64–66, 88, 93, 94, 96, 101; opposition to, 104, 108, 109, 144, 145, 229; problems with, 28, 29, 40, 46–50, 242, 243; and relief, 27, 33, 39, 40; and representation, 103–105; and self-support, 35; and social justice, 126, 127; support for, 34; and trust fund, 98, 99; as unsustainable, 160, 161, 163, 185, 221, 223, 224; value of, 16,

Polysemy, 16, 20, 21, 58, 59, 105, 234. *See also* Rhetoric

R

Race, 22, 44, 46–50, 105, 122–124, 228, 229, 242, 243
Rangel, Charles, 140
Reagan, Ronald, 57, 68
Realism/reality: and representation, 108; and rhetoric, 6, 8, 27, 62, 234, 235
Reich, Robert, 73
Reid, Harry, 179
Reischauer, Robert, 98
Representation: 105, 106; and aesthetics, 18, 107, 108, 119, 145; constraint on, 108; construction of, of population, 18, 103–106; and debate, 105, 108, 127, 137, 138, 141, 142; and ethics, 8, 106, 108, 145, 237; and inclusion/exclusion, 108, 109; and power, 105–107; processes of, 8, 108, 109; and rhetoric, 107, 108, 130; speaking for/about, 106. *See also* Rhetoric
Reserve account, 30, 38, 41, 51
Responsibility: and benefits, 77; personal, 201, 202, 236; value of, 8; and young workers, 120, 122
Retirees, political power of, 106, 112, 113, 115, 116
Retirement, 20, 22, 28, 35, 36, 48, 50
Return: and benefits, 40, 41; and investment, 71–75, 123;

long-term, 150, 151; and market, 89–92, 178–182; money's worth, 74–76, 92, 109; and privatization, 13, 78, 79, 82; rate of, 14; social, 63, 91, 92
Revolution, 61, 69, 71, 81, 117, 118
Rhetoric: constitutive function of, 5–8; ethics of, 246–248; and *kairos*, 149–154; and market talk, 14; political, 171, 172; and polysemy, 20, 21, 62–65; and public policy, 9, 11, 62, 234; and reality, 5–8, 62, 234, 235; and representation, 17, 105, 108; visual, 207–209; war, 192. *See also* Discourse
Richards, I. A., 63, 65, 66
Ricoeur, Paul, 65
Rights: -based programs, 4, 243; and benefits, 33, 36–38, 58; civil, 122, 123; contributory, 22, 42, 47, 48, 52, 53, 58, 59, 61; ownership, 84, 85, 163; and relief, 27; of women, 66
Risk: and diversification, 178, 179, 182; and insurance, 22, 44, 91; and investment, 62, 63, 133, 158, 211; and privatization, 84–86
Rivers, Lynn, 97
Roosevelt, Franklin D., 8, 26–35, 37, 41, 47, 50, 203, 206, 207, 214, 215, 216, 233, 249
Rubinow, Isaac, 24
Ryan, Paul, 199

166–170, 178, 180–182; construction of, 71, 72, 80, 158,
172–174; democratization
of, 170, 177, 178; perception
of, 131, 157, 182; returns
in, 74, 75; and risk, 90, 150;
and time, 17, 154; and trust
funds, 98, 99; as untapped
resource, 80; variability of,
90, 164, 166–168, 187, 188.
See also Markets
Summers, Lawrence, 89, 98, 139
Sustainability, 160, 161. *See also*
Solvency
Symbolic devices: fields, 10, 11;
hierarchies, 18; politics, 33,
47–49, 242, 243; resources,
18, 22, 106, 235. *See also* Discourse; Rhetoric

T

Tanner, Michael, 78, 84, 134
Technical Board on Economic Security, 26, 27
Technical sphere, 5, 124, 196, 235,
245. *See also* Public sphere
Think tanks, 10, 67–70, 190
Third Millennium, 110, 117–121,
132, 194, 237, 238, 240
Tobin, Maurice, 53
Toomey, Pat, 97
Town-Hall Meetings: 191; content
of, 217, 218, 219, 227; participation in, 207, 208; structure of, 195, 199, 200, 231,
239. *See also* Private accounts
campaign
Townsend clubs/movement, 26, 50

Townsend, Francis, 26, 29, 34, 43
Townsend Plan, 26, 29, 33, 34, 36,
42, 43
Transition costs, 92, 162, 186
Transparency, 6, 17, 79, 101
Treasury, 35, 97
Treasury bonds, 95–97, 183, 184
Trust, value of, 86, 101, 120, 133,
144, 171, 187, 188, 224, 225
Trust Fund: 51, 57; investment
of, 74; as lockbox, 154;
metaphors for, 95–99; public nature of, 34; strategic
employment of, 137, 230,
231; sustainability of, 161,
183–185, 192, 218–220. *See
also* Solvency

U

UFO factoid, 118, 119
Unemployment insurance, 29

W

Wagner, Robert, 36, 39, 45
Wall Street, 72, 73, 171, 188
Walker, David, 177, 181–183
War, rhetoric of, 192, 198, 199
War on Terror, 148, 192, 197, 198
Wealth creation, 63, 78, 82, 101.
See also Ownership
Weaver, Carolyn, 79, 85, 131
Wehner memo, 201, 202, 205, 236
Wehner, Peter, 201, 202, 236
Witte, Edward, 26, 36, 37, 39, 42,
44, 45
Worldcom, 165
Wyden, Ron, 116